My Life with
Bonnie and Clyde

My Life with
Bonnie & Clyde

Blanche Caldwell Barrow

Edited by John Neal Phillips
Foreword by Esther L. Weiser

University of Oklahoma Press : Norman

Also by John Neal Phillips

Running with Bonnie and Clyde: The Ten Fast Years of Ralph Fults (Norman, 1996)

This book is published with the generous assistance of the McCasland Foundation, Duncan, Oklahoma.

Library of Congress Cataloging-in-Publication Data

Barrow, Blanche Caldwell.
  My life with Bonnie and Clyde / by Blanche Caldwell Barrow; edited by John Neal Phillips; foreword by Esther L. Weiser
    p. cm.
  Includes bibliographical references and index.
  ISBN 978-0-8061-3715-5 (paper)
    1. Barrow, Blanche Caldwell. 2. Barrow, Clyde, 1909–1934. 3. Parker, Bonnie, 1910–1934. 4. Criminals—United States—Biography. I. Phillips, John Neal, 1949– II. Title.

HV6248.B334A3 2004
364.15'52'092273—dc22
[B]
                                                                    2004046000

The paper in this book meets the guidelines for permanence and durability of the Committee on Production Guidelines for Book Longevity of the Council on Library Resources, Inc. ∞

6 7 8 9 10

Contents

Illustrations

Maps

Foreword

IT WAS DECEMBER 1951, just before Christmas. I was having lunch with my friend Ferne at the Federal Square Grill in Grand Rapids, Michigan. We were talking about a doctor's recent recommendation that my four-year-old son, Jon, who suffered from asthma and was quite frail, might benefit from a move to a dry, warm climate. Ferne had lived in Mexico and recommended the Southwest, specifically Dallas. It was large enough to provide employment, had good medical facilities, and was not "big city," like Chicago.

However, neither one of us knew anyone in Texas, certainly no one who could provide some kind of emergency support system. I wondered what I should do. I realized I would probably have to wing it on my own and simply trust in the good Lord to provide. I felt like I was about to take a so-called leap of faith. However, the good Lord was not about to wait until I arrived in Dallas before intervening.

At that moment the cafe hostess, Tex, came by the table and said in a lovely, soft, Texas drawl, "Honey, couldn't help but overhear ya'll talkin' 'bout Dallas. Didn't mean to eavesdrop, but that's ma hometown. Kin I help?"

After we told her what we planned to do and why, Tex took my hand and led me to a phone near the cash register. Then she placed a call.

"Blanchehoney," she said, making the two words sound as one. "I have a friend here who needs a friend and a place to stay until she kin get settled in Dallas. She doesn't know a soul thar. She has a little boy with asthma. The doc wants her to try a dryer, warmer climate. What do you think?" Tex listened a moment, then turned to me.

"Honey, this is Blanche," she said, nodding toward the phone. "Blanche, this is Esther," she said. Tex handed me the receiver and stepped aside. That was my introduction to Blanche Barrow. I had no idea who the person was on the other end of the line, just somebody with a big heart named Blanche living in Texas.

Blanche gave me her address and phone number and then said, "Get on that Super Chief and head fer Dallas. Just tell the taxi driver I live in Pleasant Grove."

Jon and I stayed in Grand Rapids until after Christmas and then left for Texas. In Dallas we took a taxi, just as Blanche suggested. However, finding Pleasant Grove was another story. The driver finally stopped and asked for directions. It was way out in the country at that time. Finally, we found a neat, small white house with flowers around the front stoop and a short concrete walk from the dirt road. It was Blanche's place.

The change proved beneficial for Jon. He gained ten pounds the first month and suddenly had a lot more energy. I soon found a job and was actually planning to move to Texas permanently later in the year. However, such a move would prove unnecessary. Back in Michigan, Jon's doctor had become aware of a new drug developed for the treatment of asthma as part of a study by the University of Michigan Hospital. Jon was included in that study and his asthma was brought under control. He could finally tolerate Michigan's changing weather. So we stayed there.

Blanche and I stayed in touch over the years. Then, when economic circumstances brought me back to Dallas in the 1970s, we renewed our friendship. Initially, however, I had a little trouble locating Blanche because she had moved, apparently rather suddenly, from the Dallas area just about the time I arrived there. I kept calling her, but no one ever answered. Finally, one weekend I decided to find Blanche once and for all. With my trusty Mapsco and a listing from the phone book, I took off in search of her. However, all I found was a vacant lot in a mobile home development. I felt like Sam Spade looking for Brigid O'Shaughnessy in *The Maltese Falcon.* Lucky for me, however, the lady next door happened to come out on her porch to shake some rugs. I went over to talk to her, hoping she might be able to help.

"Blanche moved over a month ago," the lady said. "But I have her phone number. Come in and we'll call her." Those words were music to my ears.

The next thing I knew I was talking to dear Blanche and had directions to her new address near the town of Mabank, southeast of Dallas. With that I was "on the road again." Soon I was hugging Blanche in the flesh. It was a wonderful day. I found out that Bonnie Parker's niece, Rhea Leen Linder, had moved both Blanche and Bonnie's sister, Billie Jean, near Mabank so they could be near her and she could watch over them.

Shortly after Blanche and I got together again, she was diagnosed with lung cancer. A longtime smoker, Blanche had finally quit, but it was too late. I had always felt that God must have had something special in mind when Blanche and I chanced to meet way back in 1952. Suddenly I knew what it was. My children were grown. I was on my own. Therefore, it was possible for me to help care for Blanche during her last illness.

During that period, I came to know Bonnie's sister Billie; Billie's husband A. B. Moon; and Rhea Leen, who was the daughter of Buster Parker but who had been raised by Billie Jean. These people cared for Blanche. They were a group of people possessed of a tremendous sense of family love and loyalty. Billie's husband, in particular, must occupy a special place in heaven. He was so good to those two old ladies, Blanche and Billie, both of whom could be very cantankerous and demanding, and yet at other times so much fun to be around. All of this helped me to understand a different side of the Bonnie and Clyde saga.

Much time has passed. Blanche, Billie, and A. B. are all gone now. I think of them often. I am grateful to have been included in their family circle.

When Blanche died in 1988, I was named executor of her estate, such as it was. Blanche really had very few material possessions. My task was largely to make sure that debts were paid, papers were filed, and the other assorted loose ends of her life were attended to.

On the advice of my lawyer, I held on to a number of Blanche's records, just in case something ever came up. Nothing ever did, and twelve years later, I still had all of those documents boxed up and stored in my garage. I asked my lawyer if it would be all right to discard some of those items. I was told that enough time had passed and that some housecleaning would be appropriate.

I started going through all the boxes, making sure I was not about to toss something important. That is when I discovered Blanche's handwritten account of the time she and Buck Barrow had spent in the company of Bonnie and Clyde. It was almost thrown into the trash.

The account was written on an Empire Writing Tablet No. F-1024 on lined paper 8½ by 11 inches. Blanche had placed this tablet inside a large (8½-by-11) colorful Christmas card. It shows two ice-skaters on a moonlit night with a lovely home and church in the background. All is lit by a full moon, smoke is coming out of the chimney, and a horse-drawn sleigh is seen by the shore. Inside, the card reads:

> *Christmas Greetings to the One I Love:*
> *I'm sending you at Christmas time my love across the sea,*
> *and I hope that you shall hold a place in your dear heart for me.*
> *Though time and distance part us, our love shall always be secure*
> *in all its blessings which it holds for you and me."*

On the back, written in ink in Blanche's hand are the words "written in 1933 or 34 & 35 Part of my story with the Barrow gang. Blanche Barrow."

I wonder if she was thinking of Buck when she wrote those words and put them in that particular card.

Because I knew that Blanche would have wanted this story told to a wider audience and because I knew of his earlier work with the Bonnie and Clyde saga, I turned Blanche's handwritten "memoir" over to John Neal Phillips, asking him to prepare it for publication. I am glad I did.

The Blanche I knew was the antithesis of the young girl blinded by love and caught up in the tragedy of Bonnie and Clyde. She was a gardener, a lover of all creatures (whether animal or human), a builder of churches, and yes, even a Sunday school teacher. Indeed, she made certain all her Sunday school pupils left her class with their own Bible. She told me that the only thing she ever stole was a Gideon Bible from a tourist court and she wanted to be sure that none of her "kids" would have to steal a Bible. Blanche gave each of them one as they were promoted to the next class.

Blanche also had a wonderful sense of humor, Billie Jean too, something they both kept right up to the end. They were a regular comedy team. I am certain they are keeping St. Peter busy. Moreover, he had better watch out! If he ever turns his back on those two, they just might open up heaven's pearly gates and let everybody in!

ESTHER L. WEISER

Editor's Preface

THE FIRST TIME I ever heard the names Bonnie and Clyde was from my father. Sometime around the age of ten, as a result of watching the television series *The Untouchables*, I became interested in the outlaws of the 1920s and 1930s. My father had lived in Chicago during the period of Al Capone and Elliot Ness and used to regale me with his memories of those days. (He lived around the corner from the location of the infamous St. Valentine's Day Massacre.) Interspersed with tales of Chicago would be the names of other outlaws and lawmen of the day, Bonnie and Clyde among them. In my adolescent reality, I found myself mildly interested in a couple who would die together as outlaws rather than live apart.

This initial, admittedly superficial contact with America in the early part of the twentieth century nevertheless left me with something I have found eminently useful throughout my life, the knowledge that the record of a given event may not necessarily be an accurate account of that event. Because my father's memory of Chicago often differed greatly from what was being portrayed on the small screen—and it was *his* take on things that he announced loudly and clearly—I suddenly became acutely aware of the possibility of misinterpreted facts, or in some cases a complete lack of facts, especially in the hands of the entertainment industry. Since then, I have tried never to take for granted any record of fact. I know that accounts can vary and that secondary sources sometimes misinterpret details from their primary sources, and that even primary sources can leave one's head spinning because of the differences, sometimes significant, that arise from multiple accounts of the very same incident. Any historian attempting to reconstruct the past will encounter this, but the problems of sifting through the lives of a pair of intensely hunted outlaws such as Bonnie and Clyde are enormous. Not only were the fugitives and their inner circle secretive by the very nature of their existence, but the legions of law enforcement officials tracking them were secretive as well. Such a trait opens the door to the substitution of speculation, folklore, and misinformation for sound fact, some of which has been accepted for decades. Almost everyone dealing with this subject, myself included, has fallen victim to this very common phenomenon, common at least when dealing with Bonnie and Clyde. Therefore, I consider the publication of the memoir of Blanche Caldwell Barrow a major moment for students of the subject.

One may ask why we should care about the brief, tragic lives of a pair of Texans who wrought so much pain and suffering on so many innocent people. Some even complain that to discuss them or other criminals does nothing more than glorify them. However, when placed in the larger context of the socioeconomic times of the Great Depression, coupled with other factors like the culture of the Texas prison system, named the worst such institution in the nation in 1935, and the seductive nature of crime in general, there is much to be learned. If we view history as the collective memory of society, enabling us to progress into the future without encountering the same foibles that plagued our forebears, then we realize that every aspect of the past holds lessons. If we wish to eradicate crime, or at least gain control of it, then we should make a serious study of all criminals, especially Bonnie and Clyde, a couple who were not motivated in the least by money or greed, but by revenge. In his great work, *Life of Reason*, philosopher George Santayana wrote, "Those who cannot remember the past are condemned to repeat it." I do not think anyone would deny that society stands to benefit from examining its collective memory, its history, regarding crime and criminal behavior.

My boyhood fascination with underworld events, as filtered through my father, subsided as I came of age, but my interest in history did not. In college I lived overseas on a scholarship and studied firsthand the very places where society was born thousands of years ago. However, in 1980, I came back to outlaws. In that year, Andre L. Gorzell and I co-authored an essay about Bonnie Parker for the book *Legendary Ladies of Texas* (E-Heart Press, 1980). The essay was really rather inauspicious, but it led to my being introduced to former Barrow gang member Ralph Fults, who in turn introduced me to a host of others who knew Bonnie and Clyde, including Clyde's sister Marie and his sister-in-law Blanche Caldwell Barrow. The result was my book, *Running with Bonnie and Clyde: The Ten Fast Years of Ralph Fults* (University of Oklahoma Press, 1996).

Because I was privileged enough to have interviewed Blanche Barrow while conducting research for *Running with Bonnie and Clyde*, it was with particular pleasure that I accepted Esther Weiser's invitation to edit and annotate her memoir. Apart from Blanche Barrow, only Esther ever knew of the memoir's existence, and even she forgot about it until twelve years after the author's death. Perhaps the manuscript's rather caustic observations about some of the people toward whom Blanche later became very close kept her from pursuing its publication, or even revealing its existence. We may never know about that. However, concerning the value of history and the lessons to be learned from every story, even that of Bonnie and Clyde, we find a tangible thread throughout the memoir—the wholly unromantic, tension-filled life of a fugitive on the run.

Blanche Caldwell Barrow is not objective at all in her record. Hers is a most subjective viewpoint. Nevertheless, therein lies the value of her story. Her observations of those around her during her time on the run are often unflattering, usually poignant, and always from the gut. There's a sense of gritty reality throughout, with very little joy sprinkled here and there amidst long periods of grueling travels punctuated by brief periods of life-threatening activity—certainly not the stuff of romance and folklore. If ever there was a statement of the seductions and ultimate futility of crime, this is it!

Helping young girls understand the circumstances that drew the daughter of an Oklahoma farmer and part-time preacher into the netherworld of Clyde and Buck Barrow was the apparent driving force behind this document. There is also an aspect of self-examination coupled with an overall tone of explanation, perhaps directed to her father, Matt Caldwell. However, Blanche states that the intent of her memoir was to illustrate the ease with which one can become mired and very nearly consumed by some social aberration such as a life of crime, or in her case a few months of crime, a very intense few months of crime.

This was exactly what happened to Ralph Fults, who characterized his descent into juvenile delinquency and his later adult criminal behavior with the likes of Clyde Barrow and Raymond Hamilton as initially a game.

Nevertheless, it did not take long for that game to become serious business. Before he knew it he was in way over his head, and although he eventually straightened himself out, the residue of that youthful "game," as he called it, stayed with him all of his life. Certainly, such was the same for Blanche. Those few months on the run followed her wherever she went for the remainder of her nearly seventy-eight years.

In some ways one can see that Blanche Caldwell Barrow was a victim, blinded to reality by her deep, intense love for Buck Barrow, Clyde Barrow's older brother. Of Blanche's abiding loyalty to her husband, a loyalty that would lead to her involvement in robbery, murder, and a life on the run during the spring and summer of 1933, W. D. Jones, a friend and accomplice, would later observe, "I never knew love could be so strong."

On the other hand, Blanche later admitted to her own complicity in the events leading to her husband's death and her own imprisonment. "Clyde never held a gun to my head," she said in a 1984 interview. "I was there because I wanted to be." Moreover, she was quite aware of Buck's background before she married him. She even spoke of accompanying Buck on robberies before his voluntary return to prison on December 27, 1931.

Having heard these things from Blanche herself, I was somewhat surprised by the overall tone of her memoir. Throughout she maintains initial ignorance of Buck's criminal activity and paints her dead husband as an unwilling participant in nearly everything that happened between April 13 and July 29, 1933. Even as she is relating how Buck told her of killing an Arkansas town marshal, she follows by stating that Buck "loved life and hated to take it."

Blanche also casts herself as a vehemently unwilling participant in the violence and robberies. However, while it may be true that she never handled a weapon, witnesses still saw her on at least two occasions helping Buck and Clyde flee from the scene of bank robberies, perhaps even firing a weapon during one of those escapades. She also said later that she was not exactly the picture of wide-eyed innocence she was supposed to be. In addition, of the hysterical portrayal of her in the 1967 Warren Beatty–Faye Dunaway film, *Bonnie and Clyde*, Blanche said, "That movie made me out like a screaming horse's ass!" Yet, that is exactly how she portrays herself in her own memoir. Such is also the case in Jan Fortune's book *Fugitives* and in the unpublished memoir of Clyde's mother, Cumie Barrow. However, all three manuscripts were written at a time when Blanche could have easily been charged with murder, among other crimes. Indeed, the threat of a murder charge hung over Blanche all her life. No doubt this was on her mind as she began composing her memoir in her room at Camp 1 of the Missouri State Penitentiary in 1933 and may account for the discrepancy in its overall tone when compared with her later statements. Nevertheless, in many ways the Blanche of this memoir is not the same Blanche I interviewed in 1984.

The memoir appears to be a first draft, evidently never progressing to more polished stages. It is very raw. The author was not unintelligent by any means—I found her sharp-witted, thoughtful, and articulate—but she was not very well educated. The original manuscript, written in longhand on a school tablet, contains little punctuation, nearly all of which is very irregular. Throughout the text, there are numerous dots, which at first may be taken as an overuse of periods. However, because of the injuries she sustained in the Platte City, Missouri, battle of July 19, 1933, it is likely the author was placing her pencil on the line she was working on whenever she paused or looked away from the page so she would not lose her place. One can imagine her hunched over her tablet, inches from the page, focusing her one "good" eye on her work, no doubt with limited success. Still, there are other difficulties with the memoir.

Spelling is largely phonetic, sentences are lengthy run-ons, paragraphs are virtually non-existent, and while there are a few chapter headings, great long passages remain uncategorized, begging for some manner of separation from the rest of the text. The result is a rambling, at times incoherent record of events written seemingly in a cathartic state by an author wishing to exorcize some manner of demon. Indeed, despite her stated goal of warning others of the pitfalls of her early life, it may be that after writing everything down the author felt she had taken the memoir as far as she needed to and was no longer compelled to publish the work, or to even mention it afterward.

However, in 1984, she was reunited with Ralph Fults after fifty-two years, and finding he was working with me on his own account of Bonnie and Clyde, Blanche dug out her all-but-forgotten memoir and handed it to Esther L. Weiser, asking her to see if anything could be done with it. A short time later, though, the author fell ill and the memoir was once again set aside.

Once the memoir resurfaced and was examined thoroughly, it became evident that a lot of work was needed. To bring the piece to a publishable state would require careful editing. To that end, it was extremely helpful that I had already conducted so much research into the subject and had interviewed Blanche Caldwell Barrow before her death in 1988. This made it so much easier to regularize the text, adding punctuation; creating sentences, paragraphs, and chapters; and generally polishing the original without altering the tone and content of the work. (See Appendix A for a comparison of two original pages with the corresponding finished work.)

Throughout I have annotated the author's record with notes designed to help the reader understand the context of the events portrayed. Wherever possible, I have given names, dates, and locations in the Notes, along with any other pertinent information.

A number of people and organizations have helped in the development and publication of this important document. I would first like to extend my warmest regards and thanks to Esther L. Weiser, executor of the estate of Blanche Caldwell Barrow, for offering me the chance to work on the manuscript and for believing so wholeheartedly in my ability to do a good job with it. I also thank her for providing the Foreword to this book. I must also thank Lisa Hembry of the Dallas Historical Society who first suggested that I edit and annotate the memoir. I must thank Francis E. Abernethy, Ph.D., legendary Texas Folklore Society editor and all-around piney woods character, for giving me some sage advice with respect to editing this memoir. In addition, I must not forget to mention Kent Biffle of the *Dallas Morning News*, who gave me access to his rare 1969 taped interview with W. D. Jones and an even rarer letter from a former Eastham convict named Sterling Henson. Thanks as well to my longtime friend, author, and archivist parexcellence, Carol Roark of the Dallas Public Library, for helping me sift through the rather substantial holdings of the Texas/Dallas History Archives she oversees at the library's downtown location. I must also extend a very hearty thanks to James R. Knight for his impeccable new research into the subject of Bonnie and Clyde and for readily sharing it with me. To retired warden Jim Willett, formerly of the Texas Department of Criminal Justice, Institutional Division, now of the Texas Prison Museum, I wish to express my sincerest thanks for giving me and other historians such unfettered access to the old Walls prison unit, among other places, and for his continuing interest in the truth, whatever it may be. Thanks to L. J. "Boots" Hinton for his wit and friendship and for making his collections available to me. Thanks also to Buddy Barrow for sharing his photo collection and his memories of his stepfather, LC Barrow, and for letting me pick his brain so often about the very detailed research he has done on his family. In addition, to Rhea Leen Linder many thanks for helping me with stories, pictures, and other artifacts related to her aunts, Billie Jean and Bonnie Parker. I should also like to mention my wife, Andre L. Gorzell, and our daughter, Angela Phillips, both of whom have been so supportive of all my projects, including this one. Moreover, I have to offer many thanks, albeit posthumously, to Ralph Fults, who started it all for me; Blanche Caldwell Barrow, who willingly shared her story with me even when it was apparent that doing so was immensely painful; and Marie Barrow, who graciously gave of her time and allowed me unlimited access to family papers, photographs, and other heirlooms, including Cumie Barrow's unpublished manuscript, in an effort to help resolve the many unanswered questions about her brothers Clyde and Buck Barrow. Also, thanks to John Drayton and Alice Stanton and everyone at the University of Oklahoma Press for their aid and enthusiastic support. Ursula Smith deserves a word of thanks as well, for her excellent copy editing and other suggestions about the manuscript.

Others to acknowledge include: Sergeant Bobby Adams, Texas Department of Criminal Justice, Institutional Division, Eastham Unit; Phyllis Adams, Oklahoma Historical Society Newspaper Archives; Frances "Francie" Baber; T. Lindsay Baker; Wilma Blohm; Warden Major David Bone, Texas Department of Criminal Justice, Institutional Division, Wynne Unit; Polly Bower, Seneca (Mo.) Branch Library; Charles Brown, Texas Department of Criminal Justice, Public Relations Office; Jack L. Burleson, St. John's (Mo.) Bank and Trust; Linda Childress, Newton County (Mo.) Historical Society; Carolyn Chittendon, Camden County (Mo.) Library; Carolyn Couch, Oklahoma Historical Society Newspaper Archives; Kermit "Curley" Crawford; Christine [*sic*]; Michele DeLeon, Kansas City (Mo.) Public Library; Assistant Warden Joe R. Driskell, Texas Department of Criminal Justice, Institutional Division, Eastham Unit; Ola May Earnest, president, Linn County (Kans.) Historical Society Library and Museum; Robert C. Elston; Marvelle Feller; Bob Fischer; Trey Ford; Jimm Foster, Dallas Public Library, Texas/Dallas History Archives Division; Kenneth R. Fults; Ruth Fults; Liz Gaines, the Osborne Association; Michael Glennis, Springfield (Mo.) Library; William Goldman, Hempstead County (Ark.) Genealogical Society; Beverly Grant, Osborne Association; Rob Groman, Amarillo (Tex.) Public Library; Larry Grove; Jeanette Haley, Chandler County (Okla.) Library; Floyd Hamilton; Mildred Hamilton; Sherrie Langston Hardin, Joplin (Mo.) Public

Library; Mary Harris, Culver-Union (Ind.) Public Library; Johnny Hayes; Mr. and Mrs. John W. "Preacher" Hays; Betty Hobgood, Swisher County (Tex.) Library; Ken M. Holmes, Jr.; Eloise Horak, Stephenville (Tex.) Public Library; Jim Hounschell, Joplin (Mo.) Historical Society; Janice Hoyt, Pratt (Kans.) Public Library; Mike Hughes; Jack [*sic*]; Lieutenant Lonny Johnson, Texas Department of Criminal Justice, Institutional Division, Walls Unit; Sandy Jones; Linda Jorgensen; Norma Kelley, Prague (Okla.) Library; Ellis Kimsey; Shirley Kimsey; Walter M. Legg, Jr.; Charles T. "Tim" Leone; Violet Lierheimer, Audrain County (Mo.) Area Genealogical Society; Warden Charles R. Martin, Texas Department of Criminal Justice, Institutional Division, Eastham Unit; James W. "Jim" Martin, clerk of court, Bienville Parish, Louisiana; Brenda Martin-Granstra, Heron Lake (Minn.) Library; Rick Mattix; Cecil Mayes; Pat McConal; Sharol Neely, Local History and Genealogy, Springfield-Greene County (Mo.) Library; Sarah Nyman, Kansas City (Mo.) Public Library; Louise Polly Palmer, Bienville Parish (La.) Library; Dr. Robert Pierce; Teresa Pierce; John Pronk, WFAATV, Dallas; Bruce Quisenberry, Joplin (Mo.) Historical Society; Carroll Rich; James Ritchie, *Celina* (*Tex.*) *Record*; Robert F. Roseborough; Carol Ruckdeschel, Cumberland Island (Ga.) Museum; Robert H. Russell, Jr.; Luke Scoma; William B. Searles; Shauna Smith, History Museum for Springfield-Greene County, Missouri; Renay Stanard; Lieutenant Gene Stewart, Texas Department of Criminal Justice, Institutional Division, Walls Unit; Kathleen Stockmier, Irving (Tex.) Community Television Network; LaVerne Taulbee; Carol Taylor, W. Walworth Harrison Public Library, Greenville, Texas; Hilda Terry, Cleveland County (Ark.) Library; Jerry Turner, Texas Prison History Association; Carol Waller, *The Landmark*, Platte City, Iowa; Samantha Warhol, Joplin (Mo.) Public Library; Margaret Waring, Comanche (Tex.) Public Library; Dr. Robert Weesner, Dexter (Iowa) Historical Society; Lee Wilhite, Platte County (Mo.) Historical Society; Alice Withrow, Atoka County (Okla.) Library; and Mike Woltz.

I would also like to thank the following institutions for supplying the many fine photographs and other materials needed to research this subject: Atoka County Library, Atoka, Oklahoma; Barker Texas History Center, Austin, Texas; Barrow Collection; Bienville Parish Courthouse, Arcadia, Louisiana; Bienville Parish Public Library, Arcadia, Louisiana; Bryan County Heritage Association, Calera, Oklahoma; *Celina* (*Tex.*) *Record* Archive; Chickasaw Regional Library, Ardmore, Oklahoma; Crawford

Collection; Dallas Historical Society, Dallas, Texas; Dallas Public Library, Texas/Dallas History Archives Division; Denton County Public Library, Denton, Texas; *Des Moines (Iowa) Register* Photo Archives; Dexter (Iowa) Historical Society; Fairbury (Neb.) Chamber of Commerce; Trey Ford Collection; Fults Collection; Hayes Collection; Hillsboro (Tex.) Public Library; Hinton Collection; Holmes Collection; Houston County Historical Commission, Crockett, Texas; Houston (Tex.) Public Library; Joplin (Mo.) Historical Society; Joplin (Mo.) Public Library; Kaufman County Public Library, Kaufman, Texas; Leone Collection; Lorenzo de Zavalla Library, Austin, Texas; Mayes Collection; McKinney (Tex.) Public Library; Miami (Okla.) Public Library; Missouri Highway Patrol Archives; Moody Ranger Museum, Waco, Texas; Russell Collection; St. Louis County (Mo.) Public Library; Sam Houston State University Library, Huntsville, Texas; Searles Collection; Sherman (Tex.) Public Library; Tarrant County Community College District Library, Northeast Campus, Fort Worth, Texas; Temple (Tex.) Public Library; Texas Department of Criminal Justice, Institutional Division, Eastham Unit, Weldon, Texas; Texas Department of Criminal Justice, Institutional Division, Walls Unit, Huntsville, Texas; Texas Prison History Association; Texas Prison Museum, Huntsville, Texas; U.S. Government Archives, Fort Worth Branch, Fort Worth, Texas; University of North Texas Library, Denton, Texas; W. Walworth Harrison Public Library, Greenville, Texas; Wichita County Public Library, Wichita Falls, Texas.

If I omitted anyone, please forgive me. It was not intentional. I will make it up next time.

Editor's Introduction

The world was a miserable, wretched place to be in the 1930's. It was a time when death lurked around every street corner—death which could be as slow as starvation or as quick as a whistling machinegun bullet. . . . [It was a time when] everyone and everything—including the immediate future—was in doubt. . . . While a handful of men were getting rich . . . the average citizen was hard-scrabbling a meager existence [while] the staff of life was being whittled shorter and shorter with every skimpy meal.

—Billie Jean Parker Moon, 1975,
from "Bonnie, Clyde, and Me"

BLANCHE CALDWELL BARROW, the author of the following memoir, came of age during a moment in the history of the United States when a seemingly vital economy suddenly crumbled and in some parts of the country literally disappeared, resulting first in deep recession and ultimately in what is known today as the Great Depression. Her time on the run with the man she is most closely associated with, Buck Barrow, was in part a by-product of the poor economy, but there were other issues as well. Ironically, her weeks as one of the most sought-after fugitives of the 1930s roughly coincided with President Franklin D. Roosevelt's famous "Hundred Days" that produced a program of legislation designed to bring relief to the average, "hard-scrabbling" citizen described above. Nevertheless, 1933, the year the

Blanche Caldwell, left, age three, pictured with childhood friends Bertha Burr, center, and Vinia Ball, 1914. (Courtesy of Rhea Leen Linder)

Barrow brothers shot their way out of police traps from Joplin to Platte City, Missouri, remains one of the most violent of the era. There was a lot of anger. Sometimes it was manifested in hunger protests, bread riots, veterans' marches, and farm strikes. Sometimes in crime sprees.

Bennie Iva Blanche Caldwell was born New Year's Day 1911 in Garvin, Oklahoma, between Hugo and Idabel in the far southeastern part of the state. Her father was a forty-year-old farmer and sometime preacher named Matthew Fountain Caldwell. Her mother, Lillian Bell Pond, was sixteen. The only information available about the marriage is that it did not last, that Lillian left, and that Blanche was raised chiefly by her father. And, according to Blanche herself, her father spoiled her.[1]

Oklahoma had been a state for less than four years at the time of Blanche Caldwell's birth, William Howard Taft was president of the United States, and World War I was still three years in the future. In 1911 the very first Chevrolet was manufactured, Standard Oil and American Tobacco were declared monopolies and broken up by the federal government, and Mexican dictator Porfirio Diaz was deposed by revolutionaries. Edith Wharton's *Ethan Frome* was published that year, baseball great Ty Cobb won his fifth straight batting title, and the very first running of the Indianapolis 500 took place. In addition, in 1911 Marie Curie won an unprecedented second Nobel Prize, European immigration to the United States reached a peak, and the American divorce rate had risen 692 percent in just six years. The latter statistic would directly affect Blanche Caldwell, whose mother divorced and remarried numerous times in her long life, a fact that bothered Blanche more than just a little.[2] On her own, Blanche would part from three husbands, but only one by choice.

When Blanche was still a teenager, her mother forced her to marry a man named John Callaway. Callaway was apparently much older than Blanche and well acquainted with her mother. To close friends Blanche speculated that her mother thought Callaway had some money, enough anyway to perhaps acquire some it for herself by offering her daughter as part of the deal. The only thing Blanche got from the marriage, however, was abuse, both physical and emotional. Although seeing the arrangement initially as a means to freedom and independence, she quickly found it to be otherwise. Among other things, the experience left her unable to bear children.[3]

Blanche endured the marriage for a while, and then ran away, apparently to West Dallas, a poor, and at the time unincorporated, neighborhood across the Trinity River from the city. By this time, December 1929, Blanche Caldwell Callaway had acquired a young friend named Emma Lou Renfro, who may have been hiding Blanche from her husband and family.[4] Callaway had a sister living in Dallas, and Blanche, still a teenager, no doubt feared being tracked down.[5] American women in the 1920s, especially underage women, had little recourse against abusive spouses. This might account for the fact that Blanche waited until 1931 to surface and seek a divorce from Callaway. By then, however, she had also met another man.

According to Clyde Barrow's youngest sister, Marie, Blanche was living at the home of a friend, "On Borger, near the railroad tracks." One source indicates that Blanche was walking in West Dallas one day when she passed a young man. At some point, she and the young man struck up a conversation. The date was November 11, 1929. Their subsequent friendship developed quickly into deep affection and love. His name was Marvin Ivan Barrow. His friends called him Buck, but Blanche referred to him as Daddy.[6]

Just after midnight on November 30, 1929, less than three weeks after meeting Blanche, Buck was shot following a burglary in Denton, Texas, and arrested. He was tried and sentenced to four years in the Texas State Penitentiary. He began serving his sentence on January 14, 1930. In a letter written home two days later, Buck asked that Blanche write to him. (See Appendix C.) Apparently, she wrote to him often, but on March 8, 1930, less than two months after his delivery to the penitentiary system, Buck escaped from the Ferguson prison farm, near Midway, Texas, and returned to Dallas. More than a year later, following the finalization of her divorce from her first husband, Blanche married Buck Barrow. The date was July 3, 1931.[7]

It has been stated that Blanche was initially ignorant of Buck's criminal activities and that she did not realize he was an escaped convict. But that is hard to believe; she had to have known of his arrest on November 30, 1929. Buck's mother knew all along that her son had gone to prison and had subsequently escaped. In her unpublished manuscript, Cumie Barrow wrote, "When Buck escaped from the pen, he came by here and got Blanche (who was staying here) and they went off some place in a car. I think it was in a rooming house someplace, where they hid for awhile." This suggests that Blanche Barrow knew more than she admits in her own memoir. Still, whatever the extent of Blanche's initial knowledge of the nature of Buck's freedom, she, along with Buck's mother, eventually persuaded Buck to turn himself over to prison authorities, finish out his term, and start over again with a clean record. On December 27, 1931, Buck traveled to Huntsville, Texas, and surrendered to a group of very surprised prison officials.[8]

Buck Barrow served his remaining term and was issued a pardon by Governor Miriam Ferguson. He was released from prison on March 22,

1933, and reunited with his young wife the following night. Within a few days, Clyde Barrow paid a visit to Buck and Blanche. The meeting was strained and tense. By this time, Clyde, in the company of his girlfriend, Bonnie Parker, and a young man from West Dallas named W. D. Jones, was widely sought for a number of crimes ranging from auto theft to murder.

Clyde immediately began pressing Buck and Blanche to help him raid Eastham, the notorious Texas prison farm. Both Clyde and Ralph Fults had begun plotting the break-in while they were still convicts serving time there. Although mistaken in thinking that the plan was hatched to free criminal cohort Raymond Hamilton (Hamilton would not arrive at Eastham until August 1933, after Buck Barrow was dead and Blanche was in police custody), Blanche knew well of Clyde's desire to raid Eastham. And she was not eager to get involved with her brother-in-law. Still, Buck pressed the point. Eventually he and Blanche arrived at a very tenuous compromise. They would not help with the raid, but they would meet again with Clyde, Bonnie, and W. D. They would even try to convince Clyde to give himself up, even though both thought it futile.[9]

Thus, it was with some apprehension on the part of Blanche that on Wednesday, March 29, 1933, she and her husband took to the road, meeting Clyde first in Oklahoma, and then proceeding with him to Joplin, Missouri. Blanche was evidently hopeful enough about the visit to bring her camera with her, to record the images of those she could not otherwise see with any frequency.[10] Nevertheless, it would be there, in Joplin, that her fears became reality, changing her life forever.

On April 13, 1933, the day before Buck and Blanche were to return to West Dallas, six lawmen arrived at the garage apartment occupied by the Barrow brothers. A gunfight erupted. Two officers were killed and in their haste to escape, the fugitives left most of their belongings behind—including Buck's pardon papers and marriage license and Blanche's camera. Now he and Blanche were on the run with Bonnie and Clyde and their friend W. D. Jones.

In her diary, Blanche describes graphically the scene left in the wake of the bloody shoot-out. In a subsequent interview, she told of helping move the body of one of the slain officers so Clyde could get the car out of the garage.[11] Nevertheless, that was not the end of the story.

On July 19, 1933, a posse descended on Platte City, Missouri, and surrounded the tourist cabins occupied by the Barrow brothers. Again, a

Buck and Blanche Barrow near Crockett, Texas, 1931. (Courtesy of Rhea Leen Linder)

gunfight ensued and again the gang escaped. But this time Buck was mortally wounded, and Blanche was struck in the forehead with a bullet fragment and in one of her eyes with razor-sharp shards of glass.

Seeking refuge in an abandoned amusement park near Dexter, Iowa, the gang camped out for four days after their escape from Platte City. Buck drifted in and out of consciousness while Blanche, her vision greatly impaired, tried to nurse his wound. Then on July 24, 1933, just before dawn, another posse engaged the gang. Bonnie, Clyde, and W. D., all wounded, escaped. Buck and Blanche were captured—Blanche calling, "Don't die, Daddy," as she was separated from Buck. Five days later, he was dead.

Blanche was tried in Platte City, Missouri, on a charge of assault with intent to kill and was sentenced to ten years in the state penitentiary at Jefferson City. She began her memoir shortly thereafter.[12] Less than a year later, on May 23, 1934, she heard of the deaths of Bonnie and Clyde. She told reporters that she was glad they died together. In 1935, while seated in a federal courtroom with numerous other defendants (including a heavily manacled W. D. Jones), Blanche received an additional sentence of one year and one day for harboring Bonnie and Clyde; the extra time was to be served concurrently with her Missouri sentence (meaning her total sentence remained ten years).

Bonnie and Clyde on a road between Marshall, Texas, and Dallas, 1933. (Courtesy of L. J. Hinton)

By then, she had become close friends with Holt Coffey, the sheriff of Platte City, Missouri. Coffey was the officer who had launched the unsuccessful attempt to surround the Barrow brothers in 1933, the same officer Blanche was convicted of assaulting. With his help, along with that of a friendly FBI agent and the wife of a Missouri governor, Blanche's prison experience was made as comfortable as possible. It was certainly nothing to compare to the sadistic brutality suffered by her brother-in-law Clyde in the Texas penitentiary. In a letter to her mother, Blanche mentioned that she and the other female inmates were "not behind bars" and that they were allowed to make many of their own decisions, within prison regulations, of course.[13] One negative side to Blanche's sentence was the eventual loss of her injured eye. Initially, doctors were confident the eye could be saved, but a number of serious complications resulted in its loss.

Blanche was a model prisoner throughout her time in prison.[14] Indeed, she received an early release due to good behavior. On March 24, 1939, Blanche Barrow walked out of the Missouri State Penitentiary and went home to her father in Garvin, Oklahoma.

Chronology

March 14, 1903	Marvin Ivan "Buck" Barrow is born in Jones Prairie, Texas. The year 1905 on his gravestone is incorrect according to the family Bible and family members, including Marie and Cumie Barrow. When her son died, Cumie Barrow confused Buck's birth year with that of his younger sister Nell, born May 12, 1905.
March 24, 1910	Clyde Chestnut Barrow is born near Telico, Texas. The year 1909 on his gravestone is incorrect according to the family Bible and family members. In a repeat of what happened with Buck's marker (actually Buck and Clyde share the same marker), Cumie Barrow was apparently so upset at the death of Clyde that she again gave the wrong birth year to the stonecutter.
October 1, 1910	Bonnie Parker is born in Rowena, Texas. She is the third child of four born to Emma Krause and Charles Parker. The firstborn, Coley, died of crib death. Hubert "Buster" was born December 20, 1908, and Billie Jean was born December 16, 1912.
December 31, 1914	Charles Parker, Bonnie's father, dies.
1915	The Parkers move to Eagle Ford, Texas (Dallas County).

1920	Buck Barrow and Margaret Heneger marry. Twin boys are born, one of whom dies at five months of age. Barrow and Heneger divorce soon thereafter.
1921	The Barrows move to West Dallas, Texas (Dallas County). They are first listed in the city directory in 1922, but the youngest child, Marie, born May 27, 1918, said the family moved when she was three years old.
1925	Buck Barrow and Pearl Churchley are married. A daughter is born in 1926. Barrow and Churchley divorce soon thereafter.
September 25, 1926	Bonnie Parker marries Roy Glyn Thornton. Both are in their second year at Cement High School, Cement, Texas. Both quit school.
December 3, 1926	Clyde Barrow's first known arrest occurs in Dallas. He is charged with auto theft, but the charges are dropped.
1927	Blanche Caldwell is forced by her mother to marry John Callaway.
1928	Blanche Caldwell Callaway and her friend Emma Lou Renfro escape to West Dallas.
February 22, 1928	Clyde Barrow is arrested in Fort Worth for "investigation."
August 13, 1928	Buck Barrow is arrested in San Antonio for auto theft.
January 23, 1929	The Barrows (including Henry and Cumie, Buck's parents, and LC and Marie, his siblings) and the Jones family (including W. D.) travel by wagon to San Antonio for Buck's hearing. The charges against him are dropped.
October 13, 1929	Clyde and Buck Barrow and a third man are arrested on suspicion of burglarizing Buell Lumber in Dallas. Charges are dismissed.
October 24, 1929	"Black Thursday," the stock market crashes.
October 29, 1929	"Black Tuesday" brings a stock-market crash even more devastating than that of the previous week.
November 11, 1929	Buck Barrow and Blanche Caldwell Callaway meet.

[handwritten marginal notes: "Buck married twice, 1 girl"; "Bonnie & Blanche married"; "Buck & Clyde violent before Black Thursday"]

November 29, 1929	Clyde and Buck Barrow and a third man burglarize the Mark Garage in Denton, Texas. Buck is shot and captured. Clyde and the third man escape.
December 17, 1929	Buck Barrow is sentenced to four years for burglary.
January 1930	Bonnie (estranged from Roy Thornton, but not divorced) and Clyde meet for the first time at the West Dallas home of Clarence Clay, a friend of Clyde's whose sister is married to Bonnie's brother, Buster.
January 14, 1930	Buck Barrow is received at the Texas State Penitentiary in Huntsville.
February 1930	Clyde is arrested at the home of Bonnie's mother.
March 3, 1930	Clyde is sentenced to two years on each of seven counts of auto theft and burglary in Waco, Texas.
March 8, 1930	Buck Barrow and another inmate escape from the Ferguson prison farm on the Trinity River, just north of Huntsville. Barrow drives to West Dallas, picks up Blanche, and flees to the farm of his uncle Jim Muckleroy near Martinsville, Texas.
March 11, 1930	Clyde Barrow, using a gun smuggled to him by Bonnie Parker, escapes with two others from the McClelland County jail in Waco.
March 17, 1930	Clyde Barrow and his fellow escapees are captured in Middleton, Ohio, and returned to Texas.
April 21, 1930	Clyde Barrow is received at the Texas State Penitentiary at Huntsville. Over the next several weeks, he is transferred to various county jurisdictions on bench warrants.
September 18, 1930	Returning from Waco after a court appearance on a bench warrant, Clyde Barrow meets Ralph Fults in the rear of the prison transport. Fults and Barrow are both remanded to the Eastham prison farm, twenty miles north of Huntsville. That fall, responding to the brutal policies of Colonel Lee Simmons, general manager of the Texas prison system, Fults and Barrow begin making plans to one day raid Eastham.

July 3, 1931	After receiving a divorce from her first husband the month before, Blanche Caldwell marries Buck Barrow.
October 29, 1931	Clyde Barrow kills his first man, an Eastham "building tender" and convict trustee named Ed Crowder.
August 26, 1931	Ralph Fults is paroled by Texas governor Ross Sterling.
December 27, 1931	Buck Barrow voluntarily returns to prison to finish serving his term. His wife lives with the Barrow family at least through April 1932 at their residence behind the Star Service Station, the family business at 1620 Eagle Ford Road, West Dallas.
January 27, 1932	Clyde Barrow cuts off two of his own toes and is admitted to the main prison hospital in Huntsville.
February 2, 1932	Clyde Barrow is paroled by Texas governor Ross Sterling.
March 25, 1932	Clyde Barrow, Ralph Fults, and Raymond Hamilton rob the Simms Oil Refinery in West Dallas. Clyde borrows Buck's gun from Blanche for the job. Blanche warns him not to lose the weapon, or Buck " . . . will skin you alive." Clyde loses the gun.
April 1932	Clyde Barrow, Ralph Fults, and Raymond Hamilton rob the First National Bank of Lawrence, Kansas, the first such crime for any of them. The robbery is conducted to finance the planned raid on Eastham. Hamilton abruptly backs out of the planned raid, saying, "I don't know nothing about no cons on no farm."
April 14, 1932	Barrow and Fults, having now put together a gang of six, are stopped by the chief of police of Electra, Texas, and two other officials. Barrow and Fults get the drop on them and abduct the men, later abducting a fourth man, a mail carrier, in their flight from the area.
April 18, 1932	After stealing two cars in Tyler, Texas, to use in the raid on Eastham, Barrow, Fults, and Bonnie Parker get involved in an eighteen-hour flight from a posse in Kaufman County, Texas.
April 19, 1932	Fults is wounded and captured, along with Bonnie Parker, by the Kaufman County posse near Kemp, Texas. Barrow escapes.

April 20, 1932	Barrow, along with gang members Ted Rogers and Johnny Russell, raids a Celina, Texas, hardware store for weapons to use to free Fults and Parker, who are being held in the Kaufman County jail. Clyde Barrow makes at least two trips to the Kaufman County jail, once with LC Barrow and again with Blanche Barrow, to let Fults and Parker know he is working on their escape.
April 21, 1932	A posse led by the Denton County sheriff raids Barrow's hideout on Lake Dallas. Barrow, Rogers, and Russell escape. Two other gang members are captured, and all the weapons are confiscated along with the Lawrence, Kansas, bank money.
April 30, 1932	Barrow, Rogers, and Russell rob a store in Hillsboro, Texas. Rogers kills proprietor John N. Bucher. Barrow is the only one involved in this murder who is ever correctly identified. Raymond Hamilton, who is in Michigan at the time, later receives a ninety-nine-year sentence for this crime.
May 11, 1932	Fults is returned to prison.
June 15, 1932	Bonnie is "no billed," that is, no bill of indictment was returned by the grand jury, in Kaufman County and released.
August 1, 1932	Clyde Barrow, Raymond Hamilton, and another man rob the Neuhoff Meat Packing Plant, in Dallas.
August 5, 1932	Barrow, Hamilton, and at least one other man, perhaps even a fourth man, are involved in the killing of Undersheriff Eugene Moore at an outdoor dance near Stringtown, Oklahoma.
August 14, 1932	Barrow, Hamilton, and Bonnie Parker abduct Chief Deputy Sheriff Joe Johns near Carlsbad, New Mexico, leaving him by the side of the road unharmed near San Antonio, Texas, the following day.
September 1, 1932	Raymond Hamilton leaves Bonnie and Clyde and travels to Bay City, Michigan.
October 8, 1932	Raymond Hamilton returns to Texas and robs a bank in Cedar Hill, Texas (Dallas County).
October 11, 1932	A lone bandit who escapes in a car occupied by at least two other men kills grocer Howard Hall.

	Some suspect Clyde Barrow is the killer, but others do not.
November 9, 1932	Raymond Hamilton and another man rob a bank in La Grange, Texas.
November 25, 1932	Hamilton robs the bank in Cedar Hill a second time.
November 30, 1932	Clyde Barrow, along with Hollis Hale and Frank Hardy, robs a bank in Oronogo, Missouri.
December 6, 1932	Hamilton and his La Grange accomplice are arrested in Bay City, Michigan and returned to Texas.
December 25, 1932	Clyde Barrow and W. D. Jones shoot Doyle Johnson in Temple, Texas, while in the process of stealing Johnson's car. Bonnie Parker is in another car nearby. Johnson dies the next day. Frank Hardy is eventually charged with the murder, which precipitates the well-known letter written by Clyde Barrow in Hardy's defense.
January 6, 1933	Clyde Barrow kills Tarrant county deputy sheriff Malcolm Davis at 507 County Avenue, West Dallas.
January 13, 1933	A bank in Ash Grove, Missouri, is robbed.
January 26, 1933	Barrow, Jones, and Parker abduct Springfield, Missouri motorcycle officer Tom Persell, later leaving him unharmed near Joplin, Missouri. Persell, who found himself sitting on bags of money in the car, later states that his abductors spoke freely of a number of bank robberies, including the one in Ash Grove, Missouri, on January 13, 1933.
March 22, 1933	Buck Barrow is granted a full pardon from the State of Texas by Governor Miriam Ferguson. The following day Buck and Blanche are reunited.
March 25-26, 1933	Buck and Blanche Barrow pay a visit to Blanche's mother near Wilmer, Texas. During the night Clyde Barrow, Bonnie Parker, and W. D. Jones arrive. Clyde immediately begins pressing his older brother to help him raid Eastham.
March 29, 1933	Buck and Blanche leave Texas to meet Clyde in Oklahoma. After meeting, the group (Bonnie, Clyde, W. D., Buck, and Blanche) proceed to Joplin, Missouri.

April 1, 1933	After first staying in a Joplin tourist court, Blanche Barrow, the Barrow brothers, Parker, and Jones rent a garage apartment at 3347½ Oak Ridge Drive.
April 13, 1933	Newton County (Missouri) Constable Wes Harryman and Joplin (Missouri) City Motor Detective Harry McGinnis are killed trying to serve a warrant at the Joplin, Missouri, garage apartment occupied by the Barrows and W. D. Jones. All three men in the Barrow group are wounded during the gunfight.
April 14, 1933	Clyde and Buck Barrow rob a service station in Amarillo, Texas.
April 27, 1933	Ruston, Louisiana, residents H. D. Darby and Sophie Stone are abducted by the Barrow gang following Jones's theft of Darby's car. Either by accident or by design, Jones loses the group and does not rejoin them until June.
May 5, 1933	After receiving sentences of 167 years for everything from auto theft to bank robbery, Raymond Hamilton is convicted of the murder of John N. Bucher of Hillsboro, Texas (although Ted Rogers is the actual killer). Hamilton is then sentenced to an additional 99 years—for a grand total of 266 years (the 263 years usually cited plus a little-known three-year suspended sentence for auto theft that was also revoked).
May 12, 1933	Buck and Clyde attempt a bank robbery in Lucerne, Indiana. They steal nothing and have to shoot their way out of town.
May 14, 1933	Blanche takes a bus to Dallas to arrange a post–Mother's Day meeting for Bonnie, Buck, and Clyde.
May 15, 1933	The post–Mother's Day meeting takes place near Cooper, Texas.
May 19, 1933	Buck and Clyde rob a bank in Okabena, Minnesota, of approximately $2,500 However, just as in Lucerne, Indiana, the bandits, including Bonnie Parker and Blanche Barrow, have to shoot their way out of town.
May 1933	At some point between the May 15 meeting with members of the Barrow and Parker families and the June 6 meeting with Matt Caldwell, the Barrow

	gang visits Mississippi, Florida, Georgia, and several other states during a vacation of sorts.
June 6, 1933	Buck and Blanche Barrow visit Matt Caldwell, Blanche's father, in Oklahoma.
June 10, 1933	Clyde Barrow accidentally drives into the dry wash of the Salt Fork River near Wellington, Texas. He and W. D. (who has just rejoined the gang) are thrown free. Bonnie is severely burned. While trying to investigate, Collingsworth County Sheriff George Corry and Wellington City Marshal Paul Hardy are abducted and driven to Oklahoma, where a rendezvous with Buck and Blanche takes place and the officers are released.
June 11-14, 1933	The gang hides out in Pratt, Kansas.
June 15, 1933	They move to the Twin Cities Tourist Camp in Fort Smith, Arkansas.
June 18, 1933	Clyde Barrow drives to Dallas to get Billie Jean Parker Mace so she can help nurse her sister, Bonnie Parker, in Arkansas.
June 23, 1933	With Bonnie a virtual invalid in a Fort Smith, Arkansas, motor court, Buck Barrow and W. D. Jones rob the Brown Grocery in Fayetteville, Arkansas. On the return to Fort Smith, they are involved in an accident, followed immediately by a gunfight with Alma (Ark.) City Marshal Henry D. Humphrey and Deputy A. M. "Red" Salyers. Buck kills Humphrey. He and Jones then escape in the deputy's car.
July 3, 1933	After helping her sister regain her strength, and after a brief romance with W. D. Jones, Billie Jean Mace is put on a train and sent back to Dallas.
July 7, 1933	The Barrow brothers and Jones rob the National Guard armory on the campus of Phillips University in Enid, Oklahoma.
July 10-16, 1933	The Barrow gang camps on a farmer's property on the banks of the Little Sioux River in northwest Iowa.
July 18, 1933	The Barrow brothers and Jones rob three service stations within minutes in Fort Dodge, Iowa.

July 19, 1933   Buck and Blanche are wounded during a gunfight at a motor court outside of Platte City, Missouri. Buck is shot in the head; Blanche is partially blinded by flying glass. After a protracted flight from the area, the gang escapes into Iowa.

July 22, 1933   Raymond Hamilton, held in the Dallas County jail while awaiting transfer to the state penitentiary, is discovered in the process of escaping by jailer Murray Fischer and is placed in a more secure cell.

July 24, 1933   After a gunfight in an abandoned amusement park between Dexter and Redfield, Iowa, Clyde, Bonnie, and W. D., all wounded, escape. Buck and Blanche are captured.

July 26, 1933   Blanche Barrow is extradited to Missouri where she is charged with assault with intent to kill, stemming from the Platte City gunfight.

July 29, 1933   Buck Barrow dies at King's Daughters Hospital in Perry, Iowa.

August 5, 1933   Blanche Barrow appears at a preliminary hearing in Platte County, Missouri. Her bail is set at $15,000.

August 8, 1933   Raymond Hamilton is transferred to the Texas State Penitentiary at Huntsville. Two weeks later, he is transferred to the Eastham prison farm. This is nearly five months after Clyde Barrow tried to recruit Buck and Blanche to raid the farm.

August 20, 1933   Clyde Barrow and W. D. Jones rob a National Guard armory in Plattville, Illinois. Jones leaves Bonnie and Clyde not long afterward. He is later arrested near Houston, Texas.

September 4, 1933   Blanche Barrow pleads guilty in court and receives a ten-year sentence. She is transferred immediately to the Missouri State Penitentiary in Jefferson City and received as prisoner #43454. She undergoes the first of a series of ultimately unsuccessful operations designed to save her injured eye. During this same period of time Clyde Barrow and two other men, including Texas prison escapee Henry Massingale, are involved in a series of auto mishaps, followed by a brief gun battle with local officers. Later, in an attempt to get a fresh car, Massingale approaches a group of people at an outdoor church social and demands the keys to one of the cars parked nearby. While Massingale is making his demands, a woman walks up behind him and knocks the bandit out with a croquet mallet. Barrow and the other man escape.

November 22, 1933   Bonnie and Clyde are wounded in an ambush staged by the Dallas County Sheriff's Department near Sowers. Dallas County Sheriff Smoot Schmid, organizer of the failed attempt, immediately assigns one of his deputies, Bob Alcorn, to hunt Bonnie and Clyde full-time.

January 16, 1934   Bonnie and Clyde raid the Eastham prison farm, freeing five convicts (Raymond Hamilton, Henry Methvin, Hilton Bybee, J. B. French, and Joe Palmer). Palmer kills guard Major (his given name, not his title) Joseph Crowson during the raid. Another guard, Olan Bozeman, is wounded.

January 23, 1934   The Barrow gang robs a bank in Rembrandt, Iowa.

January 25, 1934   The Barrow gang robs a bank in Poteau, Oklahoma.

February 1, 1934   The Barrow gang robs a bank in Knierim, Iowa. Former Texas Ranger Captain Frank Hamer is hired by Colonel Lee Simmons, general manager of the Texas prison system, to hunt down Bonnie and Clyde. Simmons, whose brutal policies are the basis for Barrow's intense desire to raid Eastham, tells Hamer, "I want you to put Clyde and Bonnie 'on the spot' and then shoot everyone in sight." Hamer and Dallas County Deputy Sheriff Bob Alcorn soon join forces in the field.

February 12, 1934   Clyde Barrow, Raymond Hamilton, and Henry Methvin engage local authorities in a brief but intense gun battle near Reed Springs, Missouri.

February 27, 1934   Barrow gang robs the R. P. Henry & Sons Bank in Lancaster, Texas. After the robbery, Barrow and Hamilton get into an argument and part company.

March 19, 1934   Raymond and Floyd Hamilton rob the Grand Prairie State Bank in Grand Prairie, Texas.

April 1, 1934	Clyde Barrow and Henry Methvin (one of the Eastham escapees) kill motorcycle officers E. B. Wheeler and H. D. Murphy of the Texas State Highway Patrol near Grapevine, Texas. Eyewitnesses Fred and Mary Giggal see "the larger of two men" firing at the already wounded officers. (Henry Methvin is much taller and bigger than Barrow.)
April 3, 1934	The bullet-riddled body of former Eastham convict trustee Wade McNabb is found near Marshall, Texas. The Barrow gang, or at least elements of it, are no doubt responsible.
April 6, 1934	Barrow and Methvin kill Constable Cal Campbell of Commerce, Oklahoma.
April 16, 1934	The Barrow gang robs a bank in Stuart, Iowa. The getaway car is spotted speeding through Dexter, just five miles east of Stuart.
April 25, 1934	Raymond Hamilton is captured near Howe, Texas.
May 3, 1934	The Barrow gang robs a bank in Everly, Iowa.
May 23, 1934	Bonnie and Clyde are ambushed and killed eight miles south of Gibsland, Louisiana. Henry Methvin (the Eastham escapee) later admits in an Oklahoma court that he helped engineer the ambush. From the Missouri State Penitentiary for Women, Blanche Barrow says, "I'm glad they were both killed. It was the easiest way out. I'm glad it's over. It is much better they were both killed, rather than have to be taken alive."
June 15, 1934	Joe Palmer is arrested in St. Joseph, Missouri. He is extradited to Texas where he and Hamilton both receive the death sentence—Palmer for murder, Hamilton for being a habitual criminal.
July 22, 1934	Hamilton, Palmer, and Irvin "Blackie" Thompson escape from the death house inside the Texas State Penitentiary in Huntsville.
August 8, 1934	Palmer is captured in Paducah, Kentucky, and returned to Texas.
December 6, 1934	Blackie Thompson is killed in a gunfight with police near Amarillo, Texas.

January 10, 1935   Ralph Fults is pardoned by Texas governor Miriam Ferguson.

February 4, 1935   Floyd and Raymond Hamilton rob a bank in Carthage, Texas, along with another man. Later that same night the brothers narrowly escape a police trap at their hideout in Dallas. Raymond Hamilton is wounded in the neck.

February 5, 1935   Floyd Hamilton is captured in Shreveport, Louisiana.

February 16, 1935   Raymond Hamilton and Ralph Fults rob a National Guard armory in Beaumont, Texas.

February 22, 1935   Twenty-two defendants are put on trial in federal court in Dallas for harboring Bonnie and Clyde. It is a test case, the first federal harboring charges ever brought to trial. Among the defendants are Blanche Barrow and the mothers of Bonnie Parker, Clyde Barrow, and Raymond Hamilton.

February 24, 1935   Raymond Hamilton and Ralph Fults drive through a hail of bullets and narrowly escape a police ambush north of McKinney, Texas.

March 18, 1935   Ralph Fults and Raymond Hamilton pretend to abduct reporter Harry McCormick of the *Houston Press*, supposedly to let Hamilton tell his side of the story. In reality, the abduction story is staged to protect McCormick, who receives money from the outlaws for Joe Palmer's defense attorney.

March 28, 1935   Fults and Hamilton rob a bank in Prentiss, Mississippi. During their flight, Fults is wounded. Fults and Hamilton then capture a fifteen-man posse, then a six-man posse, and finally elude two hundred troops of the Mississippi National Guard before escaping to Tennessee. The governor of Mississippi declares a state of emergency. Fults and Hamilton split up in Memphis.

April 3, 1935   Members of the Texas Prison Board and the Texas state legislature launch investigations into the brutal policies of the state prison system's general manager, Colonel Lee Simmons.

April 5, 1935	Hamilton is captured in the rail yard near East Belknap, Fort Worth, Texas. He soon rejoins Palmer on death row in Huntsville.
April 10, 1935	The Osborne Commission on U.S. Prisons names the Texas prison system the worst in the nation, citing the brutal way in which convicts are handled, particularly at Eastham.
April 17, 1935	Ralph Fults is captured near Denton, Texas.
May 10, 1935	Joe Palmer and Raymond Hamilton are executed.
June 29, 1935	Ralph Fults is extradited to Mississippi.
September 2, 1935	Ralph Fults is sentenced to two fifty-year terms in Mississippi for his part in the Prentiss bank robbery. The very same day, Colonel Lee Simmons, general manager of the Texas prison system, resigns under fire.
March 24, 1939	Blanche Caldwell Barrow is released from the Missouri State Penitentiary.
March 25, 1939	Blanche's conditional commutation from the State of Missouri, signed by Governor Lloyd C. Stark, becomes effective.
April 19, 1940	Blanche Caldwell marries Edwin Bert "Eddie" Frasure in Rockwall, Texas.
September 19, 1947	Matthew Fountain Caldwell dies.
1952	Esther Weiser moves in with Blanche and Eddie Frasure.
1967	The motion picture *Bonnie and Clyde* starring Warren Beatty, Faye Dunaway, Estelle Parsons, and Gene Hackman is released.
May 11, 1969	Eddie Frasure dies.
1970-1988	Blanche Caldwell Frasure renews old friendships with the Barrows and Parkers, particularly Artie, LC, and Marie Barrow, and Billie Jean Parker Moon. During this period, Blanche also kept in close contact with Floyd Hamilton, mostly by phone, and visited Ralph Fults at least once.
December 24, 1988	Blanche Caldwell Frasure dies.

*My Life with
Bonnie and Clyde*

1

View from a Cell

Pᴇᴏᴘʟᴇ ᴏɴʟʏ ʟɪᴠᴇ ʜᴀᴘᴘɪʟʏ ever after in fairy tales. In my case, it seems it was a crime to have ever met Buck Barrow. I was brought up by a kind, loving, law-abiding father, without the aid of a mother. But when I met Buck it was a case of true love from the first. I knew I loved him more than I had ever loved anyone before, more than I could ever love anyone else for the rest of my life. And he loved me the same, if it is possible for a man to love[1] as a woman does. I don't think I am the only woman who loved a man so much. But because I loved Marvin Buck Barrow, married him, was loyal and true to him, and to my marriage vows to the bitter end, I am now serving a ten-year sentence in prison.

I am not guilty of the crime charged to me. But I am guilty of loving my husband so much I couldn't bear to have him leave me, not knowing what hour of the day or night I may receive word of him being riddled by bullets fired from some officer's machine gun. I am asking all who may read this story, was that a crime? Even though I knew my life was in danger I went with him wherever he went. Rather than live without him, I chose to face death with him.

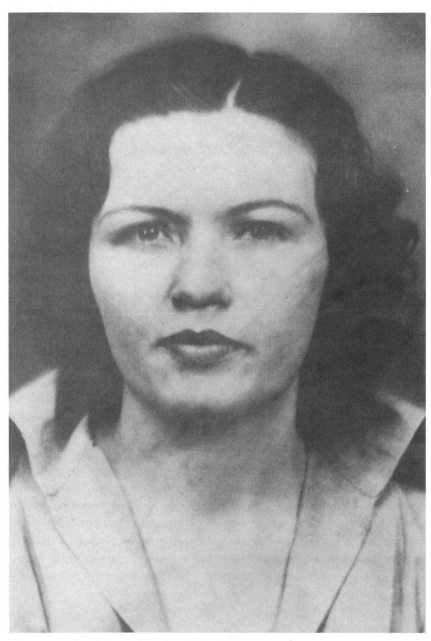

Blanche Caldwell Barrow in the Missouri State Penitentiary for Women, 1933. (Courtesy of Rhea Leen Linder)

⚙2

Marriage

Editor's Note: 1929 and 1931

On Monday, November 11, 1929, the date Blanche Caldwell Callaway met Buck Barrow, the weather in Dallas, Texas, was cloudy and 72 degrees. It was Armistice Day (now Veterans Day), exactly eleven years after the close of what was then referred to as "the Great War"—World War I. At 11 A.M., there was a moment of silence throughout the city to commemorate the event, commencing with a blast from a siren at the Adolphus Hotel on Commerce Street. Later a parade wound its way through the downtown streets and past a reviewing stand constructed on Harwood Street in front of city hall.[1]

On Elm Street, theaters and vaudeville houses planned various patriotic programs. At the Melba Theater it was possible to view, among other things, a short motion picture documentary called Over There Today, which focused on the rebuilding and restoration campaign in France since the close of the war. At the Palace Theater, where Clyde Barrow once worked as an usher, the house organist, Billy Muth, was to play a medley of songs titled "Recollections of War," followed by a program by the Highland Park High School band, fresh from its first-place triumph in a battle of the state's best bands at the Texas State Fair the previous month. In addition, local NBC radio affiliate WFAA scheduled an American Legion Armistice Day program beginning at 10:40 A.M.[2]

The Great War and its immediate legacy were still very much a part of the American psyche in 1929. The events in Dallas that day were not unlike those in most cities and communities across the United States. Indeed, so prominent were *the memories being honored that Armistice Day that there was no indication whatsoever in the news of those two days of economic doom that had passed so dramatically into history only a couple of weeks before—"Black Thursday" and the subsequent "Black Tuesday," collectively marking the start of that difficult era called the Great Depression. Nevertheless, those two days only represented the most radical of the initial stock market losses.*[3]

Between the first week of September 1929 and Armistice Day, the stock market plunged 48 percent, and the worst was yet to come. Nevertheless, the average American could not imagine such news could affect them. This was especially true in Texas, where the events on Wall Street were viewed as extremely distant "northern" problems, nothing to concern Texans.

On July 3, 1931, the day recently divorced Blanche Caldwell married Buck Barrow, the news in Texas was dominated by the ticker-tape parade for aviators Wiley Post and Harold Gatty held the day before in New York City following completion of the first ever around-the-world flight.[4] *It served to divert attention for a while from the deepening economic crisis of the burgeoning depression.*

The Texas economy, although rather diversified, was still largely agricultural, producing timber, fruit, and livestock, as well as oil and gas, among other commodities. Despite this, the vast majority of the production force at the time was made up of sharecroppers and tenant farmers, most of whom had suffered the effects of dire poverty long before the crash of 1929. Between 1920 and 1930, many of these people had quit farming and moved to urban areas in hopes of finding a better life. Indeed, it was that very reality that drove Henry and Cumie Barrow, Buck's parents, to abandon the unprofitable drudgery of working on someone else's land and move to Dallas in 1921. Between 1920 and 1930 the population of Texas had risen 25 percent, but Dallas's population almost doubled, largely due to this flight from agriculture. Nevertheless, for most of these economic refugees the relief would be short-lived. By 1931, Dallas and other Texas cities were beginning to feel the effects of the expanding recession.[5]

President Herbert Hoover, initially supported by Texans (in 1928 Texas voted Republican in a presidential election for the first time), was by 1931 finding himself largely vilified, not only by Texans but across the nation for his apparent inaction with respect to the economy. "The economy is fundamentally sound," said Hoover in October 1931. "The depression is just a passing incident in our national life." Others, whether by way of diversion or out of utter ignorance, chimed in: "I don't know anything about any depression. What depression?" announced banking mogul J. P. Morgan on returning from a European vacation. And industrialist Henry Ford said, "These are really good times!" By then,

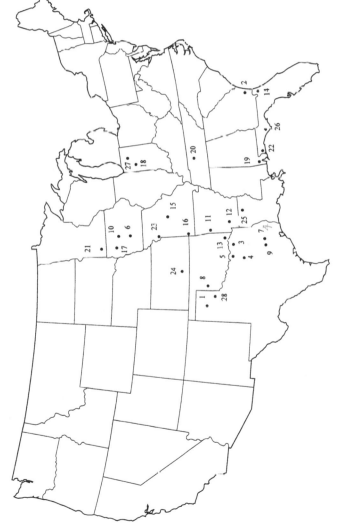

Blanche Barrow in the United States

however, unemployment stood at 8 million nationally and manufacturing had dropped 35 percent. Within a year, the latter would plunge another 25 percent. But more immediate for Texans was that fact of sagging agricultural income, which for most farmers was never very good but had fallen 25 percent since October 1929 and would pass the 50 percent mark within a year. At a time when the average national income was a mere $1,500 annually, farm households subsisted on $167 a year. [6]

In Texas and across the nation anti-Hoover sentiment was increasing. Growing communities of homeless citizens began sprouting in most large urban areas. The cardboard and scrap-wood shelters of these displaced people came to be known as "Hoovervilles." Likewise, the empty, out-turned pockets of the unemployed were called "Hoover flags," newspapers used by transients as park bench covers were called "Hoover blankets," and the various unsavory creatures snared and boiled for dinner, in lieu of anything better, were referred to as "Hoover hogs." In Texas, some tagged armadillos "Hoover hogs" but usually the term described rats. [7]

I GOT A DIVORCE from my first husband on June 5, 1931. On July 3, 1931, I married Marvin Ivan Buck Barrow at America, Oklahoma. We bought our marriage license at Idabel, Oklahoma, near where my father lived. Dad liked Buck, as did most everyone else who met him. Buck had many friends. Dad thought I would be happy. And I was. But it didn't last. I was too happy for it to last. [8]

I did not know Buck was in trouble when I met him, but if I had known, it wouldn't have kept me from loving him. So I married him and went with him to Jacksonville, Florida, for our honeymoon. Then I learned he was an escaped convict from the Texas state penitentiary at Huntsville, Texas. Of course, this cut me deeply and left me broken-hearted. It was more than I could understand. The man I loved so dearly was an escaped convict. But I loved this man who was hunted by officers of the law. I vowed he would never get in trouble again if I could help it. I begged him to reform. He said he loved me, as I did him. He said he wasn't a criminal at heart. He told me he was tired of that kind of life and since he had met and married me he wished he were free from the sentence [9] hanging over him. I told him that before we could become happy he must go back to prison and finish his sentence, which was four years for burglary. We couldn't run from place to place hiding from the law. So I begged him to give himself up and go back to prison. I was sure he wouldn't have to stay long. [10]

On December 27, 1931, after spending Christmas in Dallas, Texas, with Buck's mother, we drove to Huntsville, Texas, where the main prison is located. We drove up to the front of the building and sent for Warden W. W. Waid to come to the car. He did. Buck told him why he had come back, to give himself up and serve his time. Warden Waid was very kind to both of us and told us we had done the right thing. I was crying because I could hardly bear to leave Buck behind those cold-looking gray walls.[11]

It was like cutting my heart out with a knife to know I would be separated from him. I had sent the man I loved back to prison, which to me was almost as bad as sending him to his grave. Buck kissed me goodbye and walked up the stone steps behind the warden to his office, or wherever he needed to go to change into prison clothes and begin serving the rest of his sentence.

I hated to be away from him just a short time. I loved him so much. I knew every hour away from him would seem like years and I hardly knew how I could bear to send him back to that horrible place. But when he was free again we could be happy together for the rest of our lives. The happiness we dreamed of would be worth waiting for.

Buck's mother, two of his sisters, and one of their husbands had gone with us.[12] The sisters and husband wanted to go on one of the prison tours. Buck's mother and I weren't interested so we went to the visitors' area and waited for Buck's suit, the one he had worn to prison.

While we were there Buck came through dressed in white prison garb.[13] He was with a guard. That was almost too much for me to bear. I was unable to control myself. I began screaming and crying. Buck just smiled when he passed me. I knew I was making it harder for him. But I couldn't get myself under control. Several people were in the visitors' area, waiting to visit someone. Everyone looked at me as if I had gone crazy. Someone asked what was wrong with me. Mrs. Barrow told them the man who had walked through with a guard was my husband. Then they seemed to understand.

I went back to Dallas to stay with Buck's mother for a while. I cried all that day and night until I was sick from crying. Before returning to prison Buck had made his mother[14] and his family promise they would take care of "his baby," as he always called me. "Baby" was a pet name he had for me and I had always called him "Daddy." This may sound silly and cheap to some people—he was only eight years older than me (I was twenty when we were married and he was twenty-eight). Still, he seemed to feel that since I was so much younger than him that he had to worry about me. He was so afraid something would happen to me if he wasn't with me all the time, as if I were just a baby and needed someone to care for me.[15]

Texas State Penitentiary, Huntsville, Texas, prior to its 1943 remodeling. "I hardly knew how I could bear to send him back to that horrible place." (Texas Department of Criminal Justice)

Soon after Buck's return to prison, I went to work at a beauty shop in a town about one hundred miles from Dallas. I will not give the name of the town, or of the people for whom I worked for fear of embarrassing them. I don't want to hurt them by connecting their names with my story. They were very kind and understanding.[16]

I sold the car Buck left me and spent most of the money trying to get Buck a parole or pardon. I thought that a lawyer would do him some good. The one I hired only took my money and gave me many false promises, which did me no good.

Days and weeks went by, which seemed like years to me. In February 1932, I visited Buck and his brother Clyde, who was serving a fourteen-year sentence for several minor crimes. Mrs. Barrow was still working trying to get Clyde paroled and was sure he would be free soon. She had asked me to see him, Clyde, while I was visiting Buck. I was to tell him to be good because she was sure he would be free soon. Clyde was walking on crutches because he had cut off two of his toes with an ax while cutting wood at Eastham prison farm. He did it so he would be sent to the Walls where Buck was.[17]

Before Buck returned to prison, I met many of his friends and most of his people, including his younger brother Clyde. So I already knew him. Buck and I visited Clyde at a Texas prison farm called Eastham No. One. Buck also sent me to see him several times alone. Clyde told me many things that happened in prison. He also wanted to escape. He said he couldn't do fourteen years.[18]

On the outside, Buck had been working on Clyde's case. He supplied money to Mrs. Barrow to pay for lawyers.[19] We were sure Clyde would be given a parole when he had been in prison two years, but Clyde couldn't believe it. He begged me to bring a gun to him, but I refused. I wouldn't help him escape. But I would do anything else I could to help Buck's brother win a parole, but only if he wanted to reform and not go back to the same old law-breaking game. Clyde said if he could get out he would go straight, but he couldn't take fourteen years at Eastham. He said if he didn't make a parole soon he was going to get out of there anyway he could. He was really doing hard time.

Buck went with me twice to see Clyde. I was very worried during both those trips because Buck had escaped from another prison farm just across the river from Eastham.[20] I was afraid some one would recognize Buck and arrest him. We were about the only ones who visited Clyde, sent him

Eastham Camp 1, 1930. "Buck and I visited Clyde at a Texas prison farm called Eastham No. One." (Texas Department of Criminal Justice)

Eastham Camp 1, interior, 2001. Clyde Barrow killed his first man, Ed Crowder, behind the farthest column. "Clyde told me many things that happened in prison." (Photograph by John Neal Phillips)

money, or tried to do anything for him. His sister Nell visited him twice. His mother visited once or twice. Although Clyde knew Bonnie Parker at the time and had been keeping company with her before he went to prison, he said he only received a few letters from her while he was at Eastham.[21] Then on December 27, 1931, Buck went back to prison.

3

Buck Makes a Pardon

Editor's Note: 1932–1933

  While she waited for her husband's return from prison, Blanche Barrow worked part of the time as a licensed beautician for Buck's older sister, Artie Winkler, at the Cinderella Beauty Shoppe in Denison, Texas. She also lived for a while with Buck's parents in their cramped, three-room quarters behind the Star Service Station in West Dallas.[1]

  On February 2, 1932, Buck's younger brother Clyde was released from prison where he had been serving time for burglary and auto theft. Seething with hatred, the younger Barrow began almost immediately to finalize plans he and a fellow inmate named Ralph Fults had initiated while still incarcerated together. They were going to form a gang with the specific intention of raiding the East-ham prison farm, where both men had been held and where guards and inmates alike had viciously brutalized Barrow. By early 1933, owing to a number of circumstances, Clyde Barrow had not yet staged the raid, but as we shall see, it remained foremost in his mind. Vowing never to be taken alive, he was wanted for five murders before the first anniversary of his release from prison. And more deaths would follow.

  Nationally throughout 1932, the economy continued its downward spiral. Although people could escape for a while with movies like A Farewell to Arms *with Gary Cooper or* Red Dust *with Clark Gable and Jean Harlow, the mood of the average citizen was probably best summarized by Bing Crosby's hit song, "Buddy, Can You Spare a Dime?" Despite his support of a farm relief bill, President Herbert*

Hoover's image remained that of an ineffectual leader. "There is nothing more we can do," he said, but a growing number of Americans refused to believe it.[2]

On March 7, 1932, three thousand demonstrators demanding jobs marched on the Ford Motor Company's River Rouge plant in Michigan. Dearborn police stopped the march with tear gas, but the demonstrators pelted police with rocks and frozen mud in the zero-degree weather and then rushed Gate No. 3. Machine gun fire erupted. Four marchers were killed and sixty wounded in what has since been called "the River Rouge massacre."[3]

On May 11, three hundred World War I veterans stopped an eastbound freight train in Oregon and commandeered several boxcars so they could travel to Washington, D.C., in support of a congressional bill authorizing the early payment of a veterans' bonus, requisitioned in 1924 but not payable until 1945. The veterans wanted the money. Like most Americans at the time, they really needed it—an average of $1,000 per qualified applicant amounted to roughly the equivalent of a year's wages at an auto plant. By the time the original three hundred arrived in Washington, twenty thousand other veterans and their families had joined them. Carrying signs that read "Hard Times Are Still 'Hoovering' Over Us" and calling themselves "The Bonus Expeditionary Force," these activists camped out in a number of places throughout the capital, including along the Anacostia River flats. There they settled in to await the outcome of the congressional debate over the bill.

On June 17, the same day Bonnie Parker was "no-billed" by a Kaufman County, Texas, grand jury and released from the only jail that ever held her, the bonus bill was defeated in Congress. However, despite this, the Bonus Expeditionary Force refused to break camp and disperse. On July 28 after Washington police tried unsuccessfully to evict the veterans, violence flared. One veteran and one policeman were shot. That very afternoon President Hoover ordered the U.S. Army to remove the veterans and close their camps.

Under the command of future World War II hero General Douglass MacArthur, and against the advice of his aide, future World War II hero and future president Colonel Dwight D. Eisenhower, the army swept over the veterans and set fire to the camps. Another future World War II hero, Colonel George S. Patton, led a cavalry charge with sabers drawn. Hoover then ordered MacArthur to withdraw. The orders were ignored, a portent of MacArthur's later dealings with his superiors. "The burning Anacostia camp," wrote one reporter, "cast the city in a lurid glare that night as troops moved in to finish the job."[4]

In the end fifty veterans were wounded, a number of others killed. It was political disaster for Hoover, the last in a long series of grievances that continued to breed resentment and contempt in the average citizen. Groups like the Farmers' Holiday Association and the Dairyman's Revolt, both vowing to destroy farm products until wholesale prices rose to an equitable level, came to prominence in 1932. In addition, farm foreclosures were often forestalled by neighboring farmers, often heavily armed, who intimidated potential buyers to the point of silence and then offered pennies and nickels for the land and machinery being auctioned so that they could be restored to the original owner. That November, by a margin of nearly 58 percent, New York governor Franklin Delano Roosevelt was voted into the White House and both houses of Congress were packed with Democrats. The New Deal was about to commence.[5]

March 1933, the month of Buck Barrow's release from the Texas penitentiary, began with the ongoing incursion into China by Japan, truckloads of milk being seized and dumped by angry dairy operators in Iowa, and unemployment figures reaching 24.9 percent nationally. On March 3, the new Texas governor, Miriam A. Ferguson, ordered all banks in the state to close for five days while inspectors reviewed the soundness of each institution. The following day forty-six of the remaining forty-seven states followed suit.[6]

In addition, on that same day, March 4, 1933, Franklin Delano Roosevelt was sworn in as president of the United States. In his inaugural speech, Roosevelt asked for sweeping wartime powers to meet the economic crisis of the Great Depression. And although pointing out that the only thing to fear "is fear itself", the new president added cautiously, "Only a foolish optimist can deny the dark realities of the moment." Roosevelt also indicated the direction his policies would take by stating, "[the] practices of the unscrupulous money changers stand indicted in the court of public opinion." The very next day Roosevelt asked Congress to convene in a special session; among other things, he declared a national bank moratorium similar to that already initiated in Texas and proposed a federal guarantee of up to 50 percent of bank deposits. The famous "Hundred Days" of broad legislation aimed first at relief and then at reform had begun.[7]

On March 11, an earthquake killed 119 people in Long Beach, California. On March 15 a tornado ripped through Nashville, Tennessee, killing fifteen. By then banks had reopened nationwide, reporting record deposits following bank restructuring.[8]

In Dallas, Texas, retail stores declared Saturday, March 18, their biggest sales day since the Christmas season. Moreover, the Dallas sheriff's department announced that a recent escapee from jail in nearby Waxahachie might be on the trail of Clyde Barrow. The escapee's name was Roy Thornton, Bonnie Parker's estranged husband.[9]

The Cinderella Beauty Shoppe, 430 West Sears, Denison, Texas, 1932. "It was. . . almost closing time in the beauty shop where I was working." (Courtesy of Rhea Leen Linder)

On March 20, the State of Florida executed Giuseppe Zangara for the murder of Chicago mayor Anton Cermak, who had been mortally wounded just a little more than a month earlier as he rode in a motorcade with then President-elect Roosevelt. On the same day the jury in the Hillsboro, Texas, murder trial of Clyde Barrow's companion Raymond Hamilton was declared irrevocably deadlocked by Judge W. L. Wray. Jurors had no problem convicting Hamilton of the killing of local businessman John N. Bucher but could not agree on the penalty. A new trial was ordered.[10]

On March 22, the day Buck Barrow was released from the Texas penitentiary in Huntsville, President Roosevelt signed a measure rushed through Congress in just ten days legalizing the manufacture and sale of 3.2 percent beer. Prohibition was rapidly crumbling. In addition, on that date baseball great Babe Ruth signed an unprecedented $52,000 contract with the New York Yankees, and in Dallas, Texas, a jobless man killed his wife and then committed suicide. Within hours of the Denison, Texas, reunion of Blanche Barrow and her husband, Adolph Hitler was declared dictator of Germany, Japan's conflict with China deepened, and an

Oklahoma state bank examiner was shot to death by a bank president in Head-rick, Oklahoma.[11]

IT WAS THE AFTERNOON of March 23, 1933, almost closing time in the beauty shop where I was working.[12] I had no customers so I decided to walk to the post office, just a few blocks away, to see if there was any mail from Buck. I had not received a letter from him in several days. I was worried about him. I was afraid something terrible had happened to him or that he may be seriously ill. I could always think of so many terrible things when I did not hear from him on my regular letter day, the day I usually received mail from Buck.

I had walked a couple of blocks when a Western Union boy passed me on a bike. Something caused me to turn my head for a second. I saw him turn down the street were I worked. I had a feeling he would stop at the shop. Maybe he would have some news from Buck. I was sure it would be bad news if he did. A telegram could only mean one thing to me, very bad news from Buck, or my mother, or father. Of course, it might have meant Buck was coming home, but I had just about given up all hope of getting him paroled.

I walked on toward the post office, taking in long deep breaths of the cool crisp air. Each breath had the hint of early spring in it and felt so fresh and clean it seemed to give me new strength and courage after a busy day in the warm shop. I could not see whether the boy had stopped at the shop because I had turned onto another street a block away. Nevertheless, as I walked on I thought about that boy. I tried to make myself believe there was nothing wrong with Buck and that there would be a letter at the post office from him telling me he was okay. Anyway, why should I think anything about seeing a Western Union boy passing me on the street? I saw them pass the shop quite often every day and thought nothing of it. So why should this be any different from any other time? I tried to dismiss the thought.

There was no letter for me at the post office. I told myself that surely there would be one tomorrow and then I walked out slowly. On my way back to the shop I was deep in thought, daydreaming of how wonderful it would be to have Buck walking beside me, enjoying the pleasure of breathing the fresh clean air, which I was sure he never experienced behind those gray prison walls. When I got within a block of the shop, I almost bumped into someone. I started to apologize and only then realized it was the lady

I was working for.[13] She was all smiles and seemed to notice my embarrassment at having nearly bumped into her on the street. Someone else might have told me to watch my step, but not her. She had always been so kind and sweet to me. She just started laughing. Soon we both were laughing. She asked if I had any mail for her. I told her no and then noticed she seemed to be more than her usually happy self. I asked why she seemed so gay and why she had come to meet me.

"I have something for you that will make you very happy," she said, handing me a telegram. "He's coming home!"

I read it, but for a minute I could not speak. It was true. Buck was coming home to me. I felt as if I were going to laugh and cry all at the same time. I was so overcome with joy. I grabbed her and did a little dance around with her right there on the sidewalk. I know that people passing us, if anyone did, must have thought me crazy. But I was so filled with happiness I did not care what anyone thought. I could have shouted to the whole world that this was the happiest day of my life! Little did I know then, however, that the unhappiest day of my life would come in just a few short months. For the moment, though, I was happy.

I could hardly believe it was true, that Buck was free. Now all our plans and dreams would come true, plans of living like other normal people and of having our own home. It was too good to be true. There would be no more worries and sleepless nights caused by the fear that officers of the law would come to take Buck away from me and put him in a cold prison cell. There would be no more running away or being hunted like a fox by a pack of hounds. But I still had a lot to learn about being the wife of an ex-convict. After being in prison, one is never free to live the life of any normal person without officers of the law knowing their every move, reminding them that they once broke the law and are expected to do so again sooner or later.[14]

I looked at the telegram. It read: "Baby, I'll be home to you as soon as I can get there." God only knows what those words meant to me after waiting fifteen long, weary months. Only a few would understand, only those who have ever received word from some imprisoned loved one saying they are coming home.[15] I wondered how long Buck would have to wait before he could catch a bus and come home to me. I could hardly wait to see him.

That night I phoned the bus station and asked what time the next bus from Houston, Texas, would arrive. I was told the bus would get in around ten o'clock, and that another bus would arrive at nine the next morning. I didn't think Buck would be on the ten o'clock bus. I didn't think he would have had time to catch that one. I thought he'd arrive the next morning.[16]

I went to bed between eleven and twelve o'clock, but I could not sleep. I was too happy. Nevertheless, I wanted to go to sleep as soon as I could so the hours would not drag by. I was like some excited child on the night before Christmas, waiting to see what Santa would bring. It seemed that if I could just go to sleep, the morning would come much sooner than lying awake waiting. I soon fell asleep.

When I awoke, something was going on. The room was still dark and someone was holding me, kissing my lips and eyes, and saying, "Baby, wake up." My first words were "Daddy, is it really you, or am I still dreaming?" It was Buck.

Buck had lost no time once he sent that telegram. He arrived in Dallas at midnight, called a taxicab, and went to his mother's place. There he took off his prison-issue suit and put on his old suit, the one he wore the day he gave himself up to Warden Waid. I'd had it cleaned and pressed as soon as I returned from Huntsville, and then I packed it away for him.

After borrowing a car from his oldest brother, who also lived in Dallas, Buck along with his kid brother LC started driving north to Denison, Texas, where I was.[17] About two or two-thirty A.M. Buck woke me.

The next morning we packed my trunk and bags, loaded them in the car, and left for Dallas. It was about ten o'clock. On our way out of town, we noticed a car with two men following us. I did not recognize them, but I knew they were police officers.

Our car had been driven hard the night before and needed oil and water. We had just driven into a service station when the car that was following us whipped around and parked right in front of us. The two men jumped out with drawn shotguns. They told us to get our hands up. We did as we were told, but I wondered why they were doing this to us.

Buck and I were still in the car. LC had gotten out and was putting water in the car. The smaller of the two officers opened the door on the driver's side of our car and told Buck to get out. He did. The officer asked Buck if he and I were Clyde Barrow and Bonnie Parker.

"No!" we said as quick as we could, but they did not seem to believe us. They took Buck and LC and began shaking them down and asking how many machine guns we had in the back of the car. We did not have any guns and we told them so. We said that if they wished they could look for themselves. LC did not seem to mind the shakedown. He just went about his business, putting water in the car while the officer was searching him. LC acted as though the officer wasn't there. He had gotten so used to being arrested because of Clyde, it was nothing new to him.[18]

Buck was trying to tell the officers that he was not Clyde, but Clyde's older brother and that he had just received a pardon the day before. He showed the officer his release papers and told him he had come after me, his wife. Then the officer looked at me closely. He seemed to recognize me, although I did not recognize him. He asked if I had ever seen him before. I told him no. He said he had seen me quite often. He knew who I was and where I worked. Then he asked me if I could drive a car. I told him I could drive, but that I wasn't sure whether or not I could drive this wreck. But I said I would try. He said he would have to take the boys to the station to check up on them and ask them a few questions. I did not think I had anything to worry about. However, I knew that these were Clyde's brothers and that Buck had just gotten out of prison, so I wasn't completely sure what the police might do to them.

After putting Buck and LC in his car, the officer told me to follow. I did, although the car was in bad shape and I had never driven it before. It was quite a task for me to get used to it and for me to keep up with the officer's car. I wasn't sure where the police station was and frankly wasn't very thrilled about finding out. Still, I managed to stay close enough to their car to see where they were going and where they stopped.

When the officers stopped, I drove up beside them. They told me to drive farther down the street and I would find a place to park. One of the officers told me to stay there until he came back. I did as I was told.

I was wearing a new spring outfit. It was a golden yellow and white, with white gloves to match. When I parked and took my hands off the steering wheel, I noticed I had ruined my new white gloves. There was grease on the wheel and it turned my gloves black. Then I looked down at my white pumps. They were spotted with grease from the brakes. I wasn't very pleased about that. A mechanic had been driving the car and left grease on the steering wheel and brakes.

I waited. After an hour or so, which seemed like several hours to me, one of the officers came to the car. He seemed to want to search the car for guns. He asked me if all the luggage in the car belonged to me. I told him he could look if he wished, but I assured him he would have to help me repack everything.

He was very nice to me and seemed sorry that he had doubted us. He told me I had nothing to worry about, that the boys would be back in a short time. He did not open any of the luggage, but kidded me about having so much of it.

"A woman could always manage to have a lot of baggage when she got ready to move," the officer said, laughing. Then he said, "Mrs. Barrow, I suppose this is quite embarrassing to you."

I told him it was and that I hoped it would never happen to me again. Officers of the law before had never doubted me and I had always been respected as a lady. Naturally, being stopped by the law and taken to the police station [in a town] where most everyone knew me and where I worked was embarrassing and would cause the people for whom I worked more embarrassment.

"I hate that this had to happen here, in this small town, more because of them than for myself," I said.

I wondered how often something like this would happen to us. I prayed it would never happen again. I hoped that we could do as we had planned when Buck gave himself up and returned to prison, meaning that after he'd served the remainder of his four-year sentence (of which he had only served three months[19] before escaping) we could begin again and live our lives like normal people.

Before the officer came to the car, I prayed, "Oh God, don't let them take him away from me again." Was my happiness to be so short-lived? But as soon as the officer came to the car, he told me the boys would be back soon. Then I saw Buck and LC coming toward the car. They got in. The officer wished us luck and we drove away. I was happy once more.

Buck and LC told me the officers had seen them drive into town the night before and had been watching the car and the house, mainly because the car was from Dallas and was strange to them. They thought they might see Clyde at any time. They were always on the lookout for him. Buck and I were glad to get home to his mother's house and she was so happy to see him. She had only been able to say hello to him briefly the night before because he was in such a hurry to see me. He did not have time to talk to his mother or anyone else. I think that is why Mrs. Barrow and most of the family were so jealous of me, because Buck loved me so much. I think they felt as if I had stolen him and his love away from them. I did not want them to feel that way. Their love was far different from mine, although I believed my love was stronger than any of theirs, even his mother's love. If it was ever necessary, I knew that I would go further and suffer more for Buck than anyone in his family. But they could not understand why Buck loved me, his wife, more than them. Buck loved his mother, father, brothers, and sisters as dearly as anyone could. He was very dedicated to his family, but I came first. He told me he would give them all up, if I wanted him to. But I would never have asked that much of him. I scolded him for suggesting such a thing, especially for the sake of his mother. I was happy just to be with him and to know he loved me. I could not have asked for more from life.

No matter how poor Buck and I may be or how hard we would have to work I was happy just to have our freedom. I would have been willing to do any kind of honest work, anything to be free and with Buck. That was all that mattered to me. But Buck never wanted me to work and would not think of letting me while he was free. He seemed to feel that he would always be with me, to protect me from any harm or hard work.[20] He never thought that some day he may have to leave me alone in the world to take care of myself the best I could. But I have been capable of working and making a good honest living for my disabled father and myself since I was fifteen years old.[21] So that never worried me.

Buck didn't know that while he was gone his people forgot the wife he had left behind, the wife he loved more than anything or anyone else on earth, even them. Neither did he know that they soon forgot the promises they made to him when he returned to prison. I loved him too much to hurt him by telling him that they had broken these promises to him—that they would treat me as their own daughter and would not let me work outside of their home. He also didn't know that they had not been as kind and loving toward his wife as they had promised to be.[22]

I loved his people because he loved them. And I knew it would make him unhappy if he thought I did not love them. I would have never wanted to be guilty of killing his love for them just because of something they had done to me. I loved his people, knowing they were jealous of me and of his love for me. Although they were not always unkind to me, they often showed me I was imposing on them by living with them and not working in town to pay my rent. And they all knew this was one thing Buck would not have wanted me to do.[23]

On Saturday morning, March 25, Buck bought two Model A Ford coupes. They did not look so good, but they were cheap and the motors were okay. He was sure he could make one pay for both by overhauling the motors and giving them each a new paint job. He paid for them with the fifty dollars he received with his pardon papers when he was released from prison. He loved to work on cars, or any kind of machinery. He decided he could take care of our needs by opening a used car lot and doing this kind of work. But he was never given the chance.

That afternoon we drove one of the coupes to Wilmer, Texas, about fifteen miles south of Dallas. My mother lived about three miles from Wilmer, in the country on a small dairy farm with her husband, my stepfather. I had not seen my mother for several months and wanted to pay her a visit. Buck had a short visit with his people, now we could visit my mother.

Buck's oldest sister had given him one hundred dollars to take care of our needs until he started working. She was the only one who ever gave him anything. The rest always expected something from him all the time. And if they ever gave him any money or anything, they were always well paid for it. As long as he had anything to give, and they wanted it, they always got it—and with my permission.

My mother and stepfather were very happy to see us. So was our little white dog, which my mother was keeping for me while Buck was in prison. I wasn't able to keep him because Mrs. Barrow did not like dogs that stayed in the house and I was afraid to make him stay outside for fear he would be run over and killed by a car. Buck thought a lot of the dog and told me often in his letters not to let anything happen to our little dog. Mother was glad to keep the dog for me. It was a lot of company for her. The dog had not forgotten Buck and seemed so glad to see him. He stayed at Buck's heels whenever he went in the house or yard.[24]

That night about eleven or twelve o'clock, someone knocked on the front door downstairs. My stepfather went to the door. A young man asked him if Buck Barrow was there. He told him, yes, and asked him to come in, saying that Buck was in bed upstairs. My stepfather did not know Clyde Barrow, Bonnie Parker, or W. D. Jones[25] personally, so at first he did not know who they were.

Buck and I had not been in bed long and had just dozed off to sleep. But when they asked for Buck, their voices woke us both. We were sleeping in a bedroom on the second floor, which had been added to the small farmhouse long after the first floor had been built. We knew their voices when we first heard them.

Naturally, Buck wanted to see his brother. He had not seen him since Clyde left prison the year before.[26] So Buck went down to meet them. In a

"Bonnie was so drunk she could hardly walk." (Courtesy of Buddy Williams Barrow)

few minutes, he came back up the stairs with Clyde, Bonnie, and W. D. I was still in bed. Clyde and W. D. were both carrying sawed-off shotguns. Bonnie was so drunk she could hardly walk. All of them came over to the bed and sat down.

Bonnie greeted me. She seemed glad to see me, and I was glad to see her. I had always felt sorry for her, having to live the life she was living, never a minute's peace. She had often told me she was happier when she had something to drink. So I did not blame her for staying drunk most of the time, if it made her feel better.

The Barrows blamed her for Clyde's downfall.[27] But I knew she was not to blame for it all. She looked so tired, like she had not slept in a week. Clyde wanted to talk to Buck, so W. D. sat near a window and kept watch. I did

BLANche sAys sHe KNows BonNie wasnt to BLAme

"W. D. sat near a window and kept watch." (Courtesy of L. J. Hinton)

not think Clyde would want Buck to go with him and start living the life he was living, knowing Buck was through with hiding from the law.

I asked Bonnie to get in bed with me and try to get a little sleep, as I had heard Clyde say they would stay until just before dawn. But Bonnie seemed to want to talk instead of sleeping. She said it was so good to have a woman she knew to talk to, adding that it was so lonesome for her just being in the company of men all the time and never any women friends to talk to. I knew this was true because I had experienced a few months of that myself, after I had married Buck and before he went back to prison.[28]

Through Bonnie's chatter and laughter, I caught a few words now and then of Clyde's conversation with Buck, and I did not like what I heard. Clyde seemed to be trying to lay out a plan on a map, but I decided Buck would never go with him even if Clyde wanted him to.

I heard Clyde say, "Blanche knows where the place is and knows the country pretty well."

Then they pulled their chairs up close beside the bed and Clyde began outlining his plans. I did not like them and told him so. Clyde's plans were to go to the Eastham prison farm where Raymond Hamilton was serving a long sentence for robbery and take him away from the guards while the convicts were cutting wood or working in the fields away from the building.[29] I told him he could count Buck and me out if he thought he would get any help from us. We were not going to get mixed up in any of it.

Clyde said, "Okay, if that's the way you feel about it. But you or Buck would not get into any trouble over it. All I wanted you to do was go visit Ray and tell him where he will find everything and what time we will be there to get him. And you know all about the country around there,[30] or enough about it, to make the plan plain to Ray, where we will place the guns for him to get when he gets a signal and we will give you money enough afterwards to start you and Buck out in business and buy you a nice little home."

I told him I did not want to start our home that way because it would never do us any good. I also told him he should forget about going after Ray. I said that in a way he was a good kid and that I felt sorry for him because he had so much time to serve.

"But you are in enough trouble," I said. "And you may get him killed and get killed yourself."

"Ray would be better off if he were dead rather than have to spend the rest of his life in that 'hell hole,'" Clyde said.[31] "You have to take the chance of getting killed or your freedom." 〉 *prison worse than death*

I knew this was true. But why should Buck and I get mixed up in it?

"Why don't you try to go some place where you are not known and try to stay out of trouble?" I asked Clyde. "If you don't you know you are not going to last long, going as you are now."

"Blanche, you know I can't stop now," Clyde said. "I have gone too far already to stop. So if you are afraid you and Buck will get in trouble helping me get Ray, then I can get someone else to help me."

Raymond Hamilton. "'Ray would be better off if he were dead rather than have to spend the rest of his life in that hell hole,' Clyde said." (Phillips Collection)

"Well, Bud," I said.[32] "You will just have to get someone else, because Buck and I are not going."

Buck seemed worried about Clyde's plans too. He told Clyde he would not do anything that I thought would get us in trouble again, adding, "And what she says goes! She's the boss now you know."

Clyde did not like to hear Buck talk that way about things. But Buck also told Clyde to forget about going after Ray, that it wasn't worth the risk of Bonnie and him getting killed. Bonnie herself did not like the idea and told Clyde that Ray would not do that much for him. But of course, since Clyde wanted to do it she had nothing to say about it.[33]

The boys decided to go sit in Clyde's car and keep the motor running. The night was cold and the bedroom didn't have a heater. They also worried that they might keep my mother and stepfather awake by walking around and talking, and they did not want to do that. Besides, they could keep the car nice and warm with its heater. You could hardly hear the motor running so it would not cause any suspicion in case someone should pass the house. But at that hour of the night, no one was likely to pass anyway. And the house was quite a distance from the main highway.

Buck and Clyde told Bonnie and me to go to sleep, then went to the car with W. D. But Bonnie and I did not go to sleep. She told me everything that had happened to them in the past six months and how she wished she and Clyde were as free as Buck and I were.[34] She said she hoped we could stay that way.

About four o'clock, Buck and Clyde came back upstairs. They had another plan to talk to me about. I did not notice that Buck had been drinking. Clyde asked me if we would visit them in Joplin, Missouri, and rent an apartment or house, so they could rest up a couple or three weeks. He said they would not do anything to make the place hot and that Bonnie and I could buy whatever we wanted, furnish, and fix the place up as we pleased. We could have lots of fun doing that and when Buck and I were ready to return to Dallas, we could bring everything back with us to fix up our own house or apartment.

Clyde and Buck had already discussed this plan and worked everything out. Clyde made Buck believe we would be in no danger and that Buck would not get into trouble. Clyde said they would have plenty of money and would not have to pull any robberies for quite some time, not while we were with them anyway. And when they were away, they would take all the guns with them. There would be no guns around the place to cause us trouble. He said they would have most of the guns in the car at all times and only keep a couple rifles or shotguns inside, something they could grab and take with them to the car in case the place got any heat on it and they had to leave in a hurry. That way there would be no danger of any officers causing Buck and me trouble because of guns they may find in the apartment. And we would have nothing to be afraid of and could stand a trip to the police station in case they should want to question us. But he was sure nothing would happen because they would not do anything to cause any suspicion.

All of this had sounded very good to Buck and he could see no harm in going. So, he had already promised Clyde we would go. He thought this story would sound okay to me and that I would enjoy the trip. He also told me we would go by and see my father and bring him home with us on our way back to Texas.[35] Clyde knew how devoted I was to my father and that I had not seen him since Buck and I were married about two years before.

They could see no reason why I would not want to do this, and they thought we could help them out too. Buck also had another plan, which he did not mention just then. He thought more seriously about this plan after Clyde told him about wanting to go after Ray. Buck could not see how much trouble Clyde was in or how badly the law wanted him. Buck did not know Clyde's moves as well as I did.

While Buck was still in prison, Clyde told me most everything he had done since his own parole. What he had forgotten to tell Bonnie he'd told me. I had seen him at different times and talked to both of them when they would slip in to see Mrs. Barrow under cover of darkness, or in the early afternoon. And I realized Buck was in danger at any and all times with Clyde because the officers expected Buck to join Clyde as soon as he was released from prison and would watch his every move. I had heard an officer say this myself. But I could not make Buck or Clyde understand it.

Anyway, I refused to meet them in Joplin because I did not mean to risk losing Buck again or take the chance that Buck might want to get involved with what they called "easy money" without working for it. I wanted to keep him away from Clyde for that reason. I thought I would rather start out in our new life together without any chance that I might lose Buck again.

They argued and pleaded with me. They tried to show me how there wouldn't be any danger of Buck getting into trouble again if we went to Joplin and gave them a chance to rest up for a couple of weeks or more. But I refused to listen to any of it. Bonnie said she wished we would meet them in Joplin because she was so tired of eating in cafes or just any place they could get something to eat, and sleeping in cars most of the time, or in small tourist parks where they would not be noticed.

Bonnie did not cook and did not like to wash dishes. If they did prepare their own meals, it was Clyde who did most of the cooking.[36] But she added that if I felt I would lose Buck again after all those long weary months of waiting for him to be free, she did not want me to go against my better judgment.

So they began gathering up their guns and getting ready to leave. It was nearly light enough for people to see them leaving the place, and they did not want that to happen. I bid them both goodbye. Buck went to the car with them. W. D. had remained in the car while Buck and Clyde were talking to me about going to Joplin. As they were leaving, they said they hoped I would think it over and change my mind about meeting them in Joplin. But I did not think anything could change my mind about going. It was made up and the answer was no.

Buck was gone about twenty-five or thirty minutes. I was crying when he came back and got in bed. He began begging and pleading with me and trying to make me understand that there would be no harm done by us going to Joplin to help Clyde take a break from the life he was living. I told him I was sorry for them and would like to do something for Clyde but I could not and would not risk the chance of Buck getting in trouble again. Besides, I thought Clyde had his chance when he was released from prison, a much better one than Buck had. Clyde did not want to work or stay in one place too long. He would rather act tough and have a lot of publicity. No, he had his chance. So, let him take care of himself. Then Buck told me of his plan to try to persuade Clyde to give up the kind of life he was now living. He believed Clyde would listen to him if he could visit him for a few days.[37]

"And, Baby," Buck said, "you know how much I worry about Clyde. He is so young and I may never see him alive again if we don't go. You know I have not been with him for a long time. I want to help him live as long as I can without getting into trouble myself. And Clyde says there isn't any danger of that. So I promised him before we came back up here to talk to you about it. And he gave me some money to make the trip. And I can trade in the two cars we have for a larger and better one, if I pay a little difference. I figure if we go we can keep him from getting killed trying to take Ray out of prison. And he promised me if we would go to Joplin, he would forget about going after him. So now I've promised him and you know I have always tried to keep a promise when I make one. I don't make them if I don't think I can keep them."

I was still crying, clinging to him, begging him not to go. "Clyde isn't any younger than I am," I said. "And his young life doesn't mean any more to him than yours does to me. You shouldn't have made that promise!"

I knew when Buck did make a promise to someone he would try to keep it. But I told him that by keeping this promise he was breaking many he had made to me, that he would never again place himself in danger of getting sent back to prison, or associate with those who were hiding from the law or doing something which would get them sent to jail or prison.

But I could not make him see my view of things. He still kept saying he must keep his promise to Clyde. He was convinced he could get Clyde to stop running around killing and robbing people.

"But, Daddy," I cried, "I have talked to him like a sister should, even before he left prison. I had begged him to go straight when he was free again, but he had broken his promise that he would."

Promises meant little to Clyde. So why did Buck have to keep this one to him?

"And, Daddy," I said. "You don't realize how much trouble Clyde is in. He has already killed six or eight men[38] and he can't afford to give up now, even if he wanted to. You should know that he will shoot to kill if the officers should run in on him. And if we were with him, he would not think of you. He would only think of getting away and saving his own life. Hasn't he run away and left you before, lying in the street shot down by officers, not knowing or stopping to see if you were still alive? Didn't he run away and leave Ralph Fults and Bonnie near Kaufman, Texas, once when they had a gun battle with officers? Ralph was shot in the arm. He and Bonnie were taken to jail. He didn't even try to get Ralph a lawyer, or do anything for him. Do you think he would stop to think of what a tight place he may have you in, especially if the officers should corner him and we were with him, considering the many murders he is wanted for now? No, he wouldn't!"[39]

"But, honey," said Buck. "I am not going to break the promises I made to you. And if I thought I would get into trouble again and have to leave you, I would not think of going. But I know nothing will happen to us and we may keep Clyde from getting killed because I believe he will listen to me."

By this time, Buck had begun crying too. As I have said before in this story, Buck loved his people very dearly and worried so much about Clyde. And it was true that if Buck did not try to help him this time Clyde may be killed before Buck saw him again. Then Buck would be sorry he had broken his promise to Clyde, especially since he may have been able to save him from himself. But still I refused to allow him to go with Clyde.

Then Buck became angry and told me if I would not go, he would go alone. He knew this would hurt me deeply. Buck had said before that he would give up any of his people for me. I fought a hard battle with myself, but lost. I could not bear to have him go alone and leave me. I thought I would die of a broken heart because I did not think I could go on living without him. And I knew I would go to him if he did get in trouble sooner or later, if he wanted me to.

Ralph Fults. "Didn't he [Clyde] run away and leave Ralph Fults and Bonnie near Kaufman, Texas, once when they had a gun battle with officers?" (Phillips Collection)

So when I saw he had his mind made up to go, I decided to go with him. If he went alone I was sure he would get into trouble. Then he could never come back to me free. If I went I may be able to keep him from doing something he shouldn't. Also I thought if Buck were alone with Clyde, Clyde would try to kill his love for me.[40] So when he kept begging me to go with him, I finally promised him I would go.

He seemed very happy that I had decided to go with him. I learned later that he had been drinking. I knew we had never had a quarrel before unless he was drinking or drunk.[41]

Even after I promised to go I could not control my sobbing. I did not want my mother to hear me because she knew I had been so happy the evening before. Now, only a few hours later, I was crying and sobbing so much that I was sure I could be heard all over the house. But the thought of losing Buck seemed more than I could stand and so I told him I would go with him anywhere he should go.

Buck told me Clyde had said that if later on I still felt the same about visiting them in Joplin, to just forget about it. But Buck told him he was sure he could get me to go. Clyde said he would look for us the following Wednesday or Thursday at a place he had already picked out, a small town about twelve miles south of Muskogee, Oklahoma. Buck knew that if he told me he would go without me that I would change my mind and go. After I had said I would go, he said he did not think I would take it so hard, or that I would feel so unhappy about going. He said we would be back home in a couple of weeks, just as safe-and-sound as we were when we left. I wished I could have felt that way about it myself, but I could not. If I had held out a couple of hours longer, or all that day, our life may have been so different. He would not have gone without me, or at least he would not have gone very far without me. He would have turned around and come back before he had driven very far. But at the time I was too worried and brokenhearted about the thought of losing him. I did not stop to think before I promised to go.

We did not go back to sleep. I couldn't have slept anyway. It was daylight and time to get up. I could hear my mother in the kitchen downstairs preparing breakfast and she would soon call us.

So we got up and dressed. I washed my face in cold water from a pitcher of water mother had brought to the room the night before, when she had fixed the room for us and put extra quilts on the bed. I held a cold wet towel to my red swollen eyes and tried to act as gay and happy as I had been the evening before.

After we had eaten our breakfast, Buck asked where he could buy some liquor. He said he thought a good drink would make him feel better. My stepfather told him where he thought he might buy something to drink.[42] So he and Buck went to get it. If Buck had not been drinking the night

On the back of this photo, Blanche wrote to her father, "This was taken at Mr. Barrow's station in 1932. Me and my dog, the one I lost when we had to leave Joplin, MO. He sure was cute. I don't think you have one of these. If you do, it's ok anyway. Another won't hurt you. Ha. Ha. Your loving daughter and her dog, Snow Ball." (Courtesy of Rhea Leen Linder)

before he would have never said he would go to Joplin without me. He told me so after we had gone to Joplin, but it was too late by then.

When Buck came back from getting the liquor we started back to Dallas. He wanted to take the dog with us, but I told him to leave the dog with mother until we got back from Joplin. But he said he had not been with his wife and dog for a long time and he was going to take them both with him wherever he went. So we took the dog.

Snow Ball was the dog's name. Snow Ball seemed glad to go with us. When Buck got in the car he called the dog to get in up behind the seat. Snow Ball lay down and put both of his front feet on Buck's shoulder. Buck had taught him to ride that way when he was just a small puppy and he still remembered it. He seemed to be quite contented to be going places again.

We spent most of Sunday afternoon just driving around. Late that afternoon we drove back to Buck's mother's place. I told her what had happened the night before. She did not seem at all surprised. She said Clyde had come by to see her. He had heard about Buck being home and wanted to see him. Mrs. Barrow told him where to find Buck and me.

⬤4

Joplin

Editor's Note: April 1933

April signaled the point of no return for Buck Barrow and by association his wife, Blanche. During an ill-advised visit to Joplin, Missouri, Barrow, along with his brother Clyde and W. D. Jones, was involved in a gun battle in which two officers were killed. Jones and the Barrow brothers were all wounded but escaped with Bonnie Parker and Blanche Barrow. Two weeks later to the day, they were in the news again, involved in a highly publicized abduction and escape in Louisiana.

However, the month began with headlines about German Jews fleeing their native country in the wake of Adolph Hitler's elevation to dictator by the German Reichstag. On the fourth, the U.S. Navy dirigible Akron *was destroyed in a storm at sea. Seventy-three sailors died. Three people drowned in a Dallas, Texas, spring flood. Dust storms raged in the Texas Panhandle throughout most of the month, particularly in and around the town of Pampa.*[1]

On the tenth, President Roosevelt introduced a plan that would evolve into the Tennessee Valley Authority, allowing the federal government for the first time to produce and sell a commodity—electricity—to the public. The TVA would eventually do what no private utility could, supply electricity even at a loss if necessary. Three days later Roosevelt proposed a federal home-loan department and received word that the House had passed his $2 billion farm relief bill. By the twentieth, cotton, grain, and livestock markets were on the rise.[2]

In the movie houses, one could expect to see Our Betters *with Constance Bennett and* Tiger Shark *with Edward G. Robinson.* The Lone Ranger *and* The Jimmy

Durante Show *were popular radio programs, and songs like "Paper Moon,"
"Stormy Weather," and Duke Ellington's "Sophisticated Lady" were hits.*

*Jigsaw puzzles, mentioned by the author in her memoir, were rapidly becoming
one of the most popular and inexpensive forms of home entertainment. Jigsaw-
puzzle parties would remain a mainstay with Americans well into the 1940s.[3]*

*Crime rose sharply in April. On the third, three well-dressed men with machine
guns robbed the Adkins-Beck Packing Company of Dallas, Texas, of its $1,500
payroll. The robbery was nearly a duplicate of Clyde Barrow's robbery of the Neuhoff Brothers Packing Company the year before. In fact, in a strange coincidence,
one of the Adkins-Beck employees, Elsie Wullschleger, was working for Neuhoff
when Barrow, along with Raymond Hamilton and Ross Dyer, robbed it on
August 1, 1932. Despite the similarities, Wullschleger said the Adkins-Beck bandits
were not the same men who robbed the Neuhoff brothers.[4]*

*On the fourth, the notorious Barker-Karpis gang, including Frank Nash, robbed
the First National Bank of Fairbury, Nebraska. Two local citizens and one of the
bandits were wounded during a brief but furious gun battle. The bandit later
died. Over $100,000 was stolen and never recovered. On the thirteenth, two men
robbed the Union Savings Bank in St. Charles, Missouri. Later that very same
day, in an unrelated incident, six officers converged on the suspicious occupants of
a garage apartment in Joplin, Missouri.[5]*

MONDAY MORNING WE BEGAN getting ready to go to Joplin. Buck went to
Carl Beaty, who owned a garage and always had a number of used cars on
hand. Buck had known Carl for years and felt he would give him a good price
for the two Ford coupes if he traded them in for a bigger and better car.

In a couple of hours Buck and Carl drove a '29 Marmon sedan up to the
Barrows' filling station and called for me to look it over. I went out to see
it. Buck seemed very pleased and asked me to get in and see how I liked it.
We drove it around a few blocks, then came back. It looked good and the
motor sounded like it was in perfect shape.

Buck said, "Well, Baby, how do you like it?" I told him I liked it fine
and asked how much difference he would have to pay. He told me one
hundred dollars and said he thought it was a good buy. But Carl did not
care much about selling it because he liked the car and drove it quite a bit
himself. But since it was for Buck, he would let him have it if we both liked
it and wanted it, and we did.

Buck told me it had four good tires but the two spare tires, one on each
side, weren't very good. We would have to get at least one new spare in

case we should have a flat. Buck said he could sell it when we got back from Joplin, if we had to. So we made the trade and that afternoon Buck sent me to get the title transferred to us.[6]

Tuesday we started on our way to meet Clyde. When we drove away from the Barrow place, Mrs. Barrow was standing in the front door. We had promised we would be back in two weeks, but I felt as though I was leaving there forever and would never be free again to come and go as I wished. But I tried not to show my feelings because now Buck, the dog, and I were on our way to meet the brother Buck thought he must keep his promise to.

Everything seemed to be going nicely. The car was eating up the miles at a steady rate. But when we were only a few miles away from Sherman, Texas, the motor seemed to be running hot. We wondered if there was a leak in the radiator. We decided to stop at the first filling station we came to and have it taken care of. But soon the motor began to knock as if one of the rods was burned out. Buck had slowed down when he first noticed the motor getting hot. Now he pulled over and stopped to look at the motor and let it cool. He also wanted to check the oil. But there wasn't any to check. The oil dipstick was dry.

We could not drive the car without oil, so Buck caught a ride to a filling station after waiting what seemed like hours for someone to stop. He came back with a gallon of oil and put it in. He started the motor but the knock was still there. We drove along slowly, about ten miles an hour, but before we got to the filling station, which was only a few miles away, the rod had almost gone through the motor. We could not get the car fixed in Sherman, so we had to retrace our steps all the way back to Dallas. Because we had to drive so slowly it took us several hours.

We went to Elvin Barrow, Buck's oldest brother. Elvin worked in a garage and could get the parts needed for our car at a low price.[7] That night Buck and Elvin worked on the car as much as they could and finished the job the next day. On Wednesday, we again left Dallas to meet Clyde and Bonnie. This time we made the trip fine except for a flat tire, which delayed us for a short time in some small town in Oklahoma.

We drove to Checotah, Oklahoma, and found what we thought was the tourist camp where Clyde told us to meet him. It was late. Buck looked at most of the cars still parked outside of their garages. The rest were already inside. Still, we did not see any that looked like Clyde's Ford V-8 sedan. A few of the cabins had closed garages so we thought Clyde may be in one of those, or maybe he and Bonnie had not arrived yet. Maybe they would arrive in the morning. We also thought they may have already been there and gone.

We were sure it was the right place because we saw no other tourist park in the area. But by Thursday morning, they still had not rented a cabin there. We decided we must be at the wrong place. If so, we knew there was probably another tourist camp very close because ours was near the place Clyde had mentioned and it was the only tourist camp we saw the night before.

Buck drove out to the highway to look for another park. In a few minutes he came back and told me he had found Clyde. I was hoping he would not, but Clyde was in another park only a couple of blocks away from the one we were in. Buck then remembered that Clyde had told him about a place with nice brick cabins and closed garages. We put our bags in the car and drove around to Clyde's cabin.

They were just getting dressed when we arrived. All of them seemed very glad to see us. Inside, the cabin looked as if a cyclone had struck it. Clothes, guns, and luggage were scattered all over the small room. But Clyde and W. D. soon got everything together and in the car.

When they were ready to leave, Clyde told Buck to follow him into Muskogee, which was only about twelve miles away. But before we got to Muskogee, Clyde drove off the highway and stopped. We did the same. Clyde said he wanted Bonnie to ride with us, and for us to stop in Muskogee, and buy breakfast for the five of us. He and W. D. would be waiting a few miles outside of town. Bonnie got in.

When we got in to Muskogee, Buck drove through the main part of town. Bonnie said she felt kind of shaky riding through the busy part of any city. She and Clyde almost always tried to shun every town they could, and it had been a long time since she had ridden through the busy part of a town. It made her feel shaky, but Buck and I only laughed at her.

We stopped at a small cafe. I went in to get our breakfast, or rather lunch. It was that late. We found Clyde and W. D. parked a few miles out of town, just as Clyde had said. Bonnie got back in the car with Clyde. As she did so, she gave a sigh of relief. Clyde asked what was wrong. She told him she felt safer with him and told him how shaky she felt driving through Muskogee. Clyde only laughed and told her she would have to ride with us again before we got to Joplin. She said that would be okay.

We drove on until we found a good place to drive off the highway and eat. After we had unwrapped the food and made a table of the running boards of the cars and begun to eat, Buck said to me, "Baby, this seems like old times, doesn't it?" I laughingly told him it did, adding, "I may as well try to make the best of it since we had come this far, and just trust to fate that we will be back home in a couple of weeks as free as we were when we left. So why not try to be gay and happy for the moment?" I was happy just being with Buck because I loved him so. I would rather be dead than lose him or have to be separated from him again like I was the past fifteen months while he was in prison.

When we finished eating, Clyde, Bonnie, and W. D. got in their car. Buck and I got in ours. We drove to Vinita, Oklahoma. There Bonnie got back in the car with us. Clyde told us to stop at a Phillips filling station north of Joplin and get a cabin. Clyde and W. D. would meet us there that night or the next day. They had stopped at that particular tourist court before. The attendant, named Johnson, never seemed suspicious. Clyde said Mr. Johnson seemed like a fine fellow who would not ask any unnecessary questions. But Clyde warned us to be careful of the man who ran a grocery store near there. We would have to buy food from him or else drive into town to get what we needed. Clyde also told Buck that he would drive by the place when he and W. D. arrived, just in case something was wrong. Buck was to leave the cabin and walk along the highway when he saw Clyde's car pass, or if he heard him blow the police siren he had in his car. Clyde would pick him up, and if everything was okay he would rent a cabin for Bonnie, W. D., and himself.

Late that afternoon Buck saw Clyde's car pass. As planned, he walked out to the highway and in a few minutes returned with Clyde and W. D.

That night Clyde and I cooked supper. Buck helped too. He always seemed to think I was too small to do anything alone. He was always afraid I would cut my finger or burn myself with hot grease, so he was almost always fooling around and getting in my way. But I was already used to it.

Buck and Bonnie liked pickled pig's feet and olives. Clyde and I could not see why. We certainly didn't like that. Clyde liked french-fried potatoes and English peas cooked with a lot of cream and pepper.[8] He ate them at almost every meal except breakfast. W. D., on the other hand, would eat most anything.

I enjoyed seeing Clyde, Bonnie, and W. D. eat. I felt so sorry for them because they could not always enjoy their food for fear the cops may run in on them at any time.[9] I was glad to cook anything they wanted to eat. I hoped that Buck and I would never be like that again,[10] that we would

Clyde Barrow, 1933. "Clyde liked french-fried potatoes and English peas cooked with a lot of cream and pepper." (Courtesy of L. J. Hinton)

always be free to enjoy our life together, just as we had planned. And I hoped our freedom and happiness would last for many years. But soon I would be living the same life that Bonnie and Clyde were living.

That night (and for many nights thereafter) they did something I disliked very much. They sat up until two or three o'clock in the morning playing poker, cleaning their guns, and making so much noise that I was sure they could be heard for blocks. I told them they should not make so much noise, that it would make people suspicious. But I could not run their business and they did not seem to care what I thought about anything.

I did not know how to play cards, except for solitaire.[11] I tried to learn, just to please Buck, but I seemed to be too dumb. Instead he would almost always have me sit beside him while he was playing. He said I was good luck to him. Even then, he would try to show me what every card meant and how to play them. But when I would try to play a hand without him showing me, I would forget everything. I wouldn't know if I had won or lost, so I just stopped trying and simply sat beside him.

Sometimes I would get so sleepy. I couldn't stay awake and would rest my head on his knees and soon fall asleep. Then when everyone finally decided to go to bed, he would pick me up and put me to bed like a baby.

Clyde could hardly get Bonnie or W. D. awake the next day. He worked with them for hours, or until he got mad because they would not get up. Then he would leave them alone.

W. D. almost always slept with Clyde and Bonnie. We used to laugh at him and tell him he was afraid to sleep alone. But he would take the teasing good-naturedly. He was always jolly and never seemed to have a serious thought. But I suppose he was like most kids his age, sixteen or seventeen years old; he thought he could get a thrill from most anything, even shooting at cops. But after a few battles, he saw it wasn't fun. He also did not want to get any murder raps hung on him. I don't know for sure if he ever killed anyone or not, but Clyde got as much thrill from shooting cops as the cops did shooting or killing thieves or gangsters.

On April 1, we left the cabins and moved into a stone apartment over a double garage near Oak Ridge Drive, in the Freeman Grove addition. It was just across the county line, south of Joplin. Bonnie and I had rented the apartment the day before but we could not move in because the people who lived there could not move out until April 1.[12]

When we rented the apartment, we were told it was furnished. And it was furnished when we looked at it. It had a radio and everything else except linens. In fact, we saw two radios, so we thought one of them belonged in the apartment. Afterward we were told where to find the keys to all the doors. The next afternoon we found there was nothing but bare furniture in the apartment. We would have to get a lot of things before we could even sleep there that night. We had to have linens, blankets or quilts (or both), dishes, silverware, and everything else needed to cook and serve meals.

Clyde said he would get everything we needed and asked Buck to go with him. They came back in a few hours with six or eight large feather pillows, a feather bed, plenty of sheets and pillowcases, about fourteen quilts

"On April 1, we . . . moved into a stone apartment over a double garage near Oak Ridge Drive." (Photograph by Blanche Barrow, courtesy of Rhea Leen Linder)

and blankets, several bedspreads, dishes, silverware, and a lot of other things we needed to start keeping house. The only thing they forgot was a radio. Almost everything was new except the bed. They got it for W. D. and said he would have to sleep alone from now on.[13]

The apartment was nice enough for us. There were two bedrooms, a living room, a kitchenette with built-in furniture, and a small bathroom. Clyde told Bonnie and me that we could have a lot of fun dressing up the apartment and playing house. But most of the cleaning, cooking, and housekeeping was left to Blanche. Clyde and Bonnie's bedroom was hardly ever cleaned, nor was the bed made. Bonnie seldom got up before twelve noon or one o'clock. Of course, none of us were early birds because we stayed up so late, mostly because everyone else insisted on playing cards until all hours in the morning.

I had to have something to do, so I bought myself a bunch of jigsaw puzzles. At first, everyone laughed, but I didn't mind. I told them as soon as they worked one puzzle they would want more. And this was true! One night when Clyde had lost at poker and did not care to take any of the guns apart, he decided to help me work a puzzle. After that almost every time anyone went to town or to a drugstore for anything, he asked for more puzzles. He could hardly leave one until it was finished, day or night. Soon everyone was working them, everyone except Buck. He didn't like them. All he got from them were headaches.[14]

I think Bonnie and I almost bought out Kress's.[15] Every time we went to town we came back with our arms loaded with ashtrays, glassware, small picture frames, and anything else we saw that was pretty or that we wanted or needed, plus a lot of things we didn't need. Once we saw some twenty-cent finger rings with cut-glass sets in them and ear screws to match, but we never wore them. The rings looked real. Just for fun we bought two each. I was told later by an officer that someone identified the rings and ear screws as real diamonds taken from them in a robbery.[16] They would have been very disappointed if they ever wore them and got water on them!

Often when we were tired of staying in the house, or Clyde and W. D. were out of town, Bonnie and I would go to an afternoon movie by ourselves.[17] Buck would stay home. However, sometimes the three boys would go with us to a show at night. On these outings, we always drove our Marmon. It wasn't hot and we could park it and feel safe enough to go back to it when we were ready to go home.

Buck had driven to some small town just across the Missouri-Kansas line and bought Kansas license plates for our car because Clyde thought it best not to have Texas plates on it. He said someone may get suspicious of a Texas car and investigate to see who owned it.[18]

All of us had a lot of fun together. But to me there always seemed to be a shadow hanging over us, like a dark cloud. But since we had come this far I tried to forget about what might happen to us. I thought worrying wouldn't do any good anyway.

I usually ordered all our groceries by phone and had them delivered.[19] Sometimes Buck went for them in the car. After April 7, when the sale of beer was legalized in Missouri, we bought a case of beer nearly every day. I didn't care for beer myself but all the rest did. They enjoyed seeing who could drink the most. It wasn't that I thought I was too good to drink; I just didn't like beer or whiskey. It made me sick. I also didn't think the

Blanche drinking whiskey from a flask near Crockett, Texas, 1931. "I just didn't like beer or whiskey." (Photograph by Buck Barrow, courtesy of Rhea Leen Linder)

headache the next morning was worth the fun of getting drunk and making a silly fool of yourself.[20]

I always met the grocery store delivery boy[21] or the laundry man from the cleaners downstairs at the front. I did not like to do that. I was sure one of them would get suspicious because they were not allowed to bring the packages upstairs to the apartment. Some of the packages were almost as big as me. One time I had to argue with the laundry man about taking some clothes up myself. I told Clyde he could just as easily stay back in one of the bedrooms if he did not want any one to see him.

"Those people are always bothered with nose trouble," he said, "and may see too much if they come in."

Another reason for Clyde's concern was the fact that he had robbed one of the cleaners or laundries a few months before and he thought someone might recognize him. He wasn't taking any chances. I couldn't blame him for that, although he had not kept his promise to keep the guns out of the apartment and leave them in the car. But of course, he couldn't afford to leave them in the garage, so they were kept in a large closet in the living room or just laying around in his bedroom.

Clyde always wanted to keep the window blinds drawn so no one could see in. But we could hardly see out. I always tried to keep the blinds up in our bedroom during the day because I didn't like to be in a place where I couldn't see out. Our bedroom faced the street on the south side. Clyde and Bonnie's bedroom was on the north side.

One night not long after we had moved to the apartment, Clyde wanted to go to a small town near Joplin and look around for something. He wanted Buck to go with him. I didn't want him to go any place alone with Clyde but they told me it would be okay because they weren't going to rob anything that night, and if they did Clyde would not allow Buck to help or to have anything to do with any job he pulled. They said they would be back in a few hours, but for us to go to bed and get some sleep.

I could not keep Buck from going, even though I tried very hard. But I did not feel like having an argument with him. Anyway, he had promised me he would not help pull any job even if Clyde wanted him to. Buck did not want to go back to prison. Still, I had my doubts about what they might do.

Buck kissed me goodnight and left. We put the lights out and went to bed soon after they had gone, but I didn't go to sleep. I lay across my bed, put a pillow on the window sill, and kept myself awake looking up and down the street. I saw the private night watchman every time he made his rounds.[22] He had called at our door earlier in the month and asked if we wanted him to watch our car or to keep burglars away. We had paid him one dollar to watch our Marmon, the same amount other people in the district paid.

At the time our car had to sit on the street. There wasn't space in the double garage under our apartment. The people who lived on the same lot as us, in the large home on the corner, used half the garage. Clyde's stolen car occupied the other half. Later on, Buck rented a garage from a man next door to us. Before that Buck had asked the man who lived in the large home if he would switch with us—allowing us to use his half of the double garage under the apartment and him use the one Buck had rented for our car. We thought he could drive into it just as easy as he could the one he was using. But the man did not like the idea and refused to change with Buck. So Buck had to drive our car around in front of his house, the driveway to which was in back of our apartment. I don't remember the names of any of those people.[23]

I had watched the man on different occasions, the one who shared the garage under the apartment. Sometimes we would be up late when he got home and drove in the garage. Clyde would be cleaning guns or with the others, playing cards or working puzzles. The man would close and lock his car. Then he would stay for a few minutes, looking Clyde's car over or listening, trying to catch some of our conversation. Sometimes he would close the garage door and stand outside and listen. I had told Buck and Clyde about this but Clyde said I was just imagining things, or afraid. I wasn't afraid, just careful. I had seen these things and knew I wasn't just trying to frighten anyone. I knew that man was suspicious of something.

As I lay there watching the night watchman that night, waiting for Buck to return, I remembered other nights when I would see him peep into the garage or sometimes just stop and listen. I wondered if he may be getting suspicious too. Maybe he wanted to know why we stayed up so late at night, or maybe he'd heard the others cleaning and snapping the guns.[24]

I could not go to sleep. I just lay there awake, looking out the window and checking my watch. Hours passed. Still the boys did not come back. I thought of everything that could happen to Buck. If he was lucky enough to get back safe, I was going to ask him if we could go home.

I lay there waiting and watching for him until the light began to show in the east and cars began to appear on the streets. Soon I saw a car moving along the street below. It looked like Clyde's car but I couldn't be sure. Then the driver turned off the lights, slowed down, and drove in the driveway. Someone got out and opened the garage door. Then the car drove in.

Bonnie had not slept much, if any, and I called her when I got up and went down to meet the boys. There was a door at the foot of the stairs that opened inside the garage. I met them with their arms full of guns and rifles. I was so glad to see Buck that I did not ask many questions, only why he had stayed away so long.

After they unloaded everything onto the divan and living room floor, they told us what they had done. They had burglarized some National Guard armory. I was plenty mad about it and told them what I thought of their promises. But it didn't do much for me to get mad. There wasn't anything I could do about it.

Buck handed me a pair of army field glasses. Clyde said he knew Bonnie would not care for anything like that. She would rather have a gun. So he had given the glasses to Buck for me. Clyde began showing Bonnie all the guns and told her what he could do with one of the army rifles. It could shoot twenty times without stopping, so long as you held your finger on the trigger.[25]

I wasn't very pleased with the nice new field glasses they had given me. I would have liked them more if they had not been stolen from some armory.

Clyde told me Buck had nothing to do with the burglary, that he just sat in the car a block away. But I had my doubts about that. I believe Buck helped.

I cooked breakfast. We ate, and then went to bed. I told Buck our two weeks were about up and that I wanted to go home while we were still fine. He said we would go in a couple of days. He was ready to go home soon because he couldn't make Clyde change his ways. There was no reason for us to risk staying with him.

That afternoon, after we all woke up and had eaten dinner, Clyde wanted to drive to the country and try out the new guns. So the three boys went to the country. They came back soon after dark. Clyde seemed very pleased with his new toys. They laughingly told us about one of the guns shooting so fast that they couldn't get it to stop. They had to throw it in a small creek to stop it. That was the last time Buck went anywhere with Clyde while we were in Joplin.

That night Clyde cut the barrel and stock off one rifle. He thought it would be much easier to handle, but when he tried it the next day, it wouldn't work right. It would only shoot once instead of twenty times.[26]

Everything continued in about the same way for the next few days. Buck and I still had a few dollars left, enough to get us back home to Dallas, but Clyde's bankroll was getting low. One day he left and came back with some money. He did not say where he had gone or what he had robbed and I didn't ask any questions because I thought if they wanted me to know they would have told me. Anyway, I didn't want to know where he went or what he did.

On April 11 or 12, Clyde and W. D. left for some unknown place in Oklahoma. Clyde wanted us to stay a few days longer. Buck told him we would, but Buck had already promised me we would go home that Friday, April 14. He wanted to do a little work on our car and get it in good shape for the trip. Clyde and W. D. returned late that afternoon, but instead of one car, they had two. They had seen a Ford V-8 roadster, thought it was pretty, stole it, and put it in the garage. Surely, someone saw them drive it into the garage, I thought. Bonnie told Clyde he was crazy for doing anything like that. She said if he kept the car there, she would leave because she knew someone would call the law out to investigate. But Clyde said he would only keep it there that night, then use it the next day for a robbery and leave it some place else. They kept arguing until they both were mad enough to fight, which is what they did. And Clyde wasn't very easy with her either. He knocked her across the bedroom a couple of times but she got up and went back for more. Bonnie had tried as best she could to keep the place from getting hot. She did not want Buck and I to get into trouble and have to live the life she and Clyde were living.[27]

I asked Buck if he meant to go home Friday as he had promised. He said he didn't know. He had promised Clyde we would stay a few days longer. I wasn't very pleased about Clyde stealing another car and bringing it to the apartment. That would surely get heat on the place. I told Buck that it seemed like Clyde was just trying to get him into trouble so he would have to stay with him until he was shot down by officers, which would certainly happen to Clyde sooner or later.[28] And I told Buck that maybe he did not know whether he was going home or not, but I did! I had taken all I could stand. If he wanted to stay with his beloved brother Clyde, then he could. He could just choose between the two of us because I was leaving with him or without him! With that, he made up his mind quick, because he thought I would go alone if he didn't go with me.

Thursday morning, April 13, Buck began getting the car ready for us to leave early the following day. He worked most of the day, had the oil changed, and filled the tank with gas. Although we didn't get up early that day, we did get up earlier than usual. But Bonnie stayed in bed until noon. She didn't feel very well after the fight the night before, although she and Clyde had made up and everything was back to normal between them.

Clyde was going to take the roadster away someplace and rob something. Bonnie wanted to go with Clyde, but because she didn't feel well, Clyde wanted her to rest in bed. So she decided to stay behind. Clyde and W. D. would go alone.

All of us had the jitters and felt as if a bomb was about to explode. None of us felt good about staying in the apartment another night. Before he left, Clyde told us where we could find a good tourist park to stay and that he and W. D. would meet us there when they got back. Early Friday morning Buck and I could load our car and get ready to leave for home. The other three would watch the apartment and go someplace else if it was hot. They would be able to tell if anyone had been there.

Clyde said he and W. D. would be back sometime Thursday night and would see us before we left. He said we could draw what was left of the deposit for the lights, water, and gas, about twenty-five dollars.

I cleaned up our bedroom, the living room and bath, and had almost all our clothes ready so it would only take a few minutes for me to pack them. I cooked our lunch, but did not have the kitchen all cleaned. I also wanted to wash some of our clothes before we left for home. I would do that in the kitchen sink.

About four-fifteen or five o'clock that afternoon, Buck was just finishing the work on the car and had driven it around to the back to put it in the garage until we were ready to leave the apartment. Bonnie was sitting in the center of the living room rug recopying some of the poetry she had written. She still had on her kimono, nightgown, house slippers, and no hose. I was wearing a blue crepe dress that had once been an evening gown. I had hemmed it at the bottom to make it into a housedress to wear around in the apartment while we were there. The shoulders were lace and the back was low-cut. Like Bonnie, I wore no hose. But I did have on a pair of black kid pumps.

I was letting the clothes soak for a few minutes in the kitchen sink. I had taken my watch off and laid it in the cabinet so it wouldn't get wet. I did not want to lose or break it because Buck had given it to me just before we were married. I wanted to keep it always.

I was nervous that afternoon. I felt as though I couldn't stay in one place long. Bonnie wanted me to boil an egg for her. While it was on the stove, I took a deck of cards out and tried to settle myself down by playing solitaire before I washed the clothes. But I had no luck. Old Sol would beat me every time.

I went to see about Bonnie's egg. It was done. I broke the shell and gave it to her. My dog was at my heels wherever I went. About this time, we heard someone say, "Stop!" Then one of the garage doors opened. I looked out the living room window and saw Buck opening the other door of the garage for Clyde and W. D. I told Bonnie who it was. She said she wished she had gone with them the first time, that something must have gone wrong, or maybe they had come back after the other car. She said she would go with them now.

She and I ran down the stairs to find out why they had come back so soon. They told us they had burned the motor out in the roadster and had come back after the sedan. Clyde said Bonnie could go with them if she wanted to. W. D. could drive the roadster out of town and leave it.

Bonnie went back to finish recopying her poem.[29] She was going to finish it, then get ready to go with them. I still had the cards in my hand but had gone in the kitchen for something. Clyde and W. D. were in the garage unloading the guns from the roadster and putting them in the sedan. All of a sudden, we heard something that sounded like someone had turned a

"We heard Clyde holler, 'Oh, lordy! Let's get started!'" (From the Blanche Caldwell Barrow scrapbooks, courtesy of Rhea Leen Linder)

machine gun on the place. But the shots sounded muffled, as though they were in the garage, or behind it. I went to one of the kitchen windows but I couldn't see anyone.

We heard Clyde holler, "Oh, lordy! Let's get started!"

At first, we thought he had just accidentally discharged one of the rifles and couldn't get it to stop firing.[30] Then Buck came running up the stairs without a gun or anything.[31] He told us to get ready to leave, that the cops were there. I was still in the kitchen. Bonnie said later she fired a shot through one of the living room windows but I did not see her, or hear the glass break.[32] I didn't even know the window was broken or that any shots had been fired upstairs. I didn't know just what to do, but I didn't see why Buck and I had to leave with the other three. We hadn't done anything. But Buck said we must leave.

I thought of my purse in our bedroom. It had Buck's pardon papers, my divorce papers, and our marriage license in it. I also thought of Buck's coat with the title to our car in the pocket. I thought, "I must get those things! I cannot leave those here if we have to leave now!" But I forgot about my watch.[33]

The dog was running around as if he was trying to figure out what all the excitement was about, or what I was going to do next. He kept getting in my way. I picked him up and set him on a table in the kitchen and told him to stay there. But as I opened the swing door that led from the kitchen to the living room, he ran out and started downstairs.[34]

Then I ran into W. D. He was holding his right side. When he saw me, he caught me around the neck and then he almost fell to the floor. I nearly went down with him but I caught him around the waist and braced myself against the door jam and kept us both from falling.

He kept saying, "Blanche, they shot me! I am dying! Please do something for me!"

I had been on my way to the bedroom to get my purse and coat and Buck's coat too but I couldn't get there with W. D. holding on to me, begging me to do something for him and not to let him die. I didn't know what to do for him. Poor kid. I guess he was in a lot of pain and thought he was going to die. That upset my nerves more than ever. They weren't too steady anyway. I was too excited to know what to do next.

W. D. left Clyde alone in the garage. Buck started down the steps to see if Clyde was dead. I screamed for him not to go down. I thought he would be killed too. But he went anyway. The dog followed but came back.

By the time Buck got to the garage the shooting had stopped. Clyde hollered for us to come down so we could get away from there. Bonnie went downstairs first. I don't remember how W. D. and I ever got down to the car. I helped him onto the backseat of the sedan.

I did not see Buck or Clyde. I was almost crazy with fear, scared of Buck getting killed. But when I started around the car to look for him, I saw him running toward me. I still did not see Clyde but I saw a man lying on the garage floor. He wore a blue suit like Clyde's and his hair was brown. I thought at first that it was Clyde.[35]

Wes Harryman and his family. "I saw a man lying on the garage floor." (Courtesy of Jim Hounschell)

Buck had just moved away from the man on the floor. I ran toward him near the door. Then I heard Clyde say, "Get in the car." I don't know where he came from. My memory is just a bit hazy but I thought he meant for us to get in the officers' car that was about halfway in the door.[36] He was standing near it.

I was so excited I didn't know what I was doing. When I got to the car Clyde asked me to help him push it out of the way, so we could drive the

Harry McGinnis. "Oh, what a horrible sight. . . . [I] can still see the vision of a man lying there with what looked like his brains blown out." (Courtesy of Jim Hounschell)

sedan out of the garage. I started to push it and saw another man just outside the door. Oh, what a horrible sight to see a human body torn apart like that by shotgun bullets. I shiver now as I think of it and can still see the vision of a man lying there with what looked like his brains blown out and running down his shoulders and onto the ground. It looked as if one arm had been torn off by bullets.[37] All this I saw and more in just one glance.

As we were pushing the officers' car out of the driveway, it started rolling backwards down the hill. Buck turned it loose thinking we would do the same, but the car seemed to pull me with it. By the time I was able to let go of the car Clyde and I were out in the middle of the street.[38] I was only a few feet from him when someone started shooting from a corner of the building. I saw Clyde stagger. He had a rifle and was almost bent over double, shooting as fast as he could. I could feel bullets whiz by my head. I looked back at the garage. I didn't think I would make it back there, where Buck was. Then I saw those dead men.

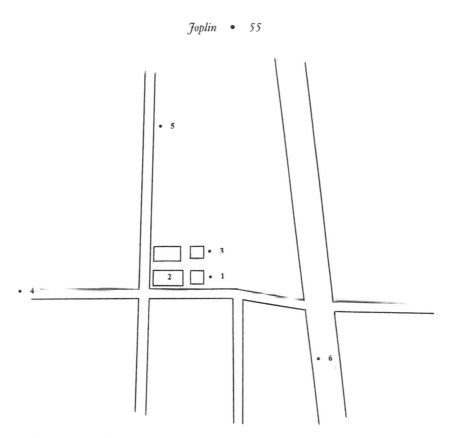

Joplin, Missouri, Shoot-out
Scale: 1 in = 85 yd
Based on a contemporary map in the editor's possession.

1. Garage apartment on 34th, occupied by the Bonnie Parker, Blanche Barrow, W. D. Jones and the Barrow brothers; 2. Main house, corner of Oak Ridge and 34th; 3. The garage where Buck Barrow's Marmon was parked; 4. West 34th; 5. Oak Ridge Drive; 6. Main Street, escape route

I let out a loud scream and started running down the hill.[39] I don't know if I thought I could outrun the bullets whizzing by me or not. Anyway, I was trying to. Suddenly the dog was beside me. He had followed me downstairs and out into the street. I kept running. The dog stayed up with me. But when I stopped, the dog kept on going. That was the last time I saw our little white dog.[40]

Buck was standing in the door calling to me to come back. Again, I thought of what I had left in the apartment in my purse. I ran back and started to go upstairs but Buck grabbed me and took me to the car. He got in with me in the back with W. D. Then Clyde got behind the wheel and stepped on the gas. We seemed to almost jump out of the garage to the street. Not one shot was fired from our car as we left, despite some of the stories told about "the Bloody Barrow Gang."[41]

Our Marmon sedan was still in the driveway where Buck had left it when he went to open the garage for Clyde or W. D. All five of us left in Clyde's Ford V-8 sedan. Clyde was driving and Bonnie was in the front seat with him.[42]

It wasn't until after we had driven away that I began to fully realize what a mess Buck and I were in. I think I must have gone insane for a few minutes. I could see all my hopes and dreams tumbling down around me, my dreams of being with my husband who I loved more than anyone or anything in the world, my dreams of having a home with him, of hoping he would always be free so we could be happy together. Now that freedom was gone. After three short weeks, it had been taken away from both of us in only a few minutes. At least two men had been killed and maybe more, I didn't know. We would be hunted for murder even though we were not guilty. We couldn't prove it then and may have been hanged for it if we had stayed. But why did we have to run away from something we did not do?

I thought of my dear old dad. What would this do to him when he read about it? I just knew it would kill him because I knew someday all of us would be torn to bits by machine guns, like the man I had seen outside the garage door and the one who lay so still inside, on the floor dead. We would be killed like that.

So this was what I had waited for all those long weary months while Buck had been in prison. I dreaded to think of how it would all end. I wished we had both been killed in the beginning. I would have gladly exchanged places with those who were left dead back there in that awful place. Our worldly troubles would be over. But now they had only just begun.

I knew then that I would not leave Buck. I hoped we would die together when our time came. I began crying and pulling my hair. I still had the deck of cards in my hand. Buck noticed them and almost broke my fingers trying to get them away from me. W. D. was trying to pet me and begging me not to cry. He was suffering himself, but was begging me to not take it so hard. Buck was trying to tell me it hurt him just as bad as it did me, but I couldn't see how it could.

W. D. asked me to find out just where he was shot. His clothes were so bloody it was hard to tell their real color. And I was almost as bad. My hands were bloody and my dress looked like a red polka-dot print instead of plain blue.

I was so nervous I couldn't get W. D.'s shirt unbuttoned, so I just tore the buttons off. We found he had been shot through the right side. The bullet had come out just above his lower rib. It looked as though it had gone between the ribs. He had lost a lot of blood. He was getting weak and sick.[43]

Clyde and Buck were both wounded too. Clyde was hit as he stood in the street after we pushed the police car out of the way, when I saw him stagger. A button on his shirt had checked the bullet and kept it from going very deep in his chest. But he was in pain and losing quite a lot of blood. He said he felt like he would faint, but he wouldn't let Buck drive.

Buck wasn't hurt bad. The bullet had only left a bruise above his heart. He was hit just as he was about to run upstairs to tell us we had to leave. He was shot before he got to the doorway on the stairs. He said at first that he thought he had been shot through the heart. He said he once heard that if someone was shot in the heart, they could hold their breath and live long enough to say a few words. He said he meant to come upstairs and tell his baby goodbye before he died. It made me cry all the more. I prayed that he would never have to tell me goodbye. If he had to be killed, then I wanted to die too. I wanted to die first or at the same time as him.

We traveled south over country roads for a while. About five miles outside of Joplin we had a flat. Rain had begun to fall. After the tire was changed, we started driving fast again. The rain and mud made traveling harder.

We found a small country store and gas station, filled with gas and oil, and bought some aspirin for W. D. He had moved up front with Bonnie and Clyde and had wrapped himself up in a blanket that was kept in the car to cover the guns. All of us were cold, especially Bonnie and me. We weren't wearing much anyway, even if it hadn't been a cold day.[44]

We moved around on country roads and over hills and finally drove down a road that came to a dead end at some farmhouse. It was after dark before we found a main road. Then we rode all night. W. D. seemed to be getting weaker all the time, but he did not lose consciousness. We were afraid he would die.

⊛ 5

Ruston

THE NEXT MORNING AT daybreak, we were in Shamrock, Texas. We were cold, hungry, and sleepy, and W. D. and Clyde had to have medicine for their wounds. We needed to stop some place for a couple hours. We pulled up to a small tourist camp, woke the owner, and got a cabin. It was a dirty place with no running water. But it had a stove, although we would have to wait until seven o'clock before the little grocery store opened nearby.

We got water and heated it. Then we bathed and dressed everybody's wounds as best we could.[1] When the store opened, I was sent to buy food. I had washed the blood from my dress as best I could, but anyone could have looked at me and known something was wrong. The morning was cold. Anyone else would have had on a coat. We were all a sorry sight to see. Still, I tried to act as if nothing was wrong. I looked at the morning papers while I waited for the storekeeper to get the food ready, but I didn't see anything about the double murders in Joplin.

After we had eaten, Clyde and W. D. tried to sleep. We discussed the battle at Joplin. In fact, that was about all we talked about, that and what we would do next. Bonnie and Clyde said they were very sorry they had gotten us into trouble. But saying they were sorry didn't do any good. Every time I closed my eyes, I could see those dead men. I told Buck about it. He said he felt the same way but that I should try and forget it. He told me about moving the man inside the garage so Clyde would not drive over him. It was bad enough to kill him without driving the car over his body. So Buck moved the man.[2]

Soon suspicious cars began driving around the camp and the men inside these cars seemed to be taking too much interest in our cabin. The place seemed to be getting too warm, so we didn't stay long. We drove out the back way.

We were on the road most of that day, staying off the main highway as much as we could. We couldn't eat anymore that day and we were too hot to rob anything. At least that's what Clyde said. He thought we would be safe if we stayed away from large towns. So we parked on a country road about ten or fifteen miles out of Amarillo, Texas, to wait until dark.

When night came, we drove into town. We had to have clothes and money and needed another car. Clyde said he would have to rob something, anything would do. He drove around for about an hour, then parked on a dark street. I hadn't seen anything worth robbing, but I didn't know anything about robbery. I wouldn't have known what to rob anyway. I was like a joke to everybody. I was often teased and laughed at because I was so dumb.

When Clyde parked, he told Buck to walk around with him. I knew they were going to rob some place, even though no one had said as much. Buck kissed me when he got out of the car and asked me not to be nervous. He seemed like he was about to cry. He seemed nervous too. I felt so sorry for him.

I started crying after he left. This would be the first time he had taken a gun and robbed someone since he'd returned to prison. He'd gone back to prison so he could stop running and hiding from the law and be a free man. Now he was facing something worse than before. Life seemed so unkind to us.

I kept watching for them to come back. I didn't have too long to wait. When I saw them, they were both running. Bonnie started the motor. We opened the car doors and they jumped in. Clyde started driving fast. I kept looking for the cops, expecting them to catch up with us at any moment. I was sure they would learn of the crime the instant it was committed. I don't remember what they said they robbed.[3] I don't even know if we left there going east, west, north, or south. I didn't care.

Just before we got off of the highway, we found a place to eat. And did we eat! Then we started traveling on country roads again. The next day we got some clothes. I lost all track of time. We drove so much and so fast, most of the day and night, sleeping only a few hours at a time. One of us always kept watch while the others slept.

We traveled through New Mexico, Kansas, Nebraska, Iowa, and Illinois, back through Missouri, Arkansas, Oklahoma, and Louisiana.[4] When the money gave out, something was robbed. I don't remember sleeping in a bed more than three or four times in the next two weeks.

"He [Jones] walked up to the car, opened the door, and got in as if he owned it." (Courtesy L. J. Hinton)

Clyde's and W. D.'s wounds were healing very well, considering the lack of care. Clyde had stolen a medical kit from some doctor's car some place. The wounds got better treatment after that.

Two weeks to the day after we left Joplin, we were driving through Ruston, Louisiana. Clyde saw a car he wanted and asked W. D. if he wanted to get it. He said he did. Clyde stopped and W. D. went to see if the keys were in it. He walked up to the car, opened the door, and got in as if he owned it. Then he waved his hand to Clyde and drove off, heading down another street that led to the highway.

Clyde waited a few seconds to see if anyone would come out of the house. We saw a man and woman run out and get into a Ford coupe.[5] Clyde started

scene from the movie

driving. He was sure he could catch up with W. D. but when we got on the highway W. D. was gone! We drove about ten miles but saw nothing that looked like the car W. D. had stolen. Therefore, Clyde turned around and started back to Ruston. He thought that maybe W. D. had stopped somewhere before he got to the highway. We still couldn't find him. But we met the man and woman in the coupe. They were trying to find W. D. too.

Clyde told W. D. what road to take after he left the main highway and where to stop if he got ahead of us. When we still did not see W. D., Clyde turned the car around again to either look for him or to chase the coupe. They had been chasing us, so Clyde decided to turn the tables.[6]

We drove over country roads through several small towns. People were standing in the streets, looking. We knew the coupe must be close to W. D. At one point, we could see where he had made a fast turn because the roads were wet in some places. Out in the country, away from the small towns, Clyde would blow the police siren he had on his car. If W. D. had left the car someplace and was waiting in the woods he would know we were looking for him by the way Clyde blew the siren. We thought we were close but we could not catch up with him.

Just outside of yet another small town, we met the man and woman in the coupe. They had given up the chase. Clyde was mad at them for following W. D. He stopped the coupe and asked them about the car they were following. At first, the man said he didn't know what Clyde was talking about. Clyde jumped out, opened the door to the coupe, and made the man get out. The man said something smart, which made Clyde even madder. He hit the man with the butt of his pistol, hit him between the shoulders, just at the base of his neck. The man went down with the blow and fell on the turtleback of the coupe. Buck and I just sat and looked on.

Bonnie jumped out of the car. She wanted to show how tough she thought she was. Clyde made the man get in our car.[7] Bonnie cursed the woman and told her to do the same. I couldn't help feeling sorry for the man and woman. They looked so frightened. Clyde took the keys to the coupe and made the man and woman sit on the front seat with Bonnie and him.[8]

We began looking for W. D. again. Again, we tried to follow his tire tracks but we couldn't tell whether or not he'd turned onto other roads. We rode for a long time looking for him, and then finally gave up hope.

We rode into Arkansas. Clyde meant to keep the man and women until after dark. They told us who they were and Clyde told them who we were. They seemed to be more frightened than ever. The man was an undertaker.

— not in the movie

The woman was a radio announcer, something about recipes or how to can fruit.[9] They begged Clyde not kill them. Clyde told them if they were careful and didn't try any funny stuff they would be released unharmed.

That afternoon Clyde drove down a country road and parked far away from the nearest house. He told the man and woman he was going to free them if they would promise to keep their backs turned until we were out of sight. They promised they would. Clyde asked the man if he had any money. He said he only had twenty-five cents. Clyde did not shake him down to see if he had more. He gave them five dollars to help them get back home or to use to wire home for more money.[10]

Clyde asked the man if he would like to embalm him when he died. The undertaker said he would not, that he hoped Clyde lived a long time. Clyde only laughed because he knew the man would like to embalm him that very minute, but was afraid to say so.[11] Clyde also said he was sorry if he hurt the man very bad. We left them there in Arkansas, but as we drove away, they turned around just enough to get our license number.[12] We knew we would soon be as hot as we were two weeks before.

I'd gotten over being so afraid every time something happened. But whenever I thought about the possibility of losing Buck, I burst out crying. I was an awful crybaby and must have been a burden to all of them. But I would have rather been shot through the heart than to have lost Buck. And I was still unsure about whether I could shoot anyone down, even if it meant their life or mine. I just didn't have the courage to fight back, even though fate had dealt me a terrible blow. I was too softhearted to take a human life. I just couldn't do it.

And I wanted to never see another gun. We couldn't sit comfortably in the car because of all the guns—guns everywhere! I got a lot of razzing because I hated guns so much. I had never been afraid of them before we got into trouble, but I knew someday they would take Buck away from me. I didn't think about what they may do to me. I didn't care. Life wouldn't mean anything to me anyway if Buck were killed. I suffered a million deaths and the very tortures of hell, day and night, with fear of losing him. Sometimes when my aching heart seemed as though it would burst, I thought of killing myself. That awful pain of fear was like a million devils tearing me apart. I was happy just to be near Buck, but if anyone can live in heaven and hell at the same time, I did. Certainly few will understand how I felt, and many may not be able to understand why I didn't fight back, loving Buck as I did and knowing some officer would shoot him down sooner or later. Buck worried a lot too. He often cursed himself for not listening to me. Now we were in over our heads. *[right there in movie]*

After the man and woman were released, late in the afternoon, we got on the main highway near Hope, Arkansas.[13] We had a choice of crossing into Louisiana by way of a toll bridge near there or using the one at Shreveport. Clyde said it would be better to cross near Hope, because he thought it would be safer. But as we entered Hope, we saw a squad car leaving town. Clyde turned down a side street so he wouldn't meet them. We were sure they were looking for us. But they saw us anyway and turned onto the same street. One of the officers put his rifle out the car, around the windshield. Clyde stepped on the gas and started cutting corners. He told Buck to shoot them through the back window. Buck raised his rifle. They were close to us and could have easily been shot, but Buck didn't fire. Neither did the officers. Clyde soon lost them by simply outdriving them.[14]

Again, we hit muddy country roads. Some were even worse than the ones we had traveled earlier in the day. We could hardy make it through the mud in some places. The ride was plenty rough, but if the officers had caught up with us, their bullets would have been worse.

We traveled south to Louisiana and crossed over to Shreveport by way of the toll bridge there. It was pretty risky, but we had to take lots of chances. From Shreveport, we continued south. It was past midnight when we stopped in the pinewoods and slept for a few hours.[15] Buck, Bonnie, and I took turns keeping watch while the others slept. We always tried to let Clyde get as much sleep as he could, because he did most of the driving.

We felt better after a little sleep. We would have to drive to Dallas to see if W. D. had gone home, or if he had been captured, or maybe killed.[16] Clyde was worried about him because the wound he'd received in Joplin had not yet healed completely. When we drove through Palestine, Texas, we bought a newspaper. Our names were in big headlines.[17]

[Haven't been w/ W. D.]

6

Friction

Editor's Note: May 1933

May was relatively quiet for the Barrow brothers. They were involved in at least two bank robberies, both rather bizarre and both attributed to others. Apart from those incidents, they apparently roamed at will through a large number of states and visited the Dallas area at least once. Otherwise, storms, more crime, and economic relief dominated the news of the month.

On the second, eighty-nine people were reported killed and another thousand injured by tornadoes in Louisiana, Arkansas, and Mississippi. On May 10, storms killed sixty-seven in Tennessee and Kentucky. On the twelfth, the day the Barrow gang sprayed Lucerne, Indiana, with automatic weapons fire following a failed robbery, flooding in central Indiana was reported as the worst in twenty years. A week later, on the very day the Barrow brothers robbed the First State Bank of Okabena, Minnesota, six were injured by heavy rain and lightning overnight. Fourteen people died when tornadoes swept through Kansas and Nebraska on the twenty-third. Two days later heavy thunderstorms struck Dallas, Texas, swelling the Trinity River to flood stage. The month closed with tornadoes touching down in rural Dallas County.[1]

A number of banks were robbed in May. In addition to those in Lucerne, Indiana and Okabena, Minnesota, already mentioned, banks in St. John, Missouri; Prague, Oklahoma; and several other cities were also looted. In Lucerne it was reported that two women, "one of them a blonde armed with an automatic rifle," fired several volleys from a moving car as they and their cohorts escaped. "This'll learn ya!" one of the women reportedly yelled from the speeding car.[2]

Apart from Nazi book burnings in Germany, the Japanese army's push toward the Chinese capital, and the opening of the Chicago World's Fair, the rest of the month's news was economic. On May 12, while the Barrow gang was shooting up Lucerne, Indiana, President Roosevelt signed the Farm Currency Act, extending immediate relief to the agricultural industry. Roosevelt also urged mortgagers to suspend farm foreclosures. Nevertheless, on the same day 900,000 independent farmers joined in a general strike, which had originated in St. Paul, Minnesota. On the fifteenth, dairy farmers blocked roads in Wisconsin and Illinois to stop milk shipments until wholesale prices rose. Two days later Roosevelt submitted a $3.3 billion employment plan to Congress.[3]

J. P. MORGAN.

The last week in May saw J. Pierpont Morgan, described as "the world's most powerful banker," appearing before the U.S. Senate Banking Committee to explain, among other things, why he had paid no income tax in 1931 and 1932. Reportedly "sweating profusely," Morgan also had to answer questions regarding an alleged list of "preferred customers" to whom he would sell securities at below market value. Among the names on the list: World War I hero General John J. "Black Jack" Pershing and former President Calvin Coolidge. Two days later, it was revealed that partners in Morgan's firm had issued themselves loans from company assets. Such revelations only served to galvanize public opinion against the banking industry and big business in general.[4]

On the next-to-last day of May, Barrow cohort Raymond Hamilton was in the Hill County (Texas) jail facing his second trial for the April 30, 1932, murder of Hillsboro store owner John N. Bucher. The night before, Mark Kitchen, a key witness against Hamilton, was abducted by two men who beat him, tied him up with barbed wire, and threatened to kill him if he testified.[5]

IN DALLAS, WHEN WE SAW Mrs. Barrow, we learned that W. D. had not been there and that nothing had been printed in the papers about him.[6] Clyde left word for W. D., saying that he would be back for him soon. Then we started driving day and night again. We traveled so fast and through so many towns and states that I lost all track of time. I often didn't even know what day it was. We lived in the car day and night with very little sleep, just driving like mad, going no place. We had to keep ahead of the cops. If we stayed in one place very long they would catch up with us, although we did stay at a lake near Warsaw, Indiana, for a few days.

When we needed money, which was often, some filling station, grocery store, or drug store was robbed. Then we'd drive three or four hundred miles before stopping to rest for a few hours. Once Buck and Clyde robbed a small-town bank.[7] They left Bonnie and me about eight or ten miles outside of town, in the country. We were to drive into town in the morning and pick them up at a certain time.[8] They stayed in the bank almost all night, waiting for it to open in the morning. They had hidden on top of the vault. When the banker came in to open the vault, he saw them. Before they could rob him, he jumped into the vault, grabbed a gun, and came out shooting. I don't think anyone was shot. We never read anything about it in the papers.[9]

By then, we'd driven in to pick them up. I don't even know what town it was, but as we rode through the outskirts an old man tried to stop the car. Clyde told Buck to shoot the man. Buck said he could not shoot an old man, or anyone else unless they were shooting at him and that it was his only way out.[10]

The old man threw a large chunk of wood in front of the car. Clyde almost hit it. If he had, it would have been too bad for all of us.[11] Clyde laid one of the rifles across Bonnie's lap, with the barrel sticking out the window. He told Bonnie to hold it up and shoot. She did. We heard later that a woman was wounded in the arm.[12] I was so scared that Buck made me lie down on the floor between the seats. I couldn't see out. That made me more afraid. In the end, they got no money and had to rob some other place before the day was gone.[13]

A few days later, Buck stole a Ford V-8 coupe so we could have our own car. He and Clyde were always arguing. They just couldn't agree on anything. Clyde wanted to go back to Dallas and get W. D. Buck told him to leave the kid alone, that he was too young. Buck said he was sure that W. D. had wanted to get way from it all or he wouldn't have kept on going after stealing the car in Ruston.

We mailed a letter to Mrs. Barrow and told her to write to us in Terre Haute, Indiana. We got a cabin there and stayed a few days until we heard from her. She told us she had heard that W. D. was home, but he had not come to see her.

We had already driven through ten or fifteen states. Now we started driving again. It was the same thing over and over. One time I was left in the coupe several miles outside of a small town while they went into town to rob a grocery store. I refused to take any part in any of the robberies. They could razz me about being afraid as much as they wanted to. I didn't care. I refused to have anything to do with killing and robbing anyone. And besides, I was afraid Buck would be killed.

The three of them went to rob the grocery store. Buck told me what to do if he should be shot and killed, or caught. But if something ever happened to him, I would not have left him to go home until I was able to see him and do all I could for him. I was always afraid Clyde would just run away and leave him if there was trouble.

Part of the time I spent driving back and forth along the road where they had left me. But mostly I just sat in the parked car and cried while they were gone. The minutes seemed like hours. I prayed Buck would be sent back to me alive and unharmed. But my prayers were not always answered.

Then I saw Clyde's car coming over a small hill. He was driving like mad and did not slow up when he got near. I knew something had gone wrong. I already had the motor running. When they passed they waved to me to follow. I did. As they passed, I saw two or three bullet holes in the back window. I immediately thought Buck had been shot because he was in the back. I was so excited for those few seconds that I am surprised I did not wreck the car. At one point, I slowed down a little but Clyde started getting way ahead of me. I stepped on the gas. The speedometer climbed to seventy-five, then eighty, and ninety. It topped out at ninety-five. I couldn't make it go faster, but I knew I had to keep up with them. The only time I took my foot off the gas was when I had to turn a corner. Clyde kept turning down side roads. I almost turned the car over a couple of times, but managed somehow to straighten out and keep up with them.[14] Finally, Clyde thought it was safe enough to stop just long enough for Buck to get in my car. He took the wheel and was I glad!

I saw blood on his hands and face and on his shoes. I almost went into hysterics and began asking what had happened and if he was hurt badly. He said he was okay. He had only been nicked in the little finger. His ring had saved the finger from being shot off. There was a dent in the ring from the buckshot. The blood on his face had come from his hand.

I asked him about his legs. He said he thought he had some buckshot in his hips and legs, but that they were not deep. He thought I could cut them out as soon as we stopped. I was relieved to know he wasn't hurt badly. Buck told me Clyde had been shot too.

We stopped when we found a place to leave the sedan with the bullet holes. We put everything in the coupe and all crowded in. I knew we could not ride like this for long. They began talking and laughing about what had happened. They told me the whole story.

They had robbed a place and taken a hostage, walking the man out to the street.[15] They told him to keep walking but the man ran into another store, got a shotgun, and started shooting at them. Bonnie was in the sedan,

The First State Bank of Okabena, Minnesota, 1933. "[T]he glass was all shot out of the coupe, but no one was hurt." (Courtesy of the First State Bank, Okabena, Minnesota)

behind the wheel.[16] Clyde jumped on the front fender and told her to start driving. She did, but almost left Buck. He caught the back fender and somehow jumped on the moving car. Clyde and Buck were shooting with their pistols but didn't hit anyone.

Clyde was lying across the hood. Bonnie said she could hardly see the road because of him climbing around on the car like a monkey. Bonnie kept laughing at Clyde because he looked so funny on the hood of the car. The man with shotgun was shooting at him. Most of the buckshot hit him in the hips. One hit his left arm but had only gone under the skin. They were well on their way before either of the boys got in the car.

We soon stopped to cut the buckshot out of Clyde and Buck and to treat their wounds. I didn't like that job because I was so afraid I may cut too deep. The small surgical knife we had was very sharp. One false move would have done more harm than if we had left the shot in. I cut nearly all of the slugs out of Buck's hips and legs. Two were so deep in the muscles of his leg that I could not get to them. Buck said they would eventually work their way out, to just leave them. He said they didn't hurt much anyway.

Rear of the old First State Bank building, Okabena, Minnesota, 2003. A gunfight erupted at the back door (lower left) on May 19, 1933, when the Barrow brothers robbed the bank. (Photograph by Esther L. Weiser)

Clyde wouldn't let Bonnie or Buck take the buckshot out of him. He said they could just stay in. And they did!

It only took a few minutes to treat the wounds. Soon we were on our way again, driving through state after state. It was always the same thing over and over. Eventually they stole another car. They were going to use it to rob something then leave it, but we traveled in the second car for a few weeks. At least we weren't so cramped anymore.

Then Clyde and Buck spotted another small-town bank and decided to try their luck again at bank robbery. Bonnie and I were left in the country with the new car. Clyde and Buck took the coupe into town. They stayed in the bank from about one o'clock in the morning until the employees arrived and it was time for the vault to open.[17]

While we were waiting for them, it began raining. Soon a hailstorm developed. The wind blew, lightning flashed, and the thunder was so loud you couldn't hear anything else. Several times the car felt as though it would be blown over. Bonnie was so frightened she hardly knew what to do. She covered her head with pillows so she couldn't see the lightning and started crying, saying she wanted to be home with her mother.[18]

I wasn't afraid of storms at that time and laughed at her fears, as they had laughed at me for being afraid of machine gun fire. Of course, it wasn't that I was afraid for myself; it was that I feared Buck would be killed. I couldn't understand why Bonnie would be so afraid of storms. She didn't act that bad when she was in a gun battle, but she feared God's work more than machine-gun fire.[19]

The storm lasted about three hours as best as I can remember. The next morning the sun was shining bright. We waited and waited for what seemed like a hundred years, like the way someone would feel waiting to be hung.[20] I had to wash my face and eyes many times to keep awake. We had tried to let each other sleep a few minutes at a time after the storm had stopped, but we couldn't sleep much. We were so worried about Clyde and Buck.

When Clyde and Buck finally arrived, the glass was all shot out of the coupe, but no one was hurt.[21] They left the coupe behind and got in the new car with us. We drove to another small town and stopped to eat breakfast. Afterward we filled the car with gas and oil. I sat on the floor most of the time. I was afraid of Clyde's fast driving, especially when we had to make a lot of turns, so I stayed on the floor, where Buck first made me sit, so I couldn't see.

They got about $100 from the bank, the most money they had made from one robbery since we had been with them. Clyde didn't like robbing banks. He thought it was too risky.[22] Instead, he liked robbing three or four filling stations, even if it meant having a bigger battle than he would have had at a bank. Buck told Clyde he would rather try and get enough money to live on for a couple of months, instead of having to rob something every day or two. But Clyde couldn't see it that way.

We started for home, Dallas, to see Mrs. Barrow. And Clyde still wanted to get W. D. back with him. The country roads we drove on were very dusty. The car was soon filled with dust. We were so dusty you could hardly tell who we were. That afternoon they decided to stop and clean up. They found a small creek far enough from any town to be safe for a couple hours. We cleaned the car, took baths, and put on what few clean clothes we had. Then we drove to a nearby town to buy food and more clothes.

The next day they were going to get another car, or maybe two. Clyde spotted a Ford V-8 roadster; he wanted it. Buck told him they should try to get a sedan so we could all be in the same car in Dallas. But Clyde said he had been looking for a roadster like that for a long time and it was too good-looking to leave. So he took it and we followed. That afternoon we changed everything to the roadster. Buck drove the sedan into the woods, some distance from the highway, and set fire to it.[23] They thought they had gotten everything out of it, but later found out they had either lost twenty-five or fifty dollars in silver, or had left it in the car.[24]

Buck hadn't found a car for us yet, so we all had to ride in the roadster. We had not been riding more than a couple hours before Buck and Clyde got into an argument about it being so crowded in the car. Buck was driving to give Clyde a chance to rest. He also wanted to drive to relieve himself from the cramped conditions. We were having to sit in each others' laps, but Buck could hardly stand it because his legs were shot up so badly. Then Bonnie started getting tired of sitting in Clyde's lap, and he was getting tired of holding her. Buck started complaining about all of us having to ride that way. Soon the argument came to blows. I was sitting between them and got hit more than they did. I was also trying to get them to stop fighting but there wasn't anything I could do.

Buck stopped the car and told Clyde to get out, that he would show him what he could do. But Clyde wouldn't fight fair. He grabbed his shotgun, the one he had killed most of his victims with. He had done that before, during an argument, so I knew he wouldn't fight fair. Otherwise, I wouldn't have tried to stop them from fighting because I thought Buck could have whipped him in a fair fight. But Buck would have never grabbed his gun. He didn't want to kill Clyde. But Clyde would shoot him if he got mad enough, and he usually got that mad. But he didn't shoot Buck that day, even though he said he was going to.[25]

If Clyde had shot Buck, he would have had to kill me too. Of course, I think that would have been a pleasure to him.[26] Anyway, it looked as though Buck and Clyde could no longer get along. And sooner or later, Clyde would kill Buck, because Clyde wouldn't fight without a gun.

When the argument was over, I asked Buck if we couldn't ride in the rumble seat. He said it would be almost as bad, but I asked him to try. It was much better than all four of us riding in one seat.

⊛7

Mother's Day

THEY WANTED ME TO go Dallas alone on Mother's Day. Originally, they had meant for all of us to drive in, but if we did that they couldn't go by and see Bonnie's mother. Bonnie and Clyde had a fight about that. She was going to shoot him, but Buck grabbed the gun out of her hand, threw it back in the car, and told her she was crazy. He always tried to separate them when they fought, especially if one of them got too rough with the other. And likewise, if Buck and I got into a fight, Clyde would butt in. But Buck and I never thought of guns when we got into an argument. If one of us had shot the other, the survivor would have committed suicide. Clyde and Bonnie would have probably done the same thing. They loved one another too much to live without each other.

So after the fight it was decided only one of us would go in to Dallas. Neither Clyde nor Buck could go and Clyde was afraid for Bonnie to go. So Buck said I could go. He knew I wouldn't be afraid. He would worry about me and hated to see me go without protection, but he knew I would be careful and not be afraid. I dressed and got ready to make the trip.

They drove me to Muskogee, Oklahoma. I could take a bus from there. They would get a cabin in Fort Smith, Arkansas, and rest up. I asked Buck not to get drunk while I was gone. He promised he wouldn't. He said they would get a good night's sleep and then drive to the spot where they were supposed to meet me, Mrs. Barrow, Mrs. Parker, and W. D. (if I could find him and he wanted to come back to Clyde). We were to meet them in northeast Texas between Commerce and Cooper at two o'clock the next day.[1] I was told to pay someone fifty dollars to drive all of us out to meet them.

They drove me to Muskogee, gave me about four hundred dollars, and told me again what to do if I should be unlucky enough to get thrown in jail. They said they would come and get me or see that I was soon released. Buck kissed me goodbye, told me to be careful, and to be sure to be at the meeting place on time. If I was more than two hours late they would know I was in jail or that something else had gone wrong. They would drive in to see Mrs. Barrow and find out what had happened. I told them I would be on time if nothing happened to me. I told them to be on time as well because I would be worried about them anyway, although I wouldn't worry so much if I knew they were not going to start drinking and get drunk. I feared what might to happen to them if they did.

They left me. I waited until they were out of sight, then called a taxi from a nearby store. At the bus station I learned that a bus had just left for Dallas. I would have to wait until about nine o'clock that night for the next one. I had the whole afternoon to myself and didn't know what to do.

I went to a show and stayed until 8:30. When I came out, I called a taxi, went back to the bus station, and waited. No one seemed to notice me. I guess I wasn't much different from anyone else. I wasn't worried about myself, but I did worry a lot about Buck. So many things could happen while I was away from him. But I believed they would do as they promised, get some sleep and get cleaned up. They really needed baths and clean clothes. And Buck and Clyde each needed a shave and a haircut.

I was glad when I got on the bus. I knew I could finally get a little sleep. In fact, I hadn't been on board long before I fell asleep. The bus driver had to wake me up when we changed buses at some town. I was so sleepy; I don't even remember where it was. I didn't even care. I could hardly wake up.

The layover there was only about ten or fifteen minutes. I went into the station cafe, ate a piece of coconut pie, and drank a glass of milk. Then I stepped into the restroom, washed my face, and put on fresh makeup. That woke me up.

When I got on the second bus, the driver from the first one came to see about me. He said he just wanted to be sure I did not miss my bus. He laughingly told the other driver to take care of me and see that I was awake when we arrived in Dallas.[2] He said I had been sleeping like a baby and that I still looked sleepy. If they had known how much sleep I had lost and how tired I really was, they would have understood why I was such a sleepyhead.

Elvin "Jack" Barrow. "I walked to Elvin's house and woke him up." (Courtesy of Buddy Williams Barrow)

The bus wasn't very crowded. I got in the back so I could lay down and have a good sleep. The night was cool. While I was asleep someone covered me with a coat. Everyone was being very kind and thoughtful to me, trying to take care of me as though I were a child. I wasn't much larger than a child. I only weighed about eighty-five pounds then, down from one hundred and eighteen just since the first of April (before we got into trouble).[3] I made the best of that trip by sleeping as much as I could.

The bus pulled into Dallas about 5:30 Monday morning. I called a taxi and had the driver drop me about three blocks from Elvin Barrow's home.[4] Then I walked to Elvin's house and woke him up. He and his family were so surprised to see me. They thought all the rest had been killed or captured, but I told them they were all right when I left them. Then I explained why I had come. They were afraid for me to stay there, but I couldn't go any place else. I called Mrs. Barrow and told her to come to Elvin's at once. She said she would as soon as she could.

We ate breakfast. I was still sleepy. I had not realized how tired I was before I got on the bus. So, I lay down on the bed to wait for Mrs. Barrow. I was asleep when she arrived, but I soon woke up. I told her to get in touch

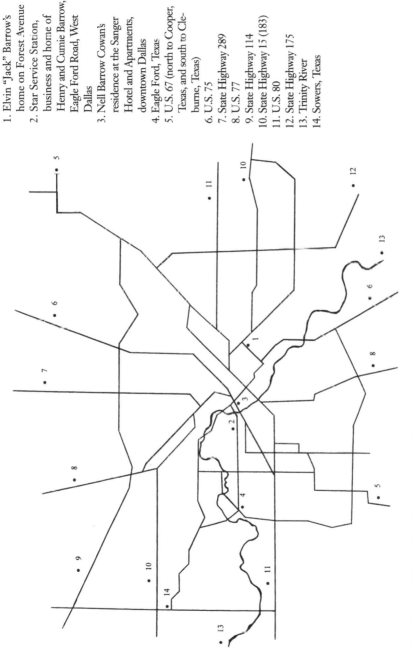

1. Elvin "Jack" Barrow's home on Forest Avenue
2. Star Service Station, business and home of Henry and Cumie Barrow, Eagle Ford Road, West Dallas
3. Nell Barrow Cowan's residence at the Sanger Hotel and Apartments, downtown Dallas
4. Eagle Ford, Texas
5. U.S. 67 (north to Cooper, Texas, and south to Cleburne, Texas)
6. U.S. 75
7. State Highway 289
8. U.S. 77
9. State Highway 114
10. State Highway 15 (183)
11. U.S. 80
12. State Highway 175
13. Trinity River
14. Sowers, Texas

Dallas, Texas, 1933; scale: 1 in = 5 mi. Based on a contemporary map in the editor's possession.

with Mrs. Parker, Bonnie's mother, and tell her to get ready to go with us to meet Clyde and Bonnie.[5] I told her everything that had happened to us since we last saw her and how we happened to get into trouble.

I told her Buck and I were both innocent of any murders. But I admitted that Buck had helped Clyde rob several places since we left Joplin. She cried so much and said she could hardly believe life could be so unkind as to throw two innocent people into the shadow of death. I tried to get her to go to Joplin and get our car and all the clothes we left there, but she was afraid it would make it harder for us. I told her we couldn't be hurt more, except to be shot and killed.

I asked her about W. D. She said she had seen him, but she did not know if he wanted to go with Clyde or not. I told her to find him if she could and have him meet me if he wanted to go back with Clyde. But I didn't blame him if he wanted to pull out of it while he still could. I just wished Buck and I could get out of it, but they knew we were with Bonnie and Clyde and would keep looking for us. We had to keep going until we were shot down.

Mrs. Barrow left to contact Mrs. Parker and see if she could find W. D. I asked Elvin if he would take us to meet Clyde and Buck in his car. Buck told me he thought he would, but Elvin said he couldn't afford to do that. He said he would love to see his brothers but he could not take the chance. He had his family to think of. Also, all the officers knew his car and may follow him, so that was out. We would have to look elsewhere for a car.

I called Nell Cowan,[6] Buck's younger sister. She came to see me and brought Buck's older sister [Artie] with her. Nell had a car. I asked her if she would drive us out to meet her brothers but she said no, she was too busy. She had to work. She wouldn't even loan her car.

I asked Nell to go to town and buy me some boots. I had a riding suit, but no boots. I couldn't find any that I liked in any of the small towns we passed through. But she wouldn't even do that! So, I got someone else to get them. I don't care to mention this person's name.

Mrs. Barrow returned with LC Barrow, Buck's youngest brother.She got hold of Mrs. Parker and she agreed to meet us.[7] But they couldn't find W. D.

I still had no car, though. It looked as if I would have to rent one but I wasn't sure how successful I would be. But I would try anyway. Then Elvin told me he knew where I could buy one for seventy-five or a hundred dollars. It wouldn't be much of a car, but we could make the trip in it. It turned out to be a Model A Ford roadster. LC said he needed a car and begged

Nell Cowan, Clyde Barrow, and Artie Winkler in Denison, Texas, 1933. "Nell Cowan, Buck's younger sister, . . . came to see me and brought Buck's older sister [Artie] with her." (Courtesy of Buddy Williams Barrow)

me to buy it. He said he would drive us out to meet Clyde and Buck. He wanted to see them so badly. That seemed the only way out, so I bought the car.

I wanted to get started or else we were going to be late. LC, Mrs. Barrow, and I left Elvin's home, met Mrs. Parker on some street corner (I don't remember where), and the four of us left Dallas. Nell wouldn't go at all.[8]

We weren't able to make it to the meeting place by two o'clock. When we finally arrived, Bonnie, Clyde, and Buck weren't there. We were afraid we'd missed them. I told LC to drive on to Cooper. Just before we got to town, though, I saw a car speeding toward us. It looked like Clyde's car. I suddenly realized they didn't know what kind of car we would have. So we stopped and I stepped out so they would see who it was. They stopped. Buck opened the door on his side of the car. He and Clyde and Bonnie were all smiles. I was never so glad to see anyone. That one day and night away from Buck seemed like months.

They told us to follow them. Clyde drove off on a country road.[9] It was muddy. When they came to a bridge across a small creek, they stopped. Everyone got out. It was like a family reunion. We were so happy to see each other. I was certainly happy to be with Buck again.

I looked them over. They didn't look like they had slept at all. Buck and Clyde still needed a shave and they had mud on their clothes. I asked Buck if he had a good night's sleep. He said no, he hadn't slept any. All three of them were drinking and they looked as though they had been on a drunk the night before.

I asked Buck what had happened. He told me they bought some whiskey before leaving Muskogee. Then Clyde decided to get in touch with Pretty Boy Floyd again.[10] He thought he might find him by visiting Pretty Boy's mother. So, they drove to Sallisaw, Oklahoma. By the time they got there, Clyde and Bonnie were crazy drunk. They stopped at a filling station to inquire how to get to the Floyd place. At first, the man at the station wouldn't tell him. Then Clyde took his hat off and asked the man if he recognized him.

The man took a good look at Clyde and said, "You aren't . . . "

"Yes," Clyde said. "I am Clyde Barrow and I want to find Pretty Boy Floyd. I promised to meet him at his mother's."

About that time, a car drove by slowly. Clyde thought it looked like a copper of some kind and asked the man at the filling station if he knew who was in the car. The man said it was the sheriff. Clyde went back to his car. They decided to come back later. Buck drove because Clyde was starting to feel sick. They didn't even get out of sight of the station before Clyde was so sick he had to get out of the car. Bonnie was nearly out cold. But Buck was sober. Bonnie and Clyde told me Buck would only take a couple of drinks because he had promised me he wouldn't get drunk. I guess it was a good thing he stayed sober, because when Clyde got out of the car and

A 1934 family reunion, including five of those present for the May 15, 1933, post–Mother's Day visit. Standing, left to right: Billie Parker Mace, Clyde Barrow, Cumie Barrow, LC Barrow. Crouching, left to right: Marie Barrow, Emma Parker, and Bonnie Parker. "[Clyde] and Buck had a nice visit with their mother . . . Bonnie also had a good visit with her mother." (Courtesy of Buddy Williams Barrow)

walked around to the back, he just passed out and fell into a ditch half-filled with mud-red water.

Buck had just fished Clyde out of the water and put him on the ground beside the car, when the sheriff drove by slowly. Buck said all he could do was just stand beside the car with his rifle in his hands, ready to shoot it out with him if he stopped and got tough. He would have hated to kill the sheriff because so far he had not had to kill anyone. He hoped the sheriff wouldn't stop. He didn't.

By then, Bonnie had gotten out of the car too. She and Clyde were both helpless. Buck finally got both of them in the car and drove them around until they felt better. Clyde and Bonnie thought the whiskey had been poisoned. They found a place to clean up a little bit, but Buck and Clyde missed the mud on their trousers. When Buck told Clyde what a close call they had, Clyde cursed himself for being such a fool. By then, it was early morning. And that's what happened to the good night's sleep they were going to get while I was on my way to Dallas.[11]

Clyde was very disappointed because W. D. did not come with us. But he and Buck had a nice visit with their mother anyway. Bonnie also had a good visit with her mother.[12] They talked about everything that had happened since they had last seen each other. But it was hard to keep the mothers from crying.

I got dressed in my riding habit and new boots. All I needed was a horse. I liked to wear them because dresses were harder to keep fit than boots and trousers.[13] When I put the boots on, I had trouble walking. It had been a so long since I'd worn any. They felt heavy. Clyde and Buck told me it would be hard to outrun any bullets with them on. And running was about the only thing I could do well. At least it was the one thing I would not refuse to do. They often laughed about me trying to outrun bullets. I told them I didn't think running from bullets was half as funny as being afraid of storms.

We laughed about a lot of things that we should have taken more seriously. But no matter how serious or dangerous the situation was, we always found something to laugh about later on. It always seemed better to laugh than to cry. We had to laugh to keep from crying.

The evening seemed to fly. LC and I had a footrace to see if I really could run with boots on. When we finished everyone laughed because I was almost out of breath.

I wished I could have visited my mother but I did not want to risk the chance of her getting killed, or accused of doing something wrong. Even though I was innocent, I had been accused of breaking the law and was a hunted woman. But I couldn't leave the man I loved so much. I wanted mother to remember me as she had last seen me, a happy girl of twenty-two. Although I was only a few months older than that now, life had changed so fast and so much, it seemed like years since I had been really free.

Buck and Clyde gave their mother a few hundred dollars. Bonnie gave her mother one hundred and twelve dollars. I gave Mrs. Barrow thirty dollars to give to my mother. It was from the money I'd been given for the trip to Dallas. We said our goodbyes and left for Florida. If I remember right, that was our only Texas visit during the month of May.[14]

8

Florida

ON OUR WAY TO Florida, we stopped more often, didn't miss so many meals, and slept more at night in beds.

That night, the Monday after Mothers Day, we drove to Shreveport, Louisiana, and got a cabin. We went to bed and didn't wake up until ten o'clock the next morning. After we had taken baths and put on clean clothes, we felt like new people. But later, after we left the camp, Clyde and Buck had an argument about staying in the tourist camp until after twelve o'clock. Buck tried to make Clyde understand we should leave earlier, but Clyde of course always knew more than anyone else. He left one of his pistols in the cabin and was mad about it. He was afraid to go back for it because the owner had acted suspicious before we left.

When we got to Minden, Louisiana, Buck began looking for a car to steal so we could leave Bonnie and Clyde. But he couldn't find one that wouldn't bring a lot of heat down on us as soon as he tried to get it. So we stayed with them.

The next day, Buck found a car in Mississippi. But we didn't leave Bonnie and Clyde. After Buck got the car and moved our things into it, we stayed with Bonnie and Clyde the rest of the day on the banks of some river. We stayed hidden from the highway with the hot car.

Clyde and Bonnie drove to a farmhouse and had them cook chicken for us. Then they got bread from a country store about eight or ten miles from where we stopped. We had a regular picnic and got our fill of fried chicken. Buck and Clyde had cooled down and so all of us stayed together.

Buck and Clyde wanted to camp there beside the river but the mosquitoes and flies were so bad that we couldn't sleep that afternoon or night. We left there and drove until about twelve or one o'clock, got a cabin, and slept.[1] In a few days we were in Florida.

We stopped at a small roadhouse before we got to Tallahassee, ate dinner, and drank some beer and wine. We stayed there a couple of hours. Soon after we left there, we pulled off the highway a few yards and parked. We then cleaned the cars out, straightened the luggage, and shifted the guns. We also covered the guns so they couldn't be seen by anyone who might look into the car when we stopped for gas.

As we were backing out to the highway, over a high embankment, Buck didn't stop fast enough and drove off the other side of the road. The car turned over once and came to rest partially on its side and partially on the roof. Buck's left hand and was caught between the top of the car and the gravel, pinning him. Luggage and guns had piled on both of us.

I wasn't hurt but I had a hard time getting everything off of me so I could get out. I had to climb through one of the windows because the door was jammed. I finally got out and tried to lift the car so Buck could get his hand and arm loose.

Clyde had already pulled onto the highway and driven off. But it wasn't long before he noticed we were not following and came back to see what had happened. I was working as hard as I could, trying to rock the car up enough to get Buck loose, but I couldn't do much good. When Clyde arrived he got out and tried to help, but even with the two of us, the car still wouldn't move. Guns were laying around everywhere. Anyone passing could have easily seen them. Two or three .45 caliber automatic pistols were laying in one of the windows as if they had been framed. But I couldn't think about getting them out of sight until Buck was freed.

Soon a car stopped with three or four soldiers in it. They got out to help us and asked if anyone was hurt. They arrived before we were able to free Buck. With the soldiers' help, the car was finally lifted up so Buck could move his hand. Then suddenly the soldiers seemed to be in a big hurry to leave. We were sure they had noticed the army rifles and pistols and would soon return with the law. We thought a battle would start at any minute.

Two other fellows stayed behind and tried to help us get the car back on the highway. One of them rubbed Buck's hand and arm with whiskey and gave him a drink of it. Clyde drove off to find a cable so we could pull our car back onto the highway. He wanted Buck to leave the car where it was and for us to get in his car and get away before the wreck was reported. But Buck told him he didn't want to leave it there. He thought leaving it would get us hot in that part of the country and we wanted to stay as cool down there as we could. Buck and I both liked Florida a lot. We had visited there once before, prior to Buck's return to prison.[2] We were thinking about staying there for a while once we got to Jacksonville. But we couldn't do that if we got hot.

Buck was sure we could somehow get the car back on the highway. But Clyde was mad because Buck was getting friendly with the two fellows who stayed behind to help. They seemed to be pretty good sports and Buck didn't think they would get too nosey or call the law.

Buck had me get in the car, start the motor, and try to get the car moving while everybody else pushed. One of the men helping us was beside the car, where he could look in and see the guns. He told me to cover them up with something just in case someone else stopped to ask questions about the wreck, so they wouldn't see the guns. I had thought they were covered but somehow the covering had slipped off.

When we finally got the car back on the highway we found that it still ran fairly good; and the dents in the fender and top weren't so noticeable, although it was a new car and those places didn't look too good. Otherwise, it was okay and we could still travel in it. But Buck could hardly drive because his hand had been pinched so badly. Consequently, I drove quite a lot. Buck only drove when we stopped in, or passed through, large towns. And even though we felt safe enough to stop and sleep at tourist camps whenever we wished, we still did a lot of driving at night.

We continued on to Jacksonville, but did not stay there as we had planned. Instead, we turned north and drove along the Atlantic coast. We stopped at a small town, Cumberland, Georgia, I believe,[3] and went in bathing and playing around up and down the beach. Then we tried to rent a furnished house for the summer, but Clyde and Buck couldn't agree on which place to take and got into another argument. After that, Buck got drunk. He didn't want to leave, so he and Clyde split up. Shortly after that, Clyde and Bonnie left town.

I was glad we were going to be alone, but my hopes were soon shattered. Buck kept drinking and talking so loud that people would stop and stare at us. I begged him to be quiet and told him we would have every cop in town after us. Before I knew it, we were arguing. He wanted to stop right on the street and fight. I was almost mad enough to fight too, but I tried to reason

"We . . . went in bathing and playing around up and down the beach. . . . Buck and I both liked Florida a lot." (Photograph by Buck Barrow, courtesy of Rhea Leen Linder)

with him instead. Finally I told him to drive to the country and let me out, that I was through if he couldn't do any better than that. I didn't want to stay with him any longer.

At first he said, "Okay. If you want to leave, then go ahead and get out now." But when I started to go he changed his mind and told me to get back in the car. I refused. With that, he started talking so loud that I had to get in with him. I wouldn't have left anyway, but I was still mad.

Suddenly Clyde and Bonnie drove up. I don't know why but they had come back to look for us, saying they had looked the town over for us. Clyde told Buck he had seen some motorcycle cops riding in town and they seemed to be checking all cars on the road. Since there was only one road leading in or out of town, he thought it best to get away while we still could. If they ever blocked the road, we would have to jump into the ocean or die fighting.

When we were out of town Buck began begging me not to leave. I was still mad and insisted I would leave him. I told him to just stop any place

Buck and Blanche in Tennessee. "We drove through South Carolina, North Carolina, Tennessee. . . ." (Photograph by Clyde Jones, courtesy of Rhea Leen Linder)

he felt like. He wanted to know how I would get home. I told him not to worry, that I could take care of myself. I said I didn't need anyone to take care of me like I was a two-year-old baby.

"But, honey, you can't go home," he said. "The cops will get you."

Blanche Barrow in Mobile, Alabama. "... then south to Alabama." (Photograph by Buck Barrow. Courtesy of Rhea Leen Linder)

"I don't care if they do," I said, even though I knew I was lying. I did care. I never wanted them to get me. The thought of going to prison seemed just as bad as being killed. I really feared prison, even though I had never been inside of one except to visit Buck or Clyde. Still I had a horror of ever going to prison.

Buck kept pleading with me not to leave. Then he said he would not let me go, that he couldn't live without me. "What would I have to live for?" he asked. He was sobering up a bit and becoming reasonable. I didn't get out. Soon our argument ended as it usually did, with each of us crying and saying how sorry we were for hurting the other.

That night we rented a nice double cabin north of Brunswick, Georgia.[4] We decided to stay there a few days if everything seemed okay. Bonnie and Clyde drove to another place on the beach to look around after we had eaten and taken our baths. Buck and I didn't want to go. Buck wanted to work on some of his guns, so we just stayed at the cabin.

Bonnie and Clyde were not gone long. Soon after they returned, Clyde went to the station to get something but stopped a few feet away, in the shadow of another little building of some kind. He had noticed two highway patrolmen parked under the station's awning. They were sitting in their car talking to the owner. Clyde caught part of the conversation, but not enough to know if the patrolmen were checking up on us. He felt sure they were, though.

Clyde came back to the cabins and told us what he'd seen. He thought we should leave, but added that he sure hated to leave those good beds without even getting to sleep in them. But he told us to get ready to leave anyway. Then he went to the woman he had rented the cabins from. He told her we had rented an apartment in town and that he wanted his money back. She agreed.

When Clyde got back with money we were ready to leave. The patrolmen were still at the station. We drove out toward Brunswick. Then, as soon as we were out of sight, we turned around and passed by the station. The patrolmen were still there. They pulled out and started chasing us, but we soon lost them.[5]

We drove almost all night. Bonnie and I drove for a couple of hours while Buck and Clyde slept. Then we drove off the road into a forest of pine trees and slept until about ten o'clock. After that, it was the same old story, afraid to stop anyplace. We kept driving, stopping only to sleep in the car. We drove through South Carolina, North Carolina, Tennessee, then south to Alabama,[6] and west through Mississippi, Louisiana, Arkansas, Oklahoma, and Texas. I think we traveled most every highway in each of those states!

Clyde wanted to go back to Dallas and get W. D. but Buck tried to talk him out of getting the kid again. Buck told Clyde that he was going to get killed fooling around with W. D. because if he ever got caught he would tell everything he knew and put Clyde on the spot. Buck said W. D. was too much of a kid to stand up under the punishment of a police grilling. He would talk to clear himself of anything if he had too. He might even talk about everything Clyde had ever done. But Clyde would not listen. He told Buck that he felt better with W. D. than with him.

"If I were you," Clyde said, "I wouldn't say anything about not trusting someone after you thought those two strangers were such good sports and you let them tell you to cover up your guns."

Clyde then wrote to his mother and told her to meet them at some appointed place, and to bring W. D. with her.

✸9

A Visit with My Father

Editor's Note: June 1933

In June Clyde Barrow, Bonnie Parker, and W. D. Jones were involved in a fiery car wreck near the Texas Panhandle town of Wellington. All three were injured but Parker was critically burned. In the aftermath, Barrow and Jones abducted two local law enforcement officers and escaped with Parker to Oklahoma where the captives were released. Later in the month Buck Barrow and W. D. Jones killed an Arkansas marshal following yet another auto accident.[1]

The rest of the month, from Wisconsin to Texas, was hot, both literally and figuratively. Severe weather still ravaged the midcontinent; on the seventh, twenty people were hurt in a Minnesota storm, but record heat was the major concern in June. Between Canada and the Rio Grande many people died of heat-related problems and crops withered away as temperatures rose and a lingering drought worsened.[2]

A variety of other stories also made headlines, including First Lady Eleanor Roosevelt's visit to Dallas, Texas, the death of silent-film star Roscoe "Fatty" Arbuckle; and congressional passage of the Glass-Steagall banking reform bill, which, among other things, guaranteed deposits of up to $2,500. There were a number of illnesses and deaths reportedly caused by bad beer and spirits. However, much of the news of the month was dominated by crime, beginning with the sometimes-Barrow-accomplice Raymond Hamilton.[3]

On June 2, Hamilton's second trial for the murder of Hillsboro, Texas, storeowner John N. Bucher resulted in another guilty verdict and this time a unanimous *opinion about the punishment, ninety-nine years in prison. For Hamilton the sentence meant little. He would receive sentences totaling 266 years before his arrival at the Texas State Penitentiary later in the summer.*[4]

On June 6, in a crime bearing similarities to the one described by Blanche in her memoir, a deputy sheriff and two citizens of Rison, Arkansas, were abducted and held at gunpoint by a gang of thieves who then tried unsuccessfully to burglarize a number of the town's businesses. On the ninth, two Chicago women (the wife and sister of bank robber Jack Gray) were charged with the May 12 attempted robbery and subsequent shooting at Lucerne, Indiana, a crime actually perpetrated by the Barrow gang. Two days later, a former accomplice of Clyde Barrow, Frank Hardy, was arrested and charged with the Christmas 1932 murder of Doyle Johnson in Temple, Texas, something Hardy had nothing to do with. Johnson was really killed by Barrow and W. D. Jones.[5]

A number of Plains states banks were robbed in June, including banks in Bokchito, Oklahoma; Seneca, Missouri; and Prescott, Kansas. On June 14, the Farmers and Merchants Bank of Mexico, Missouri, was robbed of $1,750. An hour later, a deputy sheriff and a Missouri state patrolman were killed in a gun battle at the intersection of Highways 40 and 63, north of Columbia, Missouri.[6]

On June 17, a bloody gun battle erupted in Kansas City's Union Station parking lot. Five people, including two Kansas City detectives, an Oklahoma sheriff, and an agent with the federal Department of Justice Bureau of Criminal Investigation,[7] *along with a prisoner, bank robber Frank Nash, were all killed in a failed attempt to free Nash. This became a pivotal event in depression-era crime. Known today as "the Kansas City massacre" and the "Union Station massacre," it served as an opportune anti-crime catalyst used to great effect as a public relations tool by bureau director J. Edgar Hoover to substantially increase his agency's power.*[8] *A little more than a month later, in the aftermath of the murders and the increased police and bureau of investigation presence they brought to Kansas City, a serious, somewhat childish argument in relation to that would flare between Clyde and Buck Barrow.* (See Chapter 12.)

ON JUNE 6, WE drove through Texas to Oklahoma and slept in the woods there that night. Buck and I had abandoned our sedan, the one we wrecked in Florida, and replaced it with a gray Ford V-8 sedan. We were going to visit my father the following day while Clyde went to meet his mother near Dallas. We planned to rejoin Clyde later that afternoon, near Hugo, Oklahoma.

When we awoke on the morning of the seventh, Clyde and Bonnie went to Dallas, and Buck and I drove to Goodwater, Oklahoma,[9] to see my father.

I was so happy about seeing him once more. It had been almost two years since we last met, since before my marriage to Buck.

When we got to my father's place he was in a field about a half-mile from the house, plowing. We had to wait about an hour for him to come in at noon. As he approached, I ran out to meet him. He couldn't see well enough to know who I was until I was almost touching him. His nephew saw me first (dad was staying with one of his brothers and his family).[10] He told dad I was there but he did not understand what he said because dad is almost deaf and you have to speak very loud to him. When I saw him, I noticed his hair was white as snow. I couldn't keep from crying because I knew I had caused those hairs to turn white. I loved my dad so dearly that I would have rather died than cause him one minute's suffering. It hurt so because I knew I had caused him so much grief. My love for one man, my husband, had caused me to bring grief and sorrow to the other man in my life, the other one I loved dearly—my dad. Oh God! Why did I have to cause him so much sorrow? I had turned his hair to gray and put many more lines in his dear, old kind face. His hair had once been raven black. The last time I saw dad, his hair had been streaked with gray, but now it was all white. Although dad was sixty years of age, he had not begun to show his age until a few years ago. He had been sick most of the time for the past ten years. It wasn't often that he could work. I was sure he had tuberculosis. I had thought so for years.

When he finally recognized me, he said he could hardly believe it was me. He held me in his arms, crying. I thought he would never let me go. He had read about the Joplin case, but could hardly believe anything so terrible could happen to his baby girl. I would always be just a baby to him.

We stayed a couple of hours, had dinner there. I told him as near as I could about what had happened to Buck and me. We were innocent, and yet we could not stop. We had to keep going. We hoped to someday prove our innocence and be free again. But we were just trying to kid ourselves. Deep down inside we knew we would never be free again. Sooner or later we would be killed.

We gave dad some money. He didn't want to take it, but we told him he may need it in case something should happen to me. Then he could use it to come to see me. It was alright for him to stay with his brother as long as I could buy his clothes and send him money for the few things he needed. He had spent the best part of his life working with them, and for them, and he had more than paid for his keep even though he was sick most of

Matt Caldwell, Blanche's father.
(Photograph by Blanche Barrow,
courtesy of Rhea Leen Linder)

the time. I thought he would be welcome to make his home with his brother's family for the rest of his life, in case I don't ever come back to him alive.

My aunt called me to one side and told me to be sure to leave my dad some money because the last clothes I had gotten for him early in the spring, before Buck was released from prison, were just about gone. I told her I had already given him some money and told her I would pay her for our dinner before I left. She said she did not want me to do that. She just asked me to continue sending dad clothes, or money, or both, just as I had been doing for the past five years. I told her not to worry, that I would never forget dad, and that I hoped they would take good care of him when I was dead and couldn't do anymore for him. That was the first and last money I gave dad between the time Buck got out of prison and when I was captured.

We left dad about one-thirty or two o'clock. Buck had to drive fast to make up for the lost time. We did not want to miss meeting Clyde at the appointed time. As we drove through Idabel, Oklahoma, we encountered a detour and somehow got on the wrong highway. After we realized what had happened, we had to backtrack and find the road to Hugo, Oklahoma.[11]

Then about twelve or fourteen miles from Hugo we hit some loose gravel on a sharp curve. Buck did not see the gravel in time to avoid having a wreck. The front of the car was almost ruined beyond repair. We were both shook up and bruised, but not hurt badly.

We both jumped out and removed as much of the baggage and guns as we could and hid them in a small group of bushes beside the road. Then we came back after the rest of the guns. Buck would have to take someone's car. He left me with the guns and baggage and went back to the highway to stop the first car that came by. He waited for a long time but no cars passed.

Some farmer who was working in a field nearby came over to see if anyone had been hurt, or if he could help. Buck asked him if he could drive us to town so we could get a wrecker. The farmer said he didn't have a car but he believed he could get his brother-in-law to drive us. While Buck was talking to the farmer, several cars passed. Buck wanted to get this fellow out of the way so he would not see him take a car. Then Buck asked him to sit there by our car and tell anyone who may stop that he was watching the car while the owner went to get a wrecker.

Buck came over and told me that he thought he would be able to get a car soon. He said for me to stay out of sight until he could get one. By this time, the farmer had talked to his brother-in-law, who was working in the same field. He said he would go get his car. Buck told him he was hauling liquor from Texarkana and didn't want the law to get the news about the wreck if he could help it. Buck said he would pay him fifty dollars to drive us to the nearest town. The brother-in-law returned with a Model T Ford touring car. He pulled up on the other side of the little bunch of bushes, opposite our wrecked car, near the highway in the ditch. We put everything in his car. We had the guns wrapped so no one could tell what they were.

As we rode away, a car filled with officers drove up and stopped at the wrecked car. One of the farmers saw them and told us who they were. But the officers didn't see us. If the farmers had known who we were I am sure we would have been left there with the officers.[12] But they didn't know a thing about us and so we were driven to Hugo. We had them drive us to a tourist camp. We rented a cabin, paid them, and they left us.

We could see the highway from the cabin. We watched it closely to see if Clyde would drive by, looking for us. We were sure he had given up hope of us getting to the spot where we agreed to meet him. Or maybe he thought we had grown tired of waiting for him and left. If we missed each other at Hugo, we were to meet at another small town in the northern part of Oklahoma.

We didn't see Clyde. Buck left the camp to go look for a car. He said he would be back in a few minutes if he got one. If I saw Clyde drive by, I was to stop him. Buck was hoping not to have to take a car in a little town like Hugo. It would be best not to get the country hot all over again. That's why he paid the farmer to drive us away from the wreck, to keep from putting more heat on us, and on Clyde too.

Buck came back in a few minutes. He had walked around a couple or three blocks. He hadn't been back long when I saw a car that looked like Clyde's roadster. Buck left the cabin and headed Clyde off when he turned around and started back through town. They came to the cabin; we got in the car and drove away. We had to ride in the rumble seat again, but we were glad to do so that time.

Clyde said he thought he would see us on the road but had given up hope. Then he turned around and saw Buck. Buck told him what had happened to us. Clyde wanted to know why we didn't take a car instead of paying someone to get us out of the way. Buck told him why, adding that it wasn't because he was afraid to take a car. That evening just before dark, Buck stole a V-8 coupe.

Clyde never met up with his mother and W. D. We later learned the officers were watching her too close for her to meet him. Clyde said he would drive to Dallas in a of couple days and get W. D. He'd go in at night.

✸10

Wellington

On June 9, Clyde wanted to exchange cars with Buck and me. He wanted to drive ours to Dallas. So we moved our things to the roadster. We looked on a map and found a place to meet each other. We decided to meet at a bridge between Sayre and Erick, Oklahoma. Clyde said he and Bonnie and W. D. would be there no later than one the next morning. If we should have to leave there, or if we got any heat on us, we were to place a note under one corner of the bridge and tell them where to meet us. Clyde thought Bonnie and he could make it to the bridge by dark, but asked that we stay until one and wait.

We were just about broke again. We had about seventy-five dollars between us. We divided the money with Clyde and Bonnie, and then they left us.[1]

We drove to the spot we were to wait, then drove away. We did not want someone to see us stopping there for long. They may get curious. The next afternoon we drove to within about five miles of the place and stopped for a couple of hours. Then we drove closer. We wrote Clyde a note and put it under the agreed-to corner of the bridge. In the note, we told him where we would be parked if he should arrive before dark. Dark came, but not Clyde.

We drove past the bridge and parked so we could watch both roads. We waited until midnight. Still Clyde did not come. We began to wonder if something had happened to him. We moved closer to the bridge and parked on a little road beside the creek. We were parked so Clyde could call to us from the bridge if he did not see the car. While waiting, I fell asleep. When I awoke, I heard a car honk. Buck had dozed off too, but he heard the horn first.

At first, we could not see any lights. Then we saw the lights from a car on the bridge flash on and off. Buck flashed his lights. Then we saw Clyde on the bridge, walking toward us and calling to Buck to come help him. They had turned the lights back on and we could see him plainly. He looked as if he had been in water. He was carrying his shotgun. He told us they had been in a wreck and that he thought Bonnie was dying. He also said he had two officers he had to get rid off. That really woke me up good![2]

When Clyde got to the car he told me to find W. D. and him some clothes and then try to fix a place for Bonnie to ride in the car, one that would keep her from suffering so. I asked if I should help bring Bonnie to the car. Clyde said no, he didn't want the officers to see me or our car.[3] I gathered some of Buck's clothes for Clyde and W. D. and found something to put over Bonnie. Then I fixed a place for her on the back seat as best I could. It looked like three of us would have to ride in the rumble seat.

Bonnie, Clyde, and W. D. were all hurt pretty bad. Clyde's nose was broken and his face was all cut up. He was hurt several other places too, but not as bad as his face. He was suffering a lot. W. D.'s face wasn't much better. He also had a large burned place on his leg, but he could still walk and drive. Bonnie was a mass of burns and cuts on her face, right arm, and leg. Her chin was cut to the bone. Her chest was caved in, although no ribs were broken. She was screaming and moaning like she was dying and appeared to be unconscious. All of us thought she would die before daybreak.[4] All three of them should have been in a hospital. They really needed a lot of medical care, but they wouldn't be able to get any. I thought they all might die. Each was injured internally, but Bonnie was in worse shape than the others.

Clyde told Buck he wanted him to help get the officers out of the way. He was undecided as to whether he should kill them or tie them up some place. Then he said they seemed to be pretty good fellows so he would let them live. But if anyone thought it best, then he would kill them. Buck told him he thought it best to tie them up. He said the officers had not been the cause of the wreck, so why hurt them?[5]

Buck and Clyde were gone about ten minutes. Clyde came back first. In a few minutes, Buck returned. W. D. drove the officer's car away and left it two or three miles from the bridge, just as Clyde had told him too do. Buck told me he didn't tie the officers very well. They would be able to get loose before they got hungry, that is, if someone didn't find them first.

The wrecked car in which Bonnie Parker, Clyde Barrow, and W. D. Jones were injured near Wellington, Texas, on June 10, 1933. "He [Clyde] told us they had been in a wreck and that he thought Bonnie was dying." (Courtesy of Ken Holmes, Jr.)

He left them with idea that he was coming back, saying he was going for more wire to tie them better.[6]

It was nearly dawn when we left the bridge. By daybreak, we were not far away. Clyde drove for a while, then Buck took the wheel. Clyde held Bonnie so she could lay down with her head and shoulders in his lap. It made the ride easier for her. She wasn't able to sit up at all. W. D. lay down in the rumble seat with his head in my lap.

When we pulled into a station to get gas at Canadian,[7] Texas, I covered him with a blanket. Clyde tried to cover Bonnie up enough so no one could see she was hurt. He also tried to cover his own face as much as he could with his hand and handkerchief.

We filled up with gas and crossed the bridge over the Canadian River. We thought there might be a roadblock at that bridge, but there wasn't. We were lucky. We were afraid someone had seen us pass through Canadian[8] and called ahead.

We crossed the state line back into Oklahoma. I was sent into a small-town drugstore to buy medicine, tape, and bandages. Then we drove until we found a schoolhouse located well away from the highway. We parked there for most of the day. After doctoring their cuts and burns as best we could, we gave them medicine to stop them from suffering so much, and tried to get them to sleep some. Clyde and W. D. managed to sleep, but Bonnie didn't. She would only doze, then wake up groaning with pain.

From there, we drove to Pratt, Kansas. Buck and I left Clyde and W. D. outside of town, covered Bonnie up, and drove into Pratt to find a tourist camp. When we rented a cabin, the owner asked about the third party. We told him she was my sister and was asleep, that she didn't feel so good. We told him we wanted to stop for a few days until she felt better. The owner seemed to be satisfied. It explained why she was all covered up and lying with her head and shoulder in my lap. After we put Bonnie to bed, Buck went back for Clyde and W. D. When he returned, Buck drove into the garage and closed the door. One of them was closed in the rumble seat and the other was down on the floorboard in front so no one could see either of them. W. D. was the first to recover, although one of the burns on his thigh was pretty bad. Still he didn't suffer so much with it and it soon began to heal.

We were soon broke. Buck and W. D. had to go look for something to rob, so they left.[9] I don't know where they went or what they robbed, but they came back with enough money to do for a couple of days.[10] It was taking plenty to buy medicine daily, but no one cared how much it took as long as Bonnie got well. She suffered so much.

After a few days, Clyde was feeling well enough to travel again. He sent Buck and W. D. to get a larger car.[11] Bonnie didn't feel like riding, but we were afraid to stay there any longer. Clyde said we could go to Fort Smith, Arkansas. He thought it was the best place for us to stay until Bonnie was well, if she got well. So we changed cars and left the roadster. Clyde said he would have loved to have kept it but we couldn't have two cars until we got more money. And besides, he thought he had kept it longer than he should have after making several trips to Dallas in it. So he left the roadster.

⊛11

Fort Smith

WHEN WE GOT TO Fort Smith,[1] Bonnie was worse. She had been calling for her mother and wanted to go home to her, but she knew she couldn't do that. Clyde said he would go get her mother and bring her to Fort Smith to stay with her while she was sick.[2] All of us had tried to make things as easy for her as we could, giving her as much care as possible, but we knew nothing would be as good as having her mother there to care for her. So Clyde got another car and went to Dallas for her mother, but returned instead with her sister Billie Mace.[3] Clyde also got a doctor for Bonnie—twice![4]

While we were in Ft. Smith, I laundered all our clothes. Then Buck and I went to Van Buren to buy food for all of us and medicine for Bonnie. Clyde found a place where he could buy dope for her, to give her some relief from her suffering. Her leg was getting much better but she still wanted Amytal, dope.[5]

One day, just before Clyde came back with Billie, I was sitting in the car in the garage playing the radio when I heard Bonnie and Buck cursing each other.[6] Then I heard Bonnie tell Buck to call me in, that she could whip me. I didn't know what it was all about, but I went in just the same. She jumped off the bed and began cursing me. I never found out why. All I ever learned was that she was just tired of us being with them. I had tried to be so good to her. There wasn't anything else I could do for her that I hadn't already done. I couldn't understand her angry outburst. She wanted to fight, but she was a sick woman. I would take anything she said before I

The cabin occupied by the Barrows at the Twin Cities Tourist Camp. "When we got to Fort Smith, Bonnie was worse." (Phillips Collection)

would ever strike her. I told her if she still felt the same way when she got well then we could fight it out, but not now. It would be like taking advantage of a baby. Then she said she would have Billie do her fighting for her if she should come back with Clyde and her mother. And she would tell Clyde to whip Buck, then they would leave us.[7]

Apparently, Bonnie and Buck were talking about W. D. Buck still thought Clyde should have never gone after him. Then Buck started talking about a certain officer in Texas. Buck knew him as a tough guy, not afraid of anyone. But he also knew him as someone who would play fair with those who played fair with him. Buck said he hoped Clyde would never run into that particular officer, that it would be just too bad for Clyde and anyone with him.

Bonnie got mad and said Clyde wouldn't be afraid of that officer, or of any officer. Clyde wouldn't care how tough and fast they were on the draw. He could beat them to it. Then she said she was glad W. D. was back again, that he had more nerve than both Buck and me together. Then Buck got mad when she had said I was afraid to shoot coppers and that I was just excess baggage and in the way.

If Bonnie had not been sick, Buck would have stopped her. He started to, then came to his senses. He told her that when she was well he would show her whether or not I was afraid of her. He said he would have her settle this and see to it that it was a fair fight. He would make sure there was no gun play.

"She may be afraid to shoot 'coppers,'" Buck said. "But she isn't afraid to fight fair. And just because she don't shoot 'coppers' is no sign she is afraid. She just can't bear the idea of taking a human life. She didn't grow up to be a criminal and a no-good crook like you did! If I had listened to her, we would never have been in this mess. And if Clyde would have listened to her before he left prison, you and him wouldn't be like this. I am proud of her because she don't want to do the things I have to do. And even if she wanted to shoot 'coppers' and rob people, I wouldn't let her. But she hates this kind of life, and so do I. And just because I don't want to do a lot of things isn't because I am afraid to do them. I try to use what few brains I have left. Blanche and I aren't practically crazy like you and Clyde! You should see by now you can't win. You'll get caught some time, or killed. So just lay down and shut up! When you are well, Blanche will settle this."

"Well, call her in here," Bonnie said. "And don't wait until I am well. I am well enough now!"

That's when I came in. W. D. came in about that time too. He got Bonnie back in bed. She told him what Buck had said and that she was going tell Clyde how she had been treated while he was gone.[8] She said she wouldn't have anyone but W. D. to protect her if the cops should come in. She said Clyde knew she would get no protection from us and that's why he left W. D., to take care of her.

"That's why Clyde went after him," she said. "So he would have some help, someone he could depend on when he got in a tight spot."

Buck told her she knew better than that! He said if anything should happen she knew she would be the first one put in the car and that he would fight for her just the same as he would for a sister, because Clyde loved her. Then he said she should be ashamed of her outburst.

Bonnie told us to get out and leave her alone with W. D., that he could take care of her until Clyde came back. When she jumped off the bed earlier, her burns started bleeding and hurting her again. She had to have more Amytal to put her to sleep. She told us to leave them now, because she would see to it that Clyde left us when he came back, so why wait? Buck said we would not leave them until Clyde came back, but we would rent another cabin. They would need another cabin anyway when Clyde came back with her mother, not knowing then that Billie would be arriving instead. Regardless, the situation would be the same. So, Buck rented a single and we moved in. We left the car in their garage, though, so it would be easier to put Bonnie in it if we should have to leave there in a hurry. We saw that Bonnie had every care we could give her, even after the argument.

Bonnie told Clyde everything that happened, and a lot more that she made up. I still kept on cooking their meals at their cabin, even after Billie came. I helped her cook. She didn't say anything about what Bonnie had told her, but I knew she had been told a lot because she acted so indifferent toward me, but not toward Buck.[9] Billie never started anything, so I didn't say anything about it either. I wasn't looking for trouble with her, but I wasn't running from her either. I showed her I was just as indifferent as she was. Soon she became more friendly.

Clyde started trying to get Bonnie to quit taking so much dope. They got into an argument. Clyde told us if she was still taking dope after she was well that Billie could take her back to her mother, where she apparently wanted to go. He would not stay with her now if she kept getting crazier on that stuff.[10] Bonnie wouldn't let him put medicine on the burn to heal it. She wouldn't allow anything on it but Unguentine. But it was keeping the burns too soft for them to heal. Clyde finally got some kind of acid solution that helped.[11]

One day Buck and W. D. had to go someplace and rob something. They went to Fayetteville, Arkansas. When they left they said they would be back before dark. That afternoon, when the time came for them to return, they were nowhere in sight. I couldn't help but worry about Buck whenever he was gone, but when he failed to return on time I began to worry even more. I feared he may be lying someplace in a pool of his own blood, dying. And here I was, helpless to do anything about it.

I sat by the window, watching the cars go by, but I never saw one that Buck was driving. I saw an ambulance go by, its shrill siren blowing. "Oh, God," I thought. "Could it be going after him?"[12] Darkness was slowly coming on. I could no longer see the occupants of the cars. I began to walk the floor of the small cabin. Soon Clyde came in and told me to pack up and put our bags in the roadster that was parked in our garage.

"Don't get excited now," he said. "Buck is alright! He is in our cabin, but they had to kill an officer and leave the car. They walked in and come in

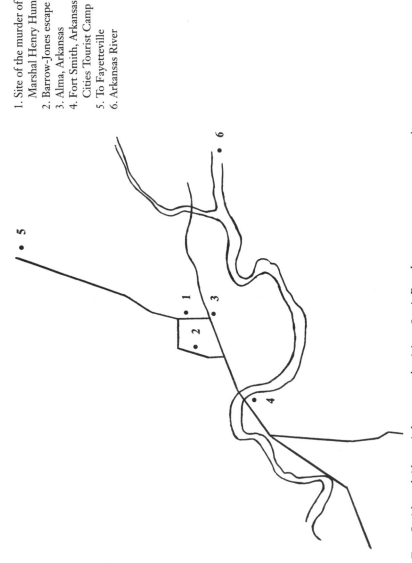

1. Site of the murder of Alma City
   Marshal Henry Humphrey
2. Barrow-Jones escape route
3. Alma, Arkansas
4. Fort Smith, Arkansas, and the Twin
   Cities Tourist Camp
5. To Fayetteville
6. Arkansas River

Fort Smith and Alma, Arkansas; scale: 1 in = 8 mi. Based on a contemporary map in the editor's possession.

the back window.[13] Both of them are alright, except they are shook up a bit. They had a wreck.

"We will have to leave, so put your bags in the car before you come to our cabin. I will drive the car in our garage and load Bonnie and our things in it. Don't act as though you are in any hurry when you are walking to our cabin."

I got everything in the car in a very short time but it was so hard for me to keep from running to Clyde's cabin to see Buck. When I got inside and saw Buck had blood on his face, hand, and arm I rushed to him. Seeing blood on him would almost drive me crazy. I knew he was hurt more than he would say.

My first words were always the same, "Oh, Daddy, are you hurt badly? "No, Baby," was the reply from him.

I was so glad to see him again and feel his arms around me. It was heavenly to be near him and know he was alive. His lower lip was busted and his face was cut in several places. One of his hands was swollen and bleeding. He said he wasn't shot, just cut up from the wreck.

"Oh, honey," Buck said. "I believe I killed a man.[14] I sure do hate it. I hope he doesn't die. I never wanted to have to kill anyone, but I am afraid this man might die if he is not already dead. I don't know if I killed him or if W. D. did it. We were both shooting at him and the other one. So if he dies, I'll be just as much to blame as anyone. I never thought I would have murder on my soul, but now I guess I will have."

He was that way. It hurt him. It was almost as if some of his own people had been shot. He loved life and didn't want to take it away from others.[15]

After getting everything in the small roadster, Clyde, Bonnie, Billie, and I drove away, leaving Buck and W. D. at the cabin.[16] Clyde would go back for them as soon as he got us out of town and hidden someplace in the woods. Buck and W. D. had stashed their rifles near Van Buren and wanted to go back for them. I wanted to stay with Buck, but he sent me on with Clyde and the others.

Clyde took us to some isolated spot southwest of town and left us some distance from the road. We fixed a place for Bonnie to lie down and then we waited. The night was so dark we could hardly see each other, but we didn't dare light a match for fear someone would see it and investigate. If a snake or lizard crawled by us, we would just sit as still as mice until they went on their way. There were mosquitoes and all kinds of other insects in the air. And the only light we had came from the lightning bugs flying around us.

Bonnie was afraid of the dark, as well as bugs and snakes. I wasn't afraid of the darkness or the insects, but I was afraid of snakes. We waited. It seemed like hours passed before Clyde, W. D., and Buck came to get us. Then the six of us rode away in the small car. They had meant to get another car but couldn't find one they could steal.

We hadn't gone far into the mountains before we began having one flat tire after another. Late that night we stopped near Antlers, Oklahoma, and slept until daybreak. Then we drove within fifteen miles of Durant, Oklahoma, and stayed far back in the woods the rest of the day. Late that afternoon we got back on the highway and went to a tourist camp where we had stayed once before. We got a double cabin and stayed there that night. The next day a larger car was stolen and the roadster was left behind. They couldn't keep two cars. Buck could not drive because of his hand and Clyde always wanted W. D. to be in the car with him.

⚙12

Platte City

Editor's note: July 1933

During July, the Barrow gang engaged a number of Missouri officers in a vicious gun battle near Platte City, Missouri. The gang escaped but Blanche and Buck Barrow were both wounded. Five days later, the gang was discovered hiding near an abandoned amusement park near Dexter, Iowa. A gunfight ensued. Clyde Barrow, Bonnie Parker, and W. D. Jones, all wounded, escaped. Buck Barrow was wounded again and captured, along with Blanche, later in the morning. On July 29, Buck Barrow died in a Perry, Iowa, hospital. His wife was extradited to Missouri to face a charge of assault with intent to kill.[1]

Apart from this, most of the month's headlines focused on aviation news. On July 9, Amelia Earhart set a new record for U.S. transcontinental flight. Charles and Anne Morrow Lindbergh were reportedly mapping new aerial routes over Labrador and Greenland. And on July 23, the day before the shoot-out near Dexter, Iowa, Wiley Post completed the first solo flight around the world. That same day, in a statement to Dallas County Sheriff Richard Allen "Smoot" Schmid, Cumie Barrow said of her sons, Clyde and Buck, "They're living on borrowed time. You know that as well as I do."[2]

In Joplin, Missouri, Hollis Hale, an accomplice of Clyde Barrow, confessed to helping Barrow and Frank Hardy rob a bank at Oronogo, Missouri, on November 30, 1932. In addition, in July, two hurricanes struck the Texas coast, cotton prices rose steadily, and one of the most visible and powerful couples in Hollywood, Mary Pickford and Douglas Fairbanks, divorced.[3]

Billie Parker Mace. "Clyde wanted to send Billie back home, but she didn't want to go." (Courtesy of the Texas/Dallas Archives Division, Dallas Public Library)

AFTER LEAVING THE CAMP near Durant, we started driving again, going no place in particular. When money was needed, some small place was robbed. When a car was needed, one was stolen. When guns and ammunition were needed, some armory was burglarized at night. We roamed over many states, leaving a trail of horror behind us, terrorizing those Clyde came in contact with and needed something from.

Bonnie was getting much better now and Clyde wanted to send Billie back home, but she didn't want to go. She and W. D. had become sweethearts not long after Clyde brought her to Fort Smith.

On the Fourth of July, we were in Pueblo, Colorado. We had spent the previous day, July 3, in the mountains near there. Afterward, we drove to

W. D. Jones. "She [Billie] and W. D. had become sweethearts." (Courtesy of L. J. Hinton)

Denison, Texas, and Billie went home.[4] Clyde had enough money to buy her a new outfit and to pay for her fare home. But she didn't want to take a bus or train so we drove to Denison and she caught the Interurban there.[5]

From Denison we started driving in circles again. It seemed as though we always drove in circles through many states—Oklahoma, Texas, New Mexico, Colorado, Nebraska, South Dakota, Minnesota, Illinois, Indiana, Ohio, Kentucky, Tennessee, Alabama, Mississippi, Louisiana, Arkansas, Kansas, Iowa, and back to Missouri.[6]

Some few days or weeks after we left Fort Smith, we stopped at a tourist camp about thirty-five miles from Enid, Oklahoma.[7] One afternoon, Clyde and Buck drove away saying they would be back late that night. I later found out they drove to Enid and burglarized an armory there.[8] But at that time, I didn't know where they had gone. They returned at about four o'clock in the morning with more guns and ammunition than I had ever seen at one time in my whole life.[9] They also had several pairs of field glasses. They said we needed the glasses to scan roads to see if they are blocked so we

"I used to sit on top of the car because I could get a better view of the surroundings." (Photograph by Buck Barrow, courtesy of Rhea Leen Linder)

don't drive into a trap. And they could be used at night when the moon shone bright and one of us was on watch. We could see at great distances with them, leaving plenty of time to wake the rest before anyone got near enough to recognize us.

I spent many nights with a pair of field glasses to my eyes, watching while the others slept. Clyde used to say that was about all I was good for, staying awake and watching. He could depend on me to stay awake no matter how sleepy I got. Often I would have to wash my face and eyes with rubbing alcohol to keep me awake.[10]

I used to sit on top of the car because I could get a better view of our surroundings. If I saw nothing suspicious I would look at the moon and stars through the field glasses. Sometimes I would sit in one position so long my feet and legs would go to sleep and I would have to get down and walk around the car several times.

While we were at the camp in Oklahoma, I found an old newspaper in the ladies washroom. In it I read about the shooting near Fort Smith, Arkansas, the one Buck and W. D. were involved in. It said one officer by the name of H. D. Humphrey of Alma, Arkansas, had died from shotgun wounds fired at him by the Barrow brothers and that the next morning a

Marshal Henry D. Humphrey. "[The newspaper] said one officer by the name of H. D. Humphrey of Alma, Arkansas, had died from shotgun wounds." (Courtesy of James R. Knight)

woman had been assaulted and beaten and that her car was then taken by the same men. I knew that last part couldn't be true because we left the area the very same afternoon[11] that Buck and W. D. had had the wreck and gun battle. Anyway, I asked Buck if he did anything like that.

"No, Baby," he said. "You know I couldn't do anything like that. And anyway, that says the woman was beaten the next day, after we left Fort Smith."

This was true and I don't believe he beat any woman. He wasn't like that.[12]

On the night of July 18, we were tired.[13] We had been driving all day, in fact many days and nights, without sleep. Surely, we could find a place where we could get one good night's rest without being disturbed. So we began looking for a camp. We drove until about eleven o'clock that night. We could see the lights of Kansas City.

"That's Kansas City, isn't it?" Buck asked Clyde. They had been arguing again and Buck had been trying to get a car most all day so we could leave them. This time we would leave them for good. Clyde was too much of a dirty rat. His own brother couldn't stay with him or get along with him without fighting two-thirds of the time. So, when Buck asked if it was Kansas City, Clyde said, "Sure, boy. This is a big town. Aren't you afraid we will meet some cops? They probably know we are this near."[14]

Just because Buck wanted to be careful, Clyde tried to make it appear that he thought Buck was just afraid.

"No. I am not afraid of meeting any cops," said Buck. "But I do know Kansas City is one of the hottest towns for people like us to stop near in the middle west.[15] What if we're near Kansas City at a camp and the cops come in looking for someone else, drunks, or car thieves? Anyone besides us could get a place hot. And we would run right into their heat without knowing it until we got into it.[16] Then we would have to shoot our way out.

"We may stop near Kansas City, but of course you haven't enough brains left to use. You had rather make someone think you are tough. Take all your guns away from you and you would throw up your hands and beg like a baby because you can't make it unless you have enough guns behind you to supply a whole army. And you will squeal on your mother if you thought it would keep you from prison or getting your neck broke. But I am not going to stay with you any longer than it takes to get a car so Blanche and I can leave you. We don't have to put up with it. We can live a lot longer away from you than we can with you.

"Luck has been with you so far. You haven't escaped just because you are smart or because you used your head. If you had used your head, you would not have had so many murders on your hands. Well, I will never have so many on mine. You can kill and not give anyone a chance, but someday you will meet someone that won't give you a chance to fire a shot."

They stopped the arguing.

We passed a place that had two brick cabins. Clyde said, "This is where we stay the rest of the night, even if we all get killed before morning." No one said anything.[17]

We drove a short distance from the camp, turned down a side road, and covered everything up so none of the guns could be seen by anyone close enough to look in the car. Buck whispered to me that we would do as they wanted that night. Then, when we left the cabins to get another car, we would get away from them forever.

Clyde and Buck were not speaking to each other, but when Clyde said some of us would have to get covered up and hide in the back of the car, Buck and W. D. got beneath some quilts and blankets.[18] I moved to the front seat with Clyde and Bonnie so I would be seen when the cabin was rented because I would have to buy food from the cafe at the filling station. Then we drove to the Red Crown Filling Station and Cabin Camp. Clyde rented both cabins. They had closed garages between them. Clyde drove into one of the garages and parked.[19]

The Red Crown Cabins, near Platte City, Missouri. "They had closed garages between them. Clyde drove into one of the garages and parked." (Photograph by William E. Searles, Phillips Collection)

After we got settled in our cabins, they wanted something to eat. So I was sent to the station for food and beer. I was given nothing but small change to pay for the food. They ordered so much food that I told them the owner would know there were more than three of us.

"Oh, they won't think anything," Clyde said. "Just get the food. We are hungry. Bring back some chicken if they have any."

When I started back with the food, the owner said he would go with me. He said he had to get our car license. It was funny he hadn't taken the number when we pulled in and rented the cabins. Anyway, I couldn't refuse to let him in the garage because most all tourist cabin people had to register.[20]

When we got to the cabin, I called for someone to open the door. Clyde opened it. I told him the man wanted the car license number. With that, the man started to go in the cabin, but Clyde told him he would open the garage door for him, adding that he couldn't go through the cabin because his wife was undressed.

After we had eaten, Buck and I went to the other cabin, the one nearest the station.[21] We took a small handbag with us, along with one rifle, several .45-caliber automatic pistols,[22] and a number of ammunition clips, all of which were wrapped in a blanket. The next morning, July 19, we slept late.

When we got up, Buck sent me to Clyde's cabin to see if they wanted anything from the station. Buck didn't go to their cabin at all. He didn't want to argue anymore with Clyde. He also told me to ask how soon they would be ready to leave.

They wanted more chicken and beer. When I asked about leaving, they said they wanted to stay another day and night. Again, they gave me small change to pay for the food. Clyde told me to see how the people acted and what I thought about them, if I thought it would be safe to stay there another night.

When I went to pay the four dollars for another night at the cabins, the owner told me I wouldn't have to pay up until four o'clock. But I paid him anyway. He told me if we changed our minds and decided to leave before four o'clock, I could have the money back. He didn't act just right to me. I told Clyde I thought he was either an officer of some kind or else he was the type that might tell the law we were there if he had the slightest suspicion about us. I didn't feel that we were safe to stay another night, but Clyde said it was just my imagination, that everything would be all right. So I said no more.

That afternoon I had to get more chicken dinners, using small change.[23] I learned that the man who had taken our license number had gone to Platte City. Of course, there wasn't anything wrong about him going to town, but somehow I felt he was checking up on us.[24] I told the others what I thought.

Late that afternoon Clyde and W. D. went to Platte City to buy medicine for Bonnie.[25] They left her in the cabin alone but asked me if I would sit in the swing near the cabin while they were gone. Buck sat inside our cabin with the window shade about half up. We didn't keep them down during the day, only at night when the lights were on. But I noticed the shades in Clyde's cabin were all drawn and had sheets of newspaper pinned to them. That was enough to make anyone get suspicious of them.[26]

Buck and I talked of what we would do when we got away from them. We could find someplace away from all this. Then Buck asked me how I would like to go to Canada. He said we could get a cabin someplace in the mountains, or in the forest, and trap that winter if we were lucky enough to live that long. I said that would be okay by me, anything to get away from all this.

That night Buck was shining my boots. I had been thinking of something I did not like to mention. I had promised him once before that I wouldn't bring it up, that I hoped I would be killed first because I didn't think I could live if he was killed. If I were not killed with him, I would have to commit that unpardonable sin, suicide. I would not want to live after he was gone. I was thinking about that because I believed there would be a battle that very night. Everyone at the station was acting funny, especially the way they all looked at me when I entered the place.

"Daddy," I said. "If I should be killed what would you do with me?"

"Why, Baby," Buck said. "You should know I would take you home if I was alive and able to drive a car. I would get you home some way."

"No, Daddy," I said. "I don't want you to take that chance. I want you to leave me someplace where my body would be found after you are gone. You would probably be killed trying to get me home. So just leave me someplace. It doesn't matter. Just so you don't get killed."

"Baby," Buck said. "You know I couldn't leave you any old place, because we want to be buried side by side when we die, no matter which one dies first. Let's don't talk about it. It hurts too bad, because I couldn't live without you and I don't like to think of losing you.

"But promise me you will never commit suicide, no matter what happens.[27] That's something God will not forgive us for. And as long as there's life, there's hope. I will never kill myself and I don't want you too. What would you do with me if I should be killed first?"

"Dad," I said. "I would take you home or stay with you until I am taken away from you. I could take you home easier than you could me. If I get caught they can't give me more than life in prison for staying with you. I haven't committed any crime unless loving you and staying with you until death parts us is a crime. And I'll stay with you, even if I am shot down or hanged afterward. I'll stay if I am alive, until the officers take me away from you, or take you from me."

And the subject was dropped.

Soon Buck climbed into bed. I went to the station to get some toilet soap and fresh towels. Before I entered the station, I noticed everyone in the place was doing a lot of talking. I could hear them and see several of them sitting around a table. But when I walked in everyone stopped talking. The place was so quiet you could have heard a pin drop. It was just as quiet as a death chamber. I knew something must be wrong. The girl who waited on me stood and stared at me for a few seconds, as if she had seen a ghost.[28] And when she did speak, she seemed to be extra polite. I told her what I wanted.

"Yes, deary," she said. "I'll get them. Is there anything else you need?"

The Red Crown Tavern. "When I walked in everyone stopped talking." (Photograph by William E. Searles, Phillips Collection)

While she was gone, I stepped on a pair of scales and dropped a penny in them. Some young fellow walked up close to me and looked to see how much I weighed. He tried to start a conversation with me. He said something about how small I was, tipping the scales at ninety-one pounds, and how I was dressed in riding boots, trousers, and a shirt. Soon the girl came back and handed me the fresh towels. Everyone acted as though I might pull out a machine gun and turn it on them at any minute. As soon as I stepped outside, the talking started again but I couldn't understand anything that was said.[29]

Every time I left the cabin, Buck would watch me. Clyde did the same thing. When I went out their rifles were almost always in their hands, or nearby in case someone grabbed me.[30] They would have come out fighting and taken me back. I always hoped it would never happen because they told me they would either get me back or die fighting, even though they were fighting amongst themselves. If they got into a tight place they would usually fight for each other. At least I knew Buck would. I had known Clyde to leave his pals, even Bonnie, when he saw a way out for himself.

I told Buck how everyone acted when I went to the station. I thought we should leave then, before it was too late. He said if we had a car we would have left earlier in the day. He said to go tell Clyde and see what he thought. I did, but he thought we would be safe until morning.

Slim's Castle. "[Clyde] sent W. D. to another place across the highway from the cabins." (Photograph by Kermit "Curley" Crawford, Phillips Collection)

"Okay," I said. "If we all get killed here tonight, you can't say I didn't warn you."

I went back to our cabin and told Buck what Clyde said.

"Well, Baby," he said. "Maybe there isn't anything wrong. If we have to stay, then we may as well get some sleep while we are here."

"Well, I have a few things to wash out," I said. "If the cops don't come before they get dry, we will have some clean clothes."[31]

So, I turned out the big light in the room and turned on a small floor lamp. Then I dressed in pajamas and did my wash. Just as I was finishing up W. D. came in and said Clyde wanted me to go get some sandwiches and beer.

"Tell him it's too late to go for more food and beer," I said. "And I'm not going out in my pj's, and I know I am not going to dress. You should have gotten food earlier if you wanted it. If they are not suspicious of us, they will be. So I'm not going!"

This made Clyde mad. He sent W. D. to another place across the highway from the cabins.[32] Soon I turned off the floor lamp and watched outside through the small glass panel of the door and window. I saw cars drive up and stop at the station. I saw people standing by their cars and pointing toward our cabins.

"Baby," Buck said. "I wish you would come to bed. If anything is going to happen, we can't stop it until it starts."

I told him I would come to bed in a few minutes. I watched some more. Everything seemed better. Some of the station lights went out about the

Sheriff Holt Coffey with shield. "Then someone knocked. . . . They told me it was the
law." (Courtesy of Rhea Leen Linder)

same time they had the night before.[33] When I got in bed Buck was
asleep. I woke him up and kissed him goodnight. I wasn't quite asleep, just
starting to doze, when someone flashed a light on our window and door.
Then someone knocked. I woke Buck and told him there was someone at
the door. Then I jumped over the foot of the bed and began putting my
clothes on. Buck told me to ask who it was and what they wanted. I did.
They told me it was the law.[34] Buck began to put his trousers and shoes
on. The man at the door told me to send out the man I had in there. I
whispered to Buck, asking what to say.

"Tell them there isn't any man in here," he said. So that's what I told
them.

"Well," the man said. "Put your trousers on and come out yourself." I
asked again what they wanted, stalling for time. I felt the end was near for
all of us. Then he asked where the men were.

Spectators examining the bullet holes on July 20, 1933. "Then the shooting stopped as suddenly as it had started." (Photograph by William E. Searles, Phillips Collection)

"Tell them the men are in the other cabin," said Buck. "And shout it loud enough so Clyde can hear you." So I told them the men were in the other cabin.[35]

"Well, come on out here yourself," the man said.

"Wait until I get my clothes on and I will come out," I said. I knew I couldn't hold out much longer and I didn't know what the next move would be. By this time, Buck was at the door. "Baby," he said. "I sure hate to have to kill him, but it looks like I am going to have to do it. So get back as close to the wall as you can and stay as close behind me as you can."

Buck grabbed one pistol, a .45, and put it in his belt, then got the rifle from beside the bed.[36] Suddenly it seemed as if the men outside were driving a car through the garage door, or trying to knock the cabin door down.[37] Then the fireworks started. I don't know who fired the first shot,[38] but I do know Buck shot at the corner of the room instead of through the door where he could have killed anyone in front of it. He had said he didn't want to kill anyone. Those who were in front of our cabin should be thankful

Clyde Barrow with a Browning automatic rifle. "I later learned that some of Clyde's shots had found their mark, passing through the officers' armored car and wounding one officer." (Phillips Collection)

they were not in front of Clyde's cabin instead. They would have been dead men because Buck could see their shadows against the window and through the glass panel in the door. He could have killed them if he had wanted too.

After he started shooting, Buck began firing through all the windows, cocking the rifle as he moved from window to window.[39] I stayed as close to Buck as I could.[40] At one point, he accidentally hit the dresser with the gunstock and broke the mirror to pieces.[41] Then the shooting stopped as suddenly as it had started. The car that seemed to be breaking down one of the garage doors started backing away with its horn screaming. We thought this meant they were calling for more help, but I later learned that some of Clyde's shots had found their mark, passing through the officers' armored car and wounding one officer in both knees. Another bullet struck the horn and caused it to blow continually.[42]

"Are you alright?" Buck called out.

"Yes," answered Clyde. "Are you both still okay?"

"Yes," we both said.

"Let's get away from here!" Clyde said.

I opened the door. I meant to go out first, hoping they would shoot at the first one so Buck would have a chance to get to the car.

"Don't do that, Baby," Buck said as I opened the door. "You will get killed. Come back."

Then we heard the motor of Clyde's car start.

"Okay," he said. "Let's go. Get the bag by the door."

I did.

"Maybe we can make it while they are reloading."

We were outside. I was about halfway to the car when a shot rang out from the station. I turned and screamed. I saw Buck fall and ran back to him.[43] I wasn't afraid anymore. If he were dead, they could shoot all the lead they had into my body. I didn't fear the bullets.

"They've killed Buck!" I shouted to Clyde.[44]

Clyde came out and asked where the shot came from. I told him. Then he picked up Buck's rifle. The barrel was so hot it blistered his hand. It was about all I could do to lift Buck up and get my arm around his waist so I could get him to the car. I lost all feeling. My body was numb. After I got him up, I couldn't even feel his weight. How I got him to the car alone I'll never know.[45] And I still had the bag in my right hand![46]

I had a little difficulty getting Buck into the car. His head bumped the side of the garage. I tried so hard not to hurt him anymore. I finally got him in the car. W. D. got in beside me. I was in the center, Buck was on my right, W. D. on my left. Clyde got in, stepped on the gas, and backed out of the garage.[47] W. D. asked for a gun.[48] Buck mumbled that he had dropped his gun and then lost consciousness. I was holding his head as close to my breast as I could, and had both my arms wrapped around him, trying to protect him should the officers shoot into the car, as I was sure they would do. My face was turned toward the right side of the car and I had my head bent as near Buck as I could. Then a hail of bullets was fired into the right

a little too vivid for a panic sit.

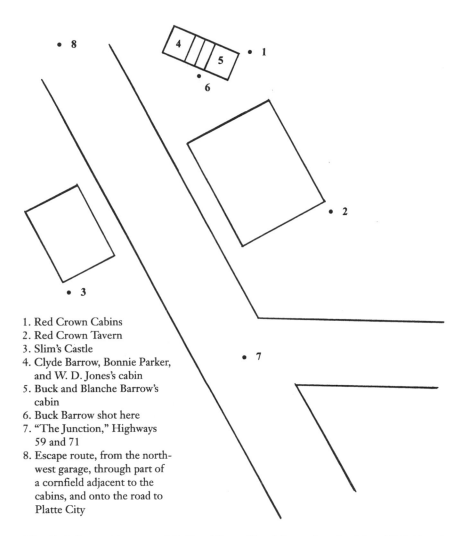

1. Red Crown Cabins
2. Red Crown Tavern
3. Slim's Castle
4. Clyde Barrow, Bonnie Parker, and W. D. Jones's cabin
5. Buck and Blanche Barrow's cabin
6. Buck Barrow shot here
7. "The Junction," Highways 59 and 71
8. Escape route, from the northwest garage, through part of a cornfield adjacent to the cabins, and onto the road to Platte City

The Red Crown Tavern and Cabins, Platte City, Missouri; scale: 1 in = 75 ft. Based on drawings by eyewitnesses Kermit "Curley" Crawford and William R. Searles.

side of the car. I couldn't protect my face because I was trying to shield Buck as much as I could. Glass broke. Something hard hit the side of my head, just above my temple.[49] It seemed to burn its way across the side of my head. I was also struck in my right arm, though I didn't feel it at the time. But none of the glass or lead hit Buck.

Then my vision suddenly faded out. All was dark. I thought my eyes had been damaged by bullets and glass. But I felt no pain. I was past feeling pain. Then, when hot blood began to stream down on my face, I thought some of it was water from my shattered eyes.

"They got my eyes!" I said. "I can't see!"
No one heard me.[50]

⊛13

Dexfield Park

I DIDN'T KNOW WHICH way we turned when we left the cabins, but we hadn't gone far when I heard Clyde say one of the rear tires was flat. Soon he turned down a side road.[1]

"This looks like an old barn," he said. "Maybe we can get to it and stay long enough to change tires."

But he couldn't. The car hit high center and bottomed out. The ruts in the road were too deep and he couldn't make the grade, especially with a flat tire. Clyde got out of the car.

"Blanche," he said. "Go to the road and watch for car lights while W. D. and I fix the tire."

I told him I couldn't see.

"My God!" he said. "Did you get shot too?"

"Yes," I said. But I told him to see how badly Buck was shot.

They struck a match and looked at both of us. Buck was conscious again. I got something from the bag to wipe the blood from his head. By this time most everything was wet with blood, as if dipped in water. The floorboard of the car was so soaked we could hear the blood gush under our feet. Buck wanted to get out of the car, saying he had to have more air. So we helped him out. He sat on the running board of the car and asked for something else to wipe the blood from his head. I felt around for the bag and got something out and gave it to him. Then I tried to wipe the blood off my face. I found that my eyes were in better shape than I originally thought. Clyde looked at them.

"The eyeballs are not busted!" he said.

I finally got my right eye cleaned out enough to barely see light. I tried to see the wound on Buck's head but couldn't tell much about it. I was afraid he would merely bleed to death if the shot had not gone far enough into his head to kill him. He didn't complain. He only said his head hurt a little and that he wanted water. When I found that I could see light with my right eye, Clyde asked me if I thought I could see car lights. I told him I thought I could.

I kissed Buck and started to feel my way to the road. I fell a couple of times before I got there, but each time I just got up and kept on going. I hated to leave Buck for even a minute but someone had to watch the road. When I kissed Buck, blood streamed down on my lips. What a sickening smell, blood and gunpowder. I got so sick I started vomiting.

While I was out by the road, acting as lookout, the car rolled off the jack and Buck fell to the ground. I heard it and stumbled back to him, trying to run. Buck just held his head. "Oh, God!" I thought. "How much more of this can I take without collapsing?" But I knew I couldn't collapse no matter what happened. I had to try and help Buck somehow, even if I couldn't see very well. About all I could do was try to protect him from more bullets with my own body. I wanted to live as long as he did. When he died, I wanted to die with him. He needed me now more than ever before. He could no longer help himself.

Buck didn't know I'd been shot. I tried to keep it from him.

It took a long time for Clyde and W. D. to get the tire fixed so we could start driving again. After we got moving, we found we had yet another flat tire. Both rear tires had been shot full of lead! They would have to get a pump from some place. Eventually we stopped at a farmhouse and borrowed what was needed.[2] We had a terrible time getting out of that part of the country.[3]

At daybreak, we were only fourteen miles from Kansas City, Missouri.[4] We stopped at a filling station to get gas.[5] Clyde told me to get Buck covered and for both of us try to lie down like we were asleep. I tried to cover us both so the station operator wouldn't see all the blood, but while we were sitting there, Buck got sick to his stomach and came out from under the covering. He didn't even know we were stopped at a station. The operator came up to the car and looked in. Clyde said he knew that guy would call Kansas City, which would make us hotter than ever. He said we wouldn't be able to get away this time. I was surprised that Clyde didn't kill that operator.

"Noah's Ark," the old covered bridge across the Little Platte River used at least three times by the fugitives during the night of July 19–20, 1933. "We had a terrible time getting out of that part of the country." (Photograph by Shirley Kimsey)

While we were under the light at the station, I could see blood all over Buck's face and head. I had wiped a lot of glass from my right eye and I could see better with it, but only if I was real close to what I was looking at. I was just as bloody as Buck. My hair was wet with blood.

We rode all that day, only stopping to get gas, except for one place where Clyde got some bandages, Mercurochrome, and alcohol.[6] He also got some aspirin for Buck and me. Then we tried to bandage Buck's head. Buck had some Amytal capsules in his pocket, but he had lost so much blood that his heart seemed too weak for him to take them. I was afraid he would die. He had taken the capsules out of the medical kit a couple of days earlier, saying someone may get shot and need them to ease the pain. He knew Clyde and Bonnie would never think to grab the kit if we got into a battle. They would always forget to put it in the car. When we needed it the most, we never had it.[7]

The only way I can describe the next few days is to say it was a living, torturing hell! I was afraid to go to sleep for fear Buck would die. I couldn't eat. Food was the last thing I could think of and when I did try to eat, it choked me.

We finally stopped in a wooded area. I later learned it was Dexfield Park, near Dexter, Iowa.[8] Buck was slowly slipping away from me and there wasn't anything I could do about it, living like a wounded, trapped animal in the woods without the care of a doctor or a bed to lie down on. Clyde fixed a

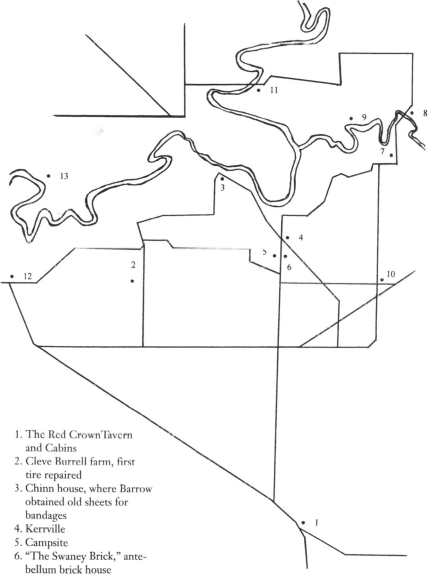

1. The Red Crown Tavern and Cabins
2. Cleve Burrell farm, first tire repaired
3. Chinn house, where Barrow obtained old sheets for bandages
4. Kerrville
5. Campsite
6. "The Swaney Brick," antebellum brick house
7. Ellis Kimsey's sighting
8. Covered bridge across the Little Platte River
9. Second tire repaired
10. Hoover
11. Mellon Bridge
12. To Platte City
13. Platte River

Escape from Platte County, Missouri; scale: 1 in = 1½ mi. Based on research conducted by Shirley Kimsey and LaVern Taulbee.

Dexfield Park, Iowa, during its heyday in the 1920s. "We finally stopped in a wooded area. I later learned it was Dexfield Park." (From the Blanche Caldwell Barrow scrapbooks, courtesy of Rhea Leen Linder)

car cushion for Buck to stretch out on beside the car, under a tree. I sat beside him. Sometimes he was so still I would feel his pulse or place my hand on his chest to see if he was still alive. He never complained, but I knew he must be suffering. We put ice on his head.[9] That seemed to give him more relief than anything else we did.

Buck begged me to lie down beside him and go to sleep. So to please him I would lie down. I was so tired, but I was afraid to go to sleep. I would always hold his wrist or put my hand over his heart. It's what he wanted me to do. Sometimes when I thought he was asleep he would reach out to me and just hold me tight, as if he couldn't let me go. But he wouldn't say anything or try to open his eyes. I could hardly keep from screaming with the fear that gripped me. How could I give him up like this? I just couldn't live if he died. I loved him too much to have to give him up, dead or alive. I wanted to go with him, whether he lived or died. If we both died together, we would die happy.

When Clyde and Bonnie went for food, they always left W. D. to watch over us.[10] W. D. told us how tired he was of the outlaw life. He said he wished he could leave and forget all about it. We told him he might have a chance to do that if he left right away and went to work someplace. No

Bonnie and Clyde camped outdoors. "We had wanted to leave the park that night." (Phillips Collection)

one knew he was with us or had his fingerprints. He was young. He could make life worthwhile for himself if he tried. And he had seen enough of this life to know it was a game that he couldn't win. You always lose in the end. If you don't die from some officer's bullets, you'll end up spending the rest of your life in prison, or go to the chair. Either way, it's death or prison in the end.

On July 23, we rode to some town nearby and Clyde got another car.[11] Our other car had eighteen bullet holes in it. Buck could hardly stand the ride. He couldn't sit up and he would get too hot and short of breath lying down in the car. We had wanted to leave the park that night and take Buck someplace where he could have a bed to lie down in, perhaps someplace with some of his people that the officers didn't know about. That way Clyde and Bonnie and W. D. could leave us. But Buck couldn't ride, so we went back to the park.[12] None of us felt very safe there, but Clyde said it was the safest place he could find. We hoped Buck would feel more like riding the next day.

That evening, about sundown, Clyde took one of the cars and drove into town with Bonnie. They left W. D. with Buck and me in the other car.

We had been trying to get Buck to eat. I asked him if he could eat some fried chicken.

"Anyone could eat fried chicken!" he said.

So Clyde brought back five fried chicken dinners and fixed a plate of food for both Buck and me.[13] I couldn't eat mine, but I held Buck's plate for him. He seemed to be feeling better. He could sit up. Then he noticed I wasn't eating anything.

"Baby," he said. "What's the use of me eating and trying to get well if you are going to starve yourself to death? The only reason I am trying to get well is because of you. If you die, I won't get well. If you hadn't been with me, I would have already been dead. I am just living for you. When you are gone, I'll go too."

I tried harder to eat and managed to swallow some of the food, but it had no taste. He got up and stood on his feet. I helped him walk a few steps.

That night we slept in the car, as we always did.[14] I sat up. Bonnie tried to get me to sleep in the front seat. I couldn't go on without food or sleep. She said she would sit by Buck and if he seemed to make any change, she would wake me. He was feeling better so I got in the front seat and lay down. But I couldn't go to sleep. I was afraid to be that far away from Buck, fearing he may miss me. So I went back to him so I could touch him and know every move he made. Buck would sometimes tear the bandage off his head and start digging into the wound with his fingernails. Sometimes it was all I could do to hold his hands away from the place.[15]

My eyes hurt a lot. I had to put drops in them every few minutes. They felt so dry and were quite swollen. Both of my eyes were still full of fine, shattered glass and there was a large piece of glass stuck in one of the pupils. Both Clyde and Bonnie had tried to get it out with tweezers, but the tweezers kept slipping off. They couldn't get enough of a grip on it to pull it out. I was also pretty weak from loss of blood.

That night all of us felt jittery. Everything got on our nerves. Whippoor-wills called and a screech owl kept coming in close to the car, hollering. I could have screamed from hearing it. But we were afraid to shoot it because someone may have come to investigate. Clyde tried to frighten it away but it always came back. I felt as if someone was slowly creeping up on us. I think the others felt the same way. Every time we heard a twig break or the leaves rustle, they would grab a gun. Finally, they went to sleep.

The rest of that night is too hard for me to describe. I can't find words to express the horror of it, although it wasn't much different from any other night after Buck was shot.

Clyde said we would start driving early the next morning. When he and W. D. woke up and got out of the car to roast some weenies left over from the night before, I lay down beside Buck with my head close to his heart and his arms holding me tight. I fell asleep for a few minutes. Then Buck moved to grab a pistol. He was talking about seeing soldiers all around us. He had the gun in his hand when I awoke. He also had W. D.'s billfold in his hand. He had taken it from W. D.'s hip pocket while he lying between the two seats.

"Baby," he said, handing me the billfold. "See what I taken from one of the soldiers that was laying here? He's drunk and I got his money!"

I looked around but could see no one but W. D. and Clyde. I knew then that Buck was feeling worse and that he didn't know what he was saying.[16] I felt his pulse. It was so weak I couldn't find it. As I started to listen to Buck's heart I heard Clyde suddenly say, "Look out!" Then he and W. D. rushed for the car, grabbed guns, and started shooting. A hail of lead hit the car.[17] Glass broke. I rolled Buck over, onto the cushion between the seats, and threw my body over his to protect him from the glass and lead. I heard W. D. say, "Clyde! I'm shot! I can't fight any longer!" I looked his way and saw blood streaming down his face. He was close, beside the car.[18]

"I'm shot too," Clyde answered. "But we gotta keep fighting."[19]

I heard Clyde curse one of the officers and say, "I'll get you for that!"[20] Then he and W. D. got in the car and tried to get away. Clyde said he couldn't drive to the highway, in the direction we'd come from, so he started backing down a hill. He backed into a ditch and got the motor hung on a tree stump. He couldn't pull out.

"Let's run," Bonnie said. Clyde told her she couldn't run, but she said she could.

"Let's go!" Clyde said.

I got Buck out of the car, but he wanted his shoes. So I put them on and tied them. I had already slipped my boots on. They were full of glass, but I didn't take the time to pull them off and get it out.

"Come on!" Clyde shouted. They were about ten feet away from the car.

I got my arm around Buck's waist and tried to follow, but when we were about twenty feet up the hill Buck fainted. I couldn't hold him up alone. He was dead weight. We both fell to the ground. Clyde, W. D., and Bonnie were still running and shooting.[21] They saw Buck faint and pull me down. I called to Clyde, but they didn't stop. I worked with Buck, trying to bring him to. When he did come to, he spoke.

Part of the posse at the outlaws' camp. Left to right: Al Gardner, who guided the group; John Drake, Sutherland city marshal; Colonel Fred Hird, U.S. marshal; and Polk County deputy sheriffs Jake Gesell, Carl Abolt, and Harold Gesell. "I heard Clyde curse one of the officers and say, 'I'll get you for that!'" (From the Blanche Caldwell Barrow scrapbooks, courtesy of Rhea Leen Linder)

"Baby," he said. "Leave me. You can get away alone. I am too tired to go on."

I got him to sit up so he could lean on me. I told him I wouldn't leave him, ever. We would both die together if I couldn't get him away. The only way I would ever leave him would be for the officers to take me away from him. And only for his sake would I give up alive.

"Baby," he said. "Please go. I love you too much to let you get killed because of me. And don't commit suicide."

"Daddy," I said. "I don't think you have to worry about me doing that. They will do it for me, because I'm not leaving you."

While I was letting him rest I emptied the glass out of my boots. My feet were already cut and bleeding. Then I helped Buck get up, putting both

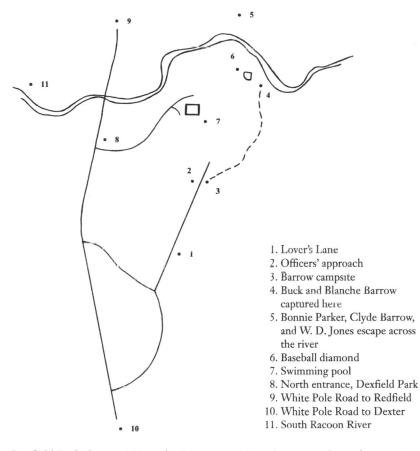

Dexfield Park, Iowa, 1933; scale: 1 in = ¼ mi. Based on maps drawn by eyewitness Marvelle Feller.

1. Lover's Lane
2. Officers' approach
3. Barrow campsite
4. Buck and Blanche Barrow captured here
5. Bonnie Parker, Clyde Barrow, and W. D. Jones escape across the river
6. Baseball diamond
7. Swimming pool
8. North entrance, Dexfield Park
9. White Pole Road to Redfield
10. White Pole Road to Dexter
11. South Racoon River

of his arms around my neck and my arm around his waist. I had to go slowly with him, almost dragging him. I had to hold onto trees to keep us both from falling down the hill, it was so steep.[22] We could only go short distances, and then he would have to sit down. He didn't seem conscious half the time.

When we got over the hill I had to let him rest because he was about to faint again. While we were stopped, I lit a cigarette for both of us. Buck joked about who could run fastest to the bottom of the hill. He bet me a quarter he could beat me. I suppose he was thinking of the many times we had foot races and would bet on who was the fastest. Sometimes I lost those races. He could run fast when he was feeling well.[23] Now he was betting he could outrun me when he couldn't even walk. He was so game about the danger we were in. I really don't think he understood.

I could hear Clyde shouting and talking but I didn't expect any help from him. I knew we were on our own.[24] I thought maybe I could get Buck away, but I had to feel my way almost to the foot of the hill where a dry creek bed lay. I had to stop again and I couldn't find anything to protect us. Buck kept begging me to leave him, but I kept on trying to get him a few steps farther.

After awhile we came to a clearing.[25] It seemed like we had covered at least a mile, over hills and rocky cliffs, but I am sure it wasn't that far, perhaps half-a-mile, if that. From the edge of the clearing, I wondered how I would ever get across such an open space and up the rise. I decided to try it.

Buck was about to pass out again. I saw a big log with a stump behind it. I thought I could sit down on the stump and let Buck lie down and rest a few minutes. We'd both be hidden behind the log. When we got to the log Buck fell, pulling me down with him. He was so weak he couldn't go any farther. He still had the same gun he was holding earlier, when he woke me up talking about soldiers. I doubted if he could use it. I tried to get it away from him, but he held on to it. He hadn't fired a shot since Platte City.

I sat down and put his head and shoulders in my lap. When Buck came to, he wanted water. I was very thirsty myself, and weak. I just had to force myself to go on. But I was afraid to leave him and try to get water from the river; afraid I couldn't get back to him. He told me not to let anyone slip up on us, that he was going to sleep.

I don't know how long we stayed there but Buck was cold and wet from the early morning dew, which was like a light rain. I was cold too. I only had on a thin silk knit blouse. We had used my skirt for bandages. Everything was covered in blood. I sat there until my feet and legs seemed paralyzed from the weight of Buck's head and shoulders. Then I heard someone walking.[26]

"There they are!" someone shouted.

I somehow pushed Buck between myself and the log. I was still trying to protect him from more bullets. By then it looked as if nearly thirty men were shouting at the sight of us. Buck came to, rolled on his stomach, and tried to shoot. I can't say if he fired any shots. But he was shot. I have no idea how he was shot without me being hit as well. But not one bullet touched me. At times, though, it seemed as if the log in front of us was being cut with a saw instead of bullets from machine guns, rifles, and shotguns.

When Buck was hit, he threw his body over mine and held me tight in his arms.

"Baby," he said. "They got me this time." Then his body relaxed. I thought he was dead. I just went mad, screaming and begging them to stop. I couldn't stand having more bullets fired into his body. I thought, "If one would only hit me and kill me instantly."

They told me to get up and have Buck get up too. But I shouted that he couldn't get up, that they'd killed him. I put my hands up, above the log. The shooting stopped for a second. Buck moved. I was so happy to know he was still alive. I lowered my hands and grabbed him.

"Baby," he said. "Don't get up. They will kill you!"

The shooting started again as we lay there, holding each other tight, murmuring to each other, "I love you, no matter what happens. I will always love you."

Suddenly, the thought that I should somehow get Buck to a hospital crossed my mind. At least that way he could die in a nice clean bed. By then, I felt sure he would die. He couldn't survive this last shock, being shot again. And I couldn't stand to see more shots fired into his precious body. I couldn't bear to see him torn to shreds before my very eyes when I might be able to save him yet. I didn't think they would let me go with Buck to the hospital and stay with him until he died, that is, if I survived. He had nothing to live for. If Buck were captured, and lived, he would be sentenced to death anyway. That would be worse than being killed outright. He was so near death. I didn't think about what might happen to me, nor did I care. Life without Buck would be worse than death to me.

"Daddy," I said. "I am going to give us up so you can go to a hospital. I can't bear to see them tear you to pieces with bullets. You can be in a clean bed."

"Don't get up, Baby," Buck said. "They will kill you."

"I don't care, Daddy," I said. "I want to go with you anyway."

"I may as well get one or two of them before I die," he said.[27]

"No, Daddy!" I said. "No! There may still be a chance and I love you so. Don't do it for me! Don't kill anyone else. They've got us anyway. Don't, because they will finish you if you try to do that and I can't stand to see them do that to you. We may have a chance to get out of it yet."

Buck told me to get up and then he dropped his gun. Again we locked ourselves in each other's arms. Then I spoke my last words to Buck.

Blanche Barrow at the time of her capture. "Then I was lifted by two men and taken away from Buck." (From the Blanche Caldwell Barrow scrapbooks, courtesy of Rhea Leen Linder)

"Daddy, whatever they do to me, I will always love you."

If the officers had put a bullet through my heart, it wouldn't have hurt any more than leaving to give up. The law would have done us a favor if they had put bullets through both our hearts at the same time.

It would have saved a lot of pain and sorrow. But they didn't. I kissed Buck goodbye.

The posse was still shooting at us. Then they stopped and I stood up with my hands raised, screaming and crying.[28] I tried to keep between them and Buck but they made me step to one side. They grabbed me. I told them Buck was dying and asked them not shoot him anymore. They went to him. I tried to get back to him. I begged them to lift him carefully and not to hurt him anymore. They wouldn't let me touch him or help with him. I was still screaming and fighting to get to him. When they got him to a car and let him down beside it, I pleaded, fought, and screamed to get to him. Two officers were holding me. Finally, one of them was kind enough to tell the other one to let me go to Buck. I went to him, knelt down beside him, and kissed him.[29]

"Daddy," I said. "Did they hurt you any worse?"

Buck Barrow, on the ground at the feet of the man bending over. "Buck was asked who he was." (From the Blanche Caldwell Barrow scrapbooks, courtesy of Rhea Leen Linder)

"No, Baby," he said.

I touched his shoulder and he told me it hurt. (Later I learned Buck had been shot six times.)[30] Then I was lifted by two men and taken away from Buck. I begged the men to let me ride in the same car with Buck, but they wouldn't allow it. Buck was asked who he was. I was asked dozens of questions before we got to the car, but I refused to answer. However, Buck started answering, so I decided if he was going to talk then I may as well give them our identification card. I took it out of the billfold in my pocket and gave it to them. I did it mainly to make them stop bothering Buck. He was suffering so.

When we got to the doctor's office in some small town nearby,[31] I saw Buck lying on the floor. He was on a stretcher without a cushion under his head. An officer told me to lie down on a wicker divan in the doctor's office. I wouldn't think of lying on that divan when Buck was only a few feet away from me, the doctor dressing his wounds. I decided these people must think I have no feelings, telling me to lie down and rest when my husband was so close to death.

I asked if Buck had been given any water. They told me he had. Then the doctor brought me a glass of water. I drank it and wanted more. The doctor handed me another glass. I thought it was water, but when I took a sip, I found it was alcohol. I couldn't drink it, not even a swallow. "Little girl," said the doctor. "You should take that. You are going to need it!" I knew he was right. But I couldn't drink the alcohol so he gave me something else, a capsule. He also gave one to Buck. The doctor was very kind to me.[32]

I wanted to go to Buck but I was told to sit down. I asked Buck if he wanted a cigarette. He said, yes, to light him one. I did and took it to him. I was still crying. I couldn't stop. I sat down beside Buck. He asked me to turn him over so the wound in his shoulder wouldn't hurt so much.[33] I did that and placed a cushion under his head. He told me to go back and sit down on the divan and stop crying because it worried him. I tried to stop crying. I told him I wanted to stop but it hurt my feelings when he told me to get up. I wanted to stay beside him as long as I could, but I didn't want to worry him or hurt him in any way. Those words were his last to me. I never heard his dear voice again. The doctor wanted to look at my eyes and took me to another room. I kissed Buck before I left.

I never knew if Buck was mad because I gave myself up. I only did it so he could die in a comfortable, clean bed and not be torn to shreds by more bullets. It wasn't that I wanted to live, or because I was afraid to die, but for his sake. Still, I know he must have suffered. He was hardly conscious of what he said.

⊛14

Mob

WHEN I CAME THROUGH the door, again handcuffs were snapped on my arms. They wouldn't allow me to get near Buck, still lying as I had left him, there on the floor. I begged to go near him just once more but was dragged out by one officer. God only knows because I can't explain the agony it caused me having to leave him. He did not answer when I called his name. I wondered if he had died while I was in the other room with that closed door between us. As they led me through the door I was crying and screaming, "Goodbye, Daddy. Goodbye."[1]

The small town was swarming with people. It looked as if they were going to mob us. Women sneered and laughed at me and posed pointed, accusing fingers at me and came to the car asking silly questions, then laughing when I shrank away from them. The officer assigned to me, the one who drove the car that took me away from there, asked them to stop being so unkind. Of course, I didn't expect anyone to be kind to me and I realized how most people felt, especially in small towns. The name "Barrow" struck fear in the minds of many because Clyde had little mercy for those who crossed him.[2]

The medicine the doctor had given me was beginning to take effect. One minute I would be screaming and crying, the next I just sat, staring ahead of me. My brain seemed blank. I could remember only one thing, that Buck had been taken away from me. One of the officers told me Buck wasn't dead and that he would be taken to a hospital. He also said I may be able to see him there.

Blanche Barrow being transferred to the Polk County jail in Des Moines. "When I came through the door, again handcuffs were snapped on my arms." (From the Blanche Caldwell Barrow scrapbooks, courtesy of Rhea Leen Linder)

I was taken to a small town[3] and kept in the courthouse because they didn't have a place in their jail for women. That afternoon I was taken to Des Moines, Iowa, and placed in jail. I didn't care what they did to me. They got a doctor and he took most of the glass from my eyes.

The rest of that day and night, as well as the next day, is still a blank to me. I was almost insane with grief and begged everyone I saw to take me to Buck. I thought he may be calling for me. At night it seemed as though I could hear him calling.

Later, when I was left alone in a cell, I tried to wash the blood out of my trousers and hair. But my right arm and hand were both so sore I could

Weapons recovered in Dexfield Park. "Clyde had little mercy for those who crossed him." (From the Blanche Caldwell Barrow scrapbooks, courtesy of Rhea Leen Linder)

hardly use them. I must have looked frightful. My hair was matted with blood and my face and eyes were swollen from glass and lead. I didn't even have a comb. But I was thankful. After all, the only thing I really wanted was Buck. When I went to bed, I soon cried myself to sleep.

I was awakened by a matron. She told me to get up and get dressed, that I was to go to the office. I asked what time it was. She told me two o'clock. I couldn't believe I had slept that long. When I was taken to an office downstairs, a bunch of officers were waiting for me there. I was told they were from Platte City, Missouri, and Kansas City and that they were going to take me back to Missouri. I didn't want to go back to Missouri. I wanted to stay there, as close to Buck as I could.

Some of the officers were not at all kind to me. Some were very kind. But as I said before, the last thing I expected was kindness from anyone. I didn't think anyone would understand my side of the story, even if they did believe

Blanche Barrow after being finger-printed at the Polk County jail, July 24, 1933. She weighed in at eighty-one pounds, down thirty-three and a half pounds in six months. "Later, when I was left alone in a cell, I tried to wash the blood out of my trousers and hair." (From the Blanche Caldwell Barrow scrapbooks, courtesy of Rhea Leen Linder)

it. No one would accept that I stayed with my husband simply because I loved him too much to allow him to go anyplace without me, even when it meant death or imprisonment for me.

After the officers spoke with me they all left the room, except for one man. He hadn't said much to me, but when he did speak he was kind, just like David R. Clevenger, the Platte County prosecuting attorney, and Constable Tom Hulett. Others had been cruel, although I didn't blame them for the way they felt. The man introduced himself. His name was Holt Coffey. He was the Platte County sheriff. He and his son had both been wounded in the gun battle of July 19.[4] I turned to face him.

"Well," I said. "Why don't you start cursing me? You are the one who got hurt. Don't you feel like killing me, like most of the rest feel?"

Blanche Barrow leaving Des Moines. "The trip back to Missouri was one of the most miserable I had ever made." (From the Blanche Caldwell Barrow scrap-books, courtesy of Rhea Leen Linder)

"I don't work that way," he said, shaking his head. "I try to be kind to everyone."

I would learn that Holt Coffey stuck by his word.

When they wanted me to sign extradition papers, I refused unless I could see Buck. They said Missouri would get me anyway. Then one of the men from Platte City promised that I would be taken to the hospital the next day to see Buck. So I signed the papers, even though I couldn't see well enough to read what they said. I'd have signed most anything to be near Buck. The next afternoon I was turned over to the Missouri officers without getting to see Buck.

Mr. Clevenger came to the jail cell to get me. Another officer, whose name I don't know, was with him. He wanted to question me, but I had little to say. I said I couldn't remember much, which was the truth, but he only thought I was lying. My mind was a blank. Even when I was alone and had tried to remember some of the things I had been asked about, I couldn't. For instance, I had been questioned a lot about where we were on the Fourth

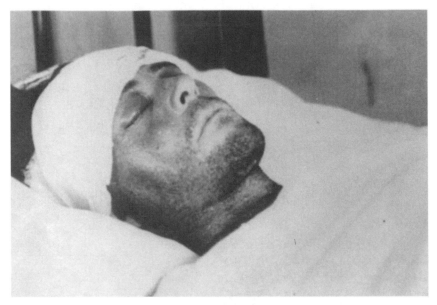

Buck Barrow in a Perry, Iowa, hospital. "The night Buck died I awoke about two o'clock in the morning." (From the Blanche Barrow scrapbooks, courtesy of Rhea Leen Linder)

of July, but try as I may, I couldn't remember.[5] I still don't remember a lot. Eventually Mr. Clevenger took pity on me and told the officer he believed I was telling the truth. So, the officer stop grilling me.[6]

The trip back to Missouri was one of the most miserable I had ever made. The next morning, July 26, I awoke in the Platte City jail. Everyone there was kind to me, although they wouldn't give me any news about Buck.

The night Buck died I awoke about two o'clock in the morning.[7] I thought I heard him calling me. It was a sign from Buck. I cried the rest of the night. I knew he must be dead. I tried to make myself believe it would be better for him if he did die now. He had nothing to live for anyway, only to face death all over again. I would have rather seen him dead than to have to spend the rest of his life in prison, or to get the death penalty, which I was sure he would get. Still, I was selfish enough to want him to live so I might have one more chance to see him.

The next morning, Sunday, I asked if he were dead, but no one would tell me. That afternoon, however, I was finally told he was dead and that his mother had been with him when he died.[8] Had it not been for thoughts of what might happen to my dear old father I am afraid I would have broken my promise to Buck and committed suicide. I wanted so much to die and be put out of my misery, but I knew that was the coward's way out. I tried to get hold of myself and take my punishment like a man, with a smile and my chin up. So far I have managed to do that.

My father wanted to come to me but I knew he had no means to do so. Besides, I didn't want him to see me in jail, and almost blind. So I wrote him and told him not to come, saying that I was all right. None of my so-called friends, or Buck's people, offered to come to me or help me in anyway, even though they could have.

Several doctors examined my eye. None of them thought it could be saved, but the Platte City doctor did all he could for me. Nearly everyone tried to help me forget my grief and keep from crying. Sheriff Coffey and his wife were very kind to me. They acted like a father and mother to me. Under the circumstances, I couldn't have asked for more kindness from my own people.

⊛15

Court

ON THE MORNING OF September 4, I appeared in court.[1] I pled guilty to assault with the intent to kill Sheriff Holt Coffey during the gun battle of July 19th. I wasn't guilty. I hadn't fired a shot that night, but I pled guilty out of ignorance, and because I feared receiving more time if I went to trial. I had nothing with which to fight my case. I was among strangers and most of them were against me. I had no money and I didn't want to testify against my dead husband. There was only my word that I was innocent,

The women's prison, Missouri State Penitentiary, Jefferson City. "I began serving my sentence on prison farm No. 1, for women." (Photograph by Blanche Barrow, courtesy of Rhea Leen Linder)

Female defendants, the Barrow-Parker harboring trial, February 22, 1935. Blanche Barrow is third from the right. "I pled guilty simply because the charges were certainly true." (Courtesy of the Texas/Dallas Archives Division, Dallas Public Library)

which few jurymen would believe. So there wasn't much left to do but plead guilty to a crime I didn't commit.[2]

I received a ten-year sentence in the Missouri penitentiary. I was told I would be eligible for a parole in two years. There was certainly no reason to believe I wouldn't be paroled. I was sure I could keep my record as clean in prison as I had in the Platte City jail.[3]

After receiving my sentence, I felt no different than before. Nothing seemed to matter anymore, except my desire to go free to my father; he had no one to support him. Other than that, I held no interest in life.

That night, at eleven o'clock, I was booked into the Missouri State Prison as convict number 43454. I began serving my sentence on prison farm No. 1, for women.

On September 9, Doctor S. P. Howard, the prison eye specialist, operated on my left eye, removing a large piece of glass from the pupil. I suffered with it until June 1934 when an exploratory operation revealed no more glass. X-rays confirmed this.[4] Nevertheless, two-thirds of the time I have suffered with that eye. Of course, it's not that I haven't had medical care. I have had every care possible. Warden J. M. Sanders and the other prison officials have tried in every way to help me, especially in dealing with my past. All have been kind to me.[5]

Clyde and Bonnie were killed on May 23, 1934.[6] I was glad they died together. That way neither one had to deal with the grief of losing the other—as I have. I think they should have been buried together. That was their last wish and the only one they asked be granted to them.[7] I suppose that if Buck and I had died together, the story would have been the same. Our wish would not have been granted either.

On February 22, 1935, I stood trial with twenty-two [*sic*] other defendants on charges of harboring Clyde Barrow and Bonnie Parker.[8] I pled guilty simply because the charges were certainly true—I had been with them, traveled with them, bought food and clothing for them. In the eyes of the law, I was guilty. I received a sentence of a year and a day, to be served along with my Missouri sentence. I am thankful for being allowed to serve my sentence that way. It was very fair.

Afterword

I HOPE BY NOW the reader understands how easily even the most innocent of persons can sometimes become trapped in a net of crime. I also hope young women and girls alike will learn from my story and avoid the pitfalls that can lead to a life of crime. It's a game you can't win. I am still in prison, forgotten by most all of my would-be friends, and Buck's people too.[1]

My father is all I have to look forward to when my time here has ended. I mean to go to him and try to make up to him for the suffering I have caused him. He is without a home and needs me. After I went to prison, I could no longer pay his expenses. His people could no longer keep him either, mainly because his daughter was in prison and a disgrace to the family name. My one hope is that my freedom doesn't come too late for me to be with him, to make his last days on Earth happy and free from worry about me. He has been faithful to me in every way he could.

Even though I failed once to turn someone away from the wrong road, I still believe an ex-convict can stay out of trouble and live an honest life, but only if they aren't afraid of work, which I am not! And even though I am blind in one eye and may be handicapped if I can't save it, I believe I can still live and work without having to turn to crime for money. In many cases, ex-convicts do return to crime, but I still think there are some who can, and will, walk the straight and narrow. I know it can be done and I want to prove it myself someday, if ever given the chance.[2]

The End. Fin.

Editor's Conclusion

BLANCHE BARROW WAS HELD in the Platte County jail in Platte City, Missouri, to await a preliminary hearing scheduled for August 5, on a charge of assault with intent to kill Sheriff Holt Coffey. Apparently at some point during her time in Platte City, Blanche's first husband, John Callaway, wrote a letter to Sheriff Coffey. The content of the letter is not entirely known but Blanche was incensed by it, writing to her mother that she wanted him to stay out of her life.[1]

Earlier, Blanche Barrow was visited by someone she had never known but grew to instantly despise, J. Edgar Hoover. The director of the U. S. Department of Justice Bureau of Criminal Investigation, later renamed the Federal Bureau of Investigation, made a special trip west to personally interrogate the wife of Buck Barrow. She had already developed a reputation for vacillating between docile uncommunicativeness and serious rants, none of which helped authorities determine the whereabouts of Bonnie and Clyde or the identity of the third man in the gang. Hoover quickly grew irritated with his bandaged, stubborn subject, threatening to gouge out her uninjured eye if she did not cooperate. She said nothing and the director left without making good his threat.[2]

To other officials, however, Blanche Barrow occasionally blurted out misleading information, including at least one bogus name for the fabled third man. The result was the arrest a few days later of Hubert Bleigh in Oklahoma. It is not known whether Blanche Barrow actually named Bleigh, who also used the alias Herbert Blythe and had a criminal record, or whether investigators merely jumped to some conclusion regarding her statement. Some have suggested Blanche Barrow mentioned a name that sounded like "Blythe." Others think, perhaps correctly, that Bleigh or Blythe was someone Blanche may have heard about or even met briefly while she was on the run with Bonnie and Clyde. She may have simply blurted out his name to win a few moments' peace during her interrogation. Unfortunately, Blanche does not mention the incident in her memoir and the subject never came up during any of her conversations with the editor.[3] Regardless, Bleigh was able to convince the authorities that he was not part of the Barrow gang. However, he could not convince them of his innocence regarding a burglary in Oklahoma.

Appearing in court for her hearing, Blanche Barrow was described as "refined of speech and manner." She waived her right to both a lawyer and a hearing. Bail was set at $15,000.[4]

In addition to the Platte County charges, she was also being considered for charges in Joplin stemming from the murders of Wes Harryman and Harry McGinnis. Platte County prosecuting attorney David R. Clevenger had to decide which jurisdiction had the best case. Clevenger decided on his own, Platte County, because so many witnesses could readily identify Blanche Barrow and still others were ready to testify that all members of the Barrow gang, including Blanche, were shooting on the night of July 19, 1933. Clevenger also wanted to hold Blanche until it could be determined whether or not Clarence Coffey, the sheriff's son, would recover from his wounds. Reportedly struck at least twice during the gunfight, young Coffey suffered one wound that was for a time considered life-threatening. When Coffey began to improve, a trial date was set for the initial charge.[5]

On September 4, Blanche Barrow appeared before Judge R. B. Bridgeman without a lawyer and entered a plea of guilty. She was asked if she wanted legal representation. "No," she answered. She was then asked if there was any reason why sentence should not be passed. "No," she answered.[12] Blanche Barrow was then assessed a ten-year sentence in the Missouri State Penitentiary. It was suggested, perhaps correctly, that the fact she had waived the cost of extradition proceedings from Iowa, as well as the cost of both a preliminary hearing and a trial, weighed in her favor. She would be eligible for parole in 1935. If parole was denied, she would still serve only five years and ten months with good behavior. And there was nothing in Blanche Barrow's manner that suggested she would be anything other than a quiet

Clarence Coffey, wounded in the Red Crown shoot-out and one of Blanche's many visitors in prison. (Photograph by Blanche Barrow, courtesy of Rhea Leen Linder)

prisoner. On the very day of her sentencing, Blanche Barrow was transported to the Missouri State Penitentiary in Jefferson City by Sheriff Coffey. There she was received as prisoner #43454.[6]

Apparently, the night of her arrival at the state prison Blanche Barrow underwent the first of a long series of procedures designed to save her injured eye. Warden J. M. Sanders had arranged for Dr. Stanley Howard, described as a Jefferson City specialist, to treat the eye. According to Blanche, Howard removed some glass from her eye, adding that it hurt for some time afterward. She also stated that the doctor and prison officials had been very nice to her.[7]

Indeed, Blanche told a number of people that her time in prison was not at all unpleasant, certainly not the type of experience her brother-in-law Clyde Barrow had endured in Texas. However, less than a year later Blanche Barrow did make a cryptic reference to the contrary in one letter, apparently following a change of prison personnel. "Things are better here now than they were before," she wrote her mother, "these people see that we have plenty

The Missouri State Penitentiary for Women, Camp 1. (Photograph by Blanche Barrow, courtesy of Rhea Leen Linder)

to eat."[8] The people to whom Blanche refers were a retired couple from Nodaway County, Missouri, a former state representative named William Job and his wife. Because of what appeared to be a genuine concern for the women under their watch, they were referred to by Blanche Barrow and her fellow inmates as "Uncle Billy" and "Aunt Clara." Blanche kept greeting cards from them in one of her scrapbooks all her life.

Nevertheless, despite better leadership, there were other concerns at the Missouri State Women's Prison. The facility was quarantined at least two times because of confirmed cases of smallpox and flu, the former being serious enough but the latter had killed hundreds of thousands worldwide just fifteen years earlier. Weather could be a concern as well. The summer of 1934 was the hottest on record in Missouri, with temperatures reaching triple digits day after day. "The heat came up from the highways in shimmering waves," wrote one historian, "like a mirage on a desert." In addition, the winters could be equally extreme. In one of her letters to her mother, Blanche mentions condensation freezing to the walls of her room at night, and occasionally she had stop writing to sweep melted droplets from the ceiling.[9]

Blanche Barrow was assigned to Camp 1, the "women's prison." The camp was located in Jefferson City, Missouri, on a high bluff overlooking the

Blanche Barrow and her prison buddy Edna Murray, "the Kissing Bandit." (Courtesy of Rhea Leen Linder)

Missouri River. A two-story stucco building with a prairie-style wooden front porch housed the eighty or so inmates. There Blanche Barrow found both the matrons in charge and the other convicts around her friendly and easygoing.[10] She was certainly one of the most notorious residents at the camp, but a few others were equally well known and most were a good deal more dangerous. One woman had murdered her abusive husband in a high-profile case. Another, convicted killer Irene McCann, was known for her spectacular jailbreaks. Edna Murray, whom Blanche befriended early on, was the infamous "Kissing Bandit." Most of the other women, like Blanche, were serving time largely because of their love for the wrong man. Still others were drug dealers or addicts.

Indeed, contraband drugs were a major commodity in the women's prison. While Blanche was incarcerated there, a well-marked, foot-worn path was found leading from the river to a hole beneath the fence around the compound. Prison officials promptly constructed a second perimeter fence between the river and the first fence in an attempt to stop the flow of drugs and other items.[11]

Blanche, still interested in photography, had her mother send her a camera, which she used throughout her prison term to record the images of those around her, the keepers as well as the kept. Some of the snapshots were mailed to friends; others wound up in her scrapbooks.

In October, the eye bandage was removed. Initially Blanche could barely see. However, by the end of the month her vision was improving, and she had had her "front teeth fixed." By December, though, she was bedridden for a week with severe eye pain. The eye was bandaged again. Blanche could only work sporadically as a kitchen helper because of recurring problems with her eye. Her condition did not improve and in January 1934, she was moved to the main prison hospital where she remained at least through March. The following month she was prescribed a topical medicine that she described as feeling like "liquid fire." Moreover, more than once in her letters she mentioned having to stop writing because of eye fatigue and pain. The following December, Blanche described her eye as being as bad as before the first operation. A year later, she was experiencing enough pain to cause her to be confined to bed once again. On January 29, 1936, she reported that her eye had swollen shut and that the specialist had informed her there was not a doctor in the country who could save it.[12]

Early in 1936, some members of the State of Missouri Board of Probation and Parole expressed interest in taking Blanche Barrow to another specialist in St. Louis, but apparently it came to nothing. She would eventually suffer complete loss of vision in the injured eye. Years later Blanche would lay blame for being denied access to the second specialist squarely on Harry S. Truman, then the junior U.S. Senator from Missouri. The reason for Truman's alleged action—or inaction—is not known, nor is there any hard evidence to support the claim, but Blanche remained convinced throughout her life that he had something to do with the inevitable loss of her eye. Blanche also stated that Truman was frequently the topic of conversation among prison officials, all of whom thought at the time he was being groomed for the White House.[13]

Throughout this period, Blanche Barrow spent an unknown number of hours hunched over a school tablet cathartically recording her memories of the brief but intense time she spent on the run with Bonnie and Clyde, W. D. Jones, and her dead husband.

When she was well enough she canned vegetables in the prison kitchen. In her spare time, apart from writing, she began reading as best she could, mostly movie magazines and self-help books at first, but then her interests broadened to subjects ranging from etiquette to reincarnation.[14] She also started keeping scrapbooks in prison. Eventually her collections filled six

Blanche Barrow in prison. Note injured eye. (Courtesy of Rhea Leen Linder)

known notebooks, the first of which bore a hand-lettered inscription on the inside cover: "News of the Dead—News of the Living Dead".

These books, which Blanche apparently continued to add to well into the 1960s, are filled with a variety of items. There are stamps, some from as far away as New Zealand, photographs, cartoons, poems clipped from the newspapers and magazines, self-help affirmations and beauty tips, an article titled "How to Be a Charming Companion," and holiday greeting cards from a number of different people ranging from friends, strangers, and relatives to people like Katherine Stark, Missouri's first lady, the family of the commissioner of the Missouri state penitentiary system, and even Sheriff Holt Coffey and his wife. The latter, a Christmas card, begins, "Darling little girl," and is signed, "Ma and Pa, Mr. and Mrs. Holt Coffey."

Blanche's father sent her a packet of postcards from Chicago. He also sent her several humorous cards, including a Christmas card collaboration with his ex-wife, Blanche's mother, which depicts part of someone's rear end poking out from behind a flap on the card. When the flap is opened, it reveals a naked Santa Claus standing in a tub fumbling with a towel. The caption reads: "Who's Behind—All This Merry Christmas Business Anyway?"

Lyrics to *"Bei Mir Bist Du Schoen,"* written in Blanche Barrow's hand. (Courtesy of Rhea Leen Linder)

In letters, she mentioned listening to a lot of "good new music" on the radio as well as a number of old songs that reminded her of Buck, although she was not specific.[15] Her scrapbooks, however, contain a substantial number of song lyrics, mostly clipped from newspapers. Among the selections she liked well enough to save were "Vote for Roosevelt Again," "Mexicali Rose," "Red Sails in the Sunset," "The Prisoner's Song," "The Yellow Rose of Texas," "Flirtation Walk," and "Ain't We Crazy?" just to name a few. She also copied in her own hand the lyrics to one of the most popular big-band tunes of the day, *"Bei Mir Bist Du Schoen,"* an old Yiddish folk song reworked for Benny Goodman's orchestra by trumpeter Ziggy Elman and sung by the Andrews Sisters.

There were occasional dances at the main prison compound with live bands as well as holiday dinners, activities that Blanche greatly enjoyed. In her scrapbooks, she placed an autographed promotional photograph of one visiting band, The Rural Ramblers. They were a five-piece group that specialized in western swing and featured a vocalist, fiddle, guitar, banjo, and bass.

Blanche loved to dance and by all accounts she was very good at it. She applied to a correspondence course in dancing that came complete with diagrams of select dance steps to place on the floor and practice. She also cut similar dance instructions and diagrams from newspapers and magazines and put them in her scrapbooks. By 1937, she had mastered popular dances like the jitterbug, rumba, samba, and tango.[16]

The men's prison, or "the big prison" as the women called it, hosted movies on Friday nights. Features like *Roll Along Cowboy* with Smith Ballew, Cecilia Parker, and Stamford Fields were standard, usually accompanied by some short musical feature such as *Who's Who* and a newsreel. The admission was five cents. Blanche attended many of these movies. She loved movies all of her life. Her scrapbooks are full of pictures and articles about movie stars like Clark Gable, Myrna Loy, Carole Lombard, William Powell, Jean Harlow, Betty Davis, and Shirley Temple.

Blanche Barrow's periodic visits to the main prison allowed her to fraternize with males. She apparently had a brief encounter of some kind with "the boy in the warden's office" in the fall of 1934. There are few details, but their relationship was evidently ended abruptly by prison officials in December.[17]

There were other suitors, some from Blanche Barrow's past, and some late arrivals, many no doubt drawn to her as much by her notoriety as by her exceptional good looks. Indeed, she apparently received numerous letters from men interested in her eventual post-prison life. Cards and letters from these numerous boyfriends she relegated to her scrapbooks.[18]

These correspondences begin with salutations like "Honey," "Darling," and "Dearest Blanche," and conclude with statements such as "Lovingly yours, Howard"; "Wish you were leaving with me, Rick"; and "I love you too much, Freddie." Other boyfriends included Mike, Eddy (not her future husband), Charles, Frank, Jack, Ray, and Tom. Another man named Bill had quite a sense of humor. Bill wrote often from some unspecified and apparently quite remote location in California. In one letter he mentions a Christmas-time visit of the wives and girlfriends of "some of these guys . . . Santa Claus sure emptied his old sack when he brought those gals to see their men. We had quite a show!" He also mentioned "mountain air" and echoes, writing, "last night I heard this guy over in the next county making love to his wife. Good old echo." In other letters Bill discusses cold nights, relatives in Houston, and his love of a certain photograph Blanche sent to him. "Just between you and I, this is strictly confidential, I am plenty proud of that picture. I will always be a sucker for white dresses on dark girls from now on!"[19]

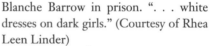

Blanche Barrow in prison. ". . . white dresses on dark girls." (Courtesy of Rhea Leen Linder)

One intriguing postcard in Blanche Barrow's collection is signed simply "N. C." Postmarked May 24, 1940, the message is a lonely lament about having been forgotten by Blanche. The unhappiness continues on the front of the card where lines like "A friend in need," "Someone cares for you," and "Why don't you write?" are written across the picture. Of course, this card was sent more than a year after Blanche's release from prison and a month after her marriage to her third and final husband, which certainly accounts for the lack of return correspondence.[20]

During her prison days Blanche Barrow's longest pen-and-ink relationship seems to have been with a young man named "Freddie." He seems to have been employed in the world of professional horse racing, although neither his exact function nor the identity of his employer is clear. There is some evidence that he may have been associated with the legendary horse War Admiral. Whatever the case, he appears to have been involved in training, writing, "terribly busy as I am running a horse."[21]

Freddie wrote often between 1936 and 1938. From the postmarks— Cincinnati, Cleveland, Lancaster (Ohio), Kansas City, Laurel (Maryland), New Orleans, and Dallas—it is clear that he traveled extensively in his job. He wrote of spending off-hours at the movies, reading, or catching up on

An extremely unusual postcard, featuring a photograph of the U.S.S. *Arizona*, sent by a boyfriend to Blanche long before the attack on Pearl Harbor (Courtesy of Rhea Leen Linder)

his sleep. He sent money to Blanche and drove her mother to see her in prison at least once. And although Blanche Barrow implies in an undated letter to her mother that Freddie had in essence led her on and then abandoned her ("guess he has gone the way all fair weather friends go"), it appears from many of his correspondences to her that the reverse was actually the case. On October 9, 1937, he wrote, "I am still wondering why I have not heard a word from you. Let me know what is the matter." Then on November 1, 1937, he added, "Dearest, Please don't wait so long to write." Eight days later he sent another letter: "Dearest Sweetheart, . . . I did not receive a letter from you last week as I expected to do. What is the matter? Are the other boyfriends taking too much of your time?" The latter question is interesting considering the fact that in the same letter Freddie mentions Blanche's jealousy over his writing to one of the other women imprisoned with her. She eventually forced him to stop writing to the other inmate.[22]

By December 26, 1937, Freddie seemed resigned, writing that he suspected Blanche no longer wanted to hear from him. He mentioned having written four previous letters with no answer, but he had nonetheless written her again because he could not get her out of his mind. He closed by wishing

Lillian Pond Horton (Blanche's mother), Blanche Barrow, and Cumie Barrow during a prison visit on August 5, 1934. Blanche chided her mother and Cumie Barrow for not helping her gain her parole. (Courtesy of Rhea Leen Linder)

her a merry Christmas and by stating that he had always suspected she would lose interest in him one day: "whatever happens remember I love you always." He wrote sporadically throughout much of 1938, then the letters ended.

Total strangers frequently wrote to Blanche Barrow. One young lady, Alba Chapman, was a friend of the daughter of J. M. Sanders, at the time warden of the Missouri State Penitentiary and later chairman of the Missouri Board of Probation and Parole. A well-known Kansas City, Missouri, good Samaritan affectionately referred to as "Mother Clark"—in her nineties at the time—kept in close contact with Blanche, writing frequently, visiting her in prison, and sending her inspirational items. But most strangers were like "Harry" from San Francisco, who wrote in 1937, "I would like to become acquainted with you very much."[23]

Blanche also heard from her first husband, John Callaway, while she was in prison. He wrote at least once and sent a gift. Her response to him, however, resulted in his never attempting to contact her again. Blanche Barrow then wrote to her mother, "I looked at John's picture and just wondered how I was ever fool enough to stay with him as long as I did. I hope he does not come near me when I am a free woman."[24]

Reporters occasionally visited Blanche. On September 10, 1936, Blanche was quoted in the *Kansas City Star* as having said, "I've seen enough of that rough and tumble life. And when I get out of here, I'm going back to my father in Oklahoma where I hope the world forgets me. Everyone who ever associated with my husband and Clyde has forgotten me, and it is no use for them to look me up."

In the first months of her prison term Blanche heard frequently from her mother and father, as well as Cumie Barrow. She also received visits at various times from all three, including one on August 5, 1934, that included Blanche's mother Lillian, Marie Barrow Francis, Joe Francis, LC Barrow and his wife, Audrey Faye Barrow, and Cumie Barrow. However, by 1935 Blanche was complaining that she had not received a letter from either her mother or Cumie Barrow in a long time. She wrote to her mother, "You can not realize how much a letter means to anyone in a place like this." She also tried repeatedly to find out about her half-sister Lucinda, who had given birth to a child in 1934. But Blanche was unable either to learn the name of the child or to obtain a picture until much later.[25]

Blanche Barrow mentioned "fair-weather friends" like "Freddie," whom she basically accused of abandoning her. She also rather angrily chided her mother and Cumie Barrow for not helping her build a file for her first parole hearing, scheduled for October 7, 1935. Among other things, she needed offers of employment, which both women had evidently first promised to help with and had then forgotten about it. "I guess he [Matt Caldwell, her father] is the only one I have left now who will try to help me get out [of prison]," she wrote her mother. Then three weeks before the hearing Blanche wrote again, "If she [Cumie Barrow] is not interested, ok. Just forget it. If she would turn me down now, she would turn Buck down. . . . I will be free from here in 1939 (with good behavior) if I have to do it all, which I am sure I will have to do."[26]

There is also a cryptic reference to an alternative identity once used by Blanche Barrow. In a letter to her mother dated April 10, 1934, Blanche wrote, "can I ever make you understand that I left that name 'Lua Talb' and the past that went with it and that I will never go by that name anymore." We can only speculate about the full meaning of this passage. It could very well have been an alias used by Blanche during her time on the run with her husband, either following his escape from the Ferguson prison

Blanche's half-sister Lucinda, West Dallas, Texas, 1934. (Courtesy of Rhea Leen Linder)

farm in March 1930 or during the flight with Bonnie and Clyde. Regardless, in yet another letter to her mother, Blanche reveals more feelings about her past life: "and don't worry about this place [prison] hurting me. I have already been hurt all they can hurt me. Nothing hurts me anymore. As for the past, I am dead too." The latter part of this statement is particularly interesting considering the inscription on the inside flap of Blanche Barrow's first scrapbook: "News of the Dead—News of the Living Dead."[27]

By spring 1936, Blanche was on better terms with her mother, perhaps because she had persuaded boyfriends like Freddie to drive Lillian to Missouri for visits. However, her relationship with Cumie Barrow seems to have come to an end (even though she is listed in Blanche's parole file as offering a place for her daughter-in-law to live). Other members of the Barrow family kept in touch, particularly LC, the youngest brother of Buck and Clyde. She had a very cordial letter from LC, written from his own

A page from one of Blanche Barrow's scrapbooks. Left to right: Ralph Fults, Blanche Barrow, Raymond Hamilton. (Courtesy of Rhea Leen Linder)

prison cell in Huntsville, Texas, in 1938, neatly tucked away in her scrapbooks at the end of her life. At the time, Blanche lamented LC's robbery conviction and subsequent sentencing to five years in the Texas penitentiary. And she expressed interest in other family members, like the youngest Barrow sibling, Marie. She clipped numerous newspaper articles related to members of the family and former gang members and placed them in her scrapbooks, including stories about Cumie Barrow's injury during a gunfight at the family service station in 1938, and LC Barrow's arrest at the East Texas farmhouse of his uncle Jim Muckleroy (the same place Blanche and Buck hid after the latter's escape from the Ferguson prison farm in 1930). There were other articles as well, including one about former Barrow cohorts Frank Hardy and Hollis Hale, accomplices in the 1932 Oronogo, Missouri, bank robbery and friends of Blanche's.[28]

One of Blanche Barrow's scrapbooks contains a page dominated by a photograph of herself, flanked by pictures of Ralph Fults and Raymond Hamilton.

Blanche also tried to find out the fate of W. D. Jones, whom she had heard nothing about since the split-up in Dexfield Park, Iowa. As late as December 1934 she was still wondering about him. "Guess the poor little innocent thing is free," she wrote her mother. "He should be in his mother's arms with a diaper on."[29] Unbeknownst to Blanche at the time, Jones was serving a fifteen-year sentence for "murder without malice" in the January 6, 1933, death of Tarrant County Deputy Sheriff Malcolm Davis. It would be a long time before he was in his mother's arms again.

Within two months of the above-mentioned letter, however, Blanche Barrow would have a chance to see W. D. Jones, if not actually speak with him. On February 22, 1935, she and Jones and twenty other defendants went on trial in Dallas, Texas, on federal charges of harboring Bonnie and Clyde. Harboring a federal fugitive was a relatively new criminal offense at the time and the "Barrow-Parker harboring trial," as it came to be known, was the government's initial test case. Five of the defendants, including Blanche Barrow, entered guilty pleas. Jones and the others took their chances with the court. In the end, all were convicted and the sentences ranged from one hour to two years. Blanche received a year and a day for harboring Bonnie and Clyde. The added sentence was to run concurrently with her Missouri conviction, meaning she would actually serve no extra time. It was part of the deal for her plea of guilty. Jones got the maximum, two years. But his sentence would also run concurrently with his other conviction, despite the innocent plea. Soon he and Blanche were back in their respective cells.[30]

Throughout 1936 and 1937, help came to Blanche Barrow from an unexpected source, Wilbur Winkler. Winkler had been married to Buck's older sister Artie. He co-owned the beauty shop in Denison, Texas, that was managed by Artie and where Blanche worked while Buck was in prison. However, the fact that Blanche's former employer, and husband of her sister-in-law, had begun working on her case probably came as a bit of a surprise because by then Winkler and Artie had divorced. In fact, by July 1937 Artie had long since left Denison and Winkler was remarried. The breakup, at least from Winkler's point of view, vacillated between annoyance and fondness. In a letter to Blanche, Winkler complained of his former wife's successful attempts to extract money and quit claim deeds from him, then stated that he felt sorry for her, and implied that he still loved her, though warily. In another letter he wrote in a self-effacing manner: "'A' is married again, you know . . . guess anything was better than I." Regardless, Winkler had been writing letters to a number of Missouri officials in Blanche Barrow's behalf and Blanche was very pleased. "He [Winkler] sure has come to the front for me and I sure do appreciate it," she wrote her mother.[31]

In letters to Missouri governor Guy Parks, as well as to Paul Rentz, commissioner of the Department of Penal Institutions for the State of Missouri, and J. M. Sanders, chairman of the State of Missouri Board of Probation and Parole, Winkler offered to pay all of Blanche Barrow's medical expenses related to treating her eye injury, to give her a job when she was released from prison, and to pay all of her travel and clothing expenses from Missouri to Texas. Winkler also asked both men to read the book *Fugitives* for proof of Blanche Barrow's innocence.

The latter statement seems to support the argument that some aspects of the portrayal of Blanche Barrow in that book, supposedly authored by Nell Barrow Cowan and Emma Parker but actually ghosted by Dallas reporter Jan Fortune, may have been fabricated to help Barrow's chances for a parole and to deter any future prosecution. This is particularly clear considering Blanche Barrow's rather candid statements made during interviews with the editor concerning her clear complicity in a series of petty robberies perpetrated with her husband before his voluntary return to prison in 1931. Moreover, regarding the image of Blanche charging off down that street in Joplin, screaming and crying (as even Blanche herself writes in her own memoir), it is more than likely that it too was a fabrication, especially since no other eyewitness accounts support the story.

In his letters to Blanche Barrow, Winkler seems deeply interested in helping her return to her pre-prison career as a beautician. He offered to contact the Texas Board of Cosmetology on her behalf and inquire as to whether she needed to keep renewing her beautician's license each year, or if she could just pay a flat fee to cover a span of years. He also asked if she was aware of a new product, "'machincless' pads for giving permanents." He offered to send her some samples to practice with, writing that he thought it was a wonderful invention.

Blanche Barrow's father was also working for her release, supplying names of potential employers that might provide his daughter with a job. A job was one of the main criteria for parole but such was not easy to obtain in the depths of the Great Depression.

Although President Roosevelt won re-election by an enormous margin in 1936, taking all but two states, the luster of the New Deal was beginning to fade. Recession and unemployment continued to linger, indeed showing few signs of ever receding despite the implementation of so many innovative relief programs beginning during the famous "Hundred Days" three years earlier. And although the industrial North was still reeling from the dire economic picture, it was independent farmers who were suffering the most, subsisting on less than 60 percent of their 1929 income. Then in 1936, the U.S. Supreme Court ruled that the Agricultural Adjustment Act was unconstitutional. The economic relief to farmers that was supplied by the AAA was thus eliminated just as raging dust storms steadily increased across the Plains states, eroding topsoil from the Dakotas to Texas. Resentment, fear, and violence frequently swelled within the ranks of an increasingly desperate working class.[32]

Demonstrations by independent farmers across the nation and the destruction of truckloads of milk by dairy operators continued to disrupt the produce industry. In 1937, a number of strikes by thousands of workers at General Motors and U.S. Steel resulted in the recognition of the exclusive right of unions to negotiate contracts, wages, and working conditions with company management. Still, the feeling persisted that bankers, business moguls, and politicians were the consummate villains of the Great Depression. The notion was reinforced in 1938 with the formation of the House Un-American Activities Committee (HUAC) and its immediate investigation of trade unions, Roosevelt's Works Progress Administration (WPA), and even the Campfire Girls. HUAC was seen by many as the tool of big business, and much public protest was raised against it, but to no avail.[33]

In the prevailing climate, it was difficult enough for ordinary citizens to find work, much less convicted felons with the last name of Barrow. Despite help from people like Wilbur Winkler and others—including Platte County (Missouri) Sheriff Holt Coffey and even Katherine Stark, wife of the governor of Missouri—Blanche Barrow remained an inmate until March 25, 1939. On that date, a conditional commutation of her ten-year prison term became effective.[34]

"Badman Barrow's Widow Quits Cell" read the headlines. The conditions set forth in the commutation included breaking no laws, associating with no person "of questionable character," nor "frequenting places of ill-repute." Blanche Barrow was also forbidden the use of alcohol and narcotics, and she had to submit a written report signed by her sponsor or a law enforcement official listing her whereabouts, employment information, and wages. She was required to submit such a report monthly until March 1941.

Blanche Barrow was also specifically ordered to leave Cole County, Missouri, and never return, an order she could easily comply with. Indeed, Blanche Barrow would have no difficulty with any aspect of the commutation. According to Warden J. M. Sanders, she had been a "model prisoner," which accounted largely for the commutation—time off with good behavior. Despite her later assertion that her early release came about as a result of friends like Sheriff Coffey and an agent with the Department of Justice Bureau of Criminal Investigation, Blanche Barrow walked out of prison because of her demeanor while she was incarcerated there, although such friendships certainly did not hurt.[35]

Regardless of the exact nature of her release, when freedom finally came for Blanche Barrow she found herself stepping into a world that was in many ways vastly different from the one she had left five and a half years earlier. As the decade of the 1930s progressed there was less focus on crime and rampaging outlaws in the news media and more emphasis on the darkening world situation. That is not to say, however, that criminal activity waned, but by 1939 many of the more notorious gangsters and outlaws like John Dillinger, Pretty Boy Floyd, the Barkers, Al Capone, Bonnie and Clyde, and all the others who made such "good copy" for reporters, had either been killed, imprisoned, or executed.[36]

In other news that broke during the years Blanche spent inside prison walls, Germany's president, Paul von Hindenburg, died and Adolph Hitler, already chancellor and dictator, assumed the German presidency as well, thus erasing any semblance of democracy. In addition, Italy and Ethiopia went to war over possession of Somalia. In 1935, the federal Works Progress Administration was organized, the Social Security Act was signed into law by President Roosevelt, and Huey P. Long, U.S. Senator from Louisiana, was assassinated in Baton Rouge. In 1936, Germany invaded the Rhineland, dust storms raged across the American Plains states, and civil war erupted in Spain.

In 1937 the world's largest dirigible, Germany's *Hindenburg*, exploded and crashed in a fiery heap near Lakehurst, New Jersey; aviatrix Amelia Earhart disappeared over the Pacific Ocean while trying to become the first woman to circumnavigate the globe by air; and the recently enacted federal minimum wage act, challenged by business interests, was upheld by the U.S. Supreme Court.

In 1938, Germany invaded Austria and ceded part of Czechoslovakia; Italy declared Libya an Italian possession; and the Japanese army pushed

Blanche and her father. (Courtesy of
Rhea Leen Linder)

further into China. In Spain, the bloody revolution led by Generalissimo
Francisco Franco expanded, threatening to topple the republican government. Although the United States remained neutral in the Spanish conflict,
many Americans volunteered to fight against Franco's fascist revolutionaries.
Nearly 50 percent of those volunteers died in Spain.

In 1939, the year of Blanche Barrow's release from the Missouri State
Penitentiary, Spain fell to Franco, Japan continued to ravage China, and
Germany invaded Poland, touching off World War II.[37]

Blanche Caldwell Barrow was released from the Missouri State Penitentiary on March 24, 1939, the day before her conditional commutation
was to officially go into effect. She left immediately for Garvin, Oklahoma,
as specified in the terms of her commutation, where she moved in with
her father. It is thought by some that she later stayed with her half-sister
Lucinda Hill, and perhaps even Buck Barrow's older sister Artie.[38]

Just six days after Blanche Barrow's release, a writer from Sherman, Texas,
named Frank E. Bronaugh wrote a letter to her proposing that she write

"a long account . . . of the intimate, detailed experiences of your life, all about how you came to know Buck Barrow, to marry him, and the unfortunate events that led up to your arrest and of your experiences in prison . . . the longer the better." Bronaugh offered to pay Blanche twenty-five dollars for the story, which was to be published in some unspecified "fact magazine." He stated that he had recently made a similar deal with Alice Davis, the mother of Floyd and Raymond Hamilton, for the stories of her two sons.[39]

It is not known what Blanche Barrow thought of the proposal, or whether she accepted the offer. She probably did not accept, but she evidently thought enough of the letter to keep it for the rest of her life. She certainly had more than enough material compiled in her own memoir, but only one person—Esther Weiser—was aware of its existence, and that was not until years later.[40] From passages in the manuscript, as well as actions later in life, it is apparent that Blanche Barrow considered her memoir much more than a cathartic experience. She wanted it published. However, as we have seen, there is much about her story that is wholly unflattering to a number of people who were still living in 1939. She may not have wanted to deal with those dynamics. Also, she was interested in distancing herself from her past, not only in compliance with her conditional commutation, but for another reason as well—a man.

It probably came as no surprise to anyone who knew her that Blanche remarried little more than a year after her release from prison. At twenty-eight years old, she was quite an attractive woman who, despite her past, still loved to laugh and apparently looked forward to what the rest of her life might hold. It was well known she had received numerous letters from prospective suitors throughout her time behind bars. That she narrowed the playing field so quickly may have startled some though, considering her feelings for her dead husband. But to others, Blanche's final choice seemed logical, even predictable.

Edwin Bert Frasure was born March 23, 1912, in Dawson, Texas, about seventy miles south of Dallas in Navarro County. Throughout his life, he was known simply as Eddie. Frasure's father was also from Navarro County but his mother was born in Alabama. Although admittedly obscure, a few correlations, or rather coincidences, can be drawn between the Frasures and the Barrows. First, two of Buck Barrow's uncles lived in Navarro County, and second, though contradicted by some members of the family, the elder Barrow men—Henry, Buck's father, and Henry's brothers James, and Frank— were all born in Alabama.[41] Of course, none of this really points to anything substantial, but more than one person observed other apparent similarities between Eddie Frasure and Buck Barrow, with respect to personality and, to a lesser extent, physical appearance.

Apart from Buck Barrow's penchant for crime and a notably violent temper, for which there can be no comparison, Eddie Frasure otherwise appeared very similar to his predecessor. By all accounts, he was very gregarious, friendly, and outgoing, as some have described Buck. Frasure also loved to joke and laugh a lot and, again like Barrow, was quite mechanically inclined. A master carpenter, both rough and finish, he eventually became supervisor of a Dallas architectural and engineering firm. He was also a talented singer and guitarist, something Buck Barrow did not have in common with him. However, another of the Barrows sang and played not only the guitar but the saxophone as well—Clyde.[42]

Although Frasure was evidently more handsome than Buck Barrow, both men nevertheless were remembered as possessing the same earthy, swarthy, almost animal attractiveness.[43] It may be hard to imagine such traits in a killer like Barrow, but people are a lot more complex than their criminal profiles would have us believe. Still, regardless of any real or supposed resemblance between the two men, Blanche became deeply attached to Frasure within months of her release from prison.

Apparently from the very beginning of his relationship with Blanche Caldwell, Eddie Frasure was, for a number of reasons, extremely wary of her association with the name of Barrow. The foremost consideration was no doubt the very real possibility of being dragged into some unsavory situation because of past associations. There was also the stigma of being an ex-convict, of which Blanche wrote, almost as a postscript to her own memoir:

> But that was not the end. The story of the parolee has yet to be told. It's a story that magazines, parole officials, and news reporters seldom mention—the story of the great obstacles faced by the ex-convict who tries to find a job, and then to merely hold on to that job once they are lucky enough to find employment. It's the story of walking until the soles of their shoes have worn through and blisters and calluses cover their feet. It's the story of looking for a job, any job, only to be told there is no room for ex-convicts, or for those whose names are so well known to the public.

Add to this the problem faced by Frasure, that of a man in love with a woman whose deep and utterly emotional past he could never be a part of

Eddie Frasure in the navy, 1943. (Courtesy of Rhea Leen Linder)

nor hope to understand. Not a little bit of jealousy was combined with Frasure's genuine fear of Blanche's past.[44] For that reason, Blanche herself tried as best she could to close the door to her past. However, as we shall see, she never let go completely. Nevertheless, Eddie Frasure never knew it, or never let it be known that he knew it. And for his benefit, Blanche kept her past to herself and made sure others around her did the same. It was the latter task that eventually led to a complete break between Blanche and her mother.

In a 1939 letter, Blanche expressed extreme displeasure with her mother's behavior during an Oklahoma visit that included Eddie Frasure. Apparently, Lillian could not stop mentioning Buck Barrow and her daughter's misadventures with the dead outlaw. Blanche, trying to avoid straining a blossoming relationship, evidently tried, rather unsuccessfully, to get her mother to abandon the topic. In her letter, written after the fact, Blanche admonished her mother for callously dredging up such "sour onions and dirty shirts" in front of her new boyfriend. Indeed at least twice before, while in prison as early as October 1933 and again the following year, she asked her mother to refrain from mentioning the past, although Blanche herself never seemed averse to writing about Buck often. Nevertheless, the incident in Oklahoma in 1939 began a serious deterioration in the relationship between Blanche and her mother. They evidently had some contact during the following three years, but after that there appears to have been a complete break.[45]

"Scarecrow." (Courtesy of Rhea
Leen Linder)

In a letter dated April 16, 1940, the director of the Missouri Board of
Probation and Parole granted permission for Blanche to marry Eddie Frasure.[46] Three days later, on April 19, the couple was married in Rockwall,
Texas. The newlyweds moved to 1601 Durant in nearby Dallas and began
their lives together as man and wife. Blanche's father, Matt Caldwell, moved
in with the Frasures. On October 7, 1942, ten months to the day after the
Japanese attack on Pearl Harbor, Eddie Frasure joined the Navy Seabees
as a construction engineer. He was thirty years old at the time. He trained
in Virginia and shipped out to the Pacific as a third-class petty officer in
the 64th Battalion, Company C, Third Platoon. Although his primary function
was that of a construction engineer, Frasure and the others in his battalion
were trained as combatants as well. Ironically, Frasure was the BAR man
for his platoon, carrying the same weapon Buck Barrow used in Platte City.

Blanche jokingly referred to another weapon in a note on the back of a
photograph of herself she once sent to Frasure while he was stationed
overseas. "Daddy, Remember you ask[ed] for this scar[e] crow [the photograph of herself]. Just put it between you and the Japanese and you'll have

the war won all by yourself—this will frighten them too [sic] *Death*." The salutation is particularly interesting. Blanche referred to Frasure with the same term of endearment she used with Buck. Frasure island-hopped all across the Pacific throughout World War II. He was discharged in 1946.[47]

During that time, Blanche went to work in Dallas as a dispatcher for the Yellow Cab Company. Her employment there may have been the reason behind her obtaining a reissue of her birth certificate on July 30, 1943, a document witnessed and signed by her mother.[48] Whether she faced the ex-convict's challenge in looking for a job that she cited at the end of her memoir cannot be known. What is known, however, is that for the rest of her life, Blanche remained under surveillance. Federal, state, and local authorities kept track of her movements and made their presence known to her in a variety of ways. The Dallas police department, in particular, liked to call Blanche periodically, especially if she moved, just to let her know they were aware of where she lived. Sometimes the callers were very arrogant and ill mannered.[49] Blanche was never known to be angered by the calls. To the contrary, she usually made jokes about them. Eddie Frasure did not think it was quite as funny. Regardless, during Frasure's years in the service, Blanche evidently worked for the cab company without incident, despite the spectral omnipresence of the authorities.

On November 2, 1946, Eddie Frasure returned to Durant Street in Dallas and the wife he had known for only three years before shipping out. His wife described the reunion like that of being newlyweds all over again, something that apparently remained so for years.[50] She retired from the Yellow Cab Company and as far as anyone knows, lived the rest of her life as a housewife, never again having to deal with being an ex-convict in search of a job.

On September 19, 1947, Blanche's father died. Besides his only child, Matt Caldwell was survived by one sister, two brothers, and a number of nieces and nephews.[51] Caldwell had lived most of his life as a farmer and logger. He was also a deeply religious man who occasionally during his long life felt the calling to bear witness to his faith. These episodes would result in brief periods of preaching as a lay minister. Over the years, these "times of calling", as he referred to them, were misunderstood by some who had the notion that Matt Caldwell was a professional preacher. He was not. He was a farmer who occasionally "testified" to small gatherings about his faith.

Eventually her father's religious convictions came to influence Blanche and her husband. Although they would never give up their love of the

Blanche Barrow in downtown Dallas, Texas. (Courtesy of Rhea Leen Linder)

occasional beer, dancing, and general "honky-tonking," as they called it, Blanche and Eddie began attending church regularly and volunteering their services there as well. Eddie, who sang in a very good barbershop quartet at the time, began singing in the church choir as well. And Blanche began teaching Sunday school.

By then, in the early 1950s, Blanche and Eddie were living in what was then a rural part of Dallas County called Pleasant Grove, at 222 Bridges. They had spent some time moving from place to place in various states because of the nature of Eddie's job as a construction engineer, but by 1951 they appear to have settled for good in the Dallas area. Prior to that time, whenever her husband's work had taken him to a new location, Blanche had gone with him. Some have said, jokingly, that she did so "to keep her good eye on him." However, those making the quip were just as quick to add that Blanche always traveled with Eddie for much the same reason she

Matt Caldwell logging near Idabel, Oklahoma, 1906. (Courtesy of Rhea Leen Linder)

traveled with Buck, "because she was a homemaker and wherever Eddie went she was going to make a home!"[52] She also no doubt had more than a little fun seeing if those keeping her under surveillance could find her. They always did.

One day late in 1951, Blanche received a long-distance call from Grand Rapids, Michigan. A friend of hers who worked at the Federal Square Grill there had been talking to one of her customers, a young single mother named Esther who was in search of a solution to her small son's health problem. The boy suffered from severe asthma and the damp, cold Michigan climate only made matters worse. Blanche's friend overheard Esther's lament and suggested she and her son move to Dallas.

"Dallas!" Esther had said. "But I don't know anybody there." The waitress said she knew someone. Before long Esther found herself on the phone in a corner of the cafe, speaking to a strange Texan named Blanche who insisted she drop everything, move with her son to Pleasant Grove, and stay with her and her husband for as long as necessary. Esther had heard of southern hospitality, but even this seemed unusual.

Blanche told Esther to catch the first train south. Once in Dallas she was to hail a cab and have it take her from Union Station, downtown, all the way to her house in Pleasant Grove, a trip of some forty-five to sixty minutes at the time. The first thing Esther saw when she arrived in front of Blanche's modest frame house at 222 Bridges in "the Grove" was a quaint white picket fence and a garden thick with brilliantly colored flowers. "Blanche didn't have a green thumb," Esther said. "She had a green arm! What a warm, welcomed sight for a couple of strangers like us."[53]

Esther and her son moved in with Blanche and Eddie. A friend of Blanche's who lived nearby was giving up her job in downtown Dallas and suggested that Esther apply for the position. She did so and got the job. Every day thereafter she walked from the Frasures' house, across a barnyard, to the neighbor's house where her son spent the day while she caught the bus at its southernmost stop and rode all the way into downtown Dallas and her new job. Blanche had seriously considered babysitting the boy. She really loved children and literally grieved because she could never bear her own. But neither she nor Eddie felt comfortable with the child's asthma, his medications, and periodic seizures. Her neighbor had some experience with such, and the deal was struck.

For several months the arrangement continued. Esther and Blanche and Eddie and all of their friends got along very well. During the entire time, the name of Barrow never came up and Esther never had any idea of her hostess's past, none whatsoever. She never dreamed this Sunday school teacher could have ever been anything but that—a Sunday school teacher, albeit one who still enjoyed "honky-tonking" every so often with her handsome, choir-singer husband.

Eventually, however, Blanche began to feel cramped in the house in "the Grove." As Esther remembered, it had more than just a little to do with Eddie. "He and I were getting along a little too well," she recalled. "And Blanche could be very jealous and possessive." One day Blanche asked Esther if she might consider moving to her own place, adding, "Eddie and me are still a bit like newlyweds. Sometimes we just like to chase each other around the house naked. And we can't do that with guests."[54] Esther got the hint and soon she and her son found there own place nearby. There were no hard feelings and everyone remained very close. It was after Esther moved out of the Frasures' house that she discovered the nature of Blanche's otherworldly past.

One day Esther received a frantic phone call at work from the neighbor who was taking care of her son. Esther's former husband, the father of her son, Jon, was at the door demanding to see the child. This sent waves of panic through Esther as it had taken a court order to take the boy out of

Michigan. She was afraid her former husband might now take their son and not return him.

"What should I do?" the neighbor asked.

"You'll have to let him see his son."

"What if he doesn't bring him back?"

"We'll deal with that when it happens," Esther responded.

After work she went to Blanche's house to hide out until the coast was clear.

Blanche noted that Esther was extremely nervous, so to take her mind off of things she began regaling her with wild tales of some woman who had got herself mixed up with a group of outlaws and killers, one of whom was the woman's husband. Initially Esther did not pay much attention to the stories, thinking to herself, "This lady sure has some imagination!" After a while, however, she began to realize Blanche was more than implying that she was the woman in the stories.

"Why are you making this up?" Esther asked.

"I'm not making it up!" Blanche answered, puzzled by Esther's reaction. With that she got up from the kitchen table and disappeared into a closet. A few minutes later, she emerged with a box of yellowing photographs, official-looking papers, and a number of old detective magazines and *Police Gazettes*. Everything was related to Bonnie and Clyde, of whom Esther knew little, apart from the fact they were once dangerous outlaws. She had never heard of Buck Barrow. But in all the pictures and in every magazine there were images of a much younger, emaciated Blanche along with Bonnie and Clyde and this Buck Barrow, who turned out to be Blanche's second husband. Esther was dumbstruck, but fascinated. As Blanche described Buck in detail, Esther was amazed at how similar he seemed to be to Eddie, especially with respect to personality. But Esther remained speechless as she sat there in utter disbelief listening to her friend, this Sunday school teacher, poring over events from another life, another world—recounting robberies, incredible escapes, the bloody bodies of slain officers, shards of glass spraying into her eyes, brain tissue oozing from her husband's head, and gunfight after gunfight. The stories flowed from Blanche much the way her memoir reads, like a catharsis. At times, it seemed as if Esther were no longer in the room, that Blanche was suddenly alone with her ghosts. Then, just as quickly as it had begun, the episode ended. Everything returned to 1952 and the box went back in the closet.[55]

Esther by then had been notified that her ex-husband had returned their child safe and sound and had left for another state. She could go home.

Eddie and Blanche at a New Year's Eve party. (Courtesy of Rhea Leen Linder)

But she never forgot how Blanche had opened so many old, secret wounds in an effort to take Esther's mind off of the present long enough to calm down. Blanche's ruse had worked, but looking back on it and considering Eddie's feeling about his wife's past, Esther suspected he knew nothing of that box in the closet.

Not long after the revelation in the kitchen, Esther received news of a new experimental drug-treatment program that her son was qualified to join. She moved back to her hometown in Michigan and over the years lost contact with Blanche.

Throughout the remainder of the 1950s and well into the 1960s, Blanche and Eddie lived what friends described as "a good life together."[56] Eddie Frasure became supervisor of George L. Dahl Architects and Engineers at 2101 North St. Paul in Dallas. He and Blanche bought property in Seagoville, Texas, at the end of Beltline Road in southeast Dallas County. There, among other things, they raised horses. Blanche was known to treat her animals as the children she could never have.

Blanche and Eddie Frasure traveled a lot. There were trips through the Plains states, to West Texas, and even to Disneyland shortly after it opened

Buck Barrow near Crockett, Texas, 1931. To some, the resemblance between Barrow and Frasure was quite evident. (Photograph by Blanche Barrow, courtesy of Rhea Leen Linder)

in the 1950s. There was also a visit to the ancient cliff dwelling in southern New Mexico called "Montezuma's Castle." As had always been the case, Blanche's camera went with her.

In the mid-sixties, much to Eddie Frasure's trepidation, Blanche's past began to interest Warner Brothers Pictures. She was contacted by a young actor and prospective producer named Warren Beatty about purchasing the rights to her name for a proposed movie about Bonnie and Clyde. There had already been a number of motion pictures made dealing in whole or in part with the lives and times of Blanche's former brother-in-law and his girlfriend, most notably Fritz Lang's *You Only Live Once* with Henry Fonda (1937) and *They Live by Night* with Farley Granger (1949). There were also some lesser films like *Gun Crazy* (1949) and the thoroughly hideous *The Bonnie Parker Story* (1958). However, Blanche had never been approached by the producers of those films, probably because her name was never used. Beatty, however, wanted to portray not only Bonnie and Clyde, but Buck and Blanche as well. And he wanted to use their real names. Blanche agreed to meet Beatty's representatives at her lawyer's office to review the proposed script.[57]

The events leading up to the production and eventual release of the 1967 movie *Bonnie and Clyde* actually began with two magazine writers. Robert Benton and David Newman had long wanted to break into the field of screenwriting. In the late 1950s, influenced by the financial success and raw filmic artistry of a series of inexpensive movies eventually identified as "the French New Wave," and led by young directors like Francois Truffaut and Jean Luc Godard, Benton and Newman began looking for a suitable subject of their own to develop in a similar fashion. They were not the only ones. Alfred Hitchcock's classic 1960 adaptation of the Robert Bloch novel, *Psycho*, was by Hitchcock's own admission influenced in every way by the French New Wave, as was Richard Lester's equally intriguing, yet quite different 1964 classic *A Hard Day's Night* starring the Beatles. Perhaps because of the fact that Benton was a native Texan and remembered stories about depression-era outlaws, the subject of Bonnie and Clyde was broached and ultimately accepted by the two writers as the topic of their screenplay.

Benton and Newman apparently conducted a lot of research and crafted an original screenplay that was relatively accurate historically yet still entertaining. They first approached Truffault and Godard with their work, but both directors passed on the project. That's when Warren Beatty entered the picture. Beatty had been making a name for himself as a leading man in movies like *Splendor in the Grass* (1960), but he was becoming more and more interested in the business side of the movie industry, particularly producing. And influenced in his own way by the French New Wave, especially with respect to independent production and distribution, Beatty would become one of the many producers and directors to emerge in the 1960s who would completely change the way the movie industry conducted business. He started by purchasing the rights to Benton and Newman's screenplay.[58] And it was that screenplay Blanche reviewed in her lawyer's office.

Blanche thought the story seemed reasonably accurate and signed a contract allowing the use of her name in the finished movie. Blanche later said she made enough money from the movie deal to pay for a new fence on her property in Seagoville.[59] Production of the movie started in 1966. Much of it was filmed on location in and around Dallas and featured performances by soon-to-be megastars like Faye Dunaway, Gene Hackman,

A local Dallas, Texas, advertisement for the 1967 motion picture *Bonnie and Clyde*.
(Courtesy of Rhea Leen Linder)

Estelle Parsons, and even a very young Gene Wilder. Blanche clipped articles
about the production and added them to her thirty-year-old scrapbooks.

When the production was filming in Dallas in Vickery Park, LC Barrow
paid a visit to the set. At one point between shots he walked up to Warren
Beatty and Gene Hackman, extended his hand, and with a wide, toothy
grin said, "Howdy there, brothers!"[60]

Blanche said that Beatty visited her home during off-hours in the production. He would sit at her piano playing a number of tunes, telling her
that if she ever needed anything, anything at all to contact him. She liked
Beatty a lot.[61] Nevertheless, she despised the movie he produced.

She indicated that by the time the script she read in her lawyer's office
made its way to the screen it had undergone an enormous transformation.
She did not recognize much of anything in the story, least of all herself. Of
Estelle Parsons's portrayal of her character, Blanche said, "That movie made
me look like a screaming horse's ass!"[62] There were also instances where
Blanche's character was freely mixed with the events and personalities of
other people—such as Mary O'Dare, also known as Mary Pitts and Mary

Mary O'Dare. (Phillips Collection)

Chambless. O'Dare was actually associated with Raymond Hamilton. She was married to a bank-robbing buddy of Hamilton's named Gene O'Dare. While O'Dare was serving a ninety-nine-year sentence in Texas, his wife became Hamilton's girlfriend. This was early 1934, after the raid on Eastham and well after Buck had been killed and Blanche imprisoned. Bonnie and Clyde and nearly everyone else then associated with the gang despised Mary O'Dare. Clyde and a cohort named Henry Methvin referred to her as "the washerwoman."[63] And Bonnie said O'Dare tried to convince her to slip knockout drops to Clyde so she and O'Dare could crack his head open, turn him in, and collect the reward. But to Clyde Barrow's thinking, the worst was when O'Dare began complaining that she should get a share of the February 27, 1934, robbery of the R. P. Henry and Sons Bank in Lancaster, Texas. That incident was folded into the movie version of Blanche's character, making it appear that she was driving a wedge between Buck and Clyde. In fact, it was Mary O'Dare, months after the death of Buck, who drove a wedge between Clyde and Raymond Hamilton. Barrow told Hamilton to dump his girlfriend or leave. Hamilton left.[64]

According to Blanche, the overall impact of the movie *Bonnie and Clyde* was that "it nearly caused my husband to divorce me. Of course, my in-laws never liked me anyway."[65]

Although the movie *Bonnie and Clyde* is certainly an exciting, fast-paced juxtaposition of violence and humor, masterfully crafted and directed by Arthur Penn, it is anything but the story of Bonnie and Clyde, much less of Buck and Blanche. Indeed, one of the initial criticisms of the movie was that it was so very inaccurate historically. Nevertheless, some may argue that such is the nature of entertainment, that if one is interested in history one shouldn't try to find it in the entertainment industry. Still, that is of little consolation to those whose lives were being represented as something purportedly approaching fact.

Such was certainly the case with the characterization of the former Texas Ranger Captain Frank Hamer, as portrayed by Denver Pyle. In the movie, Bonnie and Clyde capture Hamer and humiliate him and even beat him up. In reality, nothing even remotely like that ever happened. Indeed, the very first time Frank Hamer saw Bonnie and Clyde was the day he and five other lawmen killed them in Louisiana. Hamer did not even know what they looked like. Only one officer in the group had ever seen them before that day. Consequently, Hamer's family sued Warner brothers. The litigation was settled after a court case that included testimony from another one of the officers who killed Bonnie and Clyde, former Dallas County Deputy Sheriff Ted Hinton. When asked in court if Frank Hamer had ever been abducted by Bonnie and Clyde, Hinton responded wryly that only one entity had ever taken Frank Hamer anywhere, "and that was God! And I'm not so sure He knew what to do with him after He got him!"[66]

After the movie's release Blanche hid away as best she could and hoped the fallout from her resurrected notoriety would be minimal. Besides, she had other things on her mind. Eddie had contracted cancer and died on May 11, 1969, at age fifty-seven.

After the death of Eddie Frasure, Blanche slowly renewed friendships with her former in-laws, beginning with her old friend Artie, Buck's older sister. She started frequenting Barrow family gatherings, usually in the company of Artie. Nevertheless, it was Marie Barrow who told Blanche where to find Bonnie's sister, Billie Jean. By then, Billie Jean had dropped "Billie" from her name and was married to a man from Mesquite, Texas, named Arthur Borland Moon. Jean and her husband, whom everyone referred to simply as "Moon," also lived on Beltline Road, within a few miles of

Artie and Blanche in front of the Cinderella Beauty Shoppe, Denison, Texas, 1932. (Courtesy of Rhea Leen Linder)

Blanche. They began socializing together, eventually so much so that she rarely saw the Barrows thereafter. Marie once quipped, "Yeah, Blanche used to come by here and drink beer with us. Now she's always over at Moon's drinking beer." The last time some of the Barrows remember seeing Blanche was at LC's funeral.[67] Like Eddie Frasure, LC contracted cancer. He was sixty-six when he died.

By the early 1980s, Blanche's house and property were becoming too much for her to handle. A few years earlier for example a severe ice storm pummeled the north Texas area and a thick sheet of ice sealed Blanche in her house for two days. She finally had to telephone a neighbor to come and free her. Afterward she decided to simplify her life. She sold all her property and most of her belongings, bought a house trailer, and moved it next to Jean and Moon at a trailer park called Country Village.

In April 1984, Jean, Moon, and Blanche all decided to move to Cedar Creek Lake in nearby Kaufman County. It began with Jean's niece, Rhea Leen, suggesting that she and Moon move closer to her to make it easier to keep in touch. "Well, you better find a place for Blanche too," Jean said. And Rhea Leen did.

Blanche riding her favorite horse on her property near Seagoville, Texas. (Courtesy of Rhea Leen Linder)

The location was very near Kemp, Texas, where Clyde Barrow, Ralph Fults, and Bonnie Parker shot it out with a posse on April 19, 1932. That was the incident mentioned by Blanche early in her memoir, when Fults was wounded and captured along with Parker. However, the chief reason for the move to Cedar Creek was not to conjure memories, but to fish.

"Jean and Blanche would fish in a bucket of water," Rhea Leen once said. "But you took your life in your own hands when you fished with Blanche." The image of a 4-foot 11-inch tall, 100-pound woman with impaired vision swinging a rod that was bigger than she was and heaving a fishing line all over the 4-by-15-foot pier was the one most readily remembered. Apparently, no one would fish on the same pier with her for fear of being slapped with a rod or snagged by a baited hook. "We couldn't fish for dodging Blanche's line!" Rhea Leen remembered.[68] The only time anyone would venture within range of her was when she would knock her stool off the pier into the shallow water and someone, invariably Moon, had to retrieve it for her. This happened a lot.

One thing Moon refused to be a part of was grocery shopping with Jean and Blanche. The two women would arrive together, each take a grocery cart, and disappear down the aisles in opposite directions. But they would keep in contact by calling out to one another.

"Blanche, where are you?"

"I'm over here."

"Did you see the sale over here?"

"The bananas?"

"Yeah."

"Yeah."

"Did you get some?"

"Yeah."

"Me too."

"I'm about through."

"Me too."

When they met at the checkout counter, they often had many of the same things in their carts, especially Oreos.[69]

Both were faithful collectors of S&H Green Stamps, the old bonus program very popular between the 1950s and 1980s that was based on how much one bought at the grocery store. Stamps issued with each purchase were redeemable at Green Stamp stores for a wide variety of products ranging from small appliances, clothes, and toys to tools, camping equipment, and larger items. One day Jean and Blanche were in the checkout line at the Green Stamp store. The line was rather long and as they waited a woman in front of them kept asking Jean and Blanche to hold her place while she either exchanged an item or added to her purchases. This kept happening all the way up to the counter. Then at the cash register, the woman suddenly thought of something else she wanted. She hoisted her open purse onto the counter and turned to Jean and Blanche one last time. "Would you watch my purse while I run and grab something else?" she asked. Before she could get an answer one way or another, the woman darted off, leaving her purse in the custody of the two grandmotherly-looking strangers who happened to be convicted felons, all her cash and credit cards in plain view. Blanche turned to Jean and smiled. "If she only knew who we are!" she said. Then she and Jean burst out laughing. The woman returned and offered a brief chuckle, not really sure what was so funny.[70]

Nevertheless, it was not all fun and laughter. The plight of the ex-convict trying to reenter society, though tough enough for Blanche, especially in the early days of her freedom, was more pronounced in the lives of certain members of the Barrow family, as well as in Jean's life.[71] Even before the death

Billie Jean Parker Moon, 1968.
(Courtesy of Rhea Leen Linder)

of her sister, Jean was charged with two murders actually committed by Clyde Barrow and Henry Methvin, the heinous Easter Sunday shootings of two unsuspecting motorcycle officers of the Texas State Highway Patrol who had made the fatal mistake of approaching the wrong car at the wrong time. The story of how Jean, who was nowhere near the location at the time of the shootings, came to be charged with these crimes is strange and convoluted. Largely ignoring the testimony of two eyewitnesses who saw "the taller of two men" firing at the two lawmen on a dirt lane called East Dove Road northwest of Grapevine, Texas, Tarrant County officials (and nearly everyone else since) focused on the constantly changing story of a farmer named William Schieffer. Initially Schieffer said that although he saw the car and some people walking around it on occasion, and indeed heard the shots, he had been too far away to get a good look at the killers. Later, he was entirely unsuccessful in identifying anyone in a mug book that included pictures of Bonnie and Clyde.

The murders were particularly tragic. One of the officers, H. D. Murphy, was in training. It had been his first day on patrol. Apparently he and the other officer, E. B. Wheeler, who was one of the first men to sign on to the recently formed Texas Highway Patrol, had spotted a lone Ford V-8 parked on a side road about one hundred yards off of Highway 114.

Thinking they had found a motorist in distress, the two men turned up the road to investigate. The two main duties of the agency at the time were to monitor the weight of commercial trucks and assist stranded travelers. It seemed the perfect situation for Wheeler and his trainee. A third officer, Polk Ivy, continued along the highway.

In and around the car were Clyde Barrow, Bonnie Parker, and Henry Methvin. Out on the highway, driving behind the officers was a Dallas couple out for a drive. They saw the two officers turn up the road, joking that it would be a shame to get a ticket on Easter Sunday. Then they heard shots and saw the "taller of two men" firing into the prone bodies of the officers. The car and its occupants then sped away. By then, Polk Ivy, wondering what was taking his partner and the new man so long, had turned around. He returned to the scene shortly after the killers had left.

After appearing once in two of the four Dallas papers, the testimony of the Dallas couple appears to have been swept into the background and replaced by that of the local farmer William Schieffer, who had admittedly been too far away to get a good look at the perpetrators. Whether this shift in focus was deliberate may never be known, but there was a major problem for state officials with the account of the Dallas couple: They saw the "taller of two men," which would have been Henry Methvin, shoot the officers. The fact that Methvin was involved in a highly publicized, horribly unnecessary double murder was a very real political liability for some in Texas state government. At the time of the murders, Governor Miriam Ferguson had approved a plan that would have pardoned Henry Methvin for crimes committed in Texas in exchange for information leading to the ambush of Bonnie and Clyde. Diversion, misinformation, and political ambition all seem to have converged, and the result was William Schieffer.

From the start, the focus had been on Bonnie and Clyde, then suddenly Schieffer began saying he had been close enough to identify the killers. He named Bonnie's sister, Billie Jean, and Floyd Hamilton, Raymond Hamilton's older brother, as the murderers of Wheeler and Murphy. Billie Jean and Floyd were charged with the killings by Tarrant County prosecutors. Within days of her arrest, Billie Jean received word that her sister had been killed in an ambush in Louisiana. She attended the funeral with a heavy police escort.

Billie Jean's case actually made it to trial, but it was dismissed by a very apologetic judge when it was disclosed that a firearms expert had determined that guns in the possession of Bonnie and Clyde were used in the murders of Wheeler and Murphy. The crowd in the courtroom actually cheered when the case was thrown out.[72]

And what of Henry Methvin? Conveniently, he was not with Bonnie and Clyde when they were killed. Moreover, on August 14, 1934, he was issued a pardon from the State of Texas. Years later, in a book published on the life and career of Frank Hamer, one of the six officers who killed Bonnie and Clyde, William Schieffer is quoted as claiming to have been close enough to the murderers of Wheeler and Murphy to actually see Bonnie shoot one of the officers. Thus, Schieffer's account went from his having been too far away to identify the assailants to having crawled to within yards of the murder scene and watched every detail. The couple driving behind the officers, the ones who saw "the taller of two men" firing into the bodies, were never heard from again.[73]

Nevertheless, that was not the end of Jean's troubles. The following year she, like Blanche, was charged with harboring Bonnie and Clyde and tried in federal court in Dallas, Texas. She was convicted and sentenced to a year and a day at Alderson Federal Prison for Women in West Virginia. On her release, she returned to the Dallas area but moved frequently to avoid press and police scrutiny. On occasion, she moved outside of Dallas, usually to an aunt's home in Gladewater, Texas. Wherever she was, she lived in fear of her employers finding out to whom she was related. She worked as a beautician at the Band Box Beauty Shop in Oak Cliff and as a waitress in a number of cafes and restaurants, including the old Circle Grill in Mesquite, Texas, and Cantrell's on Harry Hines Boulevard in Dallas. While she was at Cantrell's she realized something about the owner, Tom Cantrell, she never dreamed possible. The milk deliveryman had discovered who Jean was and decided to tell Cantrell. She waited to be fired. Suddenly she heard loud voices, then saw Cantrell leading the milk deliveryman out to his truck, saying, "Get out! If you'll lie, you'll steal." He told the delivery-man never to come back and that he was going to order his milk elsewhere from then on. Evidently, Cantrell had known all along who Jean was and was feigning ignorance to the deliveryman to maintain Jean's secret.

After Jean met Arthur Moon, however, she did not have to deal with jobs and the public, and the quality of her life vastly improved. Moreover, Moon was very protective of Jean. Anytime someone called wanting to talk to "Billie Parker" he would hang up without a word. The association of the name "Billie" with that horrible past was one reason why Jean eventually dropped the name entirely. LC Barrow adopted the name "Leon" in place of his better-known given name. He chose the new name in honor of his former brother-in-law, Leon Hale, who was once married to Nell Barrow and who taught Clyde Barrow to play the saxophone.[74] For LC and other members of the Barrow family, though, it did little to stem the notoriety of the Barrow name.

Five of the seven children of Cumie and Henry Barrow spent time in prison. And two, Clyde and Buck, died at the hands of the law. Some of the other children were truly guilty of the crimes they were later convicted of, but some were simply railroaded into jail because of their last name. Before his brother Clyde was killed, it had become routine for LC to be picked up by either the Dallas police or the county sheriff's department. His reaction to his brief apprehension in Denison, described by Blanche early in her memoir, offers a glimpse of just how common such an event had already become. Shortly after Bonnie and Clyde were killed, however, the heat was turned up on LC Barrow. He had already been in jail two months at the time his brother was killed, charged with the armed robbery of three men in east Dallas. The victims told the authorities, in sworn affidavits, that Barrow was not the man who robbed them.[75] They also charged that the police persisted in having them view line-up after line-up that included LC. Each time the victims could identify no one. Finally, after they were made to view a line-up that had only one suspect, LC, the victims went to the news media and charged authorities with trying to frame Barrow. The robbery charges were suddenly dismissed.

Then LC was charged with the robbery of a drugstore in Oak Cliff. Despite the fact that the others charged in the same case asserted that LC was not involved, he was sentenced to five years in the Texas State Penitentiary. The following year he was also charged with harboring Bonnie and Clyde, along with Jean and Blanche, and received the maximum sentence, two years. Thereafter he was in and out of jail and prison, sometimes for real crimes (usually stemming from parole violations), often for imaginary crimes.[76] When he was not under arrest, he was under almost constant surveillance. For a period of time, he owned and operated a hamburger joint and pool hall for teenagers, something to keep them off the streets and out of trouble. Nevertheless, city and county officers paid almost daily visits. Once when LC made an illegal turn near Fair Park he was pulled over by the policeman following him at the time. The officer, who was very young, apparently made some off-color remark about the Barrow family's past. Muddled with anger, LC told the officer he was too young to know anything about the Barrows and to mind his "own goddamned business!" Barrow was promptly roughed up, cuffed, and arrested.[77] This went on almost all of his life.

Within days of moving to Cedar Creek Lake in 1984, Jean and Blanche were comparing notes:

"Well, I got my call," announced Blanche with a grin.

"Oh, I got mine last week!" Jean retorted.

Jean's niece asked what they were talking about. When she was told about the persistent calls from the police whenever they moved, she was outraged. Nevertheless, Jean and Blanche thought it was so funny that some officials still felt threatened by a pair of "little, old gray-haired ladies" who had not been in trouble in fifty years.

Blanche was still getting settled at her new location on Cedar Creek Lake when someone from her past knocked on her trailer door. Esther Weiser had moved back to Texas to work as special assistant to Dallas County District Clerk Bill Long. The two women renewed their friendship and told each other what had been going on in their lives for the previous three decades. Thereafter they often stayed up well into the night talking. Invariably Blanche would drift off to sleep, still sitting in her oversized recliner, a cat purring in her lap. Sometimes Esther would just stay the night at Blanche's trailer, getting up before daybreak to beat the traffic into downtown Dallas. The two women became very close. Nevertheless, Blanche's other friends never saw Esther. They heard a lot about her, but never saw her.

"It was a long time before we met [Esther]," Jean's niece, Rhea Leen said. "Blanche did not want to share her."

Likewise, Blanche spoke often of her friends, especially Jean and Moon, but seemed more than reticent to invite them to join her and Esther. Whenever Esther would suggest such a thing, Blanche usually answered with something like, "Oh, no! They're busy." This compartmentalization of friends appears to have been a lifelong trait of Blanche's. She indicates as much in her memoir, with Buck, Clyde, their mother, her own mother, and so on. She also exhibited an aptitude for pitting friends and acquaintances against each other by saying something adverse about one person in their absence to some other person, and vice versa. To some friends Blanche indicated her distrust and dislike for a well-known Dallas columnist who befriended her in the late 1960s. This writer and his wife remained rather close to Blanche all the way up to her death, sometimes taking her to Campisi's, a restaurant where she would invariably order shrimp scampi. However, to others she had nothing but good things to say about this columnist.

Blanche and Esther L. Weiser, Cedar Creek Lake, Texas, 1984.
(Courtesy of Esther L. Weiser)

Nevertheless, Blanche's little games were a lot more transparent than she thought. Once after Rhea Leen became very angry with a couple because of some comments Blanche made about them, she admitted, "Of course, there's no telling what Blanche told them about me."[78] Nevertheless, despite her flaws, people who knew her still loved her. "Here I am, warts and all!" is what she seemed to say to everyone.

Blanche loved to drive. She would take long drives all around north Texas in a white 1960s model Ford LTD sedan that everyone referred to as "The Bomb." The car was big enough by itself, but next to Blanche, it was enormous. Dressed in the same kind of riding breeches and boots she had worn in Dexfield Park, she would slip her 4-foot 11-inch frame behind the wheel, pull the seat up as far as it would go, and take off down some long series of country roads, barely able to see over the top of the dash with her one good eye. She drove fast, never used main roads, and never got lost. She seemed to know every little back road in north Texas. Indeed, her skill as a driver may account for the fact that she was able to keep up with Clyde Barrow after that unsuccessful robbery mentioned in her memoir.

During these sojourns, which usually occupied every weekend, Blanche would try out different small town cafes and restaurants. She was a connoisseur

W. D. Jones, Houston, Texas, 1969.
(Photograph by Kent Biffle, Phillips
Collection)

of country cuisine. She also liked to "go antiquing," which meant browsing every little trinket shop along the way. Her trailer was full of trinkets. She also liked costume jewelry. She had a few pieces of fine jewelry, but she had an affinity for less-expensive things.

One day in May 1984, Blanche turned on the television and saw someone she had not heard from in half a century. Ralph Fults was being interviewed by a local Dallas station on the fiftieth anniversary of the ambush of Bonnie and Clyde. "I thought he was dead," Blanche said. "I thought they hanged him over in Mississippi. The last time I saw Ralph was in the Kaufman County jail after he and Bonnie got caught near Kemp. Clyde took me down there to tell them he had a plan to bust them out of jail. I hadn't seen him since."[79]

Blanche recalled thinking as she watched Fults on the television, "That's not Ralph Fults! He was this tall, good-looking, twenty-something-year-old fellow—not an old man. And then I thought, 'Oh yeah, I guess we're all a lot older now.'" She also remembered that Fults "was very handsome, but that kid, W. D. Jones, was the best-looking one of all!"[80]

Blanche got Fults's number and phoned him. She found out he was working on a book about Bonnie, Clyde, Buck, Raymond, and all the others. She paid him a visit, driving up to his home in Mesquite in "The Bomb" to reminisce and share thoughts. She found that he had never received a death sentence in Mississippi for the bank robbery he and Raymond Hamilton had staged. It had been erroneously reported that way. He had received instead two fifty-year terms, but was pardoned during World War II. He married, raised a family, and managed to stay out of trouble. He was a grandfather who had spent a great deal of his post-prison time speaking free of charge to any church or civic group that wanted him about the wholly unglamorous, very real world of juvenile delinquency and adult criminal behavior—and how to avoid such a life. His book, he told her, would address the same issues.

Back at her trailer, Blanche dug out her own memoir. She knew that among her many other skills, her friend Esther had once worked for a publisher. And in her new capacity as special assistant to the Dallas district clerk she had access to one of the very first computer word processors, the type that filled up half a room and used 8-inch floppy disks. "Do you think you could do something with this?" Blanche asked her. Esther thought she could and took the manuscript with the idea of first transferring it to disk. Nevertheless, something made Esther forget completely about the manuscript for another fifteen years.

A short time after turning her manuscript over to Esther, Blanche got up from her chair and suddenly fell to the floor of her trailer. Her right leg had snapped. In the hospital it was determined she was in the early stages of some brittle bone disease and that her leg required surgery and a long period of convalescence to heal properly. After the surgery, Esther and Rhea Leen moved Blanche temporarily into a subsidized assisted-care facility in Oak Cliff, just across the river from downtown Dallas. It was then easy for both women, especially Esther who worked close by, to share the task of helping Blanche during her recovery. Rhea Leen and Esther alternated days and nights, visiting Blanche, making sure her needs were being met, bringing her what she wanted (including a large television set they both carried up several flights of stairs to Blanche's room). The experience marked the first time Rhea Leen and Esther met. Thereafter their meetings were brief, usually one passing the other as their respective shifts, so to speak, changed.

Others visited Blanche in Oak Cliff as well. Writer Kent Biffle and his wife, Suzanne brought her a few cartons of Pall Mall cigarettes. Biffle recalled her obvious pain as she lay in traction with raw flesh exposed around a pin inserted in her leg. Nevertheless, he said she was always jovial and up for a visit.[81]

Eventually she was able to go back to her trailer. Knowing she was going to be confined to a wheelchair for some time, Moon constructed a ramp outside the door and Esther and Rhea Leen rearranged Blanche's trailer to make it easier for her to move around in it. However, when they brought her home she was obviously displeased, not with the ramp, but with the rearrangement of her trailer. She was not unpleasant about it, but she made it clear she wanted everything back the way it was. To her memory that was the only time Esther ever saw Blanche angry, and even that did not last long.

Blanche spent her days wheeling around, putting food outside her trailer for any wild animal that might wander by, her "critters" she called them, and making clothes for her doll collection. Esther and Rhea Leen saw the critters and dolls as substitutes for the children Blanche could never have.

Blanche's health never improved. She was soon diagnosed with cancer and spent the next four years in and out of hospitals, undergoing debilitating surgery, radiation treatments, and chemotherapy. Slowly she deteriorated. Her final days were spent in intensive care in Tyler, Texas. It was while she was there that her ninety-three-year-old mother paid her a visit. How she found out where her daughter was, no one knew, but Blanche was not pleased. Even when it was clear that she had terminal cancer, she wanted nothing to do with her mother, refusing Esther's offer to contact her. Described as an ill-tempered, hard-looking, and extremely overweight woman who kept sacks of money tied in various places under her dress, Lillian stayed at the hospital for only a short time, apparently sensing she was not wanted.[82] She went to her daughter's funeral though.

Blanche Caldwell Barrow Frasure died on Christmas Eve, 1988. She was buried on a cold, damp winter's day at Grove Hill Cemetery on Samuell Drive in Dallas, the same place LC Barrow had been buried. Artie and Nell were also buried there. Moreover, in a little more than four years Ralph Fults would join them, followed a few weeks later by Jean. In 1999, Marie Barrow, the last principal of the inner circle of Bonnie and Clyde, was also buried at Grove Hill.

Across town, on the hill above West Dallas and just a few feet from Fort Worth Avenue, Clyde, Buck, Jack, Henry, and Cumie Barrow all lie together. Still farther away, near Love Field, Bonnie, her mother, and two nephews lie in three of four Parker plots purchased by Billie Jean in 1945. Only one of the plots, Bonnie's, is marked.

After Blanche's funeral, Esther, executor of the meager estate, and Rhea Leen began cleaning out the trailer and neighboring shed. They found coffee cans filled with used nails that Blanche had straightened and stored away for future use, shelves filled with rusted canned goods with no labels, a freezer full of meat and other items that were so old they were, as Rhea Leen put it, "beyond freezer burn. They were freezer dead!"

Blanche and ukelele in prison. On special occasions, such as visitor days, the inmates were not obliged to wear the prison uniform. (Courtesy of Rhea Leen Linder)

Both Rhea Leen and Esther understood what they saw, however. It was the influence of the Great Depression, recycling, thriftiness, stocking up to the point of hoarding for fear of being without. Rhea Leen remembered tough times with Jean, before Moon came along. She remembered coming home from school before Jean got off work to a cold, empty house, and finding only one can of soup in the cupboard, heating the soup and eating only half of it, saving the rest for her aunt. Esther remembered being shunned by other children when her father took a job as a janitor because his savings had been wiped out in the crash of 1929 and there were no other jobs. He always distrusted banks thereafter, refusing to do business with them, preferring to bury his money in the yard. He was not alone.

Blanche never forgot the impact of the Great Depression in her life, and she never forgot those who shared her life then, no matter how difficult and painful the memories, and no matter how much those around her, or even she herself, tried to suppress those memories. Four years before her death she said, "I talk of these incidents [with Bonnie and Clyde] as if I were not a part of any of it, like a character in a book I once read. It's the only way I keep from going crazy. Maybe we were all pretty young then, but we knew what we were doing. Clyde never held a gun to my head. I was there because I wanted to be! What's that they say in the movies? 'The show must go on!' Well, life goes on."[83]

Blanche and Buck Barrow, 1931. (Courtesy of Rhea Leen Linder)

At some point in the process of cleaning the trailer, Rhea Leen looked at Blanche's big recliner chair and remembered seeing her sitting there just before she entered the hospital for the last time. Her feet were resting on a wooden stool made for her by Clyde Barrow while he was in prison. On a TV tray in front of her was an intricately hand-tooled wooden jewelry box, also made by Barrow. Her name was carved on the lid. She had removed all her jewelry and spread it out before her—all of it. She was looking at the pieces carefully and trying them on, as if for the last time.

Blanche had lived most of her life in the shadow of four months in 1933. In addition, the pain of mortality was with her constantly, always pinching her back to reality. Nevertheless, in the end the only things that really seemed to matter were her friends, her critters, her dolls, and a few bits of paste and metal, those and the memories they carried with them.

Rhea Leen and Esther returned to the task of sifting through Blanche's life, examining boxes of receipts dating back decades, canceled checks and bank statements, rusty nails and canned goods—and one other thing, a poem:

Sometimes

Across the fields of yesterday
She sometimes comes to me
A little girl just back from play
the girl I used to be
And yet she smiles so wistfully
once she has crept within
I wonder if she hopes to see
the woman I might have been—

—Blanche Barrow, 1933

Blanche, 1932. (Courtesy of Rhea Leen Linder)

⚙Appendix A

Reproduction of Two Pages from the Original Manuscript

The passage on the following two pages replicates two pages from the original manuscript, as Blanche Barrow composed it and before the editor "regularized" it. For comparison, see pages 24–27 of this book.

Page 11 of the original handwritten manuscript. (Courtesy of Esther L. Weiser) was through with the life of hiding from the law. I ask Bonnie to get in bed with me and try to get a little sleep, as I had heard Clyde say would stay until just before dawn, but Bonnie seem to want to talk in stead of sleeping. she said it was so good to have some woman she new to talk too that it sometimes was so lonesome for her just being in the company of men all the time and never any woman friends to talk too. I new this was true because I had experienced a few months of that my self after I had married Buck and before he went back to prison. through Bonnie's chatter and laughter I caught a few words now and then of Clyde's conversation to Buck. and did not like it Clyde seem to be trying to draw a plain on a map but decided Buck would never go with his brother heather Clyde cannot if Clyde did want him too. I heard Clyde say Blanche Knew where the place is. and knew the country pretty well then. They pulled their chairs up close beside the bed and Clyde begain again lineing his plains to me. I did not like them and told him so. Clyde's plains were to get to the east ham prison farm where Raymond Hamilton was serving a long sentence for Robbery. and take him away from the gards when they were cutting wood or something in the fields away from the buildings. I told him, he could count Buck and me out. if he thought he wanted get any help from us. because we were not going to get mixed up in any of it, he said all if thats the way you feel about it, but you or Buck, would not get in to any trouble over it. all I wanted you to do was go visit Ray. and tell him where he will find every

Page 12 of the original handwritten manuscript. (Courtesy of Esther L. Weiser)

❁Appendix B

Blanche's Letter to Her Father,
November 11, 1933

On November 11, 1933, Blanche Barrow wrote to her father from the Missouri State Penitentiary. The letter appears here unedited, just as Blanche wrote it. The "best friend" Blanche mentions is Carl D. Beaty, the man who had sold Buck the '29 Marmon sedan that had carried them all to the ill-fated reunion with Bonnie and Clyde in Joplin, Missouri.

Name: M. F. Caldwell   Name: Mrs. Blanche Barrow
Relationship: Father   Box 47. Register No. 43454. No. ___
                              this week
Street Number
City: Goodwater. State: Okla.   Jefferson City, Mo. Nov. 11, 1933.

My dear dad,

Received your sweet letter yesterday noon and was so proud to hear from you. and know you are well. this leaves me feeling fine. hope you are well. I am over my cold now and my eye feels better.

Dear I received a letter from mother and Lucinda and one from Mrs. Barrow yesterday and was so proud to hear from them again. but mother was still sick and was taking Lucinda to the hospital. Mother said John had been out there. he is married again. I am proud he is. maybe he will leave me alone.

Well dear the weather is pretty cold up here. but today the sun has been shining. hope you had a nice armistice day. do you remember where we were 4 years ago today and I met Buck. I never dreamed then I would be here 4 years from then and my darling would be dead and I could never see him again. but we never know from one day to the next what will happen to us. Mrs. Barrow told me about one of Buck's and my best friends in Dallas being dead. and he is buried in the same grave yard that our darling is resting in. only a little over 3 months differences in there deaths. he was such a big healthy man. you would never think of him being *sick*. but that is something we all have to go through with. I only hope to be ready when my time comes and I can go to see my darling. Well dear I think I told you we had a dance here last Saturday night. the band boys come over with the warden and played the music for the girls to dance by. everyone seem to have a good time I know I enjoyed the music. Well dear I must go. hoping to hear from you soon. am sending lots and lots of love.

your lonely baby, Blanche

⊛Appendix C

Buck's Letter Home, January 16, 1930

On January 16, 1930, two days after arriving in Huntsville to begin his sentence, Buck Barrow wrote to his mother. The letter was probably dictated to a cell mate as Buck was illiterate.

Huntsville Tex.
Jan 16, 1930

Dear Mother and all

I will write you a few lines to let you know that I have made the trip. Mother I am in the hospital now and my legs are hurting pretty bad. It sure looks bad but I am going to take it. Mother try to get me a furlow. And don't fail to write often. And don't for get to tell Blanch to write me.

And tell me all the news that happen on the out side world. Send me some stamps and envelopes so that I can write ever day And I wish you would do the same. Mother tell sister to send my shoes and send me some more pajamas because they burn mine up.

But they well let me have some more now if you send them to me. And tell her to help me all she can to get out on a parole or a furlow while you are so sick. I hope the out side world don't for get me just because I am in the walls.

Good-by Mother and don't worry

—Marvin Barrow

Don't send me any tobbacco but send me some money Because they wont let any tobbacco come in.

⊛Appendix D

The Barrow Gang's Victims

In all, the Barrow brothers and/or their accomplices accounted for the deaths of fourteen men between the fall of 1931 and the spring of 1934. The stories behind the murders are summarized below.

Ed Crowder, Killed by Clyde Barrow, October 29, 1931

ED CROWDER WAS A convicted bank robber from Houston, Texas. Not much else is known about him prior to his prison days. Crowder was one of three "building tenders" serving Camp 1 at the Eastham prison farm when Clyde Barrow was moved there from Camp 2, probably in 1931. A building tender was a convict trustee who quite literally tended to the prison building. At each camp there were three building tenders working in eight-hour shifts. Their job was to make sure peace was maintained in the building and that everything ran smoothly. They worked closely with guards and were given quite a bit of latitude regarding the manner in which they kept the peace. Building tenders were not supposed to be armed, but most were. They carried a variety of homemade weapons, the most common being the "dirk knife," "shiv," or "shank"—knives fashioned from files stolen from the prison workshop. Some carried other weapons, including ballpeen hammers and a nasty little item called a "tough nut"—a leather glove festooned with razors.

Some building tenders were fair—tough, but fair—like Aubrey Skelley (sometimes appears as Scalley), whom Clyde Barrow befriended and made part of the original plan to raid Eastham. It was Skelley who smuggled in the guns used in the raid of January 16, 1934. Other building tenders were vicious, vindictive, and extremely dangerous. Such was the case with Ed Crowder. Described as large, hulking, and overbearing, Crowder was, among other things, a predator. He enjoyed homing in on smaller convicts, beating them, sexually assaulting them, and making them do all manner of vile things for him. Crowder raped Clyde Barrow at least once, and in return Barrow vowed to kill Crowder.

By that time Barrow was working in the Camp 1 kitchen. He could have taken a knife from there and ripped Crowder in half, but Barrow did not want to do that because the weapon would surely be traced to him. He knew his mother had been fighting to have his fourteen-year sentence reduced to the original two years. His implication in a prison murder might have jeopardized that. Barrow went to Skelley and asked to borrow his knife. Skelley talked him out of that as well. Skelley then devised a plan whereby he, a bank robber serving a long term, would take the rap for Crowder's murder knowing that nothing could, or would, be done to him. Today such a plan would never work, since convict killings are now capital crimes in the state of Texas, but in the early 1930s, such cases were commonplace and rarely if ever investigated. It might have made a difference with a "short-timer" like Barrow, but for a "heavy" like Skelley, it was nothing. In exchange for the deception, Skelley was to be included in the plan to raid Eastham—a plan that already included Ralph Fults, Joe Palmer, and Henry Methvin.

Barrow smuggled a length of galvanized pipe into the Camp 1 dormitory. He had it concealed in his pants. He waited for all the other convicts to finish their business at the open toilets and showers at the west end of the dormitory then walked back there alone. He knew such a move would lure the predator, Ed Crowder, back there with him. Barrow stood at one of the toilets pretending to urinate. When he heard Crowder approach, Barrow jerked that pipe out, wheeled around, and cracked Crowder's head wide open. Barrow then rushed back to his bunk. Skelley, waiting nearby, pulled his knife, slashed himself on the stomach, and rushed over to Crowder. Screaming and shouting, he sank the knife deep into the already dead body and backed away, clutching his bleeding, but superficially wounded abdomen. The guard, stationed outside the dormitory, asked about all the shouting. "I just killed Crowder," Skelley said. The guard said something to the effect of "good riddance" and to leave the body, that it would be cleared out later. It was Clyde Barrow's first murder.

John N. Bucher, Killed by Ted Rogers, April 30, 1932

John N. Bucher was the sixty-five-year-old owner-operator of a variety store located on the old Fort Worth Highway (Itasca Road today), just north of Hillsboro, Texas. The store was on the ground floor of a two-story building. Bucher and his wife lived upstairs. The store had long since closed for the day when at about 10:00 P.M. on the evening of April 30, 1932, a pounding came from downstairs. Someone claimed to want a guitar string, saying they were playing in a band at a nearby dance. Bucher went downstairs and let two young men into the store. He recognized them, but he probably did not know them. Their names were Johnny Russell and Ted Rogers. They were part of the gang that had planned to raid Eastham along with Clyde Barrow and Ralph Fults. By then, however, the gang had been decimated when Fults and two other gang members were captured in separate incidents. Russell, Rogers, and Barrow had barely escaped together when their hideout on Lake Dallas (now Lake Lewisville) was raided by the Denton County sheriff's department. They had left so fast that they lost everything, weapons and cash, in the raid. By the time they rolled into Hillsboro, they were flat broke and desperate.

Russell and Rogers had been in the store earlier in the day browsing with Clyde Barrow, but that night Barrow waited outside in the car. It has long been thought that the reason Barrow did not go inside was because Bucher knew Barrow, which was probably true. Indeed, there is more than one theory as to the exact nature of their association. The most popular is that Barrow knew one of Bucher's children. Nevertheless, there is another, seedier notion, which has never been substantiated—that Bucher was a fence for stolen goods and that Barrow was a longtime customer. Whatever the reason, Barrow stayed in the car while Russell and Rogers went inside, supposedly looking for a replacement guitar string.

When a string was selected, one of the men produced a ten dollar bill, knowing Bucher would have to open the safe to make change. Some reports have Bucher calling his wife at this point, for only she knew the combination. Regardless, she was apparently there in the store when Bucher opened the safe. At some point Russell and Rogers pulled guns and demanded cash and jewels. According to Rogers, who later related the story to Ralph Fults, Buck Barrow, and two other men inside the main prison at Huntsville, Texas, Bucher pulled a gun from the safe and Rogers shot him. Bucher's wife then went for the gun but Rogers grabbed her before she could reach it. He and Russell then scooped up forty dollars in cash and about fifteen hundred dollars in jewels and took off. The trio split up that night and apparently never saw each other again.

Ted Rogers was later arrested on an unrelated charge. When Raymond Hamilton, who actually resembled Rogers, was eventually tried and convicted of the Bucher murder, Rogers told Fults and the others in Huntsville that if Hamilton received the death sentence he would confess. Hamilton was sentenced to ninety-nine years instead, and Rogers remained silent. In 1934, he was caught unarmed by a convict rival in a prison shower and stabbed to death, which explains Hamilton's statement about the Bucher case at the time of his execution in 1935.

According to Blanche Barrow, Johnny Russell was killed by police in another state. Clyde Barrow, of course, was ambushed and killed along with Bonnie Parker on May 23, 1934 in Louisiana.

Eugene C. Moore, Killed by Clyde Barrow and Raymond Hamilton, August 5, 1932

Eugene C. Moore was thirty-one, married, and the father of three small children. He was born into a very wealthy family that lost everything in the Great Depression. Desperate just to feed his family, Moore gladly accepted the job of undersheriff of Atoka County, Oklahoma. He knew he was no lawman, but he needed the money and jobs were scarce. On the evening of August 5, 1932, an outdoor dance was underway near Stringtown, Oklahoma. It is often said that the dance was an indoor affair, at a dance hall. Nevertheless, according to at least one of the musicians in the band that night, the dance was outside under the night sky. There was a wooden dance platform with a riser at one end for the band. Japanese lanterns were strung overhead.

According to one report, Atoka County Sheriff Charles G. Maxwell, Deputy Sheriff Chip Miller, and Undersheriff Moore noticed a pair of men moving from one car to another, evidently preparing to steal one. It was Clyde Barrow and Raymond Hamilton, fresh from a robbery five days earlier in Dallas, Texas. They had arrived at the dance with at least one other man, possibly two. However, as the officers approached, Hamilton and Barrow were the only men they saw. One report states that Sheriff Maxwell stepped up to the driver's side of the car the two suspicious men were sitting in and said something. Without warning, gunfire erupted and

Maxwell fell to the dirt with six bullets in him. Despite this, the sheriff was able to return fire. Deputy Miller fired several shots at the assailants as frightened dancers and musicians dove from the dance platform to seek cover. None were hit. However, Eugene Moore was not so lucky. After felling Maxwell, Hamilton and Barrow turned their guns on him. He was killed instantly.

Raymond Hamilton always maintained that he never killed anyone, but this case makes his claim very tenuous. To his brother, Floyd, Raymond Hamilton admitted that he was not so sure about Stringtown. Both he and Barrow were shooting. It could have been either one, he said, or both who killed Eugene Moore. Almost three years later, Sheriff Maxwell, crippled for life by his wounds, would attend the execution of Raymond Hamilton.

Howard Hall, Killed, Perhaps by Clyde Barrow, October 11, 1932

Howard Hall was a fifty-seven year-old grocer living in Sherman, Texas. Born in 1875 in McKinney, Texas, he moved to Sherman at the age of twenty-nine. There among other things he owned his own grocery business. At some point Hall gave up his business, perhaps due to stress, and took a job as meat manager for S. R. Little Grocery.

On October 11, 1932, just before closing, a lone man walked into the store. He looked nervous. The man picked up a loaf of bread and walked to the register, asking for eggs and lunchmeat. The man then handed a dollar to grocer Homer Glaze. Glaze opened the register and when he looked up, he was staring at a blue steel (sometimes described as chrome) .45 automatic. At that point, Howard Hall stepped up and said to the bandit, "You can't do that!" The gunman became infuriated. He started backing both men toward the side entrance of the store, all the time cursing, kicking, and beating Hall. Finally, Hall tried to grab the gunman's arm and he was shot three times, the force of the blasts knocking him through the door to the sidewalk outside. The assailant stepped over Hall, shot him again, then aimed his gun at Glaze. He pulled the trigger but the gun misfired. With that, the gunman ran to a waiting car containing two other men and drove away. Hall remained conscious for a while after being taken to a nearby hospital but died shortly thereafter.

Upon hearing of the shooting, Dallas authorities sent mug shots of Clyde Barrow to Sherman, and eyewitnesses almost immediately identified him as the gunman. There is no evidence that any pictures other than Barrow's were shown to Glaze and the other eyewitness.

Eyewitness identification is not always accurate. Raymond Hamilton was convicted of the murder of John Bucher based on eyewitness identification, and he was not even in the state at the time. He was still convicted. A number of incorrect suspects would also be identified later in the Doyle Johnson case—all from eyewitness identification of mug shots, though Clyde Barrow and W. D. Jones were the true perpetrators.

Clyde Barrow always maintained he never staged a crime of any kind in Sherman. The statement carries some weight because Barrow almost always admitted to his family which crimes were his. Still, there are aspects of the robbery that sound distinctly like Barrow. He was known to rob grocery stores and he often used .45 automatics. Nevertheless, these traits are linked as well to dozens of other midwestern bandits. In addition, the nervousness of the suspect, cited in every report, would not have been characteristic of Clyde Barrow. Almost anyone who knew him, worked with him, or encountered him in any way remembered him as a very cool operator, even in the heat of a gun battle. Still, there are a lot of unanswered questions about the identity of the killer of Howard Hall, none of which diminish the tragedy of his death.

Doyle Johnson, Shot by Either Clyde Barrow or W. D. Jones on Christmas Day, 1932, Died the Following Day

Salesman Doyle Johnson was a twenty-six-year-old husband and father enjoying Christmas with his family when his wife noticed a man wearing a dark overcoat and a tan hat climb into the family car. Then she saw another man already behind the wheel. "Those men are taking the car," she cried to her husband. Johnson bolted outside where two of his in-laws were already standing beside the car shouting at the thieves.

The thieves seemed to be having trouble starting the car on the cold day. The man in the overcoat had taken over for the other thief. Finally, the engine cranked and the man behind the wheel put it in gear. Johnson jumped on the running board just as the car pulled away, reached through the open window, and started choking the driver. "Get back, man, or I'll kill you," the driver said. Johnson tightened his grip. "Stop," the man spurted, "or I'll kill you!"

Witnesses heard the discharge of two different weapons. The second shot struck Johnson in the neck, severing his spine. He died the following day.

The assailants, by their own admission, were Clyde Barrow, in the dark overcoat, and W. D. Jones, the one who first tried to start the car and then relinquished the wheel to Barrow. However, before the truth was discovered, a number of suspects were incorrectly identified, including Les Stewart, Odell Chambless, and Frank Hardy. Hardy was actually put on trial for the murder. His first trial resulted in a hung jury. His second trial had been scheduled when Jones was arrested near Houston and admitted to the killing. Clyde Barrow drafted a letter exonerating Hardy from any involvement in the Barrow gang. After typing the note, Barrow then rubbed his hands in grease and applied his hand and fingerprints to the page. The letter was never mailed, however, presumably because of the Jones confession. It remained in the Barrow family collection until sold at auction a few years ago.

Malcolm Davis, Killed by Clyde Barrow, January 6, 1933

Malcolm Davis was a resident of Grapevine, Texas. He was a veteran Tarrant County deputy sheriff, very tough, very experienced. On December 29, 1932, two men robbed the Home Bank of Grapevine. They took $2,850. A posse was quickly organized, and one of the men was soon captured. His name was Les Stewart, and he was a well-known West Dallas underworld figure. He had helped Raymond Hamilton rob a bank in Cedar Hill, Texas, on November 25, 1932. It did not take long for Deputy Davis and other Tarrant County officials to establish who the second man was, another West Dallas character named Odell Chambless. Informed that Chambless would rendezvous at a safe house in West Dallas on a certain date, Davis contacted the Dallas County sheriff's department and a task force was assembled. The house soon became the focus of their search for Chambless.

On the afternoon of January 5, 1933, Dallas County Deputy Sheriff Ed Castor paid a visit to the suspected safe house at 507 County Avenue (North Winnetka today), in West Dallas. Two of Raymond Hamilton's sisters, Maggie Fairris and Lillian McBride, lived there. Castor questioned McBride, then left. At 11 P.M. that night, more visitors arrived. Tarrant County assistant district attorney W. T. Evans, along with Tarrant County deputies Malcolm Davis and Dusty Rhodes, met two Dallas County officials, including Deputy Sheriff Fred Bradberry, in front of the house. A sixth man, J. F. Van Noy also joined the group. Sometimes described as a special ranger, other times listed as a special investigator, Van Noy was evidently acting in some multijurisdictional capacity in an attempt to solve a number of Texas crimes, including the murders of Howard Hall and Doyle Johnson.

Evans and the officers did not find McBride. She was at work in downtown Dallas. However, Maggie Fairris was there with her two small children. The men commandeered the house. Van Noy, Rhodes, and the two Dallas officers stationed themselves inside. Evans and Davis covered the back porch. For several minutes Bradberry sat on a sofa next to a front window making small talk with Fairris, who seemed nervous. At one point she left the living room to tuck her children into bed. When she returned Bradberry, ordered her to turn out all the lights. She complied, except for a small red light she insisted be left on in her children's bedroom window. Bradberry agreed.

At midnight, January 6, a Chevrolet coupe cruised slowly past the house. Seconds later it reappeared, slowing as if to stop, then picking up speed and rounding the corner. Bradberry grew suspicious of the red light and ordered it turned off. The car approached once more and stopped, engine idling, lights off. A small, lean man wearing a dark overcoat and a tan hat emerged from the driver's side of the coupe. He walked very slowly toward the front porch, both hands in the pockets of his overcoat. Bradberry had no idea who the man might be. For all he knew, it was a neighbor checking on McBride and Fairris. He told Fairris to open the door. She jerked the door open and screamed, "Don't shoot! Think of my babies!" The man on the lawn opened his coat, raised a sawed-off shotgun, and fired a blast of buckshot at the window where Bradberry was sitting. He and everyone else in the house dove to the floor, unhurt but thoroughly surprised. Chambless was not supposed to be a dangerous fugitive.

The shotgun blast brought Davis and Evans running around to the front of the house. The man with the shotgun was backing away from the house, gun raised, when Davis appeared. "Get back!" the gunman said. "Don't come any closer." Davis kept on approaching. "Don't come any closer," the gunman repeated. Davis was almost on top of the assailant when a single blast of buckshot knocked him backward onto the front porch, nine .00 buckshot pellets in his heart. Someone in the car started shooting at the house. Evans, running right behind Davis, wheeled around and dove over a neighboring fence just as a charge of buckshot narrowly missed him. The car then sped away. The gunman ran beside the house and disappeared down the alley.

Bradberry ran outside into the yard in time to see the Chevrolet coupe kicking gravel high into the air as it turned west on Eagle Ford Road. The Dallas deputy then lifted the mortally wounded Davis into his arms and carried him to his car. Bystanders had started to gather. Suddenly, Van Noy ran up and, thinking he had trapped the gunman, pulled his own weapon and fired two shots into Bradberry's car. Miraculously no one was hit. Malcolm Davis was rushed to Methodist Hospital, but the fifty-two-year-old lawman was already dead.

Wes Harryman and Harry McGinnis, Killed by Clyde Barrow, Buck Barrow, and W. D. Jones, April 13, 1933

Wes Harryman was the forty-one year-old constable of Newton County, Missouri. He was actually a farmer by trade, but farming paid next to nothing during the depression. To supplement his meager income he ran for and won the constable's seat in his district. Part of his jurisdiction was a piece of the nearby city of Joplin. Joplin was a wild town in the 1930s. . It was a well-known hangout and hideout for members of the criminal underworld—partially because it straddled several jurisdictions and partially because for a price the local authorities provided an outlaw a modicum of peace and quiet. This is not to suggest that all law officers in the Joplin area were on the take, but some were—enough so that criminals knew it as a safe haven. Nevertheless, it was evidently only safe for those who followed the rules and one of those rules was to stay clean in the area, or at least be quiet about it.

In early April, it was becoming apparent that the occupants of a garage apartment on 34th Street, near the intersection of Oak Ridge, were rather openly robbing local businesses and stealing local cars. On April 13, 1933, Wes Harryman was at his farm in Newton County when Joplin City detective Tom DeGraff and Joplin motor detective Harry McGinnis arrived. They had obtained a search warrant for the garage apartment but needed someone from the local jurisdiction to actually serve the warrant. The intersection of 34th and Oak Ridge was in Newton County and Harryman was the only Newton County official available at the time. Harryman rode off in the officers' car with Tom DeGraff at the wheel.

The three officers rendezvoused with Missouri state troopers G. B. Kahler and W. E. Grammar and proceeded to the garage apartment, the troopers following in their own car. As the apartment came into view, Harryman spotted someone at one of the two garage doors, hurrying to close it. DeGraff pulled diagonally into the short driveway to block both doors. He had not come to a complete stop before Harryman leaped from the car and rushed the door. A shotgun blast blew him to the ground. He fired one shot into the garage, then died, a massive wound in his shoulder and neck.

McGinnis leaped from the car and was actually able to jab his weapon through the opening in the garage door and squeeze off three shots before another shotgun blast hurtled him to the driveway not far from Harryman, his arm nearly ripped off.

DeGraff dove from his car, fired several shots, and then ran to the main house a few yards away from the garage apartment. "For God's sake, someone call the station," he shouted. The state troopers had already parked on the street and run to the cover of the same house. Sporadic but intense gunfire ensued. In addition to the shotgun, an automatic weapon was also fired at the three remaining officers. At one point one of the gunmen was in the street, apparently as a result of having pushed DeGraff's car out of the driveway, or perhaps he was merely looking for the other lawmen. A woman was with him. The officers fired at him. He was hit, but a button on his shirt deflected the bullet and the wound was not serious. Someone later stated that one of the officers saw a man and a woman firing intermittently from an upstairs window, but this was never mentioned at the coroner's inquests. Two people stepped outside and moved one of the downed officers, probably Harryman, apparently because his body was blocking the garage door. The officers then spotted a woman calmly walking in front of the garage and strolling off down the street. They did not know who she was or where she came from. Then a car inside the garage appeared, roaring past the dead Harryman and dying McGinnis and sped away from the scene, stopping just long enough to pick up the woman who was still walking casually down the street about a block away from the apartment.

Harryman was dead at the scene, but McGinnis was still conscious. "Where's Tom [DeGraff]," he asked. DeGraff answered. "Well, who was it that went down, the constable?" McGinnis asked. He was told it was Harryman. "Go see how he's getting along," McGinnis said. He then asked that he be taken to St. John's Hospital and that someone call his eighty-one-year-old mother. McGinnis died six hours later in the hospital. He was a likable fellow, full of jokes and laughter. Most of his friends and colleagues simply called him "the Irishman." He was a widower whose wife had been struck and killed by a car two years earlier. At fifty-three, he was engaged to be married on May 10. He was the first of two would-be grooms murdered by the Barrow gang.

Henry D. Humphrey, Shot by Buck Barrow on June 23, 1933, Died June 26, 1933

Henry D. Humphrey was city marshall of Alma, Arkansas. Like many officers discussed here, he was a farmer by trade. But in the words of Humphrey's son, Vernon, "You couldn't live off it [farming] in those days." Humphrey ran for the post of Alma City marshall and won. The regular income was a great help, but almost immediately, there was trouble. Thirty days into his term, he was abducted and beaten by bank robbers and his gun was stolen from him. The beating was bad enough but in those days lawmen paid for their own equipment. The price of a replacement gun was no small matter to a man trying to make ends meet during the Great Depression.

On June 23, 1933, the day after his abduction and beating, Humphrey received a call that a grocery store in Fayetteville, Arkansas, about fifty miles north of Alma, had been robbed by two men who were heading his way. Humphrey borrowed a pistol and contacted Deputy Sheriff A. M. "Red" Salyers. Together the two officers proceeded north on the Fayetteville road in hopes of heading off the bandits. Salyers, at the wheel of his own car, and Humphrey had not traveled too far when they passed a friend of theirs named Webber Wilson, who was driving south in the oncoming lane at a very slow speed. Right after this, another car, traveling at a high rate of speed, passed. A split-second later the officers heard a tremendous crash. The second car had careened into the rear end of Webber Wilson's slow-moving car.

Salyers turned his car around and rolled to a stop a few feet away from the wreck. Humphrey stepped from the car just as Webber Wilson was running off in the opposite direction. Then a shotgun blast rang out. The driver of the second car had opened fire on Humphrey, striking him in the chest with a load of buckshot and blowing him into the ditch. With that shot the assailant's gun had apparently jammed because he started working furiously with the ejection mechanism. This gave Salyers enough time to take his rifle and retreat to a house about a hundred yards away. From there, he began shooting with such accuracy that decades later one of the two bandits involved still vividly recalled Salyers' marksmanship. At some point automatic weapons fire raked across the area, striking a number of objects, including a strawberry field several hundred yards away. But no one was hit, including Salyers who proceeded to disrupt the killers' movements with a number of well-placed shots, slightly wounding one of the two bandits as he and his companion took off in Salyers' car. The car was later found abandoned near Van Buren, Arkansas, not far from Fort Smith.

Humphrey was taken to the hospital where he hung on for three days. But, on June 26, his killer by then long gone, Humphrey died.

Major Joseph Crowson, Shot by Joe Palmer on January 16, 1934, Died January 26, 1934

Tuesday, January 16, 1934, dawned damp and chilly. A thick fog rising from the nearby Trinity River blanketed the countryside around the Eastham prison farm, twenty miles north of Huntsville. Through the milky haze, two miles south of Camp 1, the great hulking shapes of several large brush heaps loomed here and there. Then movement, faint at first, dozens of yards away, followed by voices and the sounds of axes, handsaws, and horses. Squads of prisoners dressed in white denim lumbered toward the clearing, spreading out and getting down to the business of clearing the brush piles.

It has been said that it was really too foggy to "turn out" the convict work crews that day, too difficult to see the prisoners. That was usually the rule: the squads were "turned out" as soon as it was light enough to see them and brought back when it was too dark to see them. That also meant working the convicts in the rain, as long as it was not a heavy enough downpour to lose sight of the white or striped denim uniforms. That, of course, meant the guards also worked in the rain, sleet, and blazing sun, right along with everyone else. It was not an easy job. But that day, January 16, the crews had to turn out, fog or no fog. Wood supplies were very low and although it was not too cold that day, a front was due in soon. The camps needed to replenish their supplies.

Each squad was overseen by a group of guards collectively called "the shotgun ring," so named because of the Browning "Long Tom" shotguns they carried. Positioned at a distance, however, was the "long-arm man," or "high rider" as the convicts called him, a guard on horseback armed with a high-powered rifle. His job was to maintain his distance and watch the group as a whole. Should a convict break past the shotgun ring, the high rider would pick him off with his rifle. That is the way it was supposed to work. That was the official policy of the Texas prison system at the time, but at least two convicts in the work crews, Raymond Hamilton and Joe Palmer, were counting on the habitual disregard of that policy by one of Eastham's more notorious guards, a man noted for leaving his post to beat prisoners, a guard who had once beaten Palmer half to death, the high rider in the field that morning—Major Joseph Crowson. Although some convicts did not remember Crowson as being all that vicious, Palmer hated the guard and was about to spring a well-planned trap on him.

"Major" was Crowson's given name, not a title. Indeed the rank of major did not exist at the time in the Texas prison system. Crowson had grown up in the woods near Eastham. Several of his relatives had been guards. At least one Crowson still works for the Texas Department of Justice–Institutional Division, as the Texas prison system is known today. Nevertheless, Major Crowson started out as a barber in the town of Lovelady, Texas, not far from Eastham. However, he eventually gave up the barber's trade and signed on as the first so-called long-arm man for the Texas prison system, a position created by Colonel Lee Simmons, general manager of the system.

To raise Crowson's ire on the morning of January 16, Hamilton had "jumped squads," meaning he had left his own seventeen-man work crew and joined another, specifically Palmer's. Hamilton and Palmer, both armed, simply waited for Crowson's inevitable approach, thus affording the inmates the opportunity to disarm the one man who could have prevented the escape.

Guard Olin (or Olan) Bozeman, assigned to Palmer's squad, had already noticed Hamilton in his group. He had spotted him back at Camp 1, even before the inmates started for the fields, but decided not to pursue the matter until later, exactly what Hamilton and Palmer had hoped for. They suspected that once in the field, Bozeman would summon Crowson and either have him beat Hamilton and take him back to his squad or hold a gun on him while Bozeman whipped him. Sure enough, as soon as they arrived in the field, Bozeman called the long-arm man, the high rider Crowson. The two guards were conversing when Palmer walked up. The initial impression was that he was about to ask a question. Instead, he pulled an automatic.

"Don't you boys try to do anything," he said.

There are conflicting reports as to what happened next. Some sources indicate that Palmer deliberately shot Crowson at this point, for revenge—something Palmer himself admitted later in open court. "I killed Major Crowson," he said, "because of mistreatment to convicts." However, at least one source makes the claim that Crowson fired the first shot and that only then did Palmer open fire. Still another source quotes Palmer directly, disclosing the killer's astonishment that Crowson and Bozeman chose to fight: "I told the guards to sit still. Do not move and there will not be no shooting. I really thought the guards would stick their hands up."

Regardless, at some point Crowson was shot in the stomach by Palmer. Mortally wounded, the guard turned his horse around and rode all the way back to Camp 1 to alert the camp manager, B. B. Monzingo. Palmer then fired at Bozeman. He missed. Bozeman pulled a pistol and fired at Palmer. Palmer ducked. The bullet barely creased his temple. Palmer fired again.

The slug struck Bozeman's holstered shotgun and sliced deep into his hip. Both the mangled weapon and Bozeman fell to the ground.

Just then, someone concealed in the ravine not far away stood up and fired a volley from a Browning automatic rifle over the heads of everyone in the field. It was Clyde Barrow. Guards and prisoners alike dove for cover. Palmer turned to find Hamilton fumbling around in the mud. He had accidentally ejected the clip from his weapon.

Some have said that because of this, Hamilton never fired a shot. However, at least one eyewitness, an inmate in Palmer's squad, remembered both gunmen shooting at *and* hitting Bozeman. This may be true because even if Hamilton's clip was indeed ejected, presumably one round might have still been in the chamber.

Regardless, as soon as gunfire erupted from the creek, Hamilton, Palmer, Henry Methvin, and Hilton Bybee, all dangerous convicts serving long sentences, started running south toward the sound of a car horn. Bonnie Parker, waiting in the car on Calhoun Ferry Road, was sounding a beacon for the fleeing convicts.

Two guards (some reports say three) ran away, completely deserting their posts and the wounded Bozeman. Only one guard, Bobbie Bullock, stood his ground, perhaps preventing a devastating mass escape. "The first man to raise his head," he shouted, "will have it blown clear off!"

Nevertheless, one other convict managed to flee. J. B. French, two squads away from Palmer, Hamilton, and the others, ducked into the underbrush until things quieted down, then slipped into the woods. He was not in on the actual break and did not understand the significance of the horn. He was recaptured after midnight without ever meeting the ones responsible for his brief taste of freedom.

Eventually the wounded Bozeman mounted his horse and rode back to Camp 1 where he and Crowson were transported to a hospital in Huntsville, Texas. Bozeman recovered fully, but Crowson developed acute complications, among them pneumonia. On January 23, he mustered enough strength to dictate and sign a deathbed statement naming Palmer as his assailant. He died three days later. He was twenty-four.

Wade McNabb, Killed by Joe Palmer, March 29, 1934, His Body Recovered April 3, 1934

On February 24, 1934, convict trustee Wade McNabb, serving a twenty-five-year sentence for an August 20, 1932, armed robbery in Longview,

Texas, was released on a sixty-day furlough to visit his parents in Green-ville, Texas. Late in March, McNabb and his brother took a trip to Shreve-port, Louisiana. McNabb wanted to see the city before he had to return to Eastham, where he was a "building tender" at Camp 1. On March 29, McNabb and his brother were in a domino parlor in Gladewater, Texas, between Tyler and Marshall. At one point McNabb took off his coat, telling his brother he was hot. Shortly thereafter, someone called McNabb away from his brother. He was never seen alive again.

On April 3, 1934, crime reporter Harry McCormick of the *Houston Press*, received an anonymous letter stating that if he followed the enclosed map, the body of "one of the [Texas] prison system's worst rats could be found." The letter, described as very well written, also stated that McNabb had been "'put on the spot' because of treatment of fellow prisoners." Acting on the tip, McCormick found McNabb's body face down with his arms crossed under him in a damp clearing near Waskom, Texas. It appeared that he had been made to kneel in the soft, moist ground, then struck very hard in the head. Afterward six bullets (some reports cite four) were fired into his brain.

This was the work of Joe Palmer, escaped Eastham convict who, until Clyde Barrow's raid, had been serving twenty-five years for armed robbery. Indeed, the reason for the murder, cited in the letter, is strikingly similar to Palmer's statement regarding his reason for killing Eastham guard Major Joseph Crowson: "I killed Major Crowson . . . because of mistreatment to convicts."

Within days of his release from Eastham by Clyde Barrow, Palmer had participated in the robberies of at least two banks—one in Rembrandt, Iowa, and one in Poteau, Oklahoma. After paying his share of a fee to one of the raid's conspirators, Palmer had enough left over to "buy" McNabb a furlough. That is the correct term—"buy." It was used by convicts of the day to indicate the payment of money to a lawyer for a service, because often the payment went beyond the lawyer. After his furlough, Palmer caught up with McNabb in Gladewater, abducted him from the domino parlor, and drove him to that clearing near the Texas-Louisiana border. He then made McNabb kneel down, told him to say his prayers, and slugged him in the head. Afterward he pumped four to six slugs into his skull and walked away.

At the time of Palmer's execution more than a year later, he was asked to clear up the McNabb murder. Although Palmer made a rather eloquent statement as he stood before the electric chair, he went to his death without saying a word about Wade McNabb.

Edward Bryan Wheeler and Holloway Daniel Murphy, Killed by Clyde Barrow and Henry Methvin, April 1, 1934

On the morning of April 1, 1934, twenty-six-year-old Ed Wheeler and Doris, his wife of eighteen months, were listening to the radio and chatting over Easter Sunday breakfast. They spoke about the meaning of Easter, of life and death and of the Resurrection. At one point Wheeler made a comment about how tragic it was that the dead are so often forgotten. After breakfast, he and his wife drove to the home of Polk Ivy and his wife.

Wheeler and Ivy were partners, veterans of a relatively new state agency—the Texas Highway Patrol (now the Texas Department of Public Safety). It was formed in 1931 in response to the growing need to regulate the state's developing highway system, especially with regard to overloaded trucks, which at the time were destroying Texas highways as fast as they could be paved. In addition to this, officers of the highway patrol were responsible for enforcing traffic laws and helping stranded motorists. Wheeler was one of the original fifty officers hired by the agency.

The Wheelers and Ivys visited for a while, then Ed took his wife back home and got ready for his shift. He and Polk Ivy were in the motorcycle division. They were to begin training a new recruit that day, twenty-two-year-old Holloway Daniel Murphy. Murphy was from the town of Alto in East Texas. He had joined the force a month earlier, completed his basic training, and had just been assigned to north Texas. He and his fiancée, Maree, had already picked out an apartment in Fort Worth. They were to be married on April 13, less than two weeks from that Easter Sunday, his first day as a patrolman in the field.

Riding Harley-Davidsons, the three patrolmen rendezvoused at a service station near the Tarrant County courthouse in Fort Worth and proceeded north out of town. Polk Ivy led the trio, with Wheeler and Murphy behind, as was the custom when training a new patrolman, one veteran in the lead while other dropped back with the new officer. Their assignment, apart from checking weight limits on trucks, enforcing traffic laws, and aiding motorists, was to be on the lookout for Raymond Hamilton, Eastham fugitive who had robbed the bank in West, Texas the day before.

At three in the afternoon, the officers were traveling northwest on Texas State Highway 114, between Grapevine and Roanoke, when they passed East Dove Road. Apparently, all three patrolmen spotted the Ford V-8 parked up the road about one hundred yards from 114. Ivy had noticed it earlier, but thought nothing of it. Wheeler, however, was curious and motioned for Murphy to follow as he turned up the road to investigate.

Driving behind the patrolmen were Fred and Mary Giggal, a Dallas couple out for a drive. They had been following the officers for several minutes and noticed two of them turn off onto the side road. As they drove past East Dove Road, they saw that the officers had already dismounted and racked their bikes. The Dallas couple joked about how terrible it would be to get a ticket on such a beautiful Easter Sunday afternoon. Then they heard several loud explosions—backfires they thought at first. Then, with growing concern, they slowed down, turned their car around, and drove back to the intersection. When they arrived, they saw "the taller of two men" firing into the prone bodies of the patrolmen. Then the "smaller man" noticed the Giggals and started hurrying back to his car. The Giggals turned around and sped away in search of the third patrolman, Polk Ivy.

By this time, Ivy had noticed his colleagues were not behind him and had turned around to search for them. He soon encountered the Giggals who flagged him down and told him what they had seen. Ivy continued on to East Dove Road where he found Wheeler and Murphy alone, lying in the dirt, their motorcycles still racked. Wheeler was dead. Murphy died minutes later en route to a hospital in Grapevine.

It appears that Wheeler was shot first. His weapon was still holstered. He had no idea he was in danger. In reaction to the shooting of his partner, however, Murphy had evidently tried to arm his weapon, a shotgun he kept unloaded in a scabbard on his bike out of fear that he might one day fall and have it discharge accidentally. The shotgun was found lying near him with several unused shells strewn about.

Murphy was buried in the suit he would have worn to his wedding. His fiancée, Maree, wore her wedding dress to the funeral.

William Calvin "Cal" Campbell, Killed by Clyde Barrow and Henry Methvin, April 6, 1934

Cal Campbell was a resident of Commerce, Oklahoma, and a contractor by trade. He once had his own business but had lost everything when the depression hit. He was nearly sixty then. A single father of four, Campbell sought election to one of the Ottawa County constable seats to make ends meet. It only paid $15 a week, but in the words of his son Jim, "It kept us eating!" Campbell was elected to the position not because he was a professional lawman, which he was not, but because everyone knew him and liked him.

On the morning of April 6, 1934, Commerce City marshal Percy Boyd received word from a citizen that a car had been parked all night long on a side road just off of Highway 66 in the mining district between Commerce and Miami. Boyd asked Campbell to accompany him as he went to investigate. Campbell agreed, apparently expecting to find nothing more than a carload of drunks sleeping it off, the same thing Boyd expected to find.

Turning off Highway 66, they pulled to a stop in front of the strange car and got out. Suddenly the car took off in reverse, moving fast. Approximately one hundred yards down the road, however, the driver lost control of the car and it veered into a ditch, miring the rear wheels in mud up to the axle. Boyd and Campbell were still standing in the road, apparently dumbstruck by what they had just seen. Suddenly someone from the car was shooting. The officers pulled their weapons and returned fire. Boyd was struck in the head and knocked unconscious. Campbell, still firing, was struck in the abdomen and killed instantly, a bullet severing his spinal chord.

When Boyd regained consciousness, the taller of the two gunmen—Henry Methvin—was standing over him, coaxing him to get up. Once on his feet, Boyd was hustled over to the gunmen's car, which was still stuck. A crowd gathered as the shorter man—Clyde Barrow—began to enlist bystanders and even Boyd to try and push the car out of the ditch. Eventually a vehicle happened along, and the assailants used it to pull the car free. Boyd was loaded into the car. Besides the gunmen, the car was also occupied by a petite young woman, who sat in the front on the passenger side. The shorter man took the wheel. The larger man got in the back with Boyd. The car lurched forward and Cal Campbell was left behind, dead in the road. Boyd was later released near Fort Scott, Kansas.

✸Appendix E

Blanche's Preliminary Parole Report

Sentenced to ten years in the Missouri State Penitentiary in 1933, Blanche Barrow won her parole in March of 1939. Her work toward gaining her freedom is evident in the preliminary parole record that appears below.

Recommendations from: Dan Holman, H. L. Cohen, Alford Diceman, Paul Reinking, J. C. Briggs, B. F. McCullough, D. Lee (atty.), Milburn Mitchell, H. C. Sanders, R. L. Ives, Jeff D. McLendon, T. G. Carr, W. H. Ray, J. N. McCain, B. D. Paschall, W. J. Whitemen, Edward C. Hall, C. D. Cates, H. P. Hosey, Carl S. Preswitt, Ott Doan, W. G. Citty, Amos Taylor, Robert E. Lee.

Mrs. C. T. Barrow (home offer), Mr. & Mrs. W. J. Wilkerson (employment), W. J. Winkler offers employment.

Your sponsor is James Parsons of K. C., Mo. Judge is neutral, Pros. Atty., neu., Sheriff-Rec.

Blanche, your file is as good as it should be, the idea is just to get these people here to push your file along. There is no one who has any more right to get out of here than you have and I hope you do go. There is nothing you can do to get any better file than you already have. Around 1,000 on petitions.

—B. D. Paschall, Dallas attorney

Notes

Editor's Introduction

1. State of Texas, County of Dallas, certified copy of birth certificate 15965, Bennie Iva Blanche Caldwell. Blanche mentions in a letter to her mother, as quoted in Baker, *Blanche Barrow*, 22–23, that she can't remember her parents being together "more than a couple of days." Also, in the first chapter of Blanche Caldwell Barrow's own memoir she states, "I was brought up by a kind, loving, law-abiding father, without the aid of a mother." In an interview with the editor, October 5, 2002, Rhea Leen Linder (Bonnie Parker's niece), said that Blanche had an "everything for me" attitude, which probably stemmed from her father's attentions.

2. The divorce rate was one in eighty-five in 1905. By 1911 it had risen to one in twelve. Gordon and Gordon, *American Chronicle*, 117. In an undated letter to her mother written from her prison cell in Missouri, Blanche noted, "I want you two [mother and father] with me for once in my life, as I can't remember having you both with me at the same time for more than a couple of days." Baker, *Blanche Barrow*, 22–23.

Lillian Bell Pond was born August 25, 1895, and was already ninety-three at the time of Blanche Caldwell Frasure's death in 1988. She lived an unknown number of years afterward. Bennie Iva Blanche Caldwell's certificate of birth. Besides Caldwell, other surnames Lillian Pond used included Marcum, Horton, Pierce, and Oberlacher. This is based on addresses in the headings of Blanche Caldwell Barrow's letters to her mother as reproduced in Baker, *Blanche Barrow*, 27 and 52; on a *Dallas Evening Journal* article as reproduced in Baker, 21; and on Blanche Caldwell Frasure's death certificate, December 24, 1988. But Pond may not have actually married these men. To friends Blanche intimated that her mother was prone to merely using the last name of whomever she was living with at the time. Esther Weiser, interview by editor, October 31, 2002. Hereafter, unless otherwise noted, all interviews were conducted by the editor.

3. Blanche Barrow quoted in Weiser interview, September 8, 2001. In a letter to her mother, Blanche alluded to this, lamenting that she would never be called "mother" or "grandmother." Letter of February 28, 1936, reproduced in Baker, *Blanche Barrow*, 60–62. Later in life Blanche owned at least four dolls that some thought were treated as surrogate children. Blanche made clothes for them and spoke to them as if they were her own flesh and blood. Linder interview, October 5, 2002; Weiser interview, October 5, 2002.

From letters it can be surmised that Callaway remained in contact with Blanche's mother at least up to and during Blanche's incarceration in the Missouri State Penitentiary, long after Blanche's estrangement and subsequent divorce from Callaway. In an undated letter to her mother, Blanche asks her if Callaway still visits her. In yet another letter Blanche responds to an apparent reference by her mother to Callaway: "Well, mother, I don't care what John [Callaway] thinks of me, but that is just one more mark against him tearing my picture up. But he can't hurt me any." Callaway even wrote to Blanche while she was in prison, something Blanche was none too pleased with. Writing to her mother, Blanche stated she did not care to have anything from Callaway. Almost four months later Blanche wrote, "I hope he [Callaway] does not come near me when I am a free woman." Letters reproduced in Baker, *Blanche Barrow*, 22–23, 35, 51, 54.

4. Knowledge of Blanche's friendship with Renfro comes from information written in Blanche's hand on the back of a photograph of her and Renfro.

5. Blanche Barrow, letter to her mother, n.d., quoted in Baker, *Blanche Barrow*, 22–23.

6. Marie Barrow interview, May 1, 1998; Weiser interview, September 8, 2001. According to a letter written to her father, Blanche Barrow establishes the date she met Buck as November 11, 1929. Blanche Caldwell Barrow, letter to Matt Caldwell, November 11, 1933. See Appendix B. Because the date of Buck Barrow's arrest following a Denton, Texas, burglary has been listed in some sources as occurring in October 1929, the date in Blanche's letter would seem incorrect, but it is not. Buck was arrested shortly after midnight on November 30, 1929. *Denton (Tex.) Record-Chronicle*, November 30, 1929. See also Fortune, *Fugitives*, 32; Cumie Barrow, unpublished manuscript. The latter two sources both list October 1929 as the date of the Denton, Texas, burglary.

Supposedly the origin of Marvin Barrow's nickname, Buck, lay in the fact of his sprinting abilities. His aunt once observed him running around acting like a horse when he was just a child. Accordingly she dubbed him Buck, and the name stuck. Cumie Barrow, unpublished manuscript.

7. State of Oklahoma, Marriage License, July 2–3, 1931. In her unpublished manuscript, Cumie Barrow cites Buck's sentence as four years; Blanche also states four years in her memoir. However, the sentence is listed as five years in Fortune, *Fugitives*, 32. Buck's letter of January 16, 1930, to his mother appears in Appendix C. The letter was no doubt written by a fellow convict.

According to Cumie Barrow, Buck was illiterate. Cumie Barrow, unpublished manuscript.

8. Cumie Barrow, unpublished manuscript. Also in a 1984 interview, Blanche openly admitted to accompanying Buck on robberies while he was an escaped convict. Blanche Barrow interview, November 18, 1984.

9. For the full story of the evolution of the plot to raid Eastham, see Phillips, *Running with Bonnie and Clyde*, 33–92. In an interview by the editor on November 3, 1984, Blanche stated that she had visited Clyde a number of times while he was at Eastham, accompanied more than once by Buck, who had escaped from the Ferguson unit, just across the Trinity River from Eastham. During each visit Clyde told Blanche he couldn't stand Eastham, that he wanted to escape, then raid the farm and free as many prisoners as he could.

10. Blanche was a self-described camera buff, using a camera of some kind throughout most of her adult life. She loved taking snapshots, nothing formal or particularly aesthetic, just images of captured moments, mostly of the people closest to her. Between 1930 and 1933, she owned a handheld Kodak camera with folding bellows, probably a No. 2A Folding Autographic Brownie, manufactured between 1915 and 1926. It used 116 film and produced eight 2½-by-4¼-inch negatives per roll. She bought the camera secondhand for three dollars (the original retail price was thirteen dollars) to use mostly during road trips with Buck in 1930 and 1931.

Throughout 1932, Blanche used the camera both in West Dallas and Denison, Texas, while she waited for Buck to finish his prison term. Early in 1933, she lent the camera to Bonnie, Clyde, and W. D. Jones. With it they took some of the better-known photographs of themselves, including the infamous shot of Bonnie with a cigar clenched in her teeth. The unprocessed rolls of film containing these images, as well as the camera itself, were among the many items abandoned in Joplin, Missouri, following the shoot-out of April 13, 1933.

Blanche was then without a camera until fall 1933 when her mother mailed her own red Kodak handheld camera to her in prison. This was a less expensive fixed-focus camera, probably a No. 2A Beau Brownie, manufactured between 1930 and 1933 and available in five colors, including red. Like its folding-bellows forerunner, the Beau Brownie used 116 film.

Throughout Blanche's incarceration, she and her mother mailed the camera back and forth to each other. Blanche used it to make all her prison photographs. Her interest in taking pcitures continued after her release from prison, lasting until a few years before her death. Blanche Barrow interview, September 24, 1984; Blanche Barrow, letter to her mother, April 10, 1934, quoted in Baker, *Blanche Barrow*, 39; Weiser interviews, September 8, 2001, and October 31, 2002.

11. Blanche Barrow interview, November 3 and September 24, 1984.

12. Accompanying Blanche Barrow's original manuscript is a large, unused Christmas card, on the back of which appears in Blanche's hand, "written in 1933 or 34 & 35. Part of my story with the Barrow gang. Blanche Barrow."

13. Blanche Barrow, letter to mother, October 28, 1933, quoted in Baker, *Blanche Barrow*, 15.

14. Baker, *Blanche Barrow*, 15.

Chapter 1. *View from a Cell*

1. In the original manuscript Blanche first wrote, "me as I did him," then crossed that out and replaced it with "as a woman does."

Chapter 2. *Marriage*

1. Blanche Barrow, letter to her father Matt Caldwell, November 11, 1933; *Dallas Morning News*, November 11, 1929.

2. Fortune, *Fugitives*, 24; *Dallas Morning News*, November 11, 1929.

3. On "Black Thursday," October 24, U.S. Steel dropped from 261.75 to 193.5 and General Electric went from above 400 to 283. A consortium of bankers, including J. P. Morgan then tried desperately to drive stocks back up by deliberately paying above-market value for U.S. Steel and other stocks, but to no avail. On "Black Tuesday," October 29, there was such a sell-off of stocks that it was humanly impossible to keep up with the trading. The ticker tape flowed for hours after the market closed. By the day of Blanche and Buck's first meeting, American Can was down 54 percent, AT&T had dropped 35 percent, General Motors had lost 50 percent of its value, and U.S. Steel had sunk 63 percent. And it was only the beginning. Arnold, "The Crash, 217.

4. *Dallas Morning News*, July 3, 1931.

5. Procter, "Great Depression"; Marie Barrow interview, September 15, 1984; U.S. Census, 1920 and 1930. The population of Dallas, Texas was listed at 158,976 in 1920 and 294,734 in 1930. Although cities like Dallas would reach unemployment numbers in the double digits, the rate remained far below the national average of 25 percent. And the Barrows were actually able to open a small business in 1931, the Star Service Station at 1620 Eagle Ford Road (Singleton Road today) in West Dallas.

6. Procter, "Great Depression"; Cabell Phillips, *New York Times Chronicle of American Life*, 54, 34; Watkins, *Hungry Years*, 105, 126; Andrist, *American Heritage History*, p. 185; Kennedy, *Freedom from Fear*, 192.

7. Procter, "Great Depression"; Fults interview December 5, 1980.

8. John Callaway was Blanche's first husband. This was Buck Barrow's third marriage. At age seventeen he had married Margaret Heneger. During the marriage twin boys were born, one of whom died at five months of age. Barrow later divorced his first wife and married Pearl Churchley, by whom he fathered a girl. Eventually that marriage also ended in divorce. Blanche Caldwell Callaway was still married to her first husband when she met Buck Barrow, but the month after her divorce was finalized, she married him. Cumie Barrow, unpublished manuscript.

9. In the original manuscript, "shadow" was written here, then crossed out and replaced with "sentence" by Blanche.

10. It may have been true that Blanche did not know of Buck's record. In a letter to her father dated November 11, 1933, she reminisces about having met Buck exactly four years earlier to the day. However, Blanche couldn't

have remained ignorant for long because on November 30, 1929, less than three weeks later, Buck was wounded and arrested following a burglary in Denton, Texas. *Denton Record-Chronicle*, November 30, 1929. Furthermore, Blanche definitely knew Buck was tried, convicted, and sent to prison. Buck mentions Blanche in a letter he sent from the main prison in Huntsville, Texas. Buck Barrow, letter to family, January 16, 1930. If, as Blanche states, the revelation of her husband's escape came after she had married him (July 3, 1931), it would mean that Buck Barrow had kept his secret since March 8, 1930, the date of his escape. State of Texas, Texas Prison System, letter from William Thompson to Doug Walsh, May 17, 1932. There is evidence to suggest Blanche may have actually known all along of Buck's escape. Cumie Barrow makes it quite clear in her unpublished manuscript that she knew her son had escaped when he arrived at her home in March 1930. She described the white prison clothes Buck was wearing, how he changed out of them, and how he told her to burn them. Cumie Barrow, unpublished manuscript. In addition, in a memo from the Justice Department Bureau of Criminal Investigation to Doug Walsh of the Dallas Police Department, Jim Muckleroy told investiga-tors that his nephew, Buck Barrow, hid at his farm near Martinsville, Texas, following his prison break. In addition to the November 30, 1929, burglary for which he was sentenced to the Texas penitentiary, Buck Barrow had a number of prior arrests. On December 21, 1925, he was arrested in Houston under the name "Elmer Toms" for stealing tires. *Dallas Morning News*, April 14, 1933. This Houston arrest may be the source of some stories that Buck's younger brother Clyde had a criminal record in Houston. According to Marie Barrow, her brother Clyde neither lived in Houston nor committed any crimes there. Marie Barrow interview, August 24, 1984. By 1928, Buck Barrow was suspected of auto theft in a number of Texas cities, including Dallas, Waco, Uvalde, Waxahachie, and San Antonio. *Dallas Morning News*, April 14, 1933. Most of the charges were dropped, but San Antonio authorities arrested Buck in August 1928 after a local police officer caught him in the act of stealing a car. Cumie Barrow, unpublished manuscript. His younger sister, Marie, ten years old at the time, remembered that she and her parents traveled to San Antonio for Buck's trial. She described traveling by horse-drawn wagon and that for some reason W. D. Jones, his mother, and a couple of brothers traveled with them. The trip took a long time and the group worked their way to and from San Antonio as migrant farmhands. Marie Barrow interview, September 15, 1993. In January 1929, however, the San Antonio charges were also dismissed. Later in the year, October 13, 1929, Buck and Clyde Barrow and a friend named Frank Clause were arrested trying to burglarize a lumber company at 2521 Florence in Dallas. They were released due to lack of evidence. *Dallas Morning News*, April 14, 1933. Then on November 30, 1929, the Barrow brothers along with yet another friend, Sidney Moore, burglarized a service station in Denton, Texas. The Denton police chased them and opened fire, wounding and capturing Buck. Clyde and Sidney escaped. *Denton (Tex.) Record-Chronicle*, November 30, 1929. Despite what Blanche may have known or when she knew it, by all accounts she did press him to return to prison and finish his sentence.

11. Readers familiar with the old Walls Unit in Huntsville, Texas, with its distinctive red brick walls, may be puzzled by the reference here to gray walls. However, at the time of Buck Barrow's return to prison the original gray sandstone walls, dating from the nineteenth century, were still the only things separating the inmates from the outside world. In the 1940s those walls, by then seriously deteriorated, were encased in the red brick we see today. From atop the walls at almost any point it is possible to still see the cap of the original gray wall sandwiched between the two layers of brick.

12. In addition to Cumie and Blanche, the group traveling with Buck included sisters Marie and Nell, and Nell's second husband Luther Cowan. Marie Barrow interviews, September 25, 1993, and April 19, 1995. Cumie Barrow mentions only one sister in her unpublished manuscript. Nell is the sister implied by Fortune. Fortune, *Fugitives*, 89. The date and voluntary nature of Buck Barrow's return to prison are officially confirmed in a letter from William Thompson, chief of the Bureau of Records, Texas Prison System, to Doug Walsh of the Dallas Police Department, May 17, 1932. There is, however, a bit of confusion as to whether it was Nell's second husband, Luther Cowan, or her first, Leon Hale, who accompanied the family to Huntsville. In the two interviews mentioned above Marie interchanges the names. However, at the time there is no mention of Hale in the city directory, Nell's last name is listed as Barrow not Hale, and she's not only working at the same beauty and barber shop as Cowan but is also living in the same apartment building. Thus it was probably Cowan who went to Huntsville. *Worley's Dallas City Directory*, 1931.

When Henry and Cumie Barrow first moved to Dallas in 1921, Clyde did not live with them at the free campground but with Nell and her first husband, Leon Hale. Clyde attended Sidney Lanier School for "no more than two weeks" then got a job working at the same business where Hale was working. Hale also played saxophone in a local band at night. He is the one who taught Clyde Barrow to play saxophone. Despite his divorce from Nell, Hale remained highly regarded by the Barrows. Years later, LC, whose name was legally composed of those two letters, and only those letters, adopted the name "Leon" in honor of Hale. Marie Barrow interviews, September 15 and 25, 1993, and April 19, 1995; Buddy Barrow interview, October 26, 2002.

13. This is unusual. Standard Texas prison system procedure at the time called for escapees, or other troublemakers, to wear stripes so they would stand out from the other convicts and thus be easier for guards to keep an eye on. Ralph Fults, interview, February 1, 1981. Cumie Barrow makes mention of this, saying that upon Buck's return to prison, "They never even put him back in stripes." Cumie Barrow, unpublished manuscript.

14. In the original manuscript, "people" was written here, then crossed out and replaced with "mother" by Blanche.

15. Marvin Ivan "Buck" Barrow was born on March 14, 1903, at Jones Prairie, Texas, in Milam County. Cumie Barrow, unpublished manuscript. His

gravestone at Western Heights Cemetery in Dallas lists the year as 1905, which is incorrect. Family members concede that their mother was so upset when Buck was killed that she confused his birth year with Nell's. Evidently the same thing happened with Clyde as well. The family Bible as well as other sources lists Clyde Barrow's birth year as 1910, not 1909 as carved on the gravestone. This is supported by Cumie herself in her own unpublished manuscript. It is also supported in Fortune, who quotes Nell indicating in three different places that she was five years older than Clyde. Fortune, *Fugitives*, 3, 7, 10. The 1910 date is further supported by information supplied to Louisiana officials by Elvin "Jack" Barrow, Clyde's oldest brother, at the time of Clyde's death. Barrow declared Clyde's age to be twenty-four, indicating a 1910 birth year. Louisiana State Board of Health, Bureau of Vital Statistics, certificate of death, Clyde Chestnut Barrow.

16. The Woman for whom Blanche worked was probably Artie, the Barrows' oldest daughter and a beautician living in Denison, Texas, at the time. Artie was married to a man named Wilbur Winkler who was circulation manager for the *Denison Herald* and who owned the Cinderella Beauty Shoppe. Artie managed the shop at 430 West Sears, and it was no doubt there that Blanche worked. Cumie Barrow, unpublished manuscript; *Denison City Directory*, 1929, 1930, 1931, 1932, 1933, 1934. Some have said that it was Artie, not Wilbur Winkler, who owned the shop. Buddy Barrow e-mail, September 16, 2002.

17. Clyde was serving two counts of burglary and five counts of auto theft, all from McLennan County. His FBI file only mentions burglary; his prison record lists his offenses as "burglary, theft (14 years)." Cumie Barrow, unpublished manuscript; U.S. Department of Justice, Division of Investigation, Identification Order No. 1211, October 24, 1933; Woods, letter to Phillips, March 19, 1985. "The Walls" refers to the main prison unit at Huntsville, Texas. It has been said that Clyde Barrow axed his toes because he couldn't stand the workload at Eastham. Two other independent sources agree with the reason given here by Blanche Caldwell Barrow. Fults interview, November 5, 1980, and a letter from Sterling C. Henson to Kent Biffle, September 2, 1980.

18. Eastham is a prison farm of approximately 13,000 acres located in an oxbow of the Trinity River, twenty miles north of Huntsville. Its name is derived from that of the Eastham family, who purchased the property in 1891 and immediately began leasing it to the state as a prison farm. The state purchased the property outright in 1915. Texas Historical Commission, "Eastham Prison Farm." For a full account of the history of farm leasing and the Texas penal system, see Walker, *Penology for Profit*, 13–142. In Clyde Barrow's day there were two camps at Eastham. On his arrival there in 1930, he was housed in Camp 2, a wooden structure said to have been one of the original buildings from Eastham's preprison plantation days. Later he was transferred to Camp 1, a concrete structure located one mile north of Camp 2. It was there that Barrow killed his first man, a convict trustee who had sexually assaulted Barrow, on October 29, 1931. Among the many incidents involving Barrow, either as victim, eyewitness, or perpetrator, were fights, rapes, and murders between

convicts as well as beatings, various forms of torture, and murder committed by guards at the facility. See Phillips, *Running with Bonnie and Clyde*, for a full account. See also McConal, *Over the Wall*, 90–91; Phillips, "Raid on Eastham"; Henson, letter to Biffle, September 2, 1980; Fulsom, *Prison Stories*, 80–83; and Martin and EklandOlson, *Walls Came Tumbling Down*, 9–15.

19. Buck was robbing filling stations and oil company payrolls during this period. This revelation came up in response to an interview question about whether Blanche remembered Raymond Hamilton. She said that Raymond often wanted to accompany her and Buck during the above-mentioned robberies, but that Buck didn't like him and both thought he was too young. Blanche said she and Buck would "just drive off and leave him" Blanche Barrow interviews, September 24 and November 18, 1984.

20. On March 8, 1930, Buck had escaped from the Ferguson prison farm, near Midway, Texas. William Thompson, letter to Doug Walsh of the Dallas Police Department, May 17, 1932.

21. Ralph Fults, who arrived at Eastham with Clyde in 1930 and eventually began plotting with him to one day raid the farm, remembered it differently, saying Barrow received many letters, not only from Bonnie but from his family as well. Fults interview, February 13, 1982.

Chapter 3. *Buck Makes a Pardon*

1. *Denison City Directory*, 1931, 1932, 1933; Blanche Barrow interview, November 18, 1984; Marie Barrow interview, August 24, 1984; Fults interview, November 5, 1980.

2. Cabell Phillips, *New York Times Chronicle*, 35; Gordon and Gordon, *American Chronicle*, 316.

3. Watkins, *Hungry Years*, 127–28.

4. Ibid., 131–41. *Dallas Morning News*, July 29, 1932. MacArthur would do the same again under FDR regarding a preemptive strike against Japanese bombers being readied for a strike on the American bases in the Philippines on December 7, 1941. And he would defy President Harry Truman during the Korean War, prompting Truman to fire him.

5. Andrist, *American Heritage History*, 215.

6. *Dallas Daily Times Herald*, March 1 and 3, 1933; Gordon and Gordon, *American Chronicle*, 315; Schultz, "Great Depression," University of Wisconsin Online.

7. *Dallas Daily Times Herald*, March 4 and 5, 1933; Roosevelt's "First Inaugural Address—March 4, 1933," http://www.nationalcenter.org/FRooseveltFirst Inaugural.html; Schultz, "Great Depression."

8. *Dallas Daily Times Herald*, March 11 and 15, 1933.

9. Ibid., March 17 and 19, 1933. Thornton and Parker were married on September 25, 1926, when both were teenagers. They had not seen each other probably since 1927 or 1928 but they never divorced. Thornton eventually wound up in the Texas penitentiary where he quizzed Ralph Fults extensively about Barrow's relationship with his wife. Fults interviews, December 10, 1980, and July 18, 1981.

10. *Dallas Daily Times Herald*, February 15 and March 20, 1933. This relates directly to the visit a few days later by Bonnie and Clyde and W. D. Jones to the home of Blanche's mother near Dallas. During the visit, described by Blanche Barrow in her memoir, Clyde tries to enlist his brother Buck in a plan to raid the Eastham prison farm.

11. *Dallas Daily Times Herald*, March 22, 23, and 24, 1933. In her memoir Blanche Barrow mentions a lot of beer drinking in Missouri.

12. Cinderella Beauty Shoppe, 430 West Sears, Denison, Texas.

13. Artie Winkler, Buck and Clyde Barrow's older sister.

14. Blanche Barrow knew about this firsthand. She was an eyewitness to brother-in-law Clyde Barrow's attempts to hold a job and live a normal life following his release from prison in 1932. Some have said the experience, coupled with his nightmarish prison memories, largely shaped Clyde Barrow's actions over the subsequent two years. For the full story, see Phillips, *Running with Bonnie and Clyde*.

15. In the original text, "never more to roam" is written here, then crossed out.

16. Huntsville, where Buck Barrow was imprisoned, was one of the many stops on the Houston-to-Oklahoma City bus route. It was also the release point for all Texas convicts leaving the state prison system. Indeed, it still is.

17. Elvin W. Barrow, also known as Jack, the oldest of Buck's siblings, was born in 1894. Blanche is not specific about the location of Elvin Barrow's house. In the 1933 city directory he is listed as residing at 1308 Second Avenue, which does not exist anymore. That part of Second Avenue was eliminated when Fair Park was expanded in the 1930s to accommodate a new building for the Dallas Museum of Fine Art, which has since been moved and renamed the Dallas Museum of Art. However, in 1931 and in 1934, Barrow's residence is listed at two successive addresses on Forest Avenue (Martin Luther King Drive today), 3218 and 3210, respectively. *Worley's Dallas (Texas) City Directory*, 1931, 1933–34, 1934–35. LC Barrow was born in 1913. According to the Barrow family the letters "LC" are not initials. They represent the full first name of the youngest brother and should not be accompanied with periods, as would be the case with initials. Marie Barrow interviews, September 15 and 25, 1993.

18. LC was picked up for questioning so often, especially by the Dallas police, that there were instances when he would be detained as soon as he left the police station following a prior round of questions. Marie Barrow interview, August 1, 1998; Buddy Williams interview, August 1, 1998. There was another, more sinister side to some of these frequent arrests—extortion. In April 1934 a man named Jody called the home of Ruth Lefors, a friend of the Barrows, to report that he and another man named Sonny had been arrested for possession of alcohol. Jody rather offhandedly explained that they needed twenty-five dollars to pay Captain Phillips of the Dallas Police Department or he would file charges against them, that Phillips had actually wanted twenty-five dollars from each man but backed off to twenty-five for both men. Dallas Police Department telephone wiretap transcript, April 26, 1934, 40. Ralph

Fults and Clyde Barrow contracted a pair of Dallas policemen to act as look-outs in front of several Greenville Avenue businesses while they burglarized each one, later sharing the loot with the officers. Phillips, *Running with Bonnie and Clyde*, 66–67.

19. Actually Buck had served just a little more than seven weeks, from approximately January 16, to precisely March 8, 1930. Buck Barrow, letter to family, January 16, 1930; William Thompson, letter to Doug Walsh, May 17, 1932.

20. This sentiment, certainly not uncommon at the time, was apparently the same way Clyde Barrow felt about Bonnie Parker. In a scathing, sarcastic letter written to Raymond Hamilton after Hamilton's capture on April 25, 1934, Barrow notes, "When you started the rumor about Bonnie wanting a 'cut' of the loot you sure messed yourself up. I have always taken care of Bonnie and never asked any thief to help me." Clyde Barrow, letter to Raymond Hamilton, April 27, 1934. Also, some have indicated that Blanche Caldwell Barrow was so petite, almost like a doll, that men would often feel compelled to try and protect her. Linder and Weiser, interviews, October 5, 2002.

21. Regarding her "disabled father," later in the memoir Blanche mentions that he suffered poor eyesight, a substantial loss of hearing, and possibly tuberculosis. See Chapter 9.

22. This ia a curious complaint, for it was Buck's older sister, Artie, who gave Blanche a job and a place to stay in Denison. And Blanche was living with the Barrows in West Dallas and presumably not working outside the house at least through the middle of April 1932. And Buck Barrow would have known this. However, Blanche may have indeed felt tension from the Barrows, especially from Buck's mother who was known to have been a formidable character, to say the least. But for Blanche to write that Buck's "people forgot the wife he had left behind" is not entirely accurate. Although it might not have been to Buck's liking, his older sister had given Blanche a job, something few had the ability to give during the Great Depression. Moreover, others distinctly remember Blanche living with the Barrows at least for a while in their tiny house behind the filling station in West Dallas. According to Cumie Barrow's unpublished manuscript. "Blanche lived most of the time with me, although occasionally she spent some time with one of my daughters in Denison, Texas." Ralph Fults remembered Blanche in West Dallas as well. He and Clyde Barrow borrowed a gun from her to use in the Simms Oil Refinery robbery of March 25, 1932, something Blanche herself confirmed. Fults interviews, November 12 and December 10, 1980; Blanche Barrow interview, November 18, 1984.

In a letter to her mother, Blanche did describe an apparently pleasant Christmas in 1932 at the Barrows' place in West Dallas. She mentions baking a goose with Artie and receiving gifts from the Barrows, from her father, and even from a co-worker at the beauty shop in Denison. She mentions no gift from her mother, however, and she laments that her mother did not join her at the Barrows' for Christmas. Blanche Barrow, letter to her mother, January 14, 1933, quoted in Baker, *Blanche Barrow*, 25–26.

23. The Barrows, particularly Cumie, may have indeed been jealous of Blanche, but it was no doubt equally true that Blanche was just as jealous of them. It is known that she had a penchant for compartmentalizing her close friends and keeping them apart from one another. It was not until Blanche was seriously ill late in life that Bonnie Parker's niece and sister, who had lived next door to Blanche for a number of years, ever met Esther Weiser, who first met Blanche in 1951 and visited her sometimes daily. Weiser interviews, September 8, 2001, and October 5, 2002.

24. There is a photograph of the Barrows' youngest daughter, Marie, playing with the dog in front of the family business, the Star Service Station, which was attached to the Barrow home on Eagle Ford Road in West Dallas.

25. William Daniel Jones was most often referred to simply by the initials, W. D., but he was also known as "Deacon" and "Dub." Born in East Texas in 1916, Jones was only five or six when he moved to West Dallas with his parents, sister, and four brothers. Not long after the move, Jones's father and sister died during a flu epidemic. Jones quit school after the first grade to sell newspapers to help support the family. Because he was illiterate, he had to ask others to read the headlines for him so he'd know what to shout from his post on a downtown Dallas street corner. Jones first remembered seeing Clyde Barrow under the Houston Street viaduct. His family was camped next to the Barrows in a free campground located there. By the time he arrived at Blanche's mother's house near Wilmer, Texas, Jones had been with Barrow and Parker for three months and had been involved with Clyde in at least two murders—that of Doyle Johnson in Temple, Texas, on December 25, 1932, and of Deputy Sheriff Malcolm Davis in West Dallas on January 6, 1933. Jones, "Riding with Bonnie and Clyde"; Jones, interview by Kent Biffle, June 1969.

26. Clyde was granted a general parole on February 2, 1932. U. S. Department of Justice, Division of Investigation, Identification Order No. 1211, October 24, 1933; Woods, letter to Phillips, March 19, 1985.

27. Cumie Barrow says as much in her unpublished memoir.

28. This last statement is revealing, considering Blanche's later statements about accompanying Buck on robberies during that period. Blanche Barrow interview November 18, 1984. Moreover, Cumie Barrow states, "When Buck escaped from the pen, he came by here and got Blanche (who was staying here) and they went off someplace in a car. I think it was in a rooming house someplace, where they hid for awhile." Cumie Barrow, unpublished manuscript.

29. Raymond Hamilton was born in a tent in Oklahoma in 1913. He moved to West Dallas with his mother, brother, and sisters to join his father who'd abandoned the family briefly before turning up in Texas and sending for them. Shortly thereafter, Hamilton's father disappeared again and Raymond took to the streets to try and raise money for his family. Raymond knew the Barrows because his family (and many others) bought water from them at their filling station. Blanche Barrow remembered Hamilton as very young and eager to travel with her and Buck when they were staging holdups in the months following Buck's escape from the Ferguson prison farm. Buck didn't

like Hamilton. "We'd just drive off and leave him," Blanche said. Blanche Barrow interviews September 24 and November 18, 1984. In 1932, Hamilton worked briefly with Clyde Barrow on at least two separate occasions, then struck out on his own. In December of that year he was arrested out of state and extradited to Texas. On his return he was sent on a statewide courtroom odyssey, receiving a total of 266 years in the state penitentiary for crimes ranging from auto theft to murder. See Underwood, *Depression Desperado*, and Hamilton, *Public Enemy No. 1*, for details about Raymond Hamilton. Indeed, Clyde Barrow had a plan to raid Eastham, one that he and Ralph Fults devised in 1930–1931 while both were still prisoners at Eastham, but initially it had nothing to do with Hamilton. Blanche's assertion here is quite incorrect, for two reasons. The planned raid evolved purely as an act of revenge against Eastham, the place Barrow called "that hell-hole," not to free Hamilton as so many have thought. Hamilton would eventually enter the picture, but not for some time. For the full account of the precise reasons for the raid on Eastham, see Phillips, *Running with Bonnie and Clyde*, and Phillips, "Raid on Eastham." See also McConal, *Over the Wall*, for an excellent account of the actual 1934 raid. There is also another, more immediate reason why Blanche is incorrect here: Hamilton was not at Eastham. During the meeting she describes on the evening of March 25–26, 1933, Raymond Hamilton was in the Hill County jail in Hillsboro, Texas, facing murder charges. According to Hamilton biographer Sid Underwood, as well as numerous contemporary newspaper sources, Hamilton had escaped from the Hill County jail two days earlier but was recaptured less than an hour later. He was in Hillsboro on the night of March 25–26 and did not arrive at the Eastham prison farm until August 8, 1933, nearly five months later. By then, Buck Barrow was dead, Blanche Barrow was in jail, and W. D. Jones had left Bonnie and Clyde. Underwood, *Depression Desperado*, 32, 38–39; *Dallas Morning News*, March 18–25, 1933; *Dallas Daily Times-Herald* March 18–25, 1933; *Dallas Evening Journal*, August 9, 1933.

30. Blanche had been to Eastham a number of times, sometimes in the company of Buck, who at the time was an escapee from another farm just across the Trinity River from Eastham. Clyde told her then, while he was still at Eastham, of his desire to raid Eastham. Blanche Barrow interview, November 3, 1984. In a letter to his mother, written three weeks before cutting two of his toes off with an ax, Clyde Barrow refers to such visits: "Make her [Blanche] bring you down here." Clyde Barrow, quoted from a letter to his mother December 3, 1931, in Cumie Barrow's unpublished manuscript.

31. In 1935, the Texas prison system was named the worst in the nation by the Osborne Association, an independent organization founded by a former warden of New York state's Auburn prison. The group, which still exists today, monitored and rated U.S. prisons and published its findings in annual reports. William Cox, Osborne Association secretary, specifically named Eastham as one of the most brutal prisons in the state system. Quoted in the *Houston Press* on April 10, 1935, he spoke of a "black picture of harsh and brutal treatment, particularly at Eastham. The methods of punishment now in force are

unworthy of a prison system which claims to be taking advantage of modern methods of handling prisoners." The announcement prompted a state investigation which ultimately led to the resignation of Colonel Lee Simmons, the general manager of the Texas prison system. See the *Houston Press*, April 3, 4, and 10 and September 2, 1935.

32. "Bud" was a nickname frequently used by Clyde. There is a note from Barrow to his brother LC, signed "Bud." When New Mexico lawman Joe Johns was released following his 1932 abduction, he reported the identities of the driver of the car and his girlfriend as "Bud" and "Honey." *Roswell Daily Record*, August 15, 1932. W. D. Jones said Barrow and Parker insisted that he refer to them as "Bud" and "Sis." Jones, interview by Biffle, June 1969.

33. W. D. Jones said Barrow always dominated the decision-making process. Jones, interview by Biffle, June 1969. Although Clyde Barrow definitely wanted to raid Eastham, whether Hamilton was there or not, it is apparently equally true that he wanted to free Raymond Hamilton, *wherever* he was. It is therefore possible that Blanche is mixing the memories of two different plans. There is evidence that Barrow was involved in smuggling hacksaw blades to Hamilton in the Hill County jail in January 1933. *Dallas Daily Times-Herald*, January 8, 1933. It is also known that Barrow was being kept apprized of Hamilton's whereabouts. Floyd Hamilton interview July 18, 1981; Mildred Hamilton interview, July 18, 1981; Hamilton, *Public Enemy No. 1*, 27. Clyde Barrow later grew to hate Hamilton, even to the point of plotting to kill him. This rancorous feeling was shared by others in the Barrow circle. "I hope they catch Raymond," said a Barrow friend in 1934, when Hamilton was a fugitive on the run, "and string him up in front of old lady Hamilton!" When Hamilton was recaptured on April 25, 1934, Cumie Barrow and Emma Parker expressed different feelings, however. "I hate that they caught him [Raymond Hamilton]," said Parker to Barrow. Dallas Police Department telephone wiretap transcript, April 21, 1934, 19; April 27, 1934, 49.

34. By March 1933, Bonnie had been involved in a wild chase and gun battle in the company of Ralph Fults and Clyde Barrow, had been in and out of jail in Kaufman County, Texas, and was an accessory in a number of other crimes, including the murder of Deputy Sheriff Malcolm Davis on January 6, 1933. By then, Barrow was wanted for five murders—those of John N. Bucher in Hillsboro, Texas, on April 30, 1932; Undersheriff Eugene Moore in Atoka County, Oklahoma, on August 5, 1932; Howard Hall in Sherman, Texas, on October 11, 1932; Doyle Johnson in Temple, Texas, on December 25, 1932; and Deputy Sheriff Malcolm Davis in Dallas County on January 6, 1933. See Phillips, *Running with Bonnie and Clyde*, for the full story.

35. At that time Matt Caldwell was staying with relatives in Oklahoma.

36. This is borne out by the fact that Barrow worked in the Camp 1 kitchen at Eastham in his final month there. He started out working the fields with everyone else but was later moved into the kitchen. This same source also stated that Barrow deliberately had himself removed to the fields in January 1931 so he could sustain an injury serious enough to get him sent to the prison hospital

in Huntsville. The reason, according to this and other sources, was to see his brother Buck. Henson letter to Kent Biffle, September 2, 1980.

37. Actually, despite his earlier vow to one day raid Eastham, Clyde Barrow tried to go straight when he was paroled. He first helped his father make preparations to put an addition onto the service station, then traveled to Framingham, Massachusetts, to take a job and get away from his past in Texas. However, he quickly grew homesick and returned to Dallas to work for United Glass and Mirror, one of his former employers. It was then that local authorities began picking Barrow up almost daily, often taking him away from his job. There was a standing policy at the time to basically harass ex-cons. Barrow was never charged with anything, but he soon lost his job. He told his mother, in the presence of Blanche Barrow and Ralph Fults, "Mama, I'm never gonna work again. And I'll never stand arrest, either. I'm not ever going back to that Eastham hell hole. I'll die first! I swear it, they're going to have to kill me." Fults interview, November 12, 1980; Blanche Barrow interview, November 18, 1984. Barrow's mother also mentions police harassment in her unpublished manuscript. Mrs. J. W. Hays, wife of former Dallas County Sheriff's Deputy John W. "Preacher" Hays, said, "if the Dallas police had left that boy [Clyde Barrow] alone, we wouldn't be talking about him today." Mrs. J. W. Hays interview, April 20, 1980.

W. D. Jones later said that he could think of no reason why Buck would have talked with Blanche of a plan to persuade Clyde to reform, "except to satisfy her." Jones added, "Ain't no way he could have talked him [Clyde] into it [surrendering]. And I think Buck was old enough to know that." Jones, interview by Biffle, June 1969.

38. Clyde had, by this time, been involved in the deaths of six men: Ed Crowder, John Bucher, Undersheriff Eugene Moore, Howard Hall, Doyle Johnson, and Deputy Sheriff Malcolm Davis. He was directly involved in the murders of Crowder, Moore, Johnson, and Davis. Ted Rogers killed Bucher, but Barrow was there. Blanche Barrow interview, November 18, 1984; Fults interviews, November 12, 1980, and February 13, 1982; Jack Hammett interview, February 20, 1982. Barrow maintained he was not involved in the Hall killing. Cumie Barrow, unpublished manuscript.

39. Ralph Smith Fults, born 1911 in north Texas, was nineteen when he first met Clyde Barrow, chained at the neck in the rear of a transport truck bound for the Texas State Penitentiary at Huntsville. Both were then assigned to Eastham where the brutal conditions, substantiated by a 1935 state investigation, brought Fults and Barrow to the point of forming a pact to one day raid the prison farm. In Barrow's own words to Fults, "I'd like to shoot all these damned guards and turn everybody loose." Fults, initially unimpressed by the diminutive Barrow, later noted the change he witnessed. "I seen him change from a schoolboy to a rattlesnake. He got real bitter." Fults interviews, March 8, 1981, and June 12, 1984. This is echoed by members of the Barrow family who noted a distinct difference in Barrow's personality after his 1932 parole. According to his sister Marie, "Something awful sure must have happened to

him in prison, because he sure wasn't the same person when he got out." Marie Barrow interview, September 25, 1993. See also, Fortune, *Fugitives*, 90.

On April 19, 1932, Ralph Fults and Bonnie Parker were captured near Kemp, Texas, after a brief gun battle that included Clyde Barrow. Barrow escaped. Some sources have asserted that Raymond Hamilton was with Barrow in Kaufman County, but the record is clear that is was Fults. *McKinney (Tex.) Daily Courier Gazette*, April 21, 1932; *Denton Record-Chronicle*, April 21, 1932. Eyewitnesses confirm this as well. Legg, letter to Phillips, September 1, 1982. In her unpublished memoir, Clyde's mother incorrectly lists another outlaw, Ralph Alsup, as the man captured in Kaufman County along with Bonnie Parker. Alsup indeed ran with Clyde Barrow and Ralph Fults. He was part of the Lake Dallas Gang of 1932, but he wasn't in Kaufman County on April 19, 1932. To distinguish him from Ralph Fults, Blanche Barrow referred to Alsup as the "other Ralph." Blanche Barrow interview, November 3, 1984. In prison and in the underworld Alsup was known by the nickname "Fuzz," because of his short haircut. Fults interview, February 1, 1981.

Later statements by Blanche and others contradict her assertion here that Clyde abandoned Fults in Kaufman County. At the time, Barrow and Fults had a gang with four other members at a hideout on Lake Dallas (Lake Lewisville today). When Fults was shot, Barrow made a break for it with the idea of returning with the others and staging a jailbreak. In 1980, while reading an account of the shoot-out that stated Clyde had abandoned Bonnie and that she was angry about it, Ralph Fults said, "Oh bull! We knew Clyde would go get them other guys and come back for us." Fults interview, November 5, 1980. This is born out by eyewitness Walter M. Legg, Jr., who was part of the posse that captured Parker and Fults and who stated, "they [Parker and Fults] were real cool and not at all upset." Legg, letter to Phillips, September 1, 1982. Barrow made at least two trips to the Kaufman County jail, one with Blanche, to reassure Parker and Fults. Blanche Barrow interview, September 24, 1984; Fults interview, February 1, 1981. Fults remembered LC Barrow visiting once as well. See Phillips, *Running with Bonnie and Clyde*, 87–95, for the full story.

40. Jones later said, "He [Clyde] didn't mean to do Buck no harm. He just couldn't see that far ahead." Of Blanche, he said, "She was a good little girl— good-hearted. She begged Buck not to go. She slipped into a trap. Blanche was just an innocent little girl who got mixed up in something—a love affair. I never knew that love could be so strong." Jones, interview by Biffle, June 1969.

41. Some have suggested that Buck Barrow "was virtually an alcoholic." Milner, *Lives and Times of Bonnie and Clyde*, 10.

42. Prohibition was still in effect in many states, including Texas, although the new Roosevelt administration had already brought about the legalization of 3.2 percent beer and was moving to repeal prohibition altogether. Gordon and Gordon, *American Chronicle*, 315. Blanche Barrow's mother, Lillian, and her husband, Reg Horton, were evidently heavy drinkers. In at least one letter to her mother, Blanche makes reference to such: "You may not have taken one drink this year, but I bet you have drunk a half-gallon a day. Ha." Blanche

Barrow, letter to her mother, January 29, 1936. And to Horton she writes, "Mr. Horton, I bet you stayed safe this Xmas, and I know you have stayed drinking." Blanche Barrow, letter to her mother, January 14, 1933.

Chapter 4. *Joplin*

1. *Dallas Daily Times-Herald*, 1, 4, 5, 26, and 30, 1933.
2. Ibid., April 10, 13, and 20, 1933; Tobin, *Great Projects*, 138–51.
3. Andrist, *American Heritage History*, 212.
4 *Dallas Daily Times-Herald*, April 3, 1933.
5. *Fairbury (Neb.) News*, April 4, 1933; *Sunday World-Herald Magazine*, March 30, 1969; *Dallas Daily Times-Herald*, April 14, 1933.
6. The title to the Marmon was one of the many items recovered after the Joplin shoot-out. The fact that Beaty's name was associated with the car created some tense moments for the Dallas mechanic. However, when Jopin authorities contacted the Dallas police department, Will Fritz, at the time a detective lieutenant, confirmed that ownership of the car had indeed been legally transferred to Buck Barrow on March 29, 1933. Beaty was in the clear. *Joplin (Mo.) Globe*, April 16, 1933.
7. Elvin "Jack" Barrow, the first of the Barrows to move to Dallas, worked at a shop located at 3214 Forest Avenue (today, Martin Luther King Boulevard). *Worley's City Directory*, 1931, 1933–34.
8. According to W. D. Jones, Clyde was also very fond of hot chocolate and marshmallows. "And that's a pretty good deal right there!" Jones added. Jones, interview by Biffle, June 1969. See also Fortune, *Fugitives*, 156.
9. Despite their many robberies, Jones said they were often so broke that they frequently had to "postpone" meals. "Sometimes we didn't even have enough to get a cup of coffee or a doughnut," he said. Jones, interview by Biffle, June 1969.
10. The statement, "I hoped that Buck and I would never be like that again," is revealing. It implies, as Blanche later confirmed, that there was much more to the story of her relationship with Buck prior to his return to prison than had been previously stated. While Clyde was at Eastham, Blanche accompanied Buck on a series of robberies before she and Cumie Barrow were finally able to convince him to surrender and finish serving the rest of his prison term. Blanche Barrow interviews, September 24 and November 18, 1984. During that period Blanche and Buck hid at a number of locations, including the farm of Barrow's uncle Jim Muckleroy in Martinsville, Texas. U.S. Department of Justice, memo to Doug Walsh, Dallas police department, May 4, 1933.
11. Blanche always used the abbreviation "Sol" when referring to the game of solitaire. It is not clear if this term was actually meant as an abbreviation, or whether it was a nickname for the game, perhaps popularly used in the day or merely personal to her. Nevertheless, for clarity it was changed to the complete spelling here and in nearly every other instance by the editor.
12. The address of the apartment was 3347½ Oak Ridge Drive. The apartment's owner, Paul Freeman, stated that two women and a man rented the

house, adding that one of the women said her husband was J. W. Callahan, a civil engineer from Minnesota, and that the other woman was her sister. *Joplin (Mo.) Globe*, April 14, 1933.

Clyde Barrow did not choose Joplin at random. It was known then as "a wide-open town," used by members of the underworld like Pretty Boy Floyd, the Barker brothers, and Alvin Karpis as a safe haven. Hounschell, *Lawmen and*, 45–48; *Joplin (Mo.) Globe*, October 1, 1967; Penland, "Bonnie and Clyde," *Joplin (Mo.) Metropolitan*, March 1985. However, Joplin was not controlled by the underworld. Law enforcement appears to have been very capable and incorrupt there. It seems that Joplin was a popular outlaw haven because of location. It was a fair-sized town that happened to be minutes from the Oklahoma and Kansas state lines. Hounschell, e-mail to Phillips, February 4, 2002.

13. Much has been made about a supposed physical relationship between Clyde Barrow and W. D. Jones, largely because of the sleeping arrangements. But no one who knew them ever thought such a relationship existed. "If Clyde didn't like girls," said his sister Marie, "what the hell was he doing with Bonnie all that time?" Marie Barrow interview, September 25, 1993. The case of Jones sharing a room with Parker and Barrow was one of many ploys Barrow used to deceive potential eyewitnesses as to the exact number of people traveling with him. Other examples include Bonnie switching cars before entering a town, something Blanche has already mentioned, and instances where one or more of them would hide beneath blankets on the floorboard, or on the backseat of the car. Blanche describes the latter more than once later in the text.

14. Jigsaw puzzles became very popular depression-era diversions because they were so inexpensive. Jigsaw-puzzle parties with people chatting and fitting pieces together were extremely common well into the 1940s. Andrist, *American Heritage History*, 212.

15. S. H. Kress & Co. 1896–1980, a chain of Main Street five-and-dime stores.

16. It was reported that five diamonds, taken from Harry Bacon by two men during the robbery of the Neosho Milling Company, were found hidden in several places in the apartment following the shoot-out of April 13, 1933. *Joplin (Mo.) Globe*, April 14, 1933; *Dallas Dispatch*, April 21, 1933. A money bag from McDaniel National Bank in Springfield, Missouri, was also found. According to Shauna Smith, curator of the History Museum for Springfield-Greene County, there was no robbery of that bank reported in that era. However, McDaniel National Bank had recently been purchased by the Union National Bank of Springfield (December 8, 1931) and no doubt transferred funds in its own bags to the parent institution as well as to other banks in the area, such as the Bank of Ash Grove, Missouri, twenty-two miles northwest of Springfield. The latter bank was robbed on January 12, 1933, by three unmasked men driving a Ford V-8. The take was reportedly $3,600.58. Initially Pretty Boy Floyd was blamed for the robbery, but that notion was soon dropped. Hulston, *100 Years*, 44–45; *Ash Grove (Mo.) Commonwealth*, January 19, 1933. However, it is equally possible that Clyde Barrow, W. D. Jones, and some other man (or perhaps

Bonnie, incorrectly identified as a man, or maybe Frank Hardy or Hollis Hale who had helped Barrow rob a bank in Oronogo, Missouri, three months earlier) robbed the Bank of Ash Grove. Indeed, there is evidence to support this. Just a few days later, on January, 26, 1933, a Springfield, Missouri, motorcycle officer named Thomas Persell was abducted by Barrow, Parker, and Jones and taken for a ride to Joplin. During the journey Persell noted that he was sitting on sacks of money in the backseat of his abductors' Ford V-8 and that all three fugitives spoke of "several recent bank robberies familiarly." Persell specifically mentioned the bank at Ash Grove. The McDaniel National bank bag found in the Joplin garage apartment may have come from the Ash Grove Bank. *Springfield (Mo.) News-Leader*, April 14, 1933; *Dallas Morning News*, January 28, 1933.

17. Among the movies in release that month were *She Done Him Wrong*, starring Mae West; *Tonight Is Ours*, with Frederick March and Claudette Colbert; and Edward G. Robinson in *Tiger Shark*. *Dallas Morning News*, April 1–30, 1933.

18. The small town was Girard, Kansas, at the intersection of Highways 7 and 57, approximately thirty-five miles northwest of Joplin. No doubt the only reason for actually paying for a new set of plates was the fact that Buck's car was legitimately owned and because it would be visible so much of the time. Clyde Barrow always stole his license plates. He was known to keep a dozen or more sets of plates from different states in his car. That way wherever he went he could become a local citizen by changing his plates. Very soon Buck would be doing the same.

19. The owner of Snodgrass Grocery at 2226 Main Street, Clyde Snodgrass, Sr., remembered them as "nice customers who carried on like ordinary folks." *Joplin (Mo.) Globe*, April 13, 1975.

20. Despite her earlier dislike for beer and whiskey, many years later Blanche became known for her love of a few beers, especially while fishing. Marie Barrow interview, August 24, 1984; Linder interview, October 5, 2002; Weiser, October 5, 2002.

21. Herman H. Biggs, the delivery boy, remembered not being allowed to carry the groceries into the apartment. He also maintained that it was Bonnie who telephoned and then met him on the stairs. *Joplin (Mo.) Globe*, April 13, 1975.

22. The watchman was a man by the name of Mack Parker. *Joplin (Mo.) Globe*, April 14, 1933.

23. From other sources, it is known that a Harold Hill owned "the large home on the corner," and Sam Lanford owned the house next door at 3339 Oak Ridge: *Joplin (Mo.) Globe*, April 14, 1933; Hounschell, *Lawmen and Outlaws*, 45.

24. According to Frank Hamer, former Texas Ranger, the group "drank heavily and were quite noisy. Several complaints were filed against them." Quoted in Frost and Jenkins, *I'm Frank Hamer*, 191.

25. This was probably one of Clyde Barrow's favorite weapons, the Browning automatic rifle, or BAR. It was capable of firing a twenty-shot magazine of 30.06 ammunition in under three seconds. Harding, *Weapons*, 76.

26. This was apparently the first attempt by Barrow to make what he later called his "scatter-gun," a sawed-off Browning automatic rifle with three clips welded together, enabling it to fire fifty-six times without reloading, according to one source. Jones, "Riding with Bonnie and Clyde," 162. A sawed-off Browning automatic rifle was recovered in Dexfield Park near Dexter, Iowa, after the shoot-out on July 24, 1933.

27. The car was stolen on Wednesday, April 12, 1933 from Earl Stanton in Miami, Oklahoma. *Joplin (Mo.) Globe*, April 16, 1933. Some say Bonnie and Clyde were nearly always "agreeable" with each other, though they did have arguments. According to W. D., "I've seen them fall out over a can of sardines . . . but I never heard them call each other bad names." Jones, "Riding with Bonnie and Clyde," 164.

28. Others saw it differently. "He [Clyde Barrow] didn't mean to do Buck no harm. He just couldn't see no further ahead," Jones said. Jones, interview by Biffle, June 1969. And according to their mother, "Clyde tried to get him [Buck] to go home, or go out and get a tourist camp . . . the place was getting a little too warm for them and they might have trouble." Cumie Barrow's unpublished manuscript.

29. Bonnie's unfinished poem, "Suicide Sal,' was found on a writing tablet with pen and ink nearby. *Springfield (Mo.) News-Leader*, April 14, 1933.

30. Several days earlier Clyde had apparently fired one of the Browning automatic rifles in the apartment by accident. Cumie Barrow, unpublished manuscript.

31. Some, like Cumie Barrow, say Buck was already upstairs. Cumie Barrow, unpublished manuscript. W. D. Jones said that Buck opened the garage door for Clyde and him and that the roadster had a flat tire. He then stated that while the three men were standing there looking at the tire, Buck suddenly yelled, "Law," and that both Buck and Clyde began shooting. Dallas County Sheriff's Department, Jones, Voluntary Statement B-71, November 18, 1933. Joplin City Detective Tom DeGraff testified that he saw only two gunmen in the garage and that the shorter of the two had a shotgun. *Joplin (Mo.) Globe*, April 15, 1933.

32. This is contrary to Jones's statement that "Bonnie never packed a gun . . . during the five big gun battles I was with them, she never fired a gun." Jones, "Riding with Bonnie and Clyde," 162. Parker once shot herself in the foot while handling one of Clyde's guns. U.S. Department of Justice, memo to Doug Walsh, Dallas Police Department, May 4, 1933. She also reportedly held a sawed-off shotgun on Springfield officer Tom Persell on January 26, 1933. *Springfield (Mo.) News- Leader*, April 14, 1933. On May 12, 1933, someone firing wildly from the getaway car following an attempted bank robbery in Lucerne, Indiana, wounded two bystanders. Witnesses claimed at least one woman was shooting. Some said two women (which would have meant Bonnie and Blanche) opened fire from within the car. "[T]he women did a large part of the shooting and probably all of it," the *Pharos-Tribune* reported on May 13, 1933. Later in the year Parker covered two men in Dallas County

while she and Barrow commandeered a fresh car following a gun battle. *Dallas Morning News*, November 23, 1933.

33. The purse was left behind, along with all the papers therein. Among the other things left for authorities to sift through was a badge issued by the Police and Sheriff's Association of North America, a bag containing clippings and assorted compositions, and a writing tablet with pen and ink lying nearby. *Springfield (Mo.) News-Leader*, April 14, 1933. There were also some rolls of unprocessed film. From the photographs that were later printed, a Springfield motorcycle officer named Tom Persell was able to identify the fugitives who abducted him on January 26, 1933, and drove him to Joplin before releasing him. Persell particularly noted the "peculiar radiator cap" of the V-8 seen in many of the shots. He said a woman in the group held a sawed-off shotgun on him, as did the driver of the car used to transport him. He also said that all three used a lot of profanity and spoke of "several recent bank robberies familiarly," *Springfield (Mo.) News- Leader*, April 14 and 16, 1933; Edwards, "A Tale Tom Persell Lived to Tell"; *Dallas Morning News*, January 28, 1933.

34. Blanche Barrow later said that she had trained the dog to run to the car on command in case of an emergency. However, when she got downstairs to the garage, Blanche realized the dog had run into the street instead of jumping into the car. Blanche Barrow interview, November 3, 1984.

35. This was probably Newton County Constable Wes Harryman, who made it all the way to the west garage door, the one Buck was trying to close, when he was felled by a shotgun blast fired at point-blank range. It was determined that he died instantly. An examination of his weapon showed he had fired one shot. Harryman was actually a farmer by trade. He had taken the job of constable merely to make ends meet during the Great Depression. Because the apartment was in Newton County (Joplin occupies parts of two counties), Harryman was included in the raid for jurisdictional reasons. Only he could serve the search warrant. Harryman was forty-one. *Joplin (Mo.) Globe*, April 15, 1933.

36. The five officers involved in the raid had arrived in two cars. One, occupied by Missouri State Patrolmen G. B. Kahler and W. E. Grammar, had stopped on 34th, just west of the apartment. The other, driven by Joplin City Detective Tom DeGraff, had turned onto the shallow driveway and rolled to a stop at an angle, blocking both garage doors. DeGraff later said he was trying to drive into the west garage to prevent the door from being closed but was too late. It was already nearly closed. Newton County Constable Wes Harryman and Joplin Motor Car Detective Harry McGinnis were riding with DeGraff. DeGraff told Harryman to get to the door before it was closed. Harryman jumped out of the car while it was still rolling and was shot when he reached the door. McGinnis then got out of the car and he too was shot, multiple times. DeGraff parked, got out, fired a few shots then sought cover behind a nearby corner. *Joplin (Mo.) Globe*, April 15, 1933. It was just after this that Blanche came downstairs. It was DeGraff's car she saw. Also, the fact that she describes both Clyde *and* Buck outside the garage lends credence to Jones's assertion that both brothers were shooting, especially since DeGraff only saw

two gunmen at any given time and both he and trooper Kahler described trading shots with "a man with a shotgun" when that man stepped out of the garage. Buck's mother also said he was shooting, then contradicts herself on the next page by stating that Clyde and W. D. said Buck didn't fire a weapon in Joplin. Cumie Barrow, unpublished manuscript; Dallas County Sheriff's Department, Jones, Voluntary Statement B-71, November 18, 1933; *Joplin (Mo.) Globe*, April 15, 1933.

37. This was Joplin Motor Car Detective Harry McGinnis. He'd fired three shots before being struck multiple times. His right arm was nearly severed at the elbow, four No. 1 buckshot pellets penetrated his left side, and a bullet had struck him in the face. *Joplin (Mo.) Globe*, April 15, 1933. McGinnis was transported to a hospital where he died several hours later from shock and loss of blood. McGinnis, who was born in Nevada, Missouri, had been with the Joplin police for eight years. He was very popular and described as friendly and light-hearted. A widower, McGinnis was engaged to be married the following month. He was fifty-three. *Joplin (Mo.) Globe*, April 14, 1933.

38. Blanche said her dress got caught on the car. Blanche Barrow interview, November 18, 1984. An eyewitness, Fred Pitman, described seeing the car rolling down the hill and "a girl running after it." The car crashed into a tree, tearing off one of its doors. The eyewitness then heard a machine gun. He heard fifty to sixty shots. A man then called to the girl, "Come back here," and she ran back inside the garage. *Joplin (Mo.) Globe*, April 15, 1933.

39. Blanche said later that after helping Clyde push the police car out of the way, she went back to the sedan in the garage to get in with Bonnie and W. D. It was then that she noticed her dog, Snowball, was gone. Blanche Barrow interviews, September 24 and November 3, 984. She also stated that she helped Clyde and W. D. move the car, but in her manuscript she implies it was Clyde and Buck, not W. D., she helped. The fact that she returned to the garage is confirmed by the testimony of the eyewitness. *Joplin (Mo.) Globe*, April 15, 1933.

40. This very account, that of Blanche running hysterically from the apartment, has been mentioned elsewhere, perhaps originating with Jan Fortune's account in *Fugitives*, 152. Cumie Barrow mentions it as well in her unpublished manuscript. But Blanche said later that she never screamed and ran hysterically down the street, but that she stepped from the garage a second time and walked down the street, calmly calling her dog. By then, the dog was long gone. Blanche Barrow interviews, September 24 and November 3, 1984. This latter account is supported by the complete lack of testimony during the two inquests regarding someone running down the street, screaming. Also, there is no testimony supporting the assertion that shots were fired from the apartment upstairs. *Joplin (Mo.) Globe*, April 15, 1933. Of her portrayal in the 1967 movie, *Bonnie and Clyde*, Blanche said, "That movie made me out like a screaming horse's ass!" Blanche Barrow interview, November 18, 1984. "I was too busy moving bodies [to act hysterical]," Blanche herself said. Quoted by Rhea Leen Linder, Linder interview, October 5, 2002. Her image in this memoir, as well as in *Fugitives* and in Cumie Barrow's manuscript, was fashioned at a

time when Blanche could have easily been charged with the Joplin murders. That may account for the great difference in tone between Blanche, the young convict in the Missouri State Penitentiary, and Blanche, the elder ex-fugitive. Indeed, at least one of Blanche Barrows' champions, Wilbur Winkler, the Denison man who co-owned (along with Artie Barrow Winkler) the Cinderella Beauty Shoppe, used *Fugitives* to try to obtain a parole for Blanche from the Missouri Board of Probation and Parole. In letters to the Platte County prosecutor and the judge involved in Blanche's case, Winkler alluded to the book's description of Blanche in Joplin in an effort to win their support for her release: "Blanch [*sic*] ran hysterical [*sic*] thru [*sic*] the gunfire down the street carrying [her] dog in her arms," Winkler wrote. He even sent copies of the book to them–and to others. Winkler, letter to David Clevenger, January 17, 1936; Winkler, letter to the Hon. R. B. Bridgeman, January 17, 1936.

41. Blanche said later she was not in the car when it drove out of the garage. On returning to the garage she found that her dog was not in the car and she went out in the street to look for it. She said Clyde picked her up after driving out of the garage. She never found her dog. Blanche Barrow interview, November 18, 1984.

42. The sedan was stolen from Robert Roseborough in Marshall, Texas, between December 24, 1932, and January 26, 1933—after Jones had joined the group but before the abduction of Springfield motorcycle patrolman Tom Persell. Roseborough was an insurance agent in East Texas who had been making sales calls when he made a quick milk run at lunchtime for his mother. Roseborough recounted that in the few moments it took him to pull up to his mother's house, go inside and place the milk in the icebox, and return to the front door his car had disappeared. The next time he saw it was after it had been found abandoned in Oklahoma, after the Joplin shoot-out. Roseborough said it had blood stains in it and the bipod from a Browning automatic rifle was bolted to the dash. Roseborough interview, July 11, 1984. This car appeared in a number of photographs of the Barrow gang that were printed from unprocessed film recovered in Joplin. It was from the car's license plate that authorities traced it to Roseborough. It was also through these very same pictures, many of which were printed in newspapers and magazines of the day, that Springfield motorcycle patrolman Tom Persell was able to finally identify the trio who had abducted him nearly three months earlier. Not only did he recognize the people, he also pointed out two other things appearing in many of the photographs: "the peculiar radiator cap" of the Ford V-8 and his stolen service revolver. The latter was a distinctive Russian-made .45. It had cost Persell $50. His monthly salary was $105. Edwards, "A Tale Tom Persell Lived to Tell."

43. Jones thought he had been hit twice and that one of the bullets was still inside him. Later, in Texas, Clyde took an elm branch, wrapped gauze around it, and poked it straight into the wound in Jones's side and out the hole in his back. With that, Jones was satisfied the gunshot wound was clean. Jones, "Riding with Bonnie and Clyde," 165. There were reports that Jones had been hit in the head in Joplin, but he was not. Jones, interview by Biffle, June 1969.

44. Temperatures were only reaching highs in the thirties in Missouri and the Texas Panhandle on April 13 and 14. The lows were below freezing, 24 degrees in Amarillo, the fugitives' distination, on the morning of April 14. *Dallas Morning News*, April 14, 1933.

Chapter 5. *Ruston*

1. Jones has said his wounds were not treated until later, in Amarillo. Dallas County Sheriff's Department, Jones, Voluntary Statement B-71, November 18, 1933.

2. This is also mentioned by Buck's mother. Cumie Barrow, unpublished manuscript.

3. This was probably the reported robbery of the Phillips 66 Station at 18th Avenue and Polk in Amarillo, Texas. Approximately twenty-five dollars was taken by two armed men on foot early on the evening of April 14, 1933. *Amarillo Daily News*, April 15, 1933.

4. According to Frank Hamer, former Texas Ranger, "Barrow played a circle from Dallas to Joplin, Missouri, to Louisiana, and back to Dallas. Barrow never holed up in one place; he was always on the go; and he traveled farther in one day than any other fugitive that I have ever followed." Frank Hamer, quoted in Webb, *Texas Rangers*, 540.

5. The owner, H. Dillard Darby, thirty-five, saw the car pulling away from his rooming house, the L. K. Brooks residence on North Trenton, and ran after it. Darby ran up to the black Chevrolet and tried to jump on the running board but by then Jones had turned the corner and was going too fast. Darby ran back inside the rooming house to telephone the sheriff. After that, he emerged from the house a second time and gave chase with Sophie Stone. Blanche may have missed, or forgotten Darby's reported first appearance. *Ruston (La.) Daily Leader*, April 28, 1933. There is some question as to where Stone came from. Most sources state that she too roomed at the L. K. Brooks residence. But in a 1968 interview, Stone said she "had her car parked in front of a boarding house across from the high school," where she taught home economics, and that "after lunch I saw Mr. Darby come running out of the boarding house, shouting that someone had stolen his car." *Dallas Morning News*, March 18, 1968. Some even suggested Stone and Darby were a couple. Fortune, *Fugitives*, 161. Stone said, "Mr. Darby was a married man. And we were certainly *not* going together" [Stone's emphasis]. *Dallas Morning News*, March 18, 1968.

6. Clyde Barrow reportedly said, "Let's take 'm, for a lark!" Fortune, *Fugitives*, 162.

7. The car, described at the time as freshly stolen, was actually falling apart because of the abuse Barrow had subjected it to. "That damned car almost got us killed," said Blanche years later. Apparently the suspension was faulty. Barrow had sideswiped a parked car in Waldo, Arkansas trying to turn a corner. Blanche Barrow interview, September 24, 1984.

8. Darby said Barrow flagged him down near the town of Hico and asked if he'd seen a black Chevrolet. Darby said he got out of Stone's car and approached

Barrow. When he did, Barrow pulled a gun. The two men exchanged words and Barrow leaped out and slugged Darby, just as Blanche described. A woman, probably Bonnie, then jumped out of the car, grabbed Stone, and struck her as well. Darby said Barrow was angry because Jones had been frightened off, adding that consequently they couldn't carry out a bank robbery they had planned. *Ruston (La.) Daily Leader*, April 28, 1933. This was confirmed by Stone. *Dallas Morning News*, March 18, 1968.

9. Stone, twenty-seven, was described as the home demonstration agent for Lincoln Parish. *Ruston (La.) Daily Leader*, April 27, 1933. Stone indicated she was at the high school across from the boardinghouse at the time of the theft. She also said that when Bonnie found out Stone was a home demonstration agent, she asked if she'd prepared any food that day and to describe it because she was so hungry. *Dallas Morning News*, March 18, 1968.

10. Six miles from Waldo, Stone and Darby were released. Still fearful that they would be killed, they watched the car pull away. Suddenly it stopped. They braced themselves. But instead of bullets, a five-dollar bill appeared. Then the car sped away. *Ruston (La.) Daily Leader*, April 28, 1933; *Dallas Morning News*, March 18, 1933.

11. Stone said it was Bonnie who asked about embalming and that it was Bonnie who thought it was funny. "Clyde didn't see the humor," Stone said. *Dallas Morning News*, March 18, 1968.

12. The license plate on the stolen car was Louisiana 233-821. *Dallas Dispatch*, April 28, 1933.

13. From Ruston, Louisiana, the Barrows traveled through Dubach, Louisiana to El Dorado, Arkansas, east to Magnolia, then north to Waldo and Rosston—all in Arkansas—and finally west to Hope. *Hope (Ark.) Star*, April 28, 1933.

14. Hope, Arkansas, Police Chief Clarence Baker and officer Homer Burke saw the suspect car approach town on East Third Street from the direction of Rosston. Baker and Burke chased the car as it turned onto Second Street, north of Hazel Street. When they crossed the railroad tracks, however, the police car blew a tire. After quickly obtaining another car, the officers continued the chase. Chief Baker later said that he and Burke were close enough to see a man in the backseat of the suspect car holding a machine gun. After crossing the railroad tracks on Second Street, the car was chased past the brickyard. The suspect driver then doubled back to the south on Laurel and eventually made it back to Third Street, where he raced out of town toward Rosston. This chase was reported as occurring at 8:00 P.M. on April 27. *Hope (Ark.) Star*, April 28, 1933; *Joplin (Mo.) News Herald*, April 28, 1933.

15. North of Shreveport, in the swamps of Black Lake Bayou east of Oil City and Vivian, there was a rather elaborate hideout known to the underworld simply as the camp. Operated by a family named Chapman, "the camp" was reputedly used by such notorious outlaws as Pretty Boy Floyd, the Barker brothers, Alvin Karpis, and Bonnie and Clyde. Although it doesn't appear they used the location when Blanche was with them, there's evidence that

Bonnie and Clyde hid there, or near there, in 1934. For an excellent description of the camp, see Tattersall, *Conviction*, 259–73.

16. After abandoning Darby's car in McGee, Arkansas, Jones indeed returned to Dallas. *Ruston (La.) Daily Leader*, April 28, 1933; Jones, Dallas County Sheriff's Department, Voluntary Statement B-71, November 18, 1933.

17. The involvement of three men in the abduction of Stone and Darby, and the eventual identification of two of the men as Clyde and Buck Barrow, lent credence to the theory already posed by Joplin authorities that three men were involved in the killing of Harryman and McGinnis. *Joplin (Mo.) Globe*, April 16, 1933. Some identified the third man in Ruston as Pretty Boy Floyd. *Joplin (Mo.) News Herald*, April 28, 1933. However, Chief of Detectives Ed Portley of the Joplin Police Department said, "I want it understood that as far as the Joplin police department is concerned, we are not attempting to associate Floyd in any way whatsoever with this case." *Joplin (Mo.) News Herald*, April 28, 1933. The wording of this statement seems more like a pledge of reassurance to Floyd personally rather than to the public in general. Floyd, of course, was known to visit the Joplin area frequently. See: Unger, *Union Station Massacre*, 59–68.

Chapter 6. *Friction*

1. *Dallas Daily Times-Herald*, May 2 and 10, 1933; *Pharos-Tribune*, May 12, 1933; *Dallas Daily Times-Herald*, May 23, 25, and 29, 1933. Okabena was peppered with machine gun fire as the bandits escaped. Brothers Floyd and Anthony Strain, along with Anthony's wife, Mildred, would be convicted of this crime, but it was a Barrow job and almost a carbon copy of the Lucerne, Indiana, incident. *Fairmont (Minn.) Daily Sentinel*, May 19, 1933; *Okabena (Minn.) Press*, May 19, 1933; *Minneapolis Journal*, May 19, 1933; Boucher, *Jackson County (Minn.) History, vol. II*, 119–20. The storms and lightning, and Bonnie Parker's reaction to them, are mentioned by Blanche Barrow in her memoir. See also Fortune, *Fugitives*, 160–61, although the chronology given there appears incorrect, and other aspects of Fortune's account confuse Okabena with Lucerne.

2. *St. Louis Post-Dispatch*, May 4, 1933; *Prague (Okla.) News Record*, May 10, 1933; *Dallas Daily Times-Herald*, May 12 and June 9, 1933.

3. *Dallas Daily Times-Herald*, May 12, 1933; *Pharos-Tribune*, May 12 and 15, 1933; *Dallas Daily Times-Herald*, May 17, 1933.

4. *Dallas Daily Times-Herald*, May 24, 25, and 27, 1933.

5. *Dallas Daily Times-Herald*, May 30, 1933. Just a few days later, Buck Barrow would use barbed wire to tie up two officers following their abduction by Clyde and W. D. Jones near Wellington, Texas. Reportedly, Buck's use of the wire irritated Clyde. "You didn't have to do that!" he snapped. Jones, "Riding with Bonnie and Clyde," 165.

6. This visit might actually be the visit mentioned by Cumie Barrow in her manuscript, the one she said took place three days after Mother's Day (that is, on May 17, 1933). Cumie Barrow wrote that Bonnie and Clyde and Blanche and Buck drove to West Dallas and visited with her as they sat,

parked on the driveway outside the Barrow filling station. Cumie Barrow closed the passage by writing, "I never saw Buck but one more time after that before he was shot [in Platte City, Missouri, July 19, 1933]." The "one more time" mentioned by Cumie Barrow was probably the visit near Commerce, Texas, after Mother's Day. However, there's reason to believe Cumie Barrow is wrong about the date of the West Dallas meeting. For one thing, Blanche states that she and the other three fugitives were camped on a riverbank in Mississippi on May 17. Given this, it is likely that Cumie Barrow is confused about the date and that the visit she describes actually occurred in late April and is indeed the same one Blanche refers to here, especially since Blanche writes that the later Commerce visit was the only trip to Texas made by the four fugitives in May. Cumie Barrow, unpublished manuscript; *Fairmont* (*Minn.*) *Daily Sentinel*, May 19, 1933.

7. This was probably the attempted robbery of the Lucerne State Bank in Lucerne, Indiana, on Friday, May 12, 1933. It was reported that two men broke into the bank the night before, climbed on top of the vault, and waited for morning. At 7:30 A.M. on the twelfth, cashier Everett Gregg arrived and began setting up cash drawers and getting ready for business. Within minutes bookkeeper Lawson Selders arrived and also went to work. Approximately thirty minutes later Gregg stepped into the vault. At that moment Selders heard a noise and saw "a roughly- dressed young man" stand up and train two pistols at him, telling him to raise his hands. However, rather than obey, Selders dashed into the vault to join his colleague. The intruder fired a shot at Selders but only succeeded in attracting the attention of Ed Frushour, who happened to be walking past the bank. *Pharos-Tribune*, May 12, 1933.

8. Several witnesses saw the bandits in Lucerne on May 11, the day before the robbery attempt. Then at 7 A.M. on the morning of May 12, Ellsworth Hoover and Ura Witters both saw the soon-to-be getaway car, a Ford V-8, with Indiana plates, parked in front of their homes. Two women, one blonde and one brunette, were sitting in the car. Hoover, who walked to work each day, paused on his way and spoke briefly with the women. Witters would later try to stop the fleeing vehicle with a large chunk of wood. Ibid.

9. The technique of hiding overnight in a bank was not particularly new. Eight days earlier, on May 4, 1933, the St. John Community Bank in eastern Missouri was similarly robbed by three men who waited all night in the bank. A fourth accomplice was in the car outside. *Dallas Daily Times-Herald*, May 4, 1933; *St. Louis Post-Dispatch*, May 4, 1933. On May 8, 1933, three unmasked men took only five minutes to grab $1,400 from the Prague National Bank in Prague, Oklahoma, lock most of the witnesses in the vault, and escape in a Ford V-8 with two hostages. The hostages were then released outside of town. *Prague* (*Okla.*) *News Record*, May 10, 1933.

There is no indication in the initial reports that either Everett Gregg or Lawson Selders, the two employees inside the bank, ever fired at the intruders. When one of the intruders fired the first shot inside the bank, Ed Frushour, who was walking past the bank, stopped and peered through the window. The intruder spotted Frushour and shouted at him, ordering him to enter the bank. However, he too ran away. The intruder then fired approximately four shots at the fleeing witness, three through the glass pane and one into the window casing. By this time both bank employees had armed themselves, presumably with weapons kept in the vault for just such an occasion. After the shots were fired at Frushour, the employees heard both outlaws jump down from the vault. The intruders then fired seven shots at the vault, the slugs digging into the brick and concrete bunker surrounding the vault. Then both gunmen dashed out the rear door of the bank. In their haste, they left a "repeating shotgun" behind. Once outside, one of the bandits turned and fired nine more shots at the rear of the bank building before he and his companion climbed into a waiting car occupied by two women. The intruders then sped away. *Pharos-Tribune*, May 12, 1933.

Incredibly no one was hit inside the bank, nor was the man who stopped outside the bank after the first shot was fired. However, two bystanders, Doris Miner and Ethel Jones, were wounded when the occupants of the car slowed in front of the Christian Church and fired about forty shots toward a crowd of people who had poured out of their homes to see what the excitement was about. Some witnesses reported seeing both women firing weapons. "Those who saw the bandits leave town were alike in their stories that the women did a large part of the shooting, and probably all of it during the parting fusillade." Ibid. If the statements of the eyewitnesses are true, this is the only known hard evidence that Bonnie Parker ever fired a weapon in anger, much less wounded someone. It is also an indictment of Blanche's assertion that she never handled a weapon.

10. Although Clyde usually drove, it is possible that Blanche was the driver of the car. As we shall see, she was a bit of a virtuoso, keeping up with Clyde Barrow in a second car as they sped through the countryside after a failed robbery. And according to at least one source, Bonnie Parker did not know how to drive. Bonnie's sister, Billie Jean, has said, "I never saw her [Bonnie] drive and never heard her mention driving." Billie Jean Parker Moon, unpublished handwritten observations.

11. The "old man" described here, the one who "threw a large chunk of wood in front of the car" was Ura Witters. He had heard the shooting and had indeed tried to wreck the car. The driver, reported to have been a man, turned sharply to the right onto a "soggy lawn," but successfully brought the car back onto the road and accelerated. Shortly thereafter, the fugitives encountered the crowd in front of the Christian Church and opened fire. *Pharos-Tribune*, May 12, 1933. Following the shooting, one of the women was heard to say, "This'll learn ya!" *Dallas Daily Times-Herald*, June 9, 1933.

Because of the way it is described in Fortune's *Fugitives*, it would be easy to confuse this attempted robbery with the successful robbery exactly one week later of the First State Bank in Okabena, Minnesota. Fortune seems to mix the events of both incidents here, identifying it as Okabena but actually describing what happened in Lucerne, right down to the old man with the chunk of wood—although Fortune has Bonnie refusing to shoot the old man instead of Buck. Fortune, *Fugitives*, 163. Cumie Barrow, though brief in her description, identifies the events of the Okabena robbery with more accuracy, including the date, May 19, 1933. Cumie Barrow, unpublished manuscript. Fortune lists the date as May 16, three days early. However, this may have been due to her own confusion over the events of those two weeks in May 1933. Since she has described the discussion of the Lucerne fiasco at the "Mother's Day" meeting near Commerce, Texas, but identified it as Okabena, Fortune may have reasoned that Okabena occurred before the meeting. But it did not. Lucerne happened before the meeting and seven days before Okabena. *Fairmont (Minn.) Daily Sentinel*, May 19, 1933.

12. Two women were wounded during the shooting spree in front of the Christian Church in Lucerne. Doris Miner, twenty-two, was dressing in the bedroom of her parents' home nearby when she was struck in the shoulder and grazed on the cheek. Ethel Jones, also twenty-two, was standing outside the house next door when she was wounded in the right arm. Other slugs became embedded at various points in the neighborhood around the church, one drilling straight through a telephone pole. *Pharos-Tribune*, May 12, 1933.

The car continued west out of town and turned north before reaching Road 29. It was followed by two Lucerne men, Les Powlen and Homer Hunter, in a "high- powered" car. At some point the fugitives encountered a herd of pigs and drove through them, killing two. The car then began "zig-zagging" down back roads until losing Powlen and Hunter on Road 14, west of Winamac. The Lucerne men described the bandit driver as an "expert at the wheel." Ibid.

13. This reportedly is true. No cash was stolen from the Lucerne State Bank. However, if they "had to rob another place the same day," as Blanche goes on to say, it must have resulted in a lot of money because, as she notes, the group had several hundred dollars by the following Monday when they met with their families near Commerce, Texas.

Two Chicago women, Olga Bernaka and Josephine Gray, were eventually charged with the attempt on the bank at Lucerne. Gray, described as "a petite blonde" was the wife of bank robber Jack Gray. Bernaka was Gray's sister. "There's no way you're hanging this on us," Bernaka said. Three Lucerne eyewitnesses identified both women. *Dallas Daily Times-Herald*, June 9, 1933.

14. This passage bears out what many who knew Blanche have said about her, that she was an excellent driver. She apparently loved to drive. In her later years, nearly dwarfed behind the wheel of her mammoth white LTD, dubbed "The Bomb", Blanche could drive for hours, never getting lost and seemingly aware of every little back road in north Texas. Linder and Weiser interviews, October 5, 2002.

15. This sounds very much like a similar robbery attempt in Rison, Arkansas, in June 1933. A gang reportedly consisting of four men and a woman tried unsuccessfully to burglarize a safe at Moore's Grocery Store just after midnight June 5, 1933. In the process Deputy Sheriff Wright Fore and two

other local citizens were abducted and later released. No money was taken. *Cleveland County* (Ark.) *Herald,* June 7, 14, and 21, 1933.

16. It should be recalled that, according to her sister, Bonnie Parker could not drive.

17. This was probably in Okabena, Minnesota, located in the far southwestern part of the state, near the Iowa line, and known as the "Nesting Place of Heron." The bank involved was the First State Bank. The date of the robbery was May 19, 1933. *Fairmont (Minn.) Daily Sentinel,* May 19, 1933. That was seven days after the attempt in Lucerne, Indiana, and four days after the Mother's Day meeting near Commerce, Texas. Although some of Blanche's description varies from the facts of the incident, there are many similarities, not the least of which are the reports of devastating storms the night before the robbery, just like those Blanche describes. *Minneapolis Journal,* May 19, 1933. Also, in early spring 1932, Clyde Barrow, Ralph Fults, and Raymond Hamilton visited Okabena with the idea of robbing the bank there. But they abandoned the idea because the few roads in and out of the area were blocked by snow. They then drove south to Lawrence, Kansas, and robbed a bank there. Fults interviews, December 4, 1982, and June 12, 1984. And since the 1933 Okabena robbery is almost a carbon copy of the Lucerne attempt, it warrants consideration.

18. Indeed on the night of May 18–19, heavy weather struck Minnesota, producing high winds, rain, and tornadoes in the vicinity of Okabena. Ten people were injured and fifty farms destroyed. *Minneapolis Journal,* May 19, 1933.

19. This story is also related in Fortune, *Fugitives,* 160–61. Indeed, the provenance of the Barrow brothers' involvement at Okabena appears to begin with *Fugitives,* but most of the details probably originated with one of the popular detective magazines of the day. *Fugitives* was supposedly written by Nell Cowan, Clyde's sister, and Emma Parker, Bonnie's mother, but it was actually written by a journalist for the *Dallas Evening Journal* named Jan Fortune. Although much of the information in that book really did come from the families of Bonnie and Clyde, such as the story of Bonnie's fear of thunderstorms, there are known instances where Fortune lifted much from detective magazines. To further complicate matters, Fortune often combined details from separate incidents—for instance, the old man with the log in the Lucerne robbery attempt is transplanted by Fortune to the Okabena robbery. Fortune, *Fugitives,* 163–64; *Pharos- Tribune,* May 12, 1933; *Minneapolis Journal,* May 19, 1933. However, there is corroboration for parts of the Jan Fortune version, including that dealing with Okabena. Clyde's mother, Cumie Barrow, started to write a book in 1934, but she never completed it and never published it. Cumie's youngest daughter, Marie, allowed the editor unlimited access to that manuscript when he was working on his first book, *Running with Bonnie and Clyde.* Cumie mentions there the robbery at Okabena, listing the correct date and proper details, unlike Fortune who lists May 16 as the date of the robbery and, as previously stated, mixes a number of incidents with the attempted robbery at Lucerne, Indiana, on May 12. Cumie Barrow, unpublished manuscript.

20. For a grim first-person look at the gritty reality of a condemned person waiting to be executed, see Umphrey, *Meanest Man in Texas*, 74–96. For the ritual procedures of execution in Texas, see Marquart, Ekland-Olson, and Sorenson, *The Rope*, 30–37.

21. The Barrow brothers broke into the First State Bank of Okabena the night before the robbery and hid out until morning, just as they had done in Lucerne, Indiana. Early on the morning of May 19, bank president Sam Frederickson and cashier R. M. Jones arrived and began preparations for the day's business. At some point the Barrow brothers revealed themselves to Fredrickson and Jones and ordered them into the vault. As one of the brothers loaded money into a container, the other watched for customers, herding a total of eight into the vault along with the two bank employees. During the robbery a young woman named Cleo Atz happened to walk by the bank and see what was happening. She ran next door and told her father, August Atz, who owned and operated a hardware store there. Atz took a loaded pistol and stepped out his back door to the street that ran behind the hardware store and bank. He then hid behind a wooden toolshed. A car containing two women that had been parked nearby, pulled up to the back door of the bank. When the Barrow brothers emerged from the bank, Atz opened fire. He only succeeded in blowing out the rear glass of the car, however. The brothers (one source says a woman as well) returned fire with machine guns, probably Browning automatic rifles. The toolshed was ripped apart but Atz was unhurt. The brothers then jumped in the car and it lurched forward. Before leaving Okabena, however, the bandits made a loop around the square, spraying the town with machine gun fire. Some shots reportedly "went straight through the hotel." Witnesses saw a man and at least one of the two women handling weapons in the car. *Minneapolis Journal*, May 19, 1933; *Fairmont (Minn.) Daily Sentinel*, May 19, 1933; Boucher, *Jackson County (Minn.) History, vol. II*, 119–20. As was the case in Lucerne, Indiana, it is quite probable that Blanche was the driver of the car that pulled up behind the bank, despite her assertion that she and Bonnie waited outside of town during the robbery. We have already seen that Blanche was a bit of a virtuoso at the wheel.

22. The take from the Okabena robbery varies from source to source. The *Okabena Press* on May 25 reported around $1,400 stolen. On May 19, the *Fairmont (Minn.) Daily Sentinel* listed the amount as $2,500. So does Fortune. Fortune, *Fugitives*, 163. Cumie Barrow wrote that her sons stole $1,600 in Okabena, $700 of it in silver dollars. Cumie Barrow, unpublished manuscript. Petty thieves Anthony Strain and his wife, Mildred, were arrested in Sioux City, Iowa, and charged with the Okabena robbery. Shortly thereafter, Strain's brother Floyd was arrested in South Dakota and also charged with the robbery. Vehemently protesting their innocence, all three received forty-year sentences. Boucher, *Jackson County (Minn.) History*, vol. II, 119–20.

According to W. D. Jones, there really was not a lot of money in those small-town banks during the Great Depression. Jones, "Riding with Bonnie and Clyde," 162. And many outlaws, including Clyde Barrow, Raymond Hamilton, and Ralph Fults had each tried to rob banks that had gone out of business. To Barrow there seemed to be too much risk for too little gain. However, the following year, in 1934, Barrow staged at least six daylight bank robberies: in Rembrandt, Iowa, on January 23; in Poteau, Oklahoma on January 25; in Knierim, Iowa on February 1; in Lancaster, Texas, on February 27; in Stuart, Iowa, on April 16; and in Everly, Iowa, on May 3. Of those robberies only one was in Texas, perhaps for good reason. Despite fierce opposition from such figures as Texas Ranger Captain Frank Hamer, since 1928 the Texas State Bankers Association had offered a reward of "$5,000.00 for Dead Bank Robbers—Not One Cent for Live Ones." *Dallas Morning News*, March 13, 1928. Each of the association's 1,000 member banks contributed $5 toward these rewards. In the space of six years $35,000 in rewards had been paid out. *Dallas Daily Times-Herald*, January 12, 1933. Even though some of the killings were later proved to be nothing more than frame-ups and murders for the reward, the Texas Bankers Association refused to withdraw the offer. One such case occurred in Fort Worth, Texas, in 1930 when four men were charged with framing two supposed bank robbers during a fictitious robbery of the Polytechnic Bank. *Dallas Daily Times-Herald*, April 17, 1930.

23. Apparently this was a fairly common method used by fugitives to dispose of cars (and the evidence therein). Following the robbery of the bank at Ash Grove, Missouri (mentioned by Barrow, Parker, and Jones to Springfield motorcycle officer Tom Persell after his abduction on January 26, 1933), the burned-out hulk of a Ford V-8 sedan believed used in the robbery was discovered four miles from Springfield, Missouri. *Springfield (Mo.) Press*, January 13, 1933. Clyde Barrow and Ralph Fults similarly burned a car in north Texas in April of 1932. See Phillips, *Running with Bonnie and Clyde*, 77–78.

24. According to Cumie Barrow, $700 of the $1,600 taken from the First State Bank in Okabena, Minnesota, consisted of silver dollars. Cumie Barrow, unpublished manuscript.

25. Three of Clyde Barrow's cohorts in crime described him as very quiet, calm, and thoughtful. Fults interview, November 5, 1980; Hammett interview, February 20, 1982; Jones, interview by Biffle, June 1968. Fults had a mixed view of Buck. He once described him as "solemn, sullen." Fults interview, May 21, 1983. However, on another occassion Fults, who considred himself hotheaded in those days, remembered Buck as quiet and easygoing. Fults interview, November 12, 1980. Jones said Buck was "hot-headed." Jones, interview by Biffle, June 1968. Buck's sister Marie said of him, "Buck was the meanest, most hot-tempered kid you ever saw. He'd fight at the drop of a hat." Marie Barrow interview, April 19, 1995.

26. Here Blanche first wrote, then crossed out the following: "He would have gotten me first because I wouldn't have been quick enough to shoot him face-to-face. And I would never have shot him in the back, even if he was a dirty rat and would as soon shoot someone in the back as face them. But then, if he had shot Buck and I managed to shoot him, Bonnie would have shot me anyway."

Chapter 7. *Mother's Day*

1. That would be Monday, May 15, 1933, three days after the attempted bank robbery in Lucerne, Indiana, and four days before the successful robbery of the First State Bank in Okabena, Minnesota.

2. The bus driver's concern reinforces the observation of some of Blanche's friends that because she was so petite men felt compelled to protect her and watch over her. Linder and Weiser interviews, October 5, 2002.

3. In a letter four months earlier, Blanche had complained to her mother that she was "as fat as a pig," adding, "I weigh 114½. I am getting so fat. I can't wear my clothes. Guess I will have to reduce to get in some of them." Blanche Barrow letter to mother, January 14, 1933, quoted in Baker, *Blanche Barrow*, 25–26.

4. In the 1933 city directory Elvin, or "Jack," as he was known, is listed as residing at 1308 Second Avenue, which does not exist anymore.

5. Apparently the families of these fugitives, particularly the mothers, remained very close throughout this period and for years afterward. Cumie Barrow and Emma Parker called each other frequently and invited each other over for visits on a regular basis. And their concern for Alice Davis, Raymond Hamilton's mother, is also evident. When Hamilton was captured in April 1934, Emma asked Cumie in a phone conversation, "How is his mother?" Dallas Police Department telephone wiretap transcript, April 27, 1934, 49; April 29, 1934, 64. Blanche's mother, at the time Lillian Horton, was a part of that circle as well, even long after Buck's death and Blanche's imprisonment. This is indicated in a number of Blanche's prison letters, quoted in Baker, *Blanche Barrow*, 31–33, 38, 45–46, 49–51, and 55–56.

6. By then Nell was divorced from Leon Hale, the musician who taught Clyde to play saxophone, and had married Luther J. Cowan. Cowan was a barber who met Nell when she was a beautician at May's Barber Shop and Beauty Parlor at 4907 Ross Avenue in Dallas. By 1933 they were both living at the Sanger Hotel and Apartments at 717 South Ervay and working at the Sanger Hotel Barber and Beauty Shop. *Worley's Dallas (Tex.) City Directory* 1931, 1933–34. "Just 'LC' is all I ever knew." Marie Barrow interview, September 15, 1993.

7. Cumie Barrow, who suspected a police wiretap on her phone, was circumspect in her calls. In a Dallas police wiretap transcript covering a thirteen-day period in April 1934 there are a number of cryptic remarks made by Cumie Barrow that her descendants have identified as references to, or inquiries about Bonnie and Clyde. References to "the Howards" and "cooking beans," appearing throughout the transcript, are said to be veiled references to "the kids," as they were called. Also, a slight variation to a rural Texas colloquialism was another reference. The caller would sometimes lead with, "Do you know anything?" Even today this phrase is still used by rural Texans to spark a conversation, but from the mouths of Cumie Barrow and Emma Parker it sometimes meant something else. Once, one of the Barrows' older daughters called Cumie and asked if she knew anything. Cumie remained silent for several seconds, then said, "Come over." Just a few minutes before, Cumie had done

the same thing to Emma Parker, telling her, "Come over. I have something to tell you." Dallas Police Department telephone wiretap transcript, April 30, 1934, 65. Sometimes the references weren't so veiled. "Say, do you know what we were talking about down in the cafe today? Well, they are going to leave early in the morning." Dallas Police Department telephone wiretap transcript, April 19, 1934, 13. Everyone apparently kept close to the radio and scanned the papers carefully, frequently calling the four Dallas dailies to inquire about "extras." Emma Parker once called Cumie Barrow to ask if she was listening to the radio, that the police were in the midst of a running gunfight with three men who had abandoned their car and were on foot in the Trinity River bottoms. Dallas Police Department telephone wiretap transcript, April 18, 1934, 11. That incident had nothing to do with Bonnie and Clyde as it turned out, but another telephone call did. A friend of the Barrows called to tell Cumie that he had been at the Dallas police headquarters checking on the status of his own brother who had been arrested when he overheard officers in another room talking about a gunfight in Highland Park, a city which at the time bordered Dallas to the north. Bonnie and Clyde, traveling at their usual high rate of speed, had passed a police car on Lover's Lane and had then run through a stop sign. When the police pursued them, they were fired on with a machine gun. The incident was reported in the papers the following day, but the part about the shooting was omitted. Dallas Police Department telephone wiretap transcript, April 26, 1934, 43–46; *Dallas Daily Times-Herald*, May 27, 1934.

8. In *Fugitives*, Nell is presented as the eyewitness narrator of the events of the meeting near Commerce, Texas. Fortune, *Fugitives*, 156–63.

9. According to Blanche, Clyde Barrow felt very safe in this part of Texas, especially in or around Paris because of its proximity to the Oklahoma line and the host of back roads honeycombing the area. Blanche Barrow, quoted in Weiser interview, April 18, 2003. Cumie Barrow was also known to have inquired at least once about train passage to Paris, Texas. Dallas Police Department telephone wiretap transcript, April 18, 1934, 8. Blanche herself had a relative, Ruby Caldwell, living in Gilmer, Texas, north of Tyler.

10. It is not known when and where the first attempt to contact Floyd took place. However, they apparently had met at least once prior to the encounter mentioned by Blanche, although it is thought the outlaws never worked together on any robberies. In June 1933 both Clyde and Buck tried again to find Floyd, after the wreck near Wellington, Texas, in which Bonnie Parker was so severely burned. The Barrows were hoping Floyd could provide a safe hide-out where Bonnie could recuperate. But they never located him. It was later, after he and Parker were wounded in November of that same year, that Clyde Barrow finally met up with Floyd. Floyd, or members of his family, found an underworld doctor for them. Cumie Barrow, unpublished manuscript; Marie Barrow interview, August 24, 1984.

11. According to W. D. Jones, two aspects of this story are atypical of Clyde Barrow. Although Jones was not a witness to this specific incident, he was with Barrow constantly for several months and during that time Barrow

never used his real name, especially when talking to a stranger, as with the filling-station attendant in Sallisaw, and Jones never saw Barrow drunk. Although he admitted they all drank from time to time, even Clyde, Jones said, "I never did see him [Clyde] drunk, drunk enough not to be sensible. No, I never seen him like that." Jones, interview by Biffle, June 1968. Ralph Fults echoed this, adding, "Clyde hated dope! He didn't drink and didn't smoke either, at least not while I was with him. He didn't even like to drink coffee!" Fults also remarked about pseudonyms, saying Clyde used names like "Bud" and "Jack Sherman," among others. Fults used them as well. Fults interview, December 10, 1980.

12. According to her sister, Bonnie Parker apparently stuck to small talk during these meetings—local gossip, clothes, hair styles, and food. "She was very evasive about other things." Billie Jean Parker Moon, unpublished hand-written observations.

13. Blanche apparently continued to like boots and riding pants, wearing them frequently late in life. Weiser interview, April 18, 2003.

14. The time and circumstances of this meeting have been related elsewhere with confusing and contradictory details. Buck's mother described a meeting with Bonnie and Clyde and Blanche and Buck on the driveway outside of the family filling station in West Dallas. She wrote that the meeting took place "three days after Mother's Day," May 17, and then closes the passage by writing, "I never saw Buck but one more time after that until he was shot" (in Platte City, Missouri, on July 19, 1933). Cumie Barrow, unpublished manuscript. However, on the very same page of her own manuscript, Cumie Barrow con-tradicts herself by writing that after the Okabena robbery, on May 19, five days after Mother's Day, "Clyde and Buck came by the house . . . every three or four weeks." Fortune has the meeting near Commerce taking place "on the Wednesday after Mother's Day," May 17, the same day as the meeting described above by Cumie Barrow. The events of the Commerce meeting, according to Fortune, are narrated by Nell and at least one incident related by the fugitives to their families that day would not happen until later—the robbery of the First State Bank of Okabena, Minnesota, on Friday, May 19, 1933. Fortune, *Fugitives*, 156–63; *Fairmont (Minn.) Daily Sentinel*, May 19, 1933. However, as we have seen, Fortune actually describes the events of the attempted robbery of the Lucerne State Bank, Lucerne, Indiana, on May 12, 1933, the previous Friday, but identifies it as the robbery of the First State Bank of Okabena, Minnesota. Fortune, *Fugitives*, 163; *Fairmont (Minn.) Daily Sentinel*, May 19, 1933; *Pharos-Tribune*, May 12, 1933. Blanche wrote that she arrived in Dallas on the Monday after Mother's Day, May 15 and that the Commerce meeting took place that same afternoon. She also emphasizes the fact that Nell refused to go to the meeting at all. However if, as the author writes, the visit in Com-merce was the only trip the fugitives made to Texas in May, then when did Cumie Barrow see Buck "one more time after that"? And why did she follow that statement with the contradiction that after Okabena her sons "came by the house . . . every three or four weeks"? Did the meeting on the driveway

happen exactly as Cumie Barrow suggests? Perhaps not, unless Blanche is mistaken, which may be the case. The May 1933 time frame is confusing in nearly every source, including Blanche's own manuscript. But still, it may be that Cumie Barrow is simply confused about the date and that the meeting she describes actually occurred in late April and is the same one referred to earlier by Blanche, the visit made immediately following the abductions in Ruston, Louisiana. Moreover, in the next chapter Blanche indicates that she and the other three fugitives spent nearly all day and most of the night of the May 17 camped on a riverbank in Mississippi.

Chapter 8. *Florida*

1. This would have been the night of May 17–18, Wednesday and Thursday, respectively. It is possible that the four fugitives diverted to southern Minnesota at this point in order to stage the Okabena robbery on Friday, May 19, 1933. Considering Blanche's next statement, "In a few days we were in Florida," coupled with Clyde Barrow's penchant for long drives, it is indeed possible that the Okabena robbery was sandwiched between Mississippi and Florida. The robbery of the First State Bank in Okabena, Minnesota, was nearly a carbon copy of the Lucerne incident, except for the old man with a chunk of wood, the pigs, and having to flee with no money. "Machine Gun Bandits Shoot Up Okabena; Rob Bank," read the headlines of the *Fairmont* (*Minn.*) *Daily Sentinel*, May 19, 1933.

2. Blanche and Buck actually made two trips to Florida, in March 1930 (apparently right after Buck's escape from the Ferguson prison farm) and again in 1931 on their honeymoon.

3. There is no city, town, or village named Cumberland along the Atlantic coast of Georgia. There is, however, Cumberland Island, one of several barrier islands between the Georgia mainland and the Atlantic Ocean. It is possible that Blanche is confusing the name of that island with the town she describes. But Cumberland Island, declared a National Seashore in 1972 and a National Wilderness area in 1982, is not connected by bridge to the mainland and never has been. Thus, it is unlikely that the beach described by Blanche was on Cumberland Island. It would appear that the most likely location (between Jacksonville and Brunswick, Georgia, their next destination) would have been Amelia Island, in Florida, just south of the Georgia line. On Amelia Island there are a handful of towns, any one of which might be the place mentioned by Blanche. However, two of the towns, Fernandina Beach and American Beach, are particularly suited to her description; especially Fernandina Beach, seemingly the only Amelia Island community large enough to warrant the presence of a motorcycle patrol. Also, Fernandina Beach, Florida, is just a few miles from the southern tip of Cumberland Island. Cumberland quite possibly was a name in common use by businesses in Fernandina Beach, perhaps accounting for Blanche's confusion. Carol Ruckdeschel, Cumberland Island Museum, letter to Phillips, January 22, 2002.

4. The Barrow brothers and two accomplices were once caught in the act of burglarizing a business in Atlanta, Georgia, probably in 1929. Clyde somehow eluded the officers and slipped away unseen. Buck and the two accomplices were trapped inside the business, but Buck managed to squeeze between the engine and firewall of a large delivery truck and pull the hood down over his head before he was spotted. The two accomplices were then arrested and taken to jail. Afterward, Buck emerged from his hiding place and rejoined Clyde. The two burglarized another place and went back to Texas. When Clyde Barrow and Ralph Fults were initially planning the raid on Eastham, Barrow mentioned wanting to free a couple of convicts in Georgia afterward. Fults interview, May 10, 1981. See also Phillips, *Running with Bonnie and Clyde*, 33–92, 101–02, 167–71; Phillips, "Raid on Eastham."

5. Blanche once told a story about this trip, perhaps related to this very incident, which illustrated the only known occurrence of Clyde Barrow getting completely disoriented while behind the wheel of a car. It happened after leaving Florida when, as described in the text, a police car began chasing them. Barrow was extremely tired at the time, and in the process of turning again and again and doubling back repeatedly he lost his bearings. After eluding the police car in a maze of roads Barrow then continued driving all night long toward Texas, or so he thought. When Barrow, who would let no one else drive, finally got too tired to drive farther he pulled to a stop in a wooded area. He and the others then stretched out and slept for the rest of the night, thinking they were not far from the Texas line. When the sun rose a few hours later Barrow and his band of fugitives found themselves staring at palm trees and sandy beaches. Instead of Texas, they had ventured to within a few yards of the Atlantic Ocean on the east coast of Florida. Blanche Barrow as quoted in Weiser interview, April 18, 2003.

6. Clyde took a chance each time he traveled through Alabama. One of his uncles was a lawman in that state, and Barrow had promised his family he would never commit a crime there. Marie Barrow interview, April 29, 1998. There are pictures in Blanche's scrapbooks from trips taken to Mobile, Alabama; Pensacola, Florida; and East Jacksonville, Florida. During at least one of these trips several friends accompanied her and Buck. In addition, there is photographic evidence of a trip to Nashville, Tennessee, and at least one other trip. The latter journey was in the company of W. D. Jones's older brother Clyde and his wife. Blanche Barrow scrapbooks.

Chapter 9. *A Visit with My Father*

1. These incidents occurred on June 10 and 23, respectively. For the full story of each event, see Phillips, *Running with Bonnie and Clyde*, 134–39. For a more concise and detailed look at the Arkansas killing, see also Knight, "Incident at Alma," and Knight and Davis., *Bonnie and Clyde*, 93–98.

2. *Dallas Daily Times-Herald*, June 7 and 21, 1933.

3. *Mexico (Mo.) Weekly Ledger*, June 15, 1933; *Dallas Daily Times-Herald*, June 5, and 29, 1933; *Dallas Daily Times-Herald*, June 17, 1933.

4. *Dallas Daily Times-Herald*, June 2, 1933. Hamilton's combined sentence is usually listed as 263 years. However, his brother points out a little known three- year suspended sentence for auto theft that was revoked and added to the total, making it 266 years. See Hamilton, *Public Enemy No. 1*, 18.

5. *Cleveland County (Ark.) Herald*, June 7, 14, and, 21, 1933; *Dallas Daily Times-Herald*, June 9, and 11, 1933. Frank Hardy helped Barrow and Hollis Hale rob a bank at Oronogo, Missouri, on November 30, 1932. His arrest in the Johnson killing prompted Barrow to write a letter declaring Hardy's innocence. By then, however, W. D. Jones had been arrested and confessed to the crime and the letter became unnecessary. It remained in the Barrow family possessions until it was sold at auction in the 1990s.

6. *Springfield (Mo.) Daily News*, June 30, 1933; *Pleasanton (Kans.) Observer Enterprise*, July 6, 1933; *Dallas Daily Times-Herald*, June 8 and 30, 1933; *The Mexico (Mo.) Intelligencer*, June 15, 1933. Initially it was thought the two crimes were related, but eventually authorities came to suspect they were not linked at all. Also, Pretty Boy Floyd was at first thought to have been one of two men involved in the murders. While the bank robbers appear to have escaped without a trace, two men were convicted of the killings. See *History of Audrain County, Missouri*, 222.

7. The name of the agency was later changed to the Federal Bureau of Investigation.

8. For the very best account of this incident and its aftermath, see Unger, *Union Station Massacre*. See also *Kansas City Star*, June 17, 1933.

9. In the extreme southeastern part of the state, near both the Texas and Arkansas lines.

10. The nephew referred to here is probably Jay Caldwell. By December 1933, Matt Caldwell was no longer living with his brother. Blanche Barrow letter to her mother, December 12, 1933, quoted in Baker, *Blanche Barrow*, 35.

11. Between Idabel and Durant.

12. Jones later commented that people frequently helped them, "Not because it was Bonnie and Clyde. People in them days just helped—no questions asked." Jones, interview by Biffle, June 1969.

Chapter 10. *Wellington*

1. W. D. Jones said that by the time he and Bonnie and Clyde arrived at the meeting place, early on the morning of June 11, Buck and Blanche "had lots of money," adding that they had robbed a bank while Bonnie and Clyde were picking him up in Dallas. (Jones had met Bonnie and Clyde at the Five Star Dance Hall near Bachman Dam, Dallas. Dallas County Sheriff's Department, Jones, Voluntary Statement B-71, 12.) Blanche, however, said she and Buck had been visiting relatives in Oklahoma. Blanche Barrow interview, November 18, 1984. On June 6, 1933, the day Blanche writes that she and Buck Barrow were driving "through Texas to Oklahoma" in a stolen "gray Ford V-8 sedan," the First State Bank of Bokchito, Oklahoma, was robbed of $1,407 at 1:15 p.m. by two bandits who escaped in a Ford V-8. *Dallas Daily*

Times-Herald, June 8, 1933; Allen, "The First State Bank—Bokchito, Oklahoma." Bokchito is about eighty miles west of Goodwater, where Matt Caldwell, Blanche's father, was living at the time.

2. Earlier in the evening of June 10, 1933, Clyde Barrow had been traveling at a high rate of speed seven miles north of Wellington, in the Texas Panhandle southeast of Amarillo. He apparently did not see a sign warning that the bridge across the Salt Fork River had been moved, and he careened into the nearly dry riverbed, reportedly saying, "Hold on to your hats! This is it!" Moon and Huddleston, "Bonnie, Clyde, and Me," unpublished manuscript, 12. Barrow and Jones were able to climb out of the wreck, but Parker was pinned inside. Within a few moments the car caught fire and before she could be pulled free, Parker was severely burned. A local farmer, Sam Pritchard, helped Barrow and Jones carry Parker to his farmhouse nearby. However, Pritchard became suspicious of the trio. Another man at the Pritchard house slipped away to notify the local authorities. When they arrived, in the person of Collingsworth County Sheriff George Corry and Wellington City Marshal Paul Hardy, Barrow and Jones abducted them both and escaped with Parker in Corry's car. Barrow was driving Corry's car when he arrived at the meeting place near Sayre, Oklahoma. For the full account, see Phillips, *Running with Bonnie and Clyde,* 135–37. See also Jones, "Riding with Bonnie and Clyde," 165; Fortune, *Fugitives,* 172; *Dallas Morning News,* June 12, 1933; *Amarillo (Tex.) Sunday News-Globe,* June 12, 1933.

Gladys Cartwright, the farmer's daughter, gave her own side of the story in a later interview. According to Cartwright on June 10, 1933, Sam Pritchard, his wife, daughter and son-in-law Gladys and Alonzo Cartwright, and son and daughter-in- law Jack and Irene Pritchard were all sitting on the east porch of their farmhouse in the Texas Panhandle, seven miles north of Wellington. They heard a car approaching at a high rate of speed on the road in front of the house. They heard it long before they saw it. Several moments later a Ford V-8 topped the hill and roared past them. One of the witnesses commented that it seemed the driver was going so fast he would probably miss the detour sign mounted prominently on the road. The sign rerouted motorists onto a new stretch of road leading to the new bridge across the Salt Fork of the Red River. The old road only functioned as a spur and ended at the riverbank. The bridge there had been removed. Just as suspected, the driver missed the sign and proceeded onto the old spur at top speed. Seconds later there was a grinding crash as the car plunged over the embankment and smashed into the dry riverbed. Sam Pritchard and Alonzo Cartwright ran to the wreck, about two hundred yards from the house, just as the car was igniting. They helped two men, Barrow and Jones, free a badly burned woman, Parker, from the car. Sam and Alonzo insisted on taking all three to their house for treatment. Alonzo also suggested driving to Wellington for a doctor. "No," one of the men said. "We're hot." At some point the farm family were made aware of Clyde Barrow, although none of them had ever heard of the Barrow brothers before.

"All I knew was they were hurt and needed help," said Sam Pritchard. Later they all assumed Jones was Buck. Alonzo Cartwright managed to slip away and alert Collingsworth County Sheriff George Corry. When Corry and Wellington City Marshal Paul Hardy arrived at the Pritchard house they found Bonnie Parker in bed, badly burned. The officers walked through the house and stepped outside where Barrow and Jones were waiting with weapons drawn. They disarmed the officers. Suddenly Parker leaped out of bed and ran outside. Jones, identified as Buck, thought there were other lawmen in the house or that Cladys Cartright was reaching for a gun and opened fire, striking Gladys in the hand. Barrow then shot holes in all the tires of Alonzo Cartwright's car, cuffed the officers, and took off in the sheriff's car along with Parker and Jones. Gladys Pritchard Cartwright, interview by Evelyn Ball King, quoted in King, *Collingsworth County*, 387.

3. This statement by Clyde Barrow appears to indicate he had no intention of killing Corry and Hardy. Otherwise he would not have been worried about what they might see. This also tends to contradict Blanche's later assertion that Clyde Barrow was in some sort of a quandary over whether the officers should live or die.

4. This was confirmed by Jones, who said Parker was "burned so bad none of us thought she was going to live." Jones also stated that her right leg was burned from the hip to the ankle and that bone was visible in some places. Jones, "Riding with Bonnie and Clyde," 165. Cumie Barrow described a burn deep in the knee and said that Parker's leg was "drawn up some," indicating damage to ligaments. Cumie Barrow, unpublished manuscript.

5. This more than implies that Clyde was debating whether or not to kill the officers, which may not have been the case. Every other source close to the fugitives indicated that it was Buck, not Clyde who wanted to kill Corry and Hardy. W. D. Jones said later, "Buck was all for killing the two lawmen; but Clyde, thinking how gentle they had been with Bonnie, said no." Jones, "Riding with Bonnie and Clyde," 165. Cumie Barrow quoted Buck asking, "[Are we going to] bump them off?" Cumie Barrow, unpublished manuscript. So did Fortune in *Fugitives*, 172. The abducted officers also named Buck as the one who asked, "Are we going to kill these men?" And they reported Clyde's answer as, "No, I've been with them so long I'm beginning to like them." *Dallas Morning News*, June 12, 1933. Almost two years later, Corry would testify in federal court during the Barrow-Parker harboring case that as he and Hardy were being tied up, Buck said, "Guess you were looking for the Barrow boys." "Not especially," Corry replied. "Well you got 'm anyway," Buck said. *Dallas Dispatch*, February 24, 1935.

6. When Buck returned from tying up the officers, he mentioned that he had used barbed wire. Clyde became angry. "You didn't have to do that!" he said. Jones, "Riding with Bonnie and Clyde," 165. Apparently, however, Buck's claim that he did not tie the officers very securely was true. They freed themselves in under thirty minutes and made their way to a nearby farmhouse. *Dallas Morning News*, June 12, 1933.

7. In the original text, Blanche first wrote "Pampa, Texas," here, then crossed it out and replaced it with "Canadian," a town located in the upper northeastern part of the Texas Panhandle.

8. In the original text, the author wrote "Pampa" here. However, because she had, only a few sentences above crossed "Pampa" out and replaced it with "Canadian," the editor has followed suit—replacing Pampa with Canadian. Although Pampa is not far away from Canadian, the scene as described by Blanche, including the crossing of the Canadian River, points toward the actual location being the town of Canadian. It appears Blanche accidentally left Pampa in the text here. However, an Oklahoma posse reported last seeing the fugitives turning onto the main road to Pampa. *Dallas Morning News*, June 12, 1933.

9. If Buck and Blanche "had lots of money," as Jones stated (see Note 1 of this chapter), there would have been no reason to stage any robberies. It is possible that Jones's later statement to the Dallas County sheriff's department about Buck and Blanche having robbed a bank was merely a ploy by Jones to keep him from being implicated in any later robberies.

10. There were no reported robberies or burglaries in or around the Pratt, Kansas, area between June 11 and 17, 1933, the time the Barrow gang was hiding there. They were no doubt venturing beyond the area for cash. *Pratt (Kans.) Union*, June 11–17, 1933; *Pratt (Kans.) Daily Tribune*, June 11–17, 1933. On June 14, 1933, the Farmers and Merchants Bank of Mexico, Missouri, was robbed of $1,750 by three (some say four) men who escaped in a light-blue Buick with a bullet hole in the windshield. At 3:15 P.M., an hour after the robbery, two men shot and killed Boone County Sheriff Roger Wilson and patrolman Ben Boothe of the Missouri Highway Patrol after a scuffle at the intersection of Highways 40 and 63 north of Columbia, Missouri. *Mexico (Mo.) Intelligencer*, June 15, 1933; *Mexico (Mo.) Weekly Ledger*, June 15, 1933. The scene of the shooting is approximately four hundred miles from Pratt, Kansas. The bank robbery was a few miles further to the east. Initially it was thought that the robbery and the shooting were related, but as evidence was collected it appeared to authorities the two were unrelated. *Mexico (Mo.) Intelligencer*, July 13, 1933. It did not take long, however, before the name of Charles Arthur "Pretty Boy" Floyd was being linked to both crimes. Then, just three days later, he would be connected to Kansas City's Union Station Massacre as well, the headlines reading, "Floyd Named Columbia Killer and Gunman in KC Massacre." *Mexico (Mo.) Weekly Ledger*, June 22, 1933. Floyd probably did not rob the bank in Mexico, Missouri, and it is doubtful he had anything to do with either shooting. See Unger, *Union Station Massacre*, for a detailed accounting of why Floyd was not involved. As the days and weeks rolled on, other names floated in and out of suspicion in the Columbia, Missouri, killings. A man named Ira Seybold was considered for a while when it was thought he had been too eager to plead guilty to a bank robbery in Indiana and thus avoid being sent to Missouri to face charges there. *Mexico (Mo.) Intelligencer*, June 29, 1933. In 1936 a man named George McKeever was hanged for the murders of Sheriff Wilson and Patrolman Boothe. By then he was not considered involved

in the Mexico robbery, nor was Floyd. *History of Audrain County, Missouri*, 222. For a time, however, the Barrow brothers were considered suspects in both the Mexico robbery and the Columbia murders. *Landmark*, July 21, 1933.

11. A car was stolen on June 14, 1933, in Hutchinson, Kansas, north of Pratt. *Fort Smith Southwest American*, June 26, 1933.

Chapter 11. *Fort Smith*

1. On June 15, 1933, Barrow and his group checked into the Twin Cities Tourist Camp on North Eleventh Street in Fort Smith. They rented two cabins at one dollar a day. *Fort Smith Southwest American*, June 26, 1933.

2. According to Blanche there was another reason for Clyde's journey to Dallas: He wanted another family member there because Bonnie and Blanche were not speaking and the latter refused to help the injured fugitive. Blanche Barrow, quoted in Weiser interview, October 5, 2002.

3. Barrow left Fort Smith on June 18 and returned with Billie Jean the following day. Moon and Huddleston, "Bonnie, Clyde, and Me"; *Dallas Dispatch*, February 24, 1935. Many have noted that Barrow risked his life whenever he drove to the Dallas area, but on this occasion the risk was greater. When word of Bonnie's injuries reached Dallas, some suggested that Barrow would abandon Parker. Still others correctly surmised that Barrow would try to make contact with the Parkers, and probably his own family as well. Consequently, Dallas police and the Dallas County sheriff's department were trying to remain vigilant. Hinton, *Ambush*, 54–55. A "Barrow sighting" by a local dairy farmer on June 16, 1933, prompted several Dallas County deputies and at least two Texas Rangers to converge on Mountain Creek Valley near Cedar Hill, Texas, just south of Dallas. *Dallas Daily Times-Herald*, June 16, 1933. The fact that Barrow eluded detection speaks not so much to his stealth, which was considerable, but largely to the tremendous lack of personnel and resources at the disposal of law enforcement at the time, something Barrow counted on and exploited to the fullest wherever he went.

Billie Jean Parker was one of four children born to Emma Krause and Charles Parker. Hubert "Buster," born on December 20, 1908, was the oldest living child but he was not the first-born. The oldest would have been Coley Parker, who died of crib death as an infant. Moon, unpublished handwritten history. Billie Jean, the youngest, was once married to Fred Mace, a West Dallas man with a criminal record. Mace, along with his brother Bud and Roy Thornton, Bonnie Parker's husband, were involved in a north Texas burglary ring that included the son of a former Dallas County sheriff. During one of their crimes, Fred Mace was shot and captured, along with his three accomplices. Fred, Bud, and Roy were convicted and imprisoned. However, the son of the former sheriff was quickly released, some suggesting that his powerful father had literally "bought" his son's freedom. Fults interview, February 13, 1982.

During their marriage, Billie Jean bore two children to Fred Mace. Both died in the fall of 1933, just days apart, of some unspecified stomach disorder. Fortune, *Fugitives*, 211. Billie Jean divorced Mace after he went to prison. His subsequent fate and that of his brother Bud are unknown. Roy Thornton was killed in 1937 during an attempted escape from the Eastham prison farm. *Houston Press*, October 4, 1937.

4. The presence of two doctors was confirmed by Sheriff John B. Williams. *Fort Smith Southwest American*, June 25, 1933. The owners of the tourist camp had a twenty-four-year-old daughter, Hazel Dennis, who was in the medical profession. She helped nurse Bonnie and also contacted at least one of the doctors who attended Bonnie. Later, during the 1935 Barrow-Parker federal harboring case, Hazel Dennis refused to identify Billie Jean Parker as being one of those involved in Fort Smith. Moon and Huddleston, "Bonnie, Clyde, and Me," unpublished manuscript.

5. Van Buren is just across the Arkansas River from Fort Smith, hence the reference to "twin cities" in the name of the tourist camp. The visits to the grocery store in Van Buren are reported in the local newspaper. *Fort Smith Southwest American*, June 26, 1933. The trade name, Amytal is used by Blanche here. The generic name is amobarbital, or amobarbital sodium. It is a barbiturate, administered as a sedative.

6. Tom Persell, the Springfield, Missouri, motorcycle patrolman abducted by Bonnie, Clyde, and W. D. Jones on January 26, 1933, said, "They all were profane, hardly saying anything without cussing." Edwards, "A Tale Tom Persell Lived to Tell." Evidently such is relative, however. W. D. Jones said he rarely heard Clyde swear, certainly nothing like "kids today." Jones, "Riding with Bonnie and Clyde," 164.

7. Although there was probably more to Bonnie's outburst, one of the known side effects of barbiturate withdrawal is irritability. Another indicator of barbiturate withdrawal is the psychological and physical craving for more of the drug, which Blanche described. Depending on the person, these and other symptoms may develop within eight to twelve hours after the last dose. If Barrow was in Dallas overnight picking up Billie Jean, it is possible that Bonnie was not taking the drug and beginning to exhibit symptoms of withdrawal, including irritability. Of course, Bonnie may have been genuinely sick of Buck and Blanche as well. Blanche admitted that there was friction between Bonnie and her, characterizing it as "having two women in the same kitchen—there can only be one queen bee!" Blanche Barrow, quoted by Kent Biffle during an interview with W. D. Jones, June 1969. Also, Buck's temper would have most certainly contributed to any such incident. Fortune briefly mentions Bonnie's demeanor during her convalescence, describing her as "crosser and more exacting." Fortune, *Fugitives*, 181.

8. Jones said later that to the best of his knowledge he never witnessed any sort of argument between Bonnie and Blanche. But he qualified his remark by adding, "You know, that's possible. I can't remember that far back." Jones, interview by Biffle, June 1969.

9. Billie has stated that when she arrived in Fort Smith on June 19 her sister was in a coma and did not know she was there. When at last she regained consciousness, her focus seemed to be on getting Billie away from there before

she too became trapped in a life on the run. She pestered Clyde to take Billie back to Dallas. Moon and Huddleston, "Bonnie, Clyde, and Me," 13–14.

10. Two sources close to Clyde Barrow mention his disdain for drugs. W. D. Jones said, "He (Clyde) never used dope. He didn't even smoke cigarettes. And he didn't drink too often either." Jones, interview by Biffle, June 1969. And, according to Ralph Fults, "Clyde hated dope! He didn't drink and didn't smoke either, at least not while I was with him. He didn't even like to drink coffee!" Fults interview, December 10, 1980.

11. Unguentine is a burn salve that evolved from an early-nineteenth-century product called Cooper Alum Ointment developed by two British physicians. One of the physicians moved to the United States where his descendants interested the Norwich Pharmacal Company in the formula. First advertised in medical journals as Unguentine in 1893, the salve soon became one of Norwich's leading products. By 1922, "Unguentine–The First Thought in Burns" was being produced at a rate of one ton daily. Norwich, "Unguentine." The acid solution perhaps came from the Howe Drug Store, Fort Smith. Clerks there identified photographs of Clyde Barrow as the man who purchased one pound of burn medicine. *Fort Smith Southwest American*, June 26, 1933.

12. Actually, this was probably the ambulance carrying Alma City Marshal Henry Humphrey. After being mortally wounded in the gunfight with Buck Barrow and W. D. Jones, Humphrey was picked up and driven to Van Buren, where a waiting ambulance transported the marshal to a hospital in Fort Smith. *Fort Smith Southwest American*, June 24, 1933.

13. Indeed Buck and W. D. had to leave the car. After robbing the R. L. Brown Grocery Store in Fayetteville on June 23, they rear-ended a slow-moving vehicle on Highway 71, three miles north of Alma, Arkansas. Both cars were wrecked. To compound the situation, Alma Town Marshal H. D. Humphrey suddenly arrived in a car driven by a part-time deputy, A. M. Salyers. As he stepped from the car, Humphrey was blown into a ditch by a blast from Buck Barrow's shotgun. Jones then emerged with a Browning automatic rifle and began spraying the area with slugs, trying to fell Salyers as he ran to the cover of a nearby building. No one was hit. Salyers then returned fire, slicing off the tips of two of Jones' fingers and knocking out the horn button on Salyers' own car as the two gunmen climbed in and drove off in it, the only working machine on the road. Salyers watched his car speed north, then turn west on a country road. The gunmen also made off with Humphrey's pistol. *Fort Smith Southwest American*, June 24, 1933. Of Salyers' skill as a marksman, Jones would later comment, "That man could shoot!" Jones, "Riding with Bonnie and Clyde," 165. Marshal Humphrey died three days later, on Monday, June 26, 1933.

After leaving the scene of the shooting Barrow and Jones eventually emerged on the highway where they commandeered another car. However, upon seeing that the bridge to Fort Smith was guarded, the two outlaws abandoned the car near the summit of nearby Mount Vista, walked across the Frisco railroad trestle, and continued on foot to the Twin Cities Tourist Camp. Barrow and

Jones probably arrived sometime around ten o'clock that night. Dallas County Sheriff's Department, Jones, Voluntary Statement B-71, 13–14; Cumie Barrow, unpublished manuscript.

14. In 1933 there were a number of murders that were initially wrongfully attributed to the Barrow brothers for a variety of reasons. Apart from the four lawmen actually killed by the Barrow brothers and W. D. Jones (Malcolm Davis on January 6; Wes Harryman and Harry McGinnis on April 13; and Henry Humphrey, who died on June 26), there were the murders of Sheriff Roger Wilson and Patrolman Ben Boothe near Columbia, Missouri, on June 14; and four officers were killed in Kansas City on June 17. Then there were the related murders of two Texas officers earlier in the year. Early on the morning of January 23, 1933, two men and a woman in a Ford V-8 had tried to rob two service stations in Happy, Texas. They fled toward Tulia, where Sheriff John C. Moseley waited. Moseley intercepted the would-be bandits and forced them over to the side of the road. Gunfire erupted and Moseley was killed. The trio then calmly robbed the service station they had stopped in front of and escaped. A few days later the same group killed Deputy Sheriff Joe Brown of Rhome, Texas. This crime was initially thought to be the work of Clyde Barrow, perhaps because it came so close on the heels of the Davis killing and involved two men and a woman. *Tulia Herald*, January 26 and February 2, 1933.

15. That may be, but one of the two gunmen reportedly ran up to the mortally wounded Humphrey and said angrily, "I ought to kill you." The marshal merely looked at him and replied, "I think you already have." Knight and Davis, *Bonnie and Clyde*, 95. James Knight has conducted the most thorough research into this incident. The above book and his essay, "Incident at Alma," which appeared in the winter 1997 issue of the *Arkansas Historical Review*, are to date the very best published accounts of the whole Fort Smith-Alma episode.

16. Eyewitnesses saw a man and three women speed away from the tourist camp at 10:40 p.m. on the night of June 23. *Fort Smith Southwest American*, June 26, 1933.

Chapter 12. *Platte City*

1. For the complete story of the Platte, Missouri, and Dexfield Park, Iowa, gun battles, see Phillips, *Running with Bonnie and Clyde*, 140–58.

2. *Dallas Daily Times-Herald*, July 9, 10, and 23, 1933.

3. *Kansas City Star*, July 20, 1933; *Dallas Daily Times-Herald*, July 2, 6, 13, and 22, 1933.

4. This was not the only time Billie Jean rode with her sister. In her own unfinished, unpublished memoir she describes the aftermath of a small robbery in McKinney, Texas. She only mentions Clyde, Bonnie, and herself. There is no mention of Blanche and Buck Barrow, nor of Jones. According to Billie Jean, Clyde Barrow had parked the car in a churchyard near the town square and walked away, leaving the Parker sisters in the car with the motor running. Because they were broke and needed to conserve gas, Billie Jean turned off

the motor. Barrow had not mentioned where he was going or why he had left the motor running. When he returned, he was angry because the engine was not running. He had just robbed a grocery store around the corner. Billie had not been thinking in terms of fast getaways. Barrow's anger evidently got the better of him. When he started the car, it lurched forward and got stuck in some mud. Someone helped them free the car but not before a rather large crowd had gathered around them. Bonnie Parker was afraid an officer might show up and kept telling her sister to get out of the car and mill with the crowd so she would not be caught with her and Barrow. Parker was apparently still recovering from her burns and quite ill, which might account for Billie Jean's presence. Billie described her sister as being huddled in the backseat. "She looked so afraid and so sick . . . pathetic." Moon and Huddleston, "Bonnie, Clyde, and Me," 14–16. This was probably the September 25, 1933, robbery of the C & T Grocery on South Church Street, McKinney, Texas. This was during the county fair in McKinney, which would account for the crowd gathering at the car after the robbery and Bonnie's notion that her sister could get out of the car and disappear among the faces. At the C & T Grocery, proprietor J. J. Thompson reported that a man about twenty-five years of age asked for a pack of cigarettes then pulled a Colt .45 automatic, opened the cash register on his own, and took between thirty-five and forty dollars. *McKinney (Tex.) Courier-Gazette*, September 25, 1933. Billie Jean said the amount was much less than twenty dollars.

5. Other sources, including Billie Parker, say this occurred in Sherman, Texas, eleven miles south of Denison. Moon and Huddleston, "Bonnie, Clyde, and Me," 14. See also Fortune, *Fugitives*, 181. However, Fortune states that Billie Parker was with the group for a much shorter time, June 20 to 26. Fortune, *Fugitives*, 176. That time frame appears incorrect. Even Billie mentions a two-week period. Moon and Huddleston, "Bonnie, Clyde, and Me," 14.

6. Frank Hamer mentioned detecting a circular pattern to Clyde Barrow's travels, although the extent of that circle proved far greater than even he imagined. "Barrow played a circle from Dallas to Joplin, Missouri, to Louisiana, and back to Dallas." Webb, *Texas Rangers*, 540. Of such wanderings, Bonnie's sister wrote, "They were not going anyplace in particular because they had no place to go." Moon and Huddleston, "Bonnie, Clyde, and Me," 6.

7. There is also a reference to a stay at a tourist camp in Great Bend, Kansas, 189 miles north of Enid, Oklahoma, during this period. Fortune, *Fugitives*, 181.

8. As reported in the *Enid (Okla.) Morning News* on July 9, 1933, the robbery took place on July 7. Clyde Barrow had been to Enid before. On June 26, 1933, the day Marshal Humphrey of Alma, Arkansas died, Barrow followed a doctor to his house, waited for him to go inside, then stole his car. The object was not the car, however, but the medical bag in the car. *Enid (Okla.) Morning News*, July 27, 1933; Cumie Barrow, unfinished manuscript.

9. According to Marie Barrow, her brothers and W. D. Jones decided to play a trick on Bonnie and Blanche on their return from burglarizing the

armory. In addition to all of the weapons, field glasses, and other items, the men also stole army uniforms and were dressed in them when they pulled up to the tourist camp. The two women were suitably startled, thinking the army had surrounded their cabins and crashed through the door. Marie Barrow interview , August 24, 1984.

10. Bonnie's sister described the very same thing. "I sat up many nights at the campsites, standing watch . . . a sudden sound would send Clyde scrambling for his guns and Bonnie running toward the car." Moon and Huddleston, "Bonnie, Clyde, and Me," 19. These night watches became the root of one of the more notorious bits of folklore about Clyde Barrow, the tying up of W. D. Jones. The notion that Jones was held by Barrow against his will was started by Jones himself, as a defense against prosecution. He told Dallas County sheriff's department investigators that among other things Barrow handcuffed him at night to prevent his escape. Dallas County Sheriff's Department, Jones, Voluntary Statement B-71, 15. Later, Jones clarified the issue. Barrow and he were actually connected to one another by lengths of string, as a security measure, he said. "When you pull off out in the woods, it wasn't just because he [Barrow] was thinking I'd turn on him, or shoot him. No, when I was supposed to stay awake, when he was dead tired, he's hooked it [the string] up to hisself to where any move I make, he's gonna wake up. He never made it to where if there was a gun battle or somebody run up on us that I'd have to sit there and die." Jones, interview by Biffle, June 1969.

11. In the original manuscript the author first wrote "night" here, then crossed it out and replaced it with "afternoon."

12. There is no doubt that Buck Barrow was telling Blanche the truth when he declared himself innocent of the attack and beating described in that old newspaper. Just as Buck pointed out, the assault indeed occurred the morning after the shooting, specifically at 11 A.M., more than twelve hours after the Barrow brothers and their troupe had left the Twin Cities Tourist Camp and fled to Oklahoma. The victim, Mrs. John Rogers, was beaten with a chain at her home near Winslow, Arkansas, twenty miles north of the shooting and thirty-six miles north of the Twin Cities Tourist Camp. Two eyewitnesses, including A. M. Salyers, stated that after shooting Marshal Humphrey the gunmen first sped north in Salyers' car but then turned west onto a country road approximately a quarter-mile from the shooting. Minutes later, Salyers' car was again on Highway 71, near Van Buren, south of the shooting and even further south of the Rogers's home. There Buck and W. D. pulled in front of a car driven by a man named Lofton and forced him to a stop. Lofton was accompanied by his wife. Buck and W. D. then car-jacked the Lofton vehicle, only to abandon it a short time later near the summit of Mt. Vista, overlooking the twin cities of Van Buren and Fort Smith. By then Buck and W. D. were more than thirty miles from Rogers. The fugitives had abandoned the Lofton car because the bridge to Fort Smith was under guard. Buck and W. D. waited for dark, then walked across the unguarded Frisco railroad trestle and continued on foot to the tourist camp. *Fort Smith Southwest American*, June 24, 25, and

26, 1933; Cumie Barrow, unpublished manuscript; Dallas County Sheriff's Department, Jones, Voluntary Statement B-71, 13. By the time Mrs. Rogers was attacked, the Barrows were in Oklahoma. Fortune actually states that Buck and W. D. were the ones involved in the assault of Mrs. Rogers: "Buck told us she [Mrs. Rogers] gave him the keys [to her car]," but that he and W. D. had not beaten her. Fortune, *Fugitives*, 179. Family members maintained that Buck said no such thing, "She [Fortune] made most of that stuff up in that book!" Marie Barrow, interview, August 1, 1998. Even fellow journalists were skeptical of Fortune's research. Harry McCormick, longtime crime reporter for newspapers like the *Houston Press* and the *Dallas Morning News*, once wrote in reference to the veracity of *Fugitives*, "Jan [Fortune] never let [the] truth bother her." McCormick, handwritten notation in the margin of an unpublished manuscript about Ralph Fults and the Barrow gang. Still, despite its apparent flaws, the Fortune book contains much accurate inside information and remains a good source for those well acquainted with the fact-versus-fiction nature of the subject. See also Knight and Davis, *Bonnie and Clyde*, 93–98.

13. No doubt they were tired. At eleven o'clock that very morning Buck, Clyde, and W. D. had robbed three service stations within fifteen minutes at Fort Dodge, Iowa, then abandoned their Chevrolet north of town, switched to a black Ford V-8 occupied by Bonnie and Blanche, and then drove south 280 miles to Platte City, Missouri. *Fort Dodge (Iowa) Messenger*, July 18, 21, and 25, 1933. Prior to those robberies the group was apparently camped in O'Brien County, Iowa, along the Little Sioux River. Fort Dodge Chief of Police John Lochray had traced the Chevrolet used in the robberies to Spencer, eighty miles northwest of Fort Dodge, where it had been stolen. In Spencer, Lochray interviewed a farmer from Sutherland who had encountered five people, three men and two women, camped on his property. The farmer said the group had been camped there "several days" and left on the Monday before the Fort Dodge robberies and the Platte City gun battle. The farmer approached the camp only once, finding the intruders very unfriendly. He saw no guns but one man reached for his hip when he saw the farmer walking toward him. The farmer also noticed a black Ford V-8, license number 11-2399. The same plates were used on the Chevrolet during the Fort Dodge robberies. Lochray later visited the campsite and found a number of spent shell casings from high-powered rifles and Colt .45 automatics strewn about. He also found several bandages of the same type found in the Red Crown cabins after the Platte City shoot-out. They were probably Bonnie's. *Fort Dodge (Iowa) Messenger*, July 21, 1933.

14. This sort of taunting was typical in the surreal world of convicts in Texas at the time, and no doubt elsewhere too. One former inmate at the Eastham prison farm, where Clyde Barrow had been incarcerated, described a number of such instances, often instigated by guards. One occurrence involved the inmate in question and Henry Methvin, who would be one of those released during Clyde Barrow's prison raid of January 16, 1934, and who would eventually supply information leading to the ambush of Bonnie and

Clyde on May 23, 1934. Methvin had demanded some of this other inmate's lunch. When the inmate refused, Methvin kicked horse manure onto the inmate's plate. This precipitated a fight in which guards goaded Methvin to take further action, using the same sort of banter Clyde used with Buck outside of Kansas City. Methvin was nearly beaten to death with a hoe by the other inmate. Henson, letter to Biffle, September 4, 1980.

15. Buck was absolutely right. Kansas City had long been considered a "wide open, anything goes town . . . firmly in the grip of a few determined men," Tom Pendergast, the political boss, and Johnny Lazia, the crime boss. Unger, *Union Station Massacre*, 44–47; McCullough, *Truman*, 193–207; Hamby, *Man of the People*, 170–76. Some even referred to Lazia as "de facto chief of [Kansas City] police." Hamby, *Man of the People*, 172. According to one historian, "In 1933 it was a well-established rule that all underworld visitors checked in with Johnny Lazia when they came to town . . . nothing criminal . . . happened in Kansas City without the knowledge and consent of Johnny Lazia." Unger, *Union Station Massacre*, 49. However, things had changed considerably by the time the Barrow brothers arrived at the outskirts of Kansas City, arguing and goading each other. On June 17, while the Barrow gang was hiding at the Twin Cities Tourist Camp in Fort Smith, Arkansas, frantically tending to Bonnie Parker's severe burns, four lawmen and a bank robber were shot down in a terrible hail of bullets and buckshot in the parking lot of Kansas City's Union Station. Pendergast and Lazia, who apparently knew nothing of the events leading up to the gunfight, a botched attempt to free a captured bank robber named Frank Nash, immediately began losing power. The city became awash with federal and state authorities, particularly the U.S. Department of Justice, Bureau of Criminal Investigation (later to be called the Federal Bureau of Investigation, or F.B.I.), which lost one of its agents in the gunfight. It was into this atmosphere that the Barrow brothers were driving on July 18. Buck was right, Kansas City was the hottest place in the Midwest that summer. But it was about to get hotter. Regarding the above-mentioned gunfight, the best account to date is Unger's *Union Station Massacre*.

16. In the original manuscript, Blanche first wrote "had to start shooting, of course," then crossed it out and replaced it with "got into it."

17. Jones later stated, "Clyde dominated all them around him, even his older brother, Buck. Clyde planned and made all the decisions." Jones, "Riding with Bonnie and Clyde," 162.

18. This was a usual ploy for Clyde Barrow, and it indeed caused much confusion as to the number of people involved in the upcoming gun battle. *Kansas City Star*, July 20, 1933. Fifty years later only one eyewitness had correctly deduced there was a third man in the group, a fact no one else believed. Crawford interview, April 19, 1983.

19. The Red Crown complex was situated near the intersection of Highways 71 and 59 six miles south of Platte City, Missouri, an area known at the time as "the junction." The tavern, which faced west, housed an office, a soda fountain, and a cafe, as well as a dining room that also doubled as a ballroom.

Upstairs, called "the dome," there were living quarters occupied by William Searles, the nephew of manager Neal Houser, and Searles's grandmother. The two cabins, made of brick and joined by enclosed garages, stood just north of the tavern, facing south. Searles interview, April 20, 1983; Searles, letter to Phillips, December 14, 1982. The location, near the present intersection of I-29 and Cookingham Road, just one mile west of Ferrelview, was very rural in 1933. Today the spot where the tavern and cabins once stood is in the shadow of the Kansas City International Airport. Kimsey, letter to Phillips, October 25, 2002. In fact, the Red Crown Tavern and cabins were so close to Ferrelview that gunfire could be heard quite clearly there during the battle local residents still call "the horrible nightmare." In addition to Searles's description of the Red Crown complex, others have mentioned a service station attached to the tavern, as well as a screened-in porch. Williams, "The Day Bonnie and Clyde Shot It Out." For a full account of the Platte City, Missouri, incident, see Phillips, *Running with Bonnie and Clyde*, 141–45.

Eyewitnesses stated that it was Blanche who rented the cabins, paying in advance in silver, no bills. That method of payment mildly interested manager Neal Houser, who decided to keep an eye on the group. Searles interview, April 20, 1983. Although most of the local citizens were primarily concerned with what the ongoing drought would do to their crops, mainly corn, there was a basis for the increased vigilance of people like Neal Houser. Platte County was often used as a dumping ground for the victims of gangland killings emanating from nearby Kansas City. Sometimes the murders occurred there as well. Williams, "The Day Bonnie and Clyde Shot It Out." That, coupled with the killing of four officers and one bank robber in the parking lot of Kansas City's Union Station the month before, produced many wary eyes throughout the area.

The garage Clyde chose was the westernmost one, the one to the left as one faced the cabins.

20. This was Neal Houser, actually the manager rather than the owner. The owner was Emmett Breen, a banker and developer from Parkville, Missouri, who had opened the Red Crown Tavern exactly two years to the day before the shoot-out. *Kansas City Star*, September 17, 1978. Captain William J. Baxter of the Missouri Highway Patrol later testified that he had been made aware of "some suspicious characters" at "the junction." Baxter, who frequented both the Red Crown Tavern and a filling station–convenience store called Slim's Castle, situated across the road, checked the license plate—Oklahoma 78-872—of the Barrow car and deduced that the group occupying the Red Crown cabins were outlaws of some kind. *Dallas Dispatch*, February 24, 1935; *Kansas City Star*, July 20, 1933. Local authorities had already been advised to be aware of strangers purchasing medical supplies, particularly burn medicine. When Blanche visited Platte City Drugs, the clerk contacted Sheriff Holt Coffey. By then others, including Neal Houser, had also alerted Coffey. Searles interview, April 20, 1983; *The Landmark*, May 28, 1982.

21. Blanche probably refers here to the service station at the Red Crown Tavern. However, there was another service station across the road at Slim's

Castle. Nevertheless, Buck and Blanche occupied the east cabin, to the right as one faced the building, away from Slim's Castle. Bonnie, Clyde, and W. D. shared the west cabin. The car was parked in the west cabin garage, uncharacteristically facing in. Searles interview, April 20, 1983; Crawford interview, April 19, 1983; Searles, letter to Phillips, December 14, 1982; Crawford, letter to Phillips, December 21, 1982.

22. In the original manuscript, Blanche wrote "shotgun" here, then crossed it out.

23. In the original manuscript, Blanche wrote, "And more beer and pay 4 dollars for the cabins" here, then crossed it out.

24. Houser had indeed gone to Platte City because of his guests. He notified Sheriff Holt Coffey of his suspicions and had probably already spoken to his friend Captain William Baxter of the Missouri Highway Patrol. Eventually Platte County prosecutor David Clevenger got involved. For a number of reasons, authorities in and around Platte City began to suspect the Barrow brothers were at the Red Crown. If that was true, Coffey knew he was at a disadvantage. Considering the deadly and ferocious confrontations with officers in Joplin, Missouri, and outside of Alma, Arkansas, the sheriff understood that he would be completely outgunned by the likes of Clyde and Buck Barrow.

He had been advised of two things, that Clyde Barrow seemed "bullet-proof" and that neither he nor his brother would be taken alive. Many years later, Coffey's son, Clarence recalled his father's reaction to news that the Barrow brothers were in his neighborhood: "The look on my father's face. I'll never forget that!" he said. *The Landmark*, July 21, 1933; *Kansas City Star*, September 17, 1978.

Coffey had no protective gear, no radios, no weapons to speak of other than "squirrel rifles and a few pistols." Coffey decided to enlist reinforcements. The Missouri Highway Patrol, only two years old at the time and locally represented by Baxter and his partner, L. A. Ellis, was very cooperative. Such was not the case with Jackson County Sheriff Tom Bash in nearby Kansas City. "I'm getting pretty damn tired of every hick sheriff in the country coming in here and telling me they have a bunch of desperadoes holed up and wanting help. I'm afraid there's nothing I can do for you," Bash told Coffey. Coffey argued with Bash and finally the latter decided to lend Platte County one protective shield, one "bullet-proof" car, and a few officers. Coffey suspected that Bash gave in to his demands just to get rid of him. Williams, "The Day Bonnie and Clyde Shot It Out."

25. Clyde and W. D. may have gone to Platte City Drugs, but witnesses only remember seeing a woman. *The Landmark*, May 28, 1982. In fact, some described a woman who was undoubtedly Blanche. Platte City Drugs, also called "Louie's" after owner-operator Louis Bernstein, was a pharmacy and sundries store that also had a counter and served coffee and soft drinks. So it was often populated during that sizzling hot summer with local citizens trying to beat the heat. "Of course none of us thought we knew everyone who traded with Louie's," said one patron. "And customers buying bandages and medicines

were a common occurence. But at that we didn't see many strangers, so you can see how that particular stranger—a rather good-looking gal dressed in a slinky riding habit—attracted considerable attention." Williams, "The Day Bonnie and Clyde Shot It Out."

26. Searles remembered thinking how odd it was to have the shades drawn on such a hot day. Searles interview, April 20, 1983. Indeed, witnesses described newspapers covering the windows. *The Landmark*, July 21, 1933.

27. Bonnie and Clyde had made a suicide pact. Moon and Huddleston, "Bonnie, Clyde, and Me," 10. Jones also makes reference to this, noting that one could not live without the other because "That's all they had, was to love each other." Jones, interview by Biffle, June 1969.

28. This was eighteen year-old Vivien Smitson, the night-shift waitress. "Mr. Houser and everyone who worked in the cafe were suspicious," said Smitson. "Mostly because at least two men and two women were known to be occupying the cabins but only this rather attractive woman ventured out." Williams, "The Day Bonnie and Clyde Shot it Out with the Law," Others saw at least one of the men in the cafe with Blanche, during the day when Smitson was off-duty. The man was thought to have been Buck. Crawford, April 19, 1983. However, it was probably W. D. Jones. Blanche described being in the cafe once with Jones when he playfully lifted her onto a set of scales, the same scales mentioned in the text. Jones then started kidding her about her weight. According to Blanche, it was then that she and Jones both turned around to see Sheriff Coffey staring at them. Blanche Barrow interview, November 3, 1984. Smitson only saw Blanche on the night of the shoot-out.

29. By then, Sheriff Coffey and Captain Baxter had begun to assemble a number of men on the south side of the Red Crown Tavern, including members of the Kansas City police department and other Jackson County officers. Crawford interview, April 19, 1983; Searles interview, April 20, 1983. Two sources list a posse of thirteen, including Sheriff Coffey, Deputy Lincoln Baker, Deputy George Borden, Deputy Tom Hulett, Constable Byron Fischer, and prosecutor David Clevenger from Platte County; Deputy George Highfill, Deputy James Thorpe, Deputy Lyle Smith, and Deputy William Ryan from Jackson County; and Captain William Baxter, Sergeant Thomas Whitecotton, and Patrolman L. A. Ellis from the Missouri Highway Patrol. *Kansas City Star*, July 20, 1933; *The Landmark*, July 28, 1933.

30. Blanche said the same thing to Holt Coffey, David Clevenger, and Kermit Crawford after her capture. Crawford interview, April 20, 1983.

31. According to Blanche some of the things to be washed were for Bonnie, which contradicts the idea that Blanche refused to help her, at least then. Blanche Barrow interview, November 3, 1984.

32. The place was called Slim's Castle, after owner Charles "Slim" Myers. It was a combination filling station–convenience store managed by Kermit "Curley" Crawford. Jones arrived there at approximately ten-thirty that evening. Crawford waited on him. Jones ordered five sandwiches and five soda pops. Even though Blanche makes reference to beer, Crawford was sure Jones

ordered soda pop. While Crawford was preparing the order, Jones, who had introduced himself as Jack Sherman, kept looking warily toward the Red Crown Tavern. There were a lot of cars parked and people milling around. Crawford knew there was a dance underway and may have mentioned it to Jones. Indeed there was a dance. Coffey and Baxter were waiting for it to wrap up at 11 P.M. before making a move on the cabins. Jones took the sandwiches and drinks across the street. Crawford interview, April 19, 1983.

33. The lights were soon turned on again, illuminating the cabins. Crawford interview, April 19, 1983.

34. This was Sheriff Coffey. Some say he was holding a piece of boiler plate in front of him as a shield and facing the east cabin, the one occupied by Blanche and Buck. His back was to the west cabin, a near-fatal mistake. Crawford interview, April 19, 1983. Other sources say Captain Baxter was with Coffey and that neither had shields. Instead, several Jackson County deputies had shields and they stood around Coffey and Baxter, screening them. *Kansas City Star*, July 20, 1933.

35. Clyde and W. D. heard Blanche. "That's the law," Barrow said. "Get the car started." Dallas County Sheriff's Department, Jones, Voluntary Statement B-71, 14.

36. The weapon was a Browning automatic rifle, a military weapon, one of several stolen from the National Guard armory at Enid, Oklahoma, July 7, 1933.

37. This was a vehicle described as "bullet-proof" and supplied grudgingly by Jackson County Sheriff Tom Bash. It was driven in front of the west garage door by Jackson County Deputy George Highfill, presumably to block the car inside. Searles interview, April 20, 1983; Crawford interview, April 19, 1983; *The Landmark*, May 21, 1982; Williams, "The Day Bonnie and Clyde Shot It Out with the Law."

38. Some thought Clyde Barrow fired the first shot. As Blanche was telling Sheriff Coffey the men were in the other cabin, Barrow leaped up and said, "That's the law!" He then opened the door slightly, peeked out, grabbed his gun from under the bed and fired first through the narrow clerestory windows on the garage door, then fired bursts from the front door and all the windows. Dallas County Sheriff's Department, Jones, Voluntary Statement B-71, 14; Blanche Barrow interview, November 3, 1984. Barrow's first shot grazed Coffey's neck, knocking him down. Wood splinters and shards of glass from the garage door sprayed the area. The sheriff recovered quickly, dropped his shield, and darted to the Red Crown Tavern. "And then all hell broke loose!" Crawford interview, April 19, 1983.

Coffey thought the gunfire erupted simultaneously from both cabins. He was hit in the neck, shoulder, and little finger. According to his own account, Coffey and Baxter knocked on the door, saying, "This is Sheriff Coffey. Come out. I want to talk to you." A woman answered, "As soon as we get dressed." Several minutes later the woman said, "The men are in the other cabin." Coffey replied, "You'd better come out or we are going to start bombarding." Then fire erupted from both cabins simultaneously. *Kansas City Star*, July 20, 1933; *The Landmark*, July 21, 1933; Williams, "The Day Bonnie and Clyde Shot It Out with the Law."

39. Clyde was doing the same next door. This was confirmed by Kermit Crawford, manager of Slim's Castle, who was standing on his driveway across the road from the cabins. He described the first shot from the west garage, then long shafts of flame as gunfire erupted from each of the windows in both cabins. The assembled posse also opened fire. At one point bullets raked across the pavement near Crawford. He quickly moved inside and hurried upstairs, watching the rest of the battle from the roof of Slim's Castle. Crawford interview, April 19, 1983. Sixteen-year-old Clarence Coffey, son of the sheriff, and eighteen-year-old waitress Vivien Smitson, the one who had just waited on Blanche, decided to step out onto the tavern's screened-in porch, only a few yards from the cabins, to watch the activity. They had just stepped out there when gunfire erupted. Suddenly large chunks of wood, brick, and tile from the cafe started flying everywhere. "Did we get a good view!" Smitson said years later. The waitress dropped to the floor immediately, but Coffey saw his father go down with the first burst of gunfire. "Daddy!" he screamed. Smitson reached up and jerked Coffey to the floor. By then he was wounded and spraying blood on Smitson. She dragged him into the kitchen where they hid between the counter and the stove. Smitson was struck in the head by a bullet fragment or a piece of debris that embedded itself just under the skin. Though causing her to bleed moderately she never sought treatment. Coffey, however, was wounded in the right arm and back, and grazed on the cheek, and a bullet fragment had become lodged in his scalp. The arm wound was considered life-threatening for some time. *The Landmark*, July 21, 1933; *Kansas City Star*, September 17, 1978; Williams, "The Day Bonnie and Clyde Shot It Out with the Law." One eyewitness reported that Clarence Coffey was struck in the arm while hiding in the kitchen, that an armor-piercing slug penetrated the wall of the tavern's kitchen, drilled through the stove, and struck Coffey. Searles interview, April 20, 1983.

40. Here in the original manuscript Blanche wrote, "jumping up and down, screaming, and holding my hands over my ears like a person gone mad. I know I shouldn't have done this because Buck may have thought I was shot, but I couldn't help it. I expected to see him fall dead at my feet any minute. Still I was afraid to grab a gun and start fighting too. I didn't fire a shot or even have a gun in my hands," then crossed it all out.

41. The broken mirror was mentioned in the newspaper. "Inside the cabins bullet holes were everywhere, through doors and windows, some fired from outside, some from inside. Mirrors were shattered. Several bullets went through the Red Crown Tavern." *The Landmark*, July 21, 1933. The latter statement attests to the power of the Browning automatic rifle.

42. Deputy George Highfill, the driver, had been wounded by the armor-piercing ammunition of the Browning automatic rifles. The horn had also been hit and was blowing continuously. Deputy James Thorpe, manning a machine gun mounted on the car, fired a few shots before the weapon jammed.

Highfill threw it in reverse and backed away from the cabins, one of his head-lights pointing skyward, apparently struck by gunfire as well. Some think the blowing horn caused the officers to cease fire. Hinton, *Ambush*, 65. Crawford thought the blowing horn meant the driver was dead and slumped across the wheel. The driver survived, however. Crawford interview, April 19, 1983. Another Jackson County deputy had a machine gun. It jammed immediately. Some say Thorpe's machine gun also jammed immediately and that neither weapon fired a shot. *The Landmark*, July 21, 1933.

43. Buck was holding the BAR at waist level when he was struck. As his body arced back, he fired the weapon in a sweeping motion in the air. The officers began firing. Then, "Some woman was doing a terrible amount of scream-ing." Crawford interview, April 19, 1983. The woman screaming was Blanche. She was calling to Clyde, trying to tell him to open the garage door, that Buck had been hit. She had to scream to be heard over the gunfire. Blanche Barrow interview, November 3, 1984. One report states that Buck fell three times. *Kansas City Star*, July 20, 1933.

44. Captain Baxter reported hearing someone say, "I'm shot." *Kansas City Star*, July 20, 1933. This may have been Buck, or Deputy George Highfill, or Sheriff Coffey, though the latter reportedly ignored his wounds and never sought treatment. Hinton, *Ambush*, 65.

45. One witness remembered a man and two women dragging the wounded Buck Barrow to the car. Crawford interview, April 19, 1983.

46. In the original manuscript Blanche wrote here, "when Clyde or W. D. didn't offer to help me even get him [Buck] into the car," then crossed it out. Elsewhere in the text Blanche has already mentioned Clyde Barrow coming out of the garage, something she confirmed in a later interview. Blanche Barrow interview, November 3, 1984.

47. This passage certainly indicates that both W. D. and Clyde were still outside of the car when Buck was loaded into the back seat. Presumably, either one or both could have helped carry Buck, just as Crawford stated.

48. More than one witness reported seeing all members of the gang shoot-ing. *The Landmark*, August 11, 1933.

49. The "something hard" that struck Blanche above the temple was a bul-let fragment that remained embedded in her skull just above the hairline for the rest of her life. Shards of glass lacerated one of her eyes. Blanche Barrow interview, November 3, 1984.

50. Crawford stated that not a shot was fired after Buck was loaded in the car. Crawford interview, April 19, 1983. When told of the comment, Blanche remarked, "It didn't seem like anybody stopped shooting to me!" Blanche Barrow interview, November 3, 1984. The wounds she sustained after getting in the car certainly confirm her opinion.

Chapter 13. *Dexfield Park*

1. Clyde Barrow turned down a gravel road called Farmer's Lane and stopped only a few miles from the Red Crown Cabins. No one in the posse

assembled at the tavern pursued the fugitives. Only one man wanted to, Captain Baxter's partner, Patrolman L. A. Ellis. Crawford interview, April 19, 1983; Searles interview, April 20, 1983; *The Landmark*, May 21, 1982. Baxter did telephone ahead to have bridges blocked along the Missouri River, Platte River, and Little Platte River, among other places. *Kansas City Star*, July 20, 1933. The officers then searched the cabins. Among the items recovered were a number of weapons, including three Browning automatic rifles, one of which had its barrel and stock cut down as described by Blanche, and a pistol taken from Marshal H. D. Humphrey of Alma, Arkansas. *The Landmark*, May 21, 1982. Some sources indicate the gang possessed as many as six Browning automatic rifles and forty-seven Colt .45 automatic pistols. Cartledge, "Bonnie and Clyde," 23. The five sandwiches ordered from Slim's Castle by W. D. Jones were found uneaten, but the soda bottles were all empty. Crawford interview, April 19, 1983.

2. This may have occurred on the Hoover-Ridgely Road (today Highway B) as Clyde Barrow drove toward the old covered bridge across the Little Platte River. The car was spotted there traveling north at a high rate of speed on three tires and a nearly bare rim. The following day bloody clothes, discarded bandages, and a mutilated tire were found next to a creek near Lutes Cemetery Road (now called Old River Road) on the north side of the Little Platte River. Kimsey, letters to Phillips, October 25, 2002, May 7, 2003.

3. Indeed they did! In the course of the night the fugitives made at least five stops within miles of the Red Crown Tavern, four in the vicinity of Hoover and Kerrville near the confluence of the Little Platte and Platte Rivers, and one stop on the north bank of the Little Platte near Lutes Cemetery. After backing out of the garage, Clyde Barrow cut the wheels of the bullet-riddled V-8 hard to the north and sped overland a short distance to old Highway 71, plowing through several stalks of drought-withered corn in a dusty cultivated field adjacent to the cabins. Crawford, letter to Phillips with hand-drawn map, December 21, 1982; Searles, letter to Phillips with hand-drawn map, April 21, 1983; Vivien Smitson quoted in Williams, "The Day Bonnie and Clyde Shot It Out with the Law." Clyde Barrow initially headed northwest on old Highway 71, driving past what was then called Cockriel Road (now North Winan Road), and then turning due north on the gravel road known in those days as Farmer's Lane (since eliminated south of Highway 92 and now called Bethel Road north of Highway 92). Taulbee, e-mail to Phillips, December 2, 2002; the names "Farmer's Lane" and "Cockriel Road" come from the memory of Crawford, letter to Phillips, December 21, 1982. It was apparently on Farmer's Lane that Clyde Barrow first stopped, pulling off the road to examine Buck and fix the flat tire. It was probably here that Barrow discovered that Blanche was wounded. Also, this was near the home of farmer Cleve Burrell from whom two men, probably Clyde Barrow and W. D. Jones, borrowed a pump and a jack. *The Landmark*, July 28, 1933. The fugitives then continued north on Farmer's Lane (Bethel Road) until they reached Interurban Road. There they turned right and traveled southeast for an eighth of a mile

before stopping again. Clyde Barrow appeared at the front door of Tom and Winnie Chinn's house on Interurban, saying he'd had an automobile accident and needed bandages. Winnie Chinn gave Barrow some old sheets. After leaving the Chinn house, Barrow continued southeast on Interurban until reaching the village of Kerrville. George and Frances Baber, interview by LaVern Taulbee, quoted in e-mails to Phillips, December 2, 2002, January 15, 2003. Shortly afterward the car was spotted traveling north on the Hoover-Ridgeley Road (Highway "B" today) at a high rate of speed on three tires and a bare rim. The outlaws evidently crossed the Little Platte River near there via a covered bridge built in 1878 and known locally as "Noah's Ark." Once across the river they immediately turned left on what was then called Lutes Cemetery Road. They continued along the road as it ascended a hill and disappeared into a grove of trees. In the woods beside a creek on the property of Joe Miller the troupe again stopped, fixing the second flat tire and discarding more bloody bandages and clothes. Afterward Clyde Barrow drove further west along the Lutes Cemetery Road, apparently expecting to find the old Mellon Bridge across the Platte River. The bridge was either washed out or Barrow became uncharacteristically lost because at some point he turned around and backtracked to the covered bridge and crossed once again to the south side of the Little Platte River. In Kerrville the car turned south on Cockriel Road and pulled into a field across from a picturesque red-brick antebellum mansion known locally as "the Swaney Brick." The two-story structure with its distinctive neoclassic porch and white window casings stands on a slight bluff on the east side of the road overlooking the spot across the way where Clyde Barrow stopped once again. The fugitives evidently spent most of the rest of the night there. Early on the morning of the twentieth they left the field and drove south to Hoover Road (Highway 92) and stopped somewhere near the hamlet of Hoover, discarding yet more bandages and clothes. It may have been in Hoover that they stopped for gas. Shortly thereafter they traveled north from Hoover on what today is called Highway B, back to the covered bridge. There they crossed again to the north side of the Little Platte River. But this time Barrow continued due north, passing through Ridgley then turning west on Mt. Zion Road. Residents there saw the car that morning racing toward the Platte River. In 1933 there was a bridge across the Platte River that took travelers on Mt. Zion Road through the river bottoms to Edgerton Junction on the west bank. From there, more than six hours after the gun battle, the fugitives turned north toward Iowa. Kimsey, letters and e-mails to Phillips, October 25, 2002, May 6, 2003, May 7, 2003; *The Landmark*, July 28, 1933; Taulbee e-mails to Phillips, December 2, 2002, January 15, 2003; Searles interview, April 20, 1983; Crawford interview, April 19, 1983; Searles letter to Phillips, April 21, 1983; Crawford, letter to Phillips December 21, 1982. Some have suggested the outlaws actually spent most of the night on the north side of the Little Platte River, rather than in the field across from the "Swaney Brick," then traveled straight through Ridgely the next morning without first heading back south. Kimsey, letters and e-mails to Phillips, October 25, 2002,

May 6, 2003, May 7, 2003. None of the three bridges mentioned above exist today. The Mellon Bridge, which was thought to have been washed out at the time, was never replaced and the Lutes Cemetery Road (Old River Road) ends near the east bank of the Platte River. The Mt. Zion Road Bridge washed out in the late 1930s and was never replaced. In 1965 a devastating flood destroyed the Little Platte River's historic old covered bridge. A new, uncovered bridge stands near the old location.

4. Nearly every other source, from Fortune to Hinton and beyond, has the Barrow gang far away from Platte City by morning. "By daylight Clyde had covered hundreds of miles." Fortune, *Fugitives*, 188. "After the incident at the Cleve Burrell farm . . . they took up their drive again until they had crossed into Iowa." Hinton, *Ambush*, 68. "Clyde Barrow headed north during the early hours of July 20 and crossed into Iowa." Treherne, *Strange History of Bonnie and Clyde*, 133. "Meanwhile, Clyde continued to race through the night without stopping for sleep or food. By morning, he had covered a great distance." Milner, *Lives and Times of Bonnie and Clyde*, 92.

5. The gas station could have been in Hoover, Ridgely, or Edgerton Junction, although the former is closest to Kansas City. Nevertheless, despite Blanche's concern, no reports of the incident appeared in either the Platte City newspaper or the *Kansas City Star*. By then there was already a substantial amount of finger-pointing among lawmen over the escape of the Barrow brothers. One paper laid blame for the outcome of the gunfight on the Kansas City officers, stating, "We must all confess it looks strange that four people [only Kermit Crawford ever thought there was a fifth person] surrounded in cabins by thirteen officers could get away." *The Landmark*, July 28, 1933. The fact that the car and its bloodied cargo were able to so easily traverse back and forth for several hours within miles of the Red Crown Tavern was possible perhaps because the flight took place in what was then a very rural area. Most of the residents along the way were farmers without radios and those who owned radios were doing what their less fortunate neighbors were doing that night, sitting outside on the porches of their farmhouses enjoying the evening air and spectacular full moon. Many, including young Ellis Kimsey, saw the car speeding past their homes but knew nothing of the drama behind the fleeing automobile. The earliest most of them heard of the shoot-out was the following afternoon when the *Kansas City Star* was delivered. Kimsey, letters and e-mails to Phillips, October 25, 2002, May 6 and 7, 2003; Williams, "The Day Bonnie and Clyde Shot It Out."

6. This may have been when they stopped near Mt. Ayr, Iowa (some sources say Caledonia, Iowa), where a local man named Fred Marsh saw two men and "a red-headed woman" speeding north in a small car. Marsh then discovered the partially burned remnants of bloody clothing and bandages. *Kansas City Star*, July 21, 1933. Ringgold County Sheriff L. E. Thompson received a call that a suspicious quartet, two men and two women, were parked near Caledonia. Thompson strongly suspected the presence of the Barrow brothers and was no doubt relieved when he learned they had moved on before his

arrival. Thompson said, "the gang is one of the most desperate that has ever operated here." *Fort Dodge (Iowa) Messenger*, July 21, 1933.

7. They had indeed left the medical kit, stolen earlier in the month from Doctor Fields in Enid, Oklahoma. Among the many other items found afterward in the cabins was the small chrome case containing a syringe, two needles, a vial labeled "atropine sulphate," and a vial labeled "twenty hypodermic tablets morphine sulphate." Williams, "The Day Bonnie and Clyde Shot It Out."

8. The date was Thursday, July 20, 1933. Actually, the camp was just outside of Dexfield Park, on private property that was being used by the federal Works Progress Administration, one of many agencies established by President Franklin Roosevelt to combat the Great Depression by supplying jobs to the unemployed—in this case, loggers to cut timber. Feller interview, May 5, 1983; Blohm interview, May 5, 1983. Dexfield Park had once been a very popular amusement park located just off of what was then called White Pole Auto Road, between the towns of Dexter and Redfield, not far from Des Moines, Iowa. Operating from April 1915 to April 1933, the park had been equipped with a swimming pool, a dance hall, fairground, and a baseball field where games were held every weekend. There was a popular restaurant, a shooting gallery, and ball-throwing contests where men could win a box of cigars and women could win a box of candy. Apparently some very popular jazz bands played there as well, but by the time the Barrows arrived on July 20, 1933, it was abandoned and starting to look overgrown, a victim of the Great Depression. Weesner, *History of Dexter, Iowa*, 51; Blohm interview, May 5, 1983; Feller interview, May 5, 1983. For a full account of the Dexfield Park episode, see Phillips, *Running with Bonnie and Clyde*, 145–58.

9. Every day during their stay at Dexfield Park, Clyde drove to Dexter and bought provisions, including a daily block of ice from Blohm's Grocery, Cafe, and Meat Market, founded in 1888. Blohm interview, May 5, 1983.

10. Barrow visited a number of businesses in Dexter, including Pohle Drug Store, Stanley Drug Store, and Blohm's cafe and meat market. Parker always remained in the car. To the clerks at one of the drugstores, Barrow claimed he was a veterinarian. Blohm interview, May 5, 1983; *Dexter (Iowa) Sentinel*, July 25, 1933. Dexter, Iowa, was founded in 1868 and named after a popular nineteenth century racehorse. It was well known for the manufacture of a brand of hand-cranked washing machines marketed as "the Billy-Twister," as well as hand-made cigars and a piece of farm equipment called the Dexter Hog Oiler. However, in 1933 as they rolled through Dexter's streets, Clyde Barrow and Bonnie Parker found a very tiny, very rural town that had only acquired electricity fourteen years earlier. It was the kind of place where everyone knew everyone else, and nearly everyone who saw the strangers was suspicious and fearful of them. Blohm interview, May 5, 1983; Weesner, *History of Dexter, Iowa*, 3, 30, 36, 50–51.

11. The town was Perry, Iowa, thirty-eight miles north of Dexter. There, a car belonging to Edward Stoner was stolen. *Dexter (Iowa) Sentinel*, July 25, 1933.

12. While the fugitives were away in Perry, a local man named Ed Penn discovered the Barrow camp while taking a Sunday walk along the narrow dirt access road called Lover's Lane, near the southeast corner of Dexfield Park. Initially he thought nothing of the scene, then noticed what appeared to be bloody bandages. Penn notified the Dexter town marshal, John Love, who in turn notified the county sheriff and other authorities. *Dexter (Iowa) Sentinel,* July 25, 1933. Another source, however, states that a man named Henry Nye discovered the camp on *his* property, and that it was Nye who contacted the marshal. Hutzell and Rupp, "Bonnie and Clyde," 38. Still another source mentions a man named William Brady. *Dexter (Iowa) Sentinel,* July 25, 1933.

13. The meals were purchased from Wilma Blohm at Blohm's cafe and meat market. Barrow had done this every day since his arrival in the area. Blohm's did not have facilities for take-out, so the first time Barrow ordered five dinners, Wilma Blohm suggested that she put everything in a large bowl. Thinking Barrow was an out-of-towner visiting someone locally, she believed china and silverware would not be needed. "Oh, no," said Barrow. "I want china and silverware too!" Puzzled, but compliant, Blohm supplied everything Barrow requested. Each day, the china and silverware were returned by Barrow. "I never lost one piece of silverware," Blohm later remarked. She also described Barrow as, "not overly friendly, but he was very quiet, very courteous, and very nice-looking!" Blohm interview, May 5, 1983.

14. Jones said he was the only one to sleep outside, on a car seat that had been pulled from the car. Dallas County Sheriff's Department, Jones, Voluntary Statement B-71, 15.

15. Initially, before she was able to apply bandages, Blanche was forced to put her finger in the wound to stop the bleeding. Marie Barrow interview, September 25, 1993; Cumie Barrow, unpublished manuscript.

16. Jones stated that Buck was never delirious at Dexfield Park. Dallas County Sheriff's Department, Jones, Voluntary Statement B-71, 15. It appears, however, he was not aware of this episode. He was busying himself with the wieners at the time and would soon be wounded and running for his life. Nevertheless, Buck was in such dire condition that Clyde was prepared to drive him all the way back to their mother in Texas. He and Buck had promised Cumie that if either brother was ever mortally wounded or killed, that the other one would bring him home to her, provided he was able to do so. Fortune, *Fugitives,* 191.

17. The moment Clyde called out, the shooting started. Witnesses recalled that just before the gunfire erupted one of the lawmen announced himself, saying something to the effect, "This is the law, come out here," and that this was followed immediately by someone in the camp shouting, "Get the hell out of here, you sons of bitches! We'll kill you!" *Des Moines Register,* January 22, 1968.

Throughout the night of July 23–24, lawmen had been assembling in the vicinity of the camp. A number of armed men were involved, including Marshal Love, Sheriff Clint Knee of Adel, Deputies Evan Burger and Pat Chase, and several Des Moines police officers. Apparently, there were quite a few hard-drinking local sight-seers gathered in the woods as well, some accounts listing upwards of fifty people milling about. Piper, video interview, *Remembering Bonnie and Clyde*. Burger and a volunteer, E. A. Place, editor of the local paper, the *Dexter Sentinel*, were posted at the bridge across the South Raccoon River leading to the old park's north entrance. Eight others were stationed along the wagon trail called Lover's Lane, and a six-man squad lined up in a draw near the camp. The six men included Love, Knee, and two lawmen from Des Moines–Bill Arthur and C.C. "Rags" Riley. According to Love, it was Arthur and Riley that Clyde Barrow and W. D. Jones first saw approaching on the morning of July 24, 1933. The other four had spread out nearby. The time was 5:15 A.M. *Dexter (Iowa) Sentinental*, July 25, 1933; Feller interview, May 5, 1983; *Des Moines Register*, January 22, 1968. Throughout the night, the six men waiting in the draw heard many noises emanating from the camp, pounding and other such sounds. At 1 A.M. a car started, but no one drove away from the camp. Hutzell and Rupp, "Bonnie and Clyde," p. 39. Jones stated that he worked that evening removing everything from the damaged Platte City car and transferring it to the freshly stolen car. Jones also removed ammunition from a great many pasteboard boxes and stored it in an old inner tube. He then put the ammunition-laden inner tube behind the seat of the new car and broke down all the boxes, presumably for disposal. This, he said, took quite a while. Dallas County Sheriff's Department, Jones, Voluntary Statement B-71, 15. It appears Clyde Barrow was preparing to take Buck home to West Dallas. Fortune, *Fugitives*, 190.

18. Jones stated that he did not have time to straighten up from the camp-fire before bullets started flying. Jones then jumped up and ran to the car where he was struck by a load of buckshot in the face and chest. Then two slugs hit him, one in the calf of the left leg, the other in the upper right chest. Dallas County Sheriff's Department, Jones, voluntary statement B-71, 15–16.

19. Clyde Barrow was apparently struck three times that morning, including a ricocheting bullet which struck him in the head, temporarily stunning him. Jones, "Riding with Bonnie and Clyde," 165. Clyde also took a slug in the leg and was struck in the arm and shoulder by a charge of buckshot after he got behind the wheel of one of the cars. Dallas County Sheriff's Department, Jones, Voluntary Statement B-71, 15. The shoulder wound would cause Barrow to drive over a stump left by the WPA timber cutters, disabling the car. Blanche Barrow interview, November 3, 1984. Bonnie Parker was shot twice in the abdomen. Feller interview, May 5, 1983.

20. The fire from the camp was substantial, but not deadly. C. C. "Rags" Riley was creased on the scalp, sustaining the only injury to any of the officers assembled in the posse. *Dexter (Iowa) Sentinel*, July 25, 1933. Some felt, probably correctly, that Barrow was shooting over the officers' heads, hoping to scare them away. Chapler, letter to Sanborn, May 3, 1974. That tactic was often used by Barrow. He and Ralph Fults were notably shooting above the heads of their pursuers in Kaufman County, Texas on April 19, 1932. Legg, letter to

Phillips, September 1, 1982. Evidence of the same is supported in the Dexfield Park incident by the fact that tree limbs as thick as two inches were found littering the position of the six men in the draw. Love described branches falling on him during the battle. Feller interview, May 5, 1983. Others, however, have said that topography played a part in the trajectory of the shots coming from the camp. The camp was located in a low spot below the access road called Lover's Lane and the six lawmen were positioned across the road in a draw that was also below the road. The gunfire erupting from the camp was evidently aimed in such a way as to clear the grade of the road. In doing so, the shots sailed about ten feet over the officers' heads. Still, the fire sent everyone, including spectator Kirt Piper, "to the ditches". Piper, video interview, *Remembering Bonnie and Clyde*, 1994.

21. At some point during their flight on foot, Buck and Blanche became separated from the others. All five initially struck out in a northeasterly direction, then turned north, following a fence line. But Buck and Banche stopped behind a very large tree that had been felled. Bonnie, Clyde, and W. D. continued north, making it all the way to the bank of the South Raccoon River. There Clyde left Bonnie and W. D. in some underbrush while he tried to cross the bridge guarded by Deputy Burger and E. A. Place. Parker and Jones heard gunfire, then waited so long afterward that they came to think Barrow had been killed, Jones even saying as much to Parker. At that point Parker spoke of suicide. She and Clyde had a suicide pact. Moon and Huddleston, "Bonnie, Clyde, and Me," unpublished manuscript, 20. But according to one source, Jones talked her out of it. Then within a few moments Barrow appeared. Fortune, *Fugitives*, 196. Parker, however, told her sister a much more chilling version of this story. She said when it looked as though Barrow had been killed or captured, at her request Jones raised his pistol to her head. "W. D. already had the gun to my head—cocked and his finger on the trigger," she said. Then Barrow suddenly arrived and Jones lowered the weapon. Moon and Huddleston, "Bonnie, Clyde, and Me," unpublished manuscript, 11.

22. Though separated, all five fugitives were traveling north along a fence row leading from the draw below the camp. In front of them, after first traversing up a steep hill, then down the other side, was a sheer embankment, portions of which stood sixty-five feet high, overlooking the South Raccoon River. The timber on the hill was second growth, but dense. Feller interview, May 5, 1983. John Love remarked about the problem posed in trying to pursue someone through the terrain. "We weren't very organized when we went after them," Love said. "They were up the hill from the park and I'd never really been out there. I thought [Sheriff] Clint Knee was in charge 'til I found out that he turned it over to the [Iowa] state department. After it was all over, the next day, if someone had yelled 'scat,' I'd have probably shot them. That was the way I felt." Hutzell and Rupp, "Bonnie and Clyde: Hideout in Dexter," 39.

23. Recall that Buck Barrow earned his nickname as a child because of his speed afoot. Cumie Barrow, Unpublished manuscript.

24. Many years later, when asked if she thought Clyde felt guilty about leaving her and Buck in Dexfield Park, Blanche replied, "I don't know if Clyde felt guilty . . . , but he should not have. We were shot up and holding everyone back." Blanche Barrow interview, November 3, 1984. Apparently, though, Clyde Barrow *did* feel guilty about leaving Buck and Blanche. Marie Barrow interview, September 25, 1993.

25. Blanche and Buck had found their way into the park. The old baseball field had once been located in the clearing she describes. Feller interview, May 5, 1983; *Dexter (Iowa) Sentinel*, July 25, 1933.

26. By then it was midmorning. Bonnie, Clyde, and W. D. had already crossed the river, hijacked a car, and escaped north. For the full story of their escape, see Phillips, *Running with Bonnie and Clyde*, 145–158. The group approaching Blanche and Buck included Sheriffs Clint Knee and Loren Forbes and Dr. Herschell Keller of Des Moines. *Dexter (Iowa) Sentinel*, October 5, 1967. The posse tracking Buck and Blanche had been organized at the campsite shortly after the gunfight was over and the fugitives had fled on foot. Sheriff Knee said they had better start looking for bodies in the underbrush, that the fugitives had been hit by gunfire and he needed volunteers from the local spectators milling around. More than one group was organized, including one manned by Kirt Piper and about five others. Piper's crew ascended the steep hill mentioned by Blanche then began descending "a bank of some distance" before reaching a flat open area, about fifty yards wide between the hill and the South Raccoon River. They had been following heel marks dug deep in the earth. Near the clearing was a very large tree that had been cut down, apparently by the WPA loggers. Piper and the others thought it would have been an excellent place to hide so they all started to approach the felled tree. Suddenly Blanche stood up from behind the tree. Piper said she was wearing "riding breeches, a pair of nice boots, and sun glasses, (and) she didn't look too clean." Piper, video interview, *Remembering Bonnie and Clyde*.

27. This contradicts Blanche's earlier description of Buck as being someone who "loved life and didn't want to take it away from others."

28. According to a member of the posse, Kirt Piper, Blanche said, "My husband's on the ground and he can't move." The posse demanded he get up and asked Blanche if he was armed. She did not answer. The posse kept demanding that Buck get up. Piper said through it all, "She [Blanche] was pretty hysterical." Piper interview, *Remembering Bonnie and Clyde*. At last the posse was able to approach Barrow. As Buck was lying there on the ground behind the log, a member of the posse mashed the outlaw's throat with his boot and poked a shotgun in his face. "I thought that was a little too much, and unnecessary," one bystander said. *Des Moines Register*, January 22, 1968. Buck Barrow was finally coaxed to his feet. He would walk for a while, then collapse. The posse would "drag him a few feet then he'd get his feet under him again and he'd walk a little ways. Buck had a bad pallor, a ghastly-looking pallor. His head wound was not bandaged . . ., his brain was exposed and you could tell this was a man on his last leg." Piper, video interview, *Remembering Bonnie and Clyde*.

29. Just before she was allowed to go to Buck, Blanche was photographed at least three times by Herb Schwartz of the *Des Moines Register*. The location was about one quarter of a mile from where Buck and Blanche were apprehended. Blanche is being held by Sheriff Loren Forbes in all three shots. In two of the shots she is standing quietly, looking toward Buck, who is lying on the ground nearby with a group of armed men stooping over him. In the third shot, which has been widely published, Blanche is struggling with Forbes and looking directly at the camera, screaming dramatically. In his notes, Schwartz commented that Blanche, in her semiblind state, saw him raising his camera and apparently thought it was a gun and that he was about to shoot Buck. Blanche is screaming at Schwartz. Herb Schwartz, notes, July 24, 1933.

30. Some sources indicate that Buck was shot more than once at Dexfield Park. Many years later, Blanche was still unsure how many times he was hit, only that he was shot "several times." Blanche Barrow interview, November 3, 1984. Fortune is more specific, stating that Buck was shot five times in Iowa. Fortune, *Fugitives*, 193. The doctor who treated Buck in Dexter, and later operated on him at King's Daughter's Hospital in Perry, Iowa, only mentioned one wound in addition to the head wound sustained in Platte City. The bullet causing the new wound had entered through the back, ricocheted off a rib, and become "lodged in the chest wall, posteriorly, close to the pleural cavity." Chapler, letter to Sanborn May 3, 1974.

31. Chapler-Osborn Clinic in Dexter, Iowa.

32. The physician described Blanche as "a highly tense, nervous person, . . . highly hysterical and uncooperative at times." But her demeanor changed considerably when she was allowed to sit beside Buck. "As you watched her sitting on the floor of the reception room in my office with Buck, . . . she would become quite subdued." Chapler, letter to Sanborn, May 3, 1974.

33. Buck told the doctor that the head wound sustained at Platte City did not bother him at all. Initially he had experienced headaches, but aspirin had since controlled that symptom. The doctor was amazed at how clean the head wound was, describing it as a "through-and-through head wound in the front part of the skull where no vital centers are contained." Buck told him it had been treated three or four times a day with hydrogen peroxide. The only pain Buck mentioned was that which was caused by the fresh gunshot wound in his back. Chapler, letter to Sanborn, May 3, 1974.

Chapter 14. *Mob*

1. Blanche tried to escape from the clinic. When she was taken to the examining room, she asked to go to the bathroom. A nurse had her remove all her clothes and put on a hospital gown and wrap a sheet around herself. She was then led by the nurse to the bathroom, which was located in the basement. When she reached a landing on the stairway, Blanche apparently spotted a doorway leading to the alley outside. She made a break for the door, struggling with the much larger nurse who held on tight. Soon officers arrived to help and Blanche was subdued. Thereafter, guards were posted all around

the clinic. Chapler, letter to Sanborn, May 3, 1974. Later, Blanche had no recollection of this incident. Indeed, she had no memory whatsoever of the time between her surrender in Dexfield Park and just before she was escorted from the clinic, including the moments recorded by Herb Schwartz's camera. The first thing she remembered was being suddenly aware of bruises on her arms and that she was in a clinic somewhere. She also remembered the hand-cuffs, and that they cut her wrists. Shortly thereafter she was removed to a cell. Blanche Barrow interview, November 3, 1984.

2. Things were different when it came time to transport Buck to a hospital in Perry, twenty miles away. Fearing the crowd would pose a problem, one of the officers went to the front door of the Chapler-Osborn Clinic and using a bullhorn announced that a call had just been received from a reliable source stating that Bonnie and Clyde were on their way to Dexter to free Buck. Within minutes the streets were cleared. "[Y]ou could have shot a cannon ball down through Main Street and never touched a soul," Dr. Chapler said later. Chapler, letter to Sanborn, May 3, 1974.

3. Adel, Iowa, just west of Des Moines. That same day she was transferred to the Polk County jail in Des Moines and booked. Her weight was listed at eighty-one pounds, down thirty-three and a half pounds from January. However, Blanche herself indicates in this memoir that just five days earlier, when she stepped on those scales at the Red Crown Tavern, she weighed ninety-one pounds. Regardless, she had lost a considerable amount of weight while on the run. Polk County (Iowa) Arrest Record, Blanche Barrow, July 24, 1933; Blanche's letter to her mother, January 14, 1933, quoted in Baker, *Blanche Barrow*, 25.

4. Holt Coffey was the one knocking on the door in Platte City and talking with Blanche when Clyde Barrow opened fire and grazed Coffey in the neck. Clarence Coffey, the sheriff's sixteen-year-old son, was watching from the kitchen of the Red Crown Tavern with a waitress when gunfire erupted. Young Coffey and the waitress took cover behind a cast-iron stove, but an armor-piercing bullet penetrated the hiding place, struck the boy, and broke his arm. Crawford interview, April 19, 1983; *The Landmark*, May 28, 1982.

5. The authorities may have been trying to clear up one or more crimes. For instance, the First National Bank of Clinton, Oklahoma, was robbed of $11,000 on July 3, 1933. *Chandler (Okla.) News-Publican*, July 13, 1933. And in another crime that sounds more like the bumbling Barrow gang, the Proctor State Bank of Proctor, Texas was burglarized by a group that first tried to take the 3,000-pound safe with them. But in transit to the waiting truck, the safe slipped off the dolly and literally crashed through the floor, becoming impossibly wedged. In response, the burglars took $123 in small change, 500 three-cent envelopes, and 1,000 one-cent postcards. *Comanche (Tex.) Chief*, July 7, 1933; *Stephenville (Tex.) Empire-Tribune*, July 7, 1933.

6. Another thing Blanche was questioned about was the identity of the third man in the group. Blanche may have forgotten a lot, but she certainly had not forgotten who W. D. Jones was. But she was not about to reveal his

name. Eventually she made up a name, Hubert Bleigh, no doubt to get the officers to leave her alone. The power of her words became immediately apparent when a man bearing the same name was arrested in Oklahoma. *Dexter (Iowa) Sentinel,* July 25, 1933. However, it didn't take authorities long to realize they'd been duped. Blanche said the director of the U. S. Department of Justice, Bureau of Criminal Investigation J. Edgar Hoover, personally interrogated her at one point. Blanche Barrow interview, November 3, 1984.

7. Buck Barrow's death was reported to have occurred at two o'clock the previous afternoon, twelve hours earlier. Fortune, *Fugitives,* 203.

8. Buck Barrow died of pneumonia on July 29 at King's Daughters Hospital in Perry, Iowa. Pneumonia developed after surgery had been performed to remove the bullet from his chest. Apparently throughout his stay at the hospital, Barrow vacillated between delirium and complete lucidity. A number of official visitors paraded past his bed, asking questions. One of those visitors was A. M. Salyers of Alma, Arkansas. Barrow told Salyers that he had killed Marshal Humphrey, adding that Salyers was lucky to be alive. "We were shooting to kill you both," Barrow said of the gunfight on June 23, 1933. *Dallas Dispatch,* February 24, 1935. Among those with Barrow when he died were Cumie Barrow, his mother; LC Barrow, his younger brother; Emma Parker, Bonnie Parker's mother; and Billie Jean Parker. Their trip to Iowa was paid for by a Dallas County deputy sheriff. Marie Barrow interview, August 24, 1984.

Chapter 15. *Court*

1. Platte County Circuit Court, Judge R. B. Bridgeman presiding. David R. Clevenger prosecuted the case. Blanche Barrow had no attorney. Armed officers surrounded the courthouse. Visitors unknown to the officers or other officials were not allowed inside the courthouse during the trial. *The Landmark,* June 4, 1982.

2. Upon hearing Blanche Barrow's plea, Judge Bridgeman asked if she wanted an attorney. "No," she said. Then Bridgeman asked if she knew of any reason why sentence should not be passed. "No," she said. After she was assessed the ten-year sentence, Sheriff Coffey transported her immediately to the penitentiary at Jefferson City, Missouri. *The Landmark,* June 4, 1982.

3. Apparently many local people visited Blanche Barrow in the Platte County jail during the weeks before her trial, Kermit Crawford among them. "She [Blanche] spoke so soft and was so quiet, you wouldn't think she could harm a flea," Crawford observed later. Crawford interview, April 19, 1983. This view was shared by others, including Ann Tatman Clevenger, the wife of David Clevenger, the prosecuting attorney, who described Blanche Barrow as "a very small woman, very soft-spoken, and mild. She was so very tiny that it was hard to visualize her having the strength to lift a very large weapon. Blanche Barrow probably got into trouble because she fell in love with the wrong man." *The Landmark,* June 4, 1982.

4. Here in the original manuscript Blanche first wrote, "The warden and other prison Board members have tried in vain," then crossed it out. One source

states that Blanche Barrow had at least four operations on her eye in the Missouri State Penitentiary. Fortune, *Fugitives*, 188.

5. Blanche Barrow wrote a letter to David Clevenger, Platte County prosecuting attorney, thanking him for his kindness. *The Landmark*, June 4, 1982.

6. After becoming separated from Blanche and Buck Barrow, Bonnie Parker, Clyde Barrow, and W. D. Jones continued north on foot until they reached the South Raccoon River. There was a bridge to the west, near the old access to Dexfield Park's north entrance. Barrow left Jones and Parker briefly to examine the bridge. Deputy Evan Burger and E. A. Place of the *Dexter Sentinel* were guarding the bridge and briefly engaged Barrow in a gunfight. This occurred approximately fifteen minutes after the initial gunfight at the camp. Feller interview, May 5, 1983. Barrow's BAR was disabled by gunfire and he retreated to the east, rejoining Parker and Jones. The three fugitives, all wounded, then swam across the river to the north bank. Parker later commented that "the water around us was red with our mingled blood." Moon and Huddleston, "Bonnie, Clyde, and Me," 11. Once across, Barrow used an empty gun to hijack a farmer's car. The blood-stained car was abandoned in Polk City, Iowa, and another was stolen. The second car, also blood-stained, was found in Broken Bow, Nebraska. Feller interview, May 5, 1983; *Dallas Evening Journal*, July 29, 1933. Sometime later W. D. Jones left Parker and Barrow. Jones, interview by Biffle, June 1969. Barrow and Parker were ambushed in Dallas County on November 22, 1933, but they escaped. On January 16, 1934, Barrow finally fulfilled his desire to raid the Eastham prison farm, twenty miles north of Huntsville, Texas. Five prisoners, including Raymond Hamilton, were released and one guard was killed. The raid, often Barrow's sole focus, would ultimately lead to the deaths of both him and Parker later that spring. For the full story see Phillips, *Running with Bonnie and Clyde*, 159–78; and: Phillips, "Raid on Eastham," 54–64; McConal, *Over the Wall*, 82–120; and Simmons, *Assignment Huntsville*, 114–147. Clyde Barrow returned to Iowa frequently in the first months of 1934, robbing at least four banks there: in Rembrandt on January 23, Knierim on February 1, Stuart on April 16, and Everly on May 3. Interestingly, Stuart is only five miles from Dexter, Iowa. On April 1, Barrow and one of the Eastham escapees, Henry Methvin, murdered two Texas highway patrolmen near Grapevine, Texas. Two witnesses identified "the taller of two men (Methvin)" firing into the prone bodies of the two officers. *Dallas Morning News*, April 2, 1934. On April 6, Barrow and Methvin murdered an Oklahoma constable, some witnesses identifying Barrow as the shooter. State of Oklahoma, *Methvin v. State*, A-9060, September 18, 1936. Others testified that both Barrow and Methvin had weapons and that both were shooting at the victim, Constable Cal Campbell. *Methvin v. State*, A-9060, September 18, 1936. In Louisiana, on May 23, 1934, a second attempt was made to ambush Parker and Barrow. It was successful. With the help of Henry Methvin, who arranged the trap in exchange for a pardon from the State of Texas, six lawmen opened fire on Barrow and Parker as they sat in their car on a country road eight miles south of Gibsland, Louisiana. They were killed instantly. For the full story, see Phillips, *Running with Bonnie and Clyde*, 196–219.

7. Reportedly, Bonnie Parker's mother said, "He had her for two years. Look what it got her. He's not going to have her anymore. She's mine now." Hinton, *Ambush*, 190.

8. Actually there were twenty-one other defendants, apart from Blanche. This was the Clyde Barrow–Bonnie Parker Harboring Case, U. S. Federal District Judge William H. Atwell presiding, U. S. District Court for the Northern District of Texas, Dallas, Texas. This was the test case for what was then the brand new federal law making it a crime to harbor a federal fugitive. The twenty-two defendants were John Basden, Cumie T. Barrow, LC Barrow, Audrey Faye Barrow, Blanche Barrow, Marie Barrow Francis, Joe Francis, Emma Parker, Billie Jean Parker Mace, Hilton Bybee, Joe Chambless, Alice Davis, Steve Davis, Floyd Hamilton, Mildred Hamilton, Lillian Hamilton McBride, W. D. Jones, Henry Methvin, James Mullens, Mary O'Dare, S. J. Whatley, and Beulah Praytor. The date of the trial, George Washington's birthday, was no accident. The prosecutor, Clyde O. Eastus, U. S. district attorney for the Northern District of Texas, used the occasion of Washington's birthday in addressing the jury: "Gentlemen, this trial started on the 22nd day of February, A. D. 1935—George Washington's birthday. If George Washington had lived until the 22nd day of February, this year, he would have been 203 years old. My opinion is, gentlemen of the jury, that if George Washington, the father of our country, had known or had any idea that such men and women as these you have on trial here—such a bunch of outlaws —would ever immigrate to this country, I seriously doubt whether he would have ever crossed the Delaware." Russell, "Clyde Barrow-Bonnie Parker Harboring Case," 34.

Afterword

1. The editor has seen photographs of Cumie Barrow, among others, visiting Blanche in prison. These snapshots used to be in the personal collection of Marie Barrow, but they have all been sold to various collectors and their exact whereabouts now are unknown. Nevertheless, Blanche's scrapbooks contain photos of Cumie, LC, Marie, among others visiting her in prison.

2. In concluding her memoir, Blanche wrote the following: "Oct. 7, 1935 I was given a parole hearing. By then I had been on farm No. 1 twenty-five months. My record was clear and my parole file was fairly good. I am printing one of many letters. This letter is from the man I was working for when my husband was given a pardon from the Texas penitentiary by Governor Miriam A. Ferguson." Unfortunately, no letter accompanied the manuscript, so the passage was placed here in the Notes. However, there are copies of several letters in Blanche's scrapbooks from Wilbur Winkler, the co-owner (along with Artie Barrow Winkler) of the Cinderella Beauty Shoppe where Blanche worked while Buck was in prison. The letters are variously addressed to prosecutor David Clevenger, Penal Commissioner Paul Rentz, Governor Guy Parks, and Judge R. B. Bridgeman and are dated between January and May 1936, after the hearing date mentioned by Blanche. Often referring to Jan Fortune's book, *Fugitives*, and its portrayal of Blanche as an innocent victim of blind love,

Winkler asks that Blanche be released, adding in one case, "there was never a better woman than she." Winkler, letter to Clevenger, January 17, 1936.

Blanche Barrow was denied a parole in 1935. However, described as a model prisoner, she was ultimately released in 1939. *The Landmark*, June 4, 1982. By then Blanche Barrow had developed a close friendship with Platte County Sheriff Holt Coffey, his wife, Bessie May Cannon Coffey, and an unnamed FBI agent, all of whom helped her win a parole. Blanche Barrow interview, November 3, 1984.

Editor's Conclusion

1. Blanche Barrow, letter to mother, November 1, 1933, quoted in Baker, *Blanche Barrow*, 33–34. Despite her feelings about Callaway, Blanche Barrow was in communication with his teenaged niece, whom she liked a great deal.

2. Blanche Barrow interview, November 18, 1984.

3. *Fort Smith Southwest American*, July 29, 1933; Hinton, *Ambush*, 78; Knight and Davis, *Bonnie and Clyde*, 93–98; Blanche Barrow interviews, September 24, 1984, November 3 and 18, 1984.

4. *The Landmark*, August 11, 1933.

5. Ibid., July 28, 1933; *Kansas City Star*, September 17, 1978. Coffey was initially reported wounded twice, in the right arm and grazed on the face. *Kansas City Star*, July 20, 1933. The following day, Coffey's wounds were described as being in the right arm and back, with grazes on the cheek and head. *The Landmark*, July 21, 1933. Coffey himself said he was hit four times. *Kansas City Star*, September 17, 1978.

6. *The Landmark*, June 4, 1982.

7. Blanche Barrow, letter to her mother, September 9, 1933, quoted in Baker, *Blanche Barrow*, 27, 15.

8. Linder and Weiser interview, October 5, 2002; Blanche Barrow, letter to her mother, October 28, 1933, quoted in Baker, *Blanche Barrow*, 32–33, 43–44.

9. McCullough, *Truman*, 205, 209; Blanche Barrow, letters to her mother, n.d. and January 29, 1936, quoted in Baker, *Blanche Barrow*, 20–23, 59–60.

10. Linder interview, October 5, 2002.

11. Newspaper article, no source, n. d., clipped and pasted in Blanche Barrow's Scrapbook I. The headline reads: "Build Fence to Beat Narcotic Smugglers Here, Surround Women's Prison with New Strands of Barbed Wire to Stop Flow of Contraband."

12. Blanche Barrow, letters to her mother, October 1933, April 10, 1934, January 29, 1936, quoted in Baker, *Blanche Barrow*, 28,. 43–44, 60.

13. Weiser interviews, October 5, 2002 and September 8, 2001. According to historian David McCullough, Truman, who wrote prolifically, first indicated the possibility of being considered for the vice-presidency (which by transfer of power resulted in his reaching the White House) in the summer of 1943, more than four years after Blanche Barrow left prison. McCullough, *Truman*, 292.

14. Weiser interviews, October 5, 2002, and September 8, 2001.

15. Blanche Barrow, letter to her mother, October 28, 1933, quoted in Baker, *Blanche Barrow*, 32–33. The songs could have been any of the hits between 1929 and 1933, including "Stardust," "Happy Days Are Here Again," "Life is Just a Bowl of Cherries," "When the Moon Comes Over the Mountain," "Just a Gigolo," "Stormy Weather," "It's Only a Paper Moon," and Duke Ellington's "Sophisticated Lady." Gordon and Gordon, *American Chronicle*, 318.

16. Weiser interview, October 5, 2002.

17. Blanche Barrow, letter to her mother, December 23, 1934, quoted in Baker, *Blanche Barrow*, 46–47.

18. Among the names mentioned in another source are Frank, Jack, and Ray. Blanche Barrow, letters to her mother, quoted in Baker, *Blanche Barrow*, 22, 46, 60; Weiser interview, October 5, 2002.

19. Bill Griffith, letters to Blanche Caldwell Barrow, February 8, 1936, April 7, and August 13, 1936. Bill also gives an interesting look into his recent past. Writing of his memories of Reno, Nevada, in 1931, he described "a wide open town . . . greatest collection of people from all walks of life I have ever seen. Plenty of money and everything to buy with it."

20. Perhaps the most interesting thing about that particular card is the photograph on the front, an aerial view of the battleship USS Arizona coursing past New York City. The card was mailed nearly eighteen and a half months before the Japanese attack on Pearl Harbor and depicts the famous ship prior to its remodeling which, among other things, changed the look of the crow's nests and bridge area.

21. "Freddie," postcard to Blanche Barrow, June 25, 1936.

22. Letters of July 5 and 13, and October 1, 1936; May 17, June 9, November 1 and 8, and December 26, 1937; and October 3 and 10, 1938; Blanche Barrow letter to her mother, n. d., quoted in Baker, *Blanche Barrow*, 22–23. The complete passage from Blanche's letter to her mother regarding Freddie reads, "I have not heard from Freddie for 3 weeks. Guess he has gone the way all fair weather friends go. The last I heard from him was a wire saying a letter would follow, and he would send some money right away. Also that he would try to bring you to see me next month. But suppose it was all lies, because he hasn't written since."

23. "Harry," letter to Blanche Barrow, March 11, 1937.

24. Blanche had evidently received a photograph of her first husband from her mother, who was still friendly with Callaway. Blanche returned the picture. Blanche Barrow, letters to her mother December 31, 1935, and February 28, 1936, quoted in Baker, *Blanche Barrow*, 54, 61.

25. Blanche Barrow, letters to her mother, September 1, 1935, February 28, 1936, and October 28, 1934, quoted in Baker, *Blanche Barrow*, 49–51, 60–62, 32–33.

There is some confusion about Lucinda and her firstborn. Born in Kansas in either 1915 or 1916, Lucinda Marcum was Blanche's half-sister, the daughter of Lillian Bell Pond. Blanche Barrow, unpublished handwritten history; State of Texas, standard birth certificate, Betty Sue Hill. By the early 1930s, Lucinda, also known as "Senda," was married to John Hill, a laborer from Coleman County, Texas. The couple lived variously in Ferris, Albany, Stamford, and West Dallas, Texas, among other places. They moved whenever and wherever work was available. Lucinda gave birth to at least five children, including a boy early in 1934. It was this child, evidently Lucinda's first, that Blanche tried repeatedly to find out about while she was serving time in Missouri. Among other things, she asked her mother whether a gift from her, a pair of baby booties, had ever arrived. It does not appear, however, that Blanche received any substantial news of the child until 1936 when a picture was finally sent to her. Blanche Barrow, letters to her mother, quoted in Baker, *Blanche Barrow*, 55–57, 60–62. Among Blanche's scrapbooks, papers, and other records was a handwritten list of her half-sister's children indicating that Lucinda's first child was born in 1935. But the aforementioned letters say otherwise. It is possible that Blanche mistakenly listed the year as 1935 in her handwritten history of the Marcum family, but it is also possible that the child born in 1934 did not survive (which might explain Blanche's difficulty in obtaining information about the infant). There are no references to Lucinda, John Hill, or any of their children in Blanche's papers beyond the late 1940s.

26. Blanche Barrow, letters to her mother, April 20, 1934, and September 14, 1935, quoted in Baker, *Blanche Barrow*, 45–46. 52–53. But many were doing a lot for Blanche Barrow's file, including Cumie Barrow who had offered a place for her former daughter-in-law to live. See Appendix E.

27. Blanche Barrow, letters to her mother, April 20, 1934, and November 1, 1933, quoted in Baker, *Blanche Barrow*, 44, 34.

28. LC Barrow, letter to Blanche Barrow, March 8, 1938. "How is your health! And has your eyes ever got well! I so hope they have. More than anything else in the world I want to see you well and happy. I know that is what he [Buck] would wish. So keep that pretty little head of yours up and think of the future . . . you have a lot of life in front of you." LC Barrow was arrested October 30, 1934, for robbing the Dougherty Drug Store at 2009 Beckley in Dallas. He was convicted and sentenced despite claims from Homer Dillingham, who confessed to the crime, that Barrow was not involved. *Dallas Evening Journal*, October 30, 1934; *Dallas Dispatch*, December 23, 1934; *Dallas Daily Times-Herald*, December 2, 1934.

29. Blanche Barrow, letter to her mother, December 23, 1934, quoted in Baker, *Blanche Barrow*, 47.

30. See Note 8, Chapter 15, for the identity of the twenty-two accused. Jones, interview by Biffle, June 1969; Weiser interview, September 8, 2001, October 5, 2002.

31. Winkler, letter to Blanche Barrow, July 26, 1937. Winkler stated that he had remarried, adding, "haven't seen any of the folks in Dallas in some time. Artie held me up for $25 for giving me a quit claim deed to the house, and that really finished me with her, for since divorcing she asked me for a quit claim deed to the west Dallas place and I sent it by return mail, and in

addition released her insurance policy so that she could cash it in for about $400, and now she hijacks me for a quit claim deed. Tried to get $75. I feel sorry for her, but when they start robbing those who love them, it is time to beware." Winkler, letter Blanche Barrow, October 11, 1937; Blanche Barrow, letters to her mother, January 5 and 29, 1936, quoted in Baker, *Blanche Barrow*, 57, 60.

32. Cabell Phillips, *New York Times Chronicle*, 485, 496–97, 240–41, 320.

33. Ibid., 237, 515–23, 278.

34. Katherine Stark is probably the one mentioned by Blanche Barrow in her letter to her mother of September 9, 1933, as quoted in Baker, *Blanche Barrow*, 27. There is a photograph and a reproduction of a painting of Mrs. Stark in the author's scrapbooks.

35. *International News Service* March 25, 1939; State of Missouri, Conditional Commutation for the State of Missouri, March 25, 1939; *Kansas City Star*, September 10, 1936; Blanche Barrow interview, November 18, 1984.

36. In 1934 John Dillinger, Baby Face Nelson, and Pretty Boy Floyd were killed by law enforcement officers. The following year Fred and Ma Barker died in a hail of gunfire.

37. Gordon and Gordon, *American Chronicle*, 359.

38. The date of Blanche's release was noted in the *Dallas Daily Times-Herald*, on March 24, 1939. Terms of the commutation began officially on March 25, 1939. She was required to abide by the terms of the commutation for a period of nearly two years, until March 3, 1941. The terms included moving to Garvin, Oklahoma, and preparing a monthly written report, signed by her sponsor or a police officer, listing her whereabouts and job status, among other things. Apparently so few women were involved in such matters that the official form referred only to the masculine gender. Thus, on Blanche Barrow's form, every "he," "his," and "him" has been crossed out by hand and replaced with "she," "hers," and "her". State of Missouri, Conditional Commutation, March 25, 1939. Artie was now living in Dallas, having moved from Denison after her divorce from Wilbur Winkler. Buddy Barrow, e-mail, September 16, 2002.

39. Bronaugh, letter to Blanche Barrow, March 30, 1939. Raymond Hamilton, involved in Clyde Barrow's raid on Eastham, was captured and sentenced to death in Texas in 1934. On July 22 of that year he and two others escaped from the death house in Huntsville, to date the only such break ever successfully staged in Texas penal history. He was captured again in April 1935 and executed on May 10 of that year. For the full story, see Phillips, *Running with Bonnie and Clyde*, 159–296. Floyd Hamilton, who had a good job as a truck driver and a respectable position in the community, was drawn into the underworld by his younger brother. The older brother helped plant the guns used in the raid on Eastham, a charge that was dismissed due to lack of evidence. He was then implicated in the murder of two Texas State Highway patrolmen. That charge was quickly proven to be an attempted frame-up and dropped. In 1935 Floyd Hamilton received the maximum sentence, two years, on federal charges of harboring Bonnie and Clyde. Blanche Barrow was among

the twenty-two defendants at the same trial. In 1938, after serving his time for harboring at the federal prison near Leavenworth, Kansas, Floyd Hamilton was habitually picked up and harassed by Dallas officers, both city and county. Consequently, like Clyde Barrow before him, he could not hold down a job. Desperate, he and another man named Ted Walters went on a crime spree, committing a number of robberies before both were captured. For his part, and mainly because of his last name, Hamilton was sentenced to a long stretch on "the Rock," Alcatraz. For the full story, see Hamilton, *Public Enemy No. 1*.

40 . Sometime in the early 1980s, Blanche handed the original manuscript to Esther Weiser, asking her to see if "something" could be done with it. However, shortly thereafter Blanche fell ill and Weiser forgot completely about the manuscript until many years later. Weiser interview, May 13, 2003.

41. Cumie Barrow wrote that Henry was born in Pensacola, Florida. Cumie Barrow, unpublished manuscript.

42. That Clyde Barrow played saxophone is by now well known. His brother-in-law Leon Hale taught him to play. One of the items retrieved from the car in Louisiana immediately after he and Bonnie were killed was an alto saxophone. However, he also played guitar. His mother mentioned this in her memoir. Blanche remembered him playing guitar, and among the items found in the abandoned Joplin garage apartment was a guitar. Cumie Barrow, unpublished manuscript; Hinton, *Ambush*, 173; Weiser interview, October 5, 2002. Also, according to her sister, Bonnie Parker played piano. Moon and Huddleston, "Bonnie, Clyde, and Me," unpublished manuscript.

43. Weiser interview, October 5, 2002; Linder interview, October 5, 2002.

44. Ibid.

45. Blanche Barrow, letter to her mother, July 12, 1939; Blanche Barrow, letters to her mother, October 1933 and April 10, 1934, quoted in Baker, *Blanche Barrow*, 28, 43–44. On July 30, 1943, Blanche, by then married to Eddie Frasure, had her birth certificate reissued. Her mother appeared as the witness, signing under the name Lillian Caldwell Horton.

46. Robert Edson, letter to Blanche Barrow, April 16, 1939, quoted in Baker, *Blanche Barrow*, 16.

47. Frasure's active service dates spanned October 7, 1942 to November 2, 1946. Odell B. Lamb, Chief Administrative Division, U.S. Navy, form FL 3–39, February 17, 1949.

48. State of Texas, County of Dallas, certified copy certificate of birth, no. 15965, July 30, 1943.

49. Weiser interview, October 5, 2002; Linder interview, October 5, 2002; Marie Barrow interview, September 15, 1993; Buddy Barrow interview, October 26, 2002. Bonnie's sister and the Barrows received similar calls.

50. When Esther Weiser lived for a while with the Frasures in 1951, Blanche referred to the relationship between her and her husband as that of newlyweds. According to Weiser, the implication was sexual. Weiser interview, September 8, 2001, October 5, 2002.

51. *Dallas Morning News*, September 19, 1947.

52. Weiser interview, October 5, 2002.

53. Ibid.

54. Ibid.

55. Weiser interview, October 5, 2002; September 8, 2001.

56. Linder interview, October 5, 2002.

57. Blanche Barrow interview, November 3, 1984.

58. Cawelti, *Focus on Bonnie and Clyde*, 2.

59. Blanche Barrow interview, November 18, 1984; Marie Barrow interview, September 25, 1993.

60. Buddy Barrow interview, October 26, 2002.

61. According to one source Blanche "was crazy about Warren." Biffle, e-mail, May 27, 2003.

62. Blanche Barrow interview, November 3, 1984.

63. Simmons, *Assignment Huntsville*, 167. The disdain for Mary O'Dare extended elsewhere as well. In a conversation with Emma Parker, Cumie Barrow said, "I just saw that stool pigeon Mary O'Dare. She tried to get the kids [Bonnie and Clyde] caught when she was with them and finally got Raymond caught." Emma responded that she would never speak to Cumie again if she let "that woman" in her house. Barrow assured her she had nothing to worry about, that she would assault O'Dare with one of her irons if she came too close. Dallas police department telephone wiretap transcript, April 28, 1934, 56. Even Hamilton's brother Floyd hated Mary O'Dare. Floyd Hamilton interview, July 18, 1981.

64. For the full story of this incident, see: Phillips, *Running with Bonnie and Clyde*, 173–78.

65. Blanche Barrow interview, November 18, 1984.

66. "Boots" Hinton interview, August 15, 2001.

67. Marie Barrow interview, August 24, 1984; Buddy Barrow, e-mail, September 16, 2002.

68. Linder interview, October 5, 2002.

69. Ibid.

70. Ibid.

71. During a 1934 telephone conversation, Billie Jean explained why she had not gone to work that day, saying, "I don't think they like me. They think I'm too hard-boiled. I can't please the public. No need trying." Later, in yet another telephone conversation, Emma Parker tells Cumie Barrow that her daughter, because of who she is [the sister of a wanted fugitive and the wife of convicted burglar Fred Mace], has been forced to leave Dallas to find a job. "I know she can find a job where she's gone. She can't find work in Dallas." Dallas Police Department telephone wiretap transcript, April 18, 1934, 6; April 29, 1934, 59.

72. *Dallas Dispatch*, May 31, 1934.

73. For the full story of this incident, see Phillips, *Running with Bonnie and Clyde*, 181–84.

74. Marie Barrow interview, April 19, 1995; Buddy Barrow interview, October 26, 2002.

75. *Dallas Daily Times-Herald*, May 25, 1934. The three men were identified as Russell Mullins, Guy Thompson, and Jim Forrester.

76. In 1954 Barrow was sentenced to two years for forging a six-dollar check. *Dallas Daily Times Herald*, October 14, 1954.

77. Buddy Barrow interview, October 26, 2002.

78. Linder interview, October 5, 2002.

79. Blanche Barrow interviews, September 24, November 3, and November 18, 1984.

80. Blanche Barrow interview, November 18, 1984. Marie Barrow added, "and he [Jones] had a bunch of good-looking brothers too!" Marie Barrow interview, September 25, 1993.

81. Biffle, e-mails, December 24 and 27, 2002, January 15, 2003.

82. Linder interview, October 5, 2002. Despite the rebuff, Lillian attended her daughter's funeral.

83. Blanche Barrow interview, November 3, 1984.

Bibliography

Public Documents

Dallas County Sheriff's Department. W. D. Jones, Voluntary Statement #B-71, November 18, 1933. Dallas Public Library, Texas/Dallas History Archives.

Dallas Police Department. Mug book. Dallas Public Library, Texas/Dallas History Archives.

Dallas Police Department, File #6048. Clyde Chestnut Barrow. Dallas Public Library, Texas/Dallas History Archives.

Dallas Police Department. Handwritten transcript of telephone wiretaps of the Barrow, Brown, Lefors, and Parker residences, April 18, 1934–April 30, 1934. Dallas Public Library, Texas/Dallas History Archives.

Fort Worth Police Department. File #4316, Clyde Barrow. Dallas Public Library, Texas/Dallas History Archives.

Louisiana State Board of Health, Bureau of Vital Statistics. Certificate of Death, Clyde Chestnut Barrow, May 23, 1934.

Polk County (Iowa) Arrest Record. Blanche Barrow, July 24, 1933.

State of Missouri, Board of Probation and Parole. Letter from Robert C. Edson, director, to Mrs. Blanche Barrow, April 16, 1940.

State of Missouri. Conditional Pardon, Blanche Caldwell Barrow, March 22, 1939.

State of Oklahoma, McCurtain County, Marriage License and Certificate, issued July 2, 1931, recorded July 11, 1931, page 280, Marriage record 16.

State of Oklahoma, *Methvin v. State*, No. A9060, Criminal Court of Appeals of Oklahoma, September 18, 1936. Barker Texas History Center.

State of Texas, County of Dallas. Certified copy certificate of birth, no. 15965, July 30, 1943.

State of Texas, Texas Department of Health, Bureau of Vital Statistics, Standard certificate of birth, Betty Sue Hill, November 22, 1944.

State of Texas, Texas Prison System. *"Annual Report for the Year Ending December 31, 1929."* Barker Texas History Center.

State of Texas, Texas Prison System. File #63527, Clyde Barrow. Barker Texas History Center.

State of Texas, Texas Prison System. File #72718, Hilton Bybee. Barker Texas History Center.

State of Texas, Texas Prison System. File #54953, Charlie Frazier. Barker Texas History Center.

State of Texas, Texas Prison System. File #70383, Ralph Fults. Barker Texas Archives.

State of Texas, Texas Prison System, File #65949, Henry Methvin. Barker Texas History Center.

State of Texas, Texas Prison System. File #61455, Joe Palmer. Barker Texas History Center.

State of Texas, Texas Prison System. File #69384, Roy Thornton. Barker Texas History Center.

State of Texas, Texas Prison System. Letter from William M. Thompson to Doug Walsh, May 17, 1932. Dallas Public Library, Texas/Dallas History Archives.

State of Texas, Texas Prison System. Minutes of the Texas Prison Board, March 1 and August 3, 1930. F. L. Tiller, secretary. Barker Texas History Center.

State of Texas, Texas Prison System. Special Escape Report, Raymond Hamilton, January 16, 1934. Barker Texas History Center.

U. S. Department of Justice, Bureau of Criminal Investigation. Identification Order No. 1211, October, 24, 1933. Dallas Historical Society.

U. S. Department of Justice, Bureau of Criminal Investigation. Memo to Doug Walsh, May 4, 1933. Dallas Public Library, Texas/Dallas History Archives.

U. S. Department of the Navy. Odell B. Lamb, U. S. Navy, form FL 3-39, February 17, 1949.

Books

Andrist, Ralph K., ed. *The American Heritage History of the 20's and 30's.* New York: American Heritage Publishing Co., 1970.

Baker, Eugene, ed. *Blanche Barrow, The Last Victim of Bonnie and Clyde: Prison Letters from 1933 to 1936. From the Collection of Mary Ann and Robert E. Davis.* Waco: Texian Press, 2001.

Boucher, Colleen, ed. *Jackson County (Minn.) History.* Vol. II. Jackson, Minn.: Jackson County Historical Society, 1979.

Cawelti, John G., ed. *Focus on Bonnie and Clyde.* Englewood Cliffs, N.J.: Prentice-Hall, Inc., 1973.

Cox, William. *Osborne Association Annual Report on U.S. Prisons, 1935. New York:* Osborne Association, 1935.

Dallas City Directory, 1921 through 1934-1935. Dallas: Worley Publishing, 1921–1935.

Denison (Texas) City Directory, 1929 through, 1934, Dallas: Worley Publishing, 1929–1934.

Fortune, Jan I. *Fugitives: The Story of Clyde Barrow and Bonnie Parker, as Told by Bonnie's Mother (Emma Krause Parker) and Clyde's Sister (Nell Barrow Cowan).* Dallas: Ranger Press, 1934.

Frost, H. Gordon, and John H. Jenkins. *"I'm Frank Hamer": The Life of a Texas Peace Officer,* Austin: State House Press, 1993.

Fulsom, Louise Adams. *Prison Stories: The Old Days.* Weldon: self published, 1998.

Gordon, Lois, and Alan Gordon. *American Chronicle, Year by Year through the Twentieth Century.* New Haven, Conn.: Yale University Press, 1999.

Halperin, Jerome A. *United States Pharmacopoeial Dispensing Information, 1997. 17th ed., Volume 1, Drug Information for the Health Care Professional.* Rockville, Md.: U.S. Pharmacopoeial Convention, 1997.

Hamby, Alonzo L. *Man of the People: A Life of Harry S Truman,* New York: Oxford University Press,1995.

Hamilton, Floyd. *Public Enemy #1.* Dallas: Acclaimed Books, 1978.

Harding, David. *Weapons.* New York: St. Martin's Press, 1980.

Hinton, Ted, as told to Larry Grove. *Ambush: The Real Story of Bonnie and Clyde.* Austin, Tex.: Shoal Creek, 1979.

History of Audrain County, Missouri. St. Louis: O. P. Williams and Co., 1986.

Hounschell, Jim. *Lawmen and Outlaws: 116 Years in Joplin History.* Joplin, Mo.: Joplin Historical Society, 1993.

Hulston, John K. *100 Years: Bank of Ash Grove, 1883–1983.* Springfield, Mo.: Fay Printing, 1983.

Kennedy, David M. *Freedom from Fear: The American People in Depression and War, 1929–1945.* New York: Oxford University Press, 1999.

King, Evelyn Ball. *Collingsworth County, 1890–1984.* Dallas, Tex.: Taylor Publishing, 1985.

Knight, James R., with Jonathan Davis. *Bonnie and Clyde: A Twenty-First Century Update.* Austin, Tex.: Eakin Press, 2003.

Marquart, James W., Sheldon Ekland-Olson, and Jonathan R. Sorenson. *The Rope, the Chair, and the Needle: Capital Punishment in Texas, 1923–1990.* Austin: University of Texas Press, 1994.

Martin, Steve J., and Sheldon Ekland-Olson. *Texas Prisons: The Walls Came Tumbling Down.* Austin: Texas Monthly Press, 1987.

McConal, Patrick M. *Over the Wall: The Men behind the 1934 Death House Escape.* Austin, Tex.: Eakin Press, 2000.

McCullough, David. *Truman.* New York: Simon & Schuster, 1992.

McDonald, William L. *Dallas Rediscovered.* Dallas: Dallas Historical Society, 1978.

Milner, E. R. *The Lives and Times of Bonnie and Clyde*. Carbondale: Southern Illinois University Press, 1996.

Paxton, William M. *Annals of Platte County (Missouri)*. Platte City, Mo.: Platte County Historical Society, 1978.

Phillips, Cabell. *The New York Times Chronicle of American Life from the Crash to the Blitz, 1929–1939*. New York: Macmillan, 1969.

Phillips, John Neal. *Running with Bonnie and Clyde: The Ten Fast Years of Ralph Fults*. Norman: University of Oklahoma Press, 1996.

Polk's Greater Dallas City Directory, 1960, 1970. Dallas: R. L. Polk, 1960, 1970.

Simmons, Lee. *Assignment Huntsville: Memoirs of a Texas Prison Officer*. Austin: University of Texas Press, 1957.

Tattersall, Peter D. *Conviction: A True Story*. Montclair, N.J.: Pegasus Rex Press, 1980.

Treherne, John. *The Strange History of Bonnie and Clyde*, London: Jonathan Cape, 1984.

Tobin, James. *Great Projects: The Epic Story of the Building of America from Taming the Mississippi to the Invention of the Internet*. New York, Free Press, 2001

Umphrey, Don. *The Meanest Man in Texas: A True Story Based on the Life of Clyde Thompson*. Nashville, Tenn.: Thomas Nelson Publishers, 1984.

Underwood, Sid. *Depression Desperado: The Chronicle of Raymond Hamilton*, Austin, Tex.: Eakin Press, 1995.

Unger, Robert. *The Union Station Massacre: The Original Sin of J. Edgar Hoover's FBI*. Kansas City: Andrews McMeel Publishing, 1997.

Walker, Donald R. *Penology for Profit: A History of the Texas Prison System 1867–1912*. College Station: Texas A&M University Press, 1988.

Wallis, Michael. *Pretty Boy: The Life and Times of Charles Arthur Floyd*. New York: St. Martin's Press, 1992.

Watkins, T. H. *The Hungry Years: A Narrative History of the Great Depression in America*. New York: Henry Holt Company, 1999.

Webb, Walter Prescott. *The Texas Rangers: A Century of Frontier Defense*, 2d ed., Austin: University of Texas Press, 1965.

Weesner, Robert, ed. *History of Dexter, Iowa*. Dexter: Dexter Historical Society, 1979.

Articles and Essays

Arnold, Thurman. "The Crash: What It Meant." In Isabel Leighton, ed. *The Aspirin Age, 1919–1941*. New York: Simon & Schuster, 1949.

Cartledge, Rick. "Bonnie and Clyde." *Machine Gun News*, volume 11, no. 7, July 1993, 12–15.

Edwards, Robert. "A Tale Tom Persell Lived to Tell." *Springfield (Mo.) News-Leader*, January 25, 1997.

Gast, Dorothy. "Bonnie and Clyde No Heroes, Victim Says," *Kansas City Star*, September 17, 1978.

Jones, W. D. "Riding with Bonnie and Clyde." *Playboy Magazine*, November 1968, 151–65.

Knight, James R. "Incident at Alma." *Arkansas Historical Review*, vol. 61, no. 4, (winter 1997), 399–426.

McCormick, Harry, as told to Mary Carey. "The Impossible Interview." *Argosy Magazine*, vol. 25, no. 2 (February 1958), 42–43, 68–74.

Penland, Curtis. "Bonnie and Clyde: The Vacation That Became a Gun Battle." *Joplin Metropolitan*, vol. 23, no. 3 (March 1985), 43–44.

Phillips, John Neal. "Raid on Eastham." *American History Magazine*, vol. 35, no. 4 (October 2000), 54–64.

Texas Historical Commission. "Eastham Prison Farm," Texas State Historical Marker, County Road 230, Weldon, Texas.

Tolbert, Frank X. "Taken for a Ride by Bonnie and Clyde." *Dallas Morning News*, March 18, 1968.

Williams, Francis. "The Day Bonnie and Clyde Shot It Out with the Law in Ferrelview." *Discover North*, vol. 8, no. 3, (mid-March to mid-April 1974), 4–16.

Newspapers

Amarillo (Tex.) Daily News
Amarillo (Tex.) Sunday News-Globe
Ash Grove (Mo.) Commonwealth
Austin (Tex.) American Statesman
Chandler (Okla.) News-Republican
Cleveland County (Ark.) Herald
Comanche (Tex.) Chief
Daily Oklahoman
Daily Oklahoma Times
Dallas Daily Times-Herald
Dallas Dispatch
Dallas Evening Journal
Dallas Morning News
Denton (Tex.) Record-Chronicle
Des Moines Register
Dexter (Iowa) Sentinel
Enid (Okla.) Morning News
Fairbury (Neb.) News
Fairmont (Minn.) Daily Sentinel
Fort Dodge (Iowa) Messenger and Chronicle
Fort Smith Southwest American
Hope (Ark.) Star
Houston Press
International News Service
Jackson (Minn.) Republic

Joplin (Mo.) Globe
Joplin (Mo.) News Herald
Landmark, Platte City, Mo.
McKinney (Tex.) Daily Courier Gazette
Mexico (Mo.) Intelligencer
Mexico (Mo.) Weekly Ledger
Minneapolis Journal
Okabena (Minn.) Press
Pharos-Tribune, Logansport, Ind.
Pleasanton (Kans.) Observer Enterprise
Prague (Okla.) News Record
Pratt (Kans.) Daily Tribune
Pratt (Kans.) Union
Ruston (La.) Daily Leader
Southwest American, Fort Smith, Arkansas.
Springfield (Mo.) Daily News
Springfield (Mo.) News-Leader
Springfield (Mo.) Press
Stephenville (Tex.) Empire-Tribune
Sunday World-Herald Magazine of the Midlands
Wellington (Tex.) Leader

Unpublished Manuscripts and Correspondence

Allen, James G. "The First State Bank–Bokchito, Oklahoma." Unpublished manuscript held by the Bryan County Heritage Association, Calera, Oklahoma.

Barrow, Blanche Caldwell. Letter to Matt Caldwell, November 11, 1933.

———. Letters to her mother. January 14, 1933; January 29, 1936; July 12, 1939.

———. Unpublished handwritten history of Marcum family.

———. Four unpublished scrapbooks.

Barrow, Buck. Letter to family, January 16, 1930.

Barrow, Buddy Williams. E-mail to John Neal Phillips, September 16, 2002.

Barrow, Cumie T. Unpublished manuscript, 1933–1934.

Biffle, Kent. E-mails to John Neal Phillips, December 24 and 27, 2002.

Bronaugh, Frank E. Letter to Blanche Barrow, March 30, 1939

Chapler, Keith M, M.D. Letter to Debra Sanborn, May 3, 1974. Dexter (Iowa) Historical Society.

Crawford, Kermit "Curley." Letter to John Neal Phillips, December 21, 1982.

Griffith, Bill. Letters to Blanche Barrow, February 8, April 7, and August 13, 1936.

Henson, S. C., a. k. a. Joe Wood. Letter to Kent Biffle, September 2, 1980.

Hounschell, Jim. E-mail to John Neal Phillips, February 4, 2002.

Hutzell, Diane, and Cheri Rupp. "Bonnie and Clyde: Hide-Out in Dexter." Dexter (Iowa) Historical Society.

Kimsey, Shirley I. E-mail to John Neal Phillips, May 6, 2003.
———. Letters to John Neal Phillips, October 25, 2002; May 7, 2003.
Legg, Walter M., Jr. Letter to John Neal Phillips, September 1, 1982.
Mattix, Rick. E-mail to John Neal Phillips, April 1, 2003.
McCormick, Harry. Unpublished manuscript dealing with Ralph Fults, 1956–66.
Moon, Billie Jean Parker. Unpublished handwritten history of the Parker and Krause families, 1985.
———. Unpublished handwritten observations about Bonnie Parker.
———, and Joyce Huddleston, as told to Clint Kelley. "Bonnie, Clyde, and Me."unpublished essay.
Ruckdeschel, Carol. Cumberland Island Museum. Letter to John Neal Phillips, January 22, 2002.
Russell, Bud. "The Clyde Barrow–Bonnie Parker Harboring Case." Unpublished manuscript, 1935.
Sanborn, Debra. "The Barrow Gang's Visit to Dexter." Unpublished essay. Dexter (Iowa) Historical Society.
Schwartz, Herb. Notes accompanying a series of photographs made in Dexfield Park, July 24, 1933. *Des Moines Register*.
Searles, William R. Letter to John Neal Phillips, December 14, 1982; April 21, 1983.
Taulbee, LaVern. E-mails to John Neal Phillips, December 2, 2002; January 15, 2003.
Winkler, Wilbur. Letters to Blanche Barrow July 26, 1937, and October 11, 1937.
———. Letter to R. B. Bridgeman, January 17, 1936.
———. Letter to David Clevenger, January 17, 1936.
———. Letter to Paul V. Renz, May 30, 1936.
Woods, S. O., Jr. Texas Department of Corrections (now TDCJ-ID), letter to John Neal Phillips, March 19, 1985.

Interviews

Baber, George and Frances. Eyewitnesses. Interview by LaVern Taulbee, Platte County, Missouri, November 19, 2002.
Barrow, Blanche Caldwell. Wife of Buck Barrow. Interviews by John Neal Phillips, Kaufman County, Texas, September 24, 1984, November 3 and 18, 1984.
Barrow, Buddy Williams. Clyde Barrow's nephew, LC Barrow's stepson. Interviews by John Neal Phillips, Dallas, August 1, 1998; October 26, 2002.
Barrow, Marie. Clyde Barrow's youngest sister. Interviews by John Neal Phillips, Dallas, August 24, 1984; September 15, 25, and 30, 1993; November 18, 1993; May 25, 1994; April 19, 1995; April 29, May 1, August 1, September 12, and November 30, 1998.
Blohm, Wilma. Dexter, Iowa, resident. Interview by John Neal Phillips, Dexter, Iowa, May 5, 1983.

Carey, Mary. Colleague of newspaperman Harry McCormick. Interview by John Neal Phillips, Dallas, December 8, 1985.

Christine. Post-prison friend of W. D. Jones. Interview by John Neal Phillips, Dallas, May 25, 1984.

Crawford, Kermit "Curley." Platte City, Mo. resident. Interview by John Neal Phillips, Kansas City, April 19, 1983.

Feller, Marvelle. Dexter, Iowa, resident. Interview by John Neal Phillips, Dexter, May 5, 1983.

Ford, Trey. Historian. Interview by John Neal Phillips, Dallas, June 6, 1984.

Fults, Ralph S. Barrow gang member. Interviews by John Neal Phillips, Dallas, November 5 and 12, 1980; December 5 and 10, 1980; February 1, March 8 and 14, May 10, and July 18, 1981; February 13 and December 4, 1982; May 21, 1983; June 12, 1984; February 22 and April 29, 1985.

Grove, Larry. Newspaper reporter. Interview by John Neal Phillips, Dallas, April 2, 1980.

Hamilton, Floyd. Bank robber. Raymond Hamilton's older brother. Participant in the raid on the Eastham prison farm. Interview by John Neal Phillips, Dallas, July 18, 1981.

———. Bank robber. Telephone interview by Teresa Pierce, June 5, 1975.

Hamilton, Mildred. Floyd's wife. Interview by John Neal Phillips, Dallas, July 18, 1981.

Hammet, Jack. Barrow gang member. Interview by John Neal Phillips. Denton, Texas, February 20, 1982.

Hayes, Johnny. Photojournalist. Interviews by John Neal Phillips, Dallas, October 10, 1981; February 28, 1983.

Hays, John W. "Preacher." Former Dallas County deputy sheriff. Interview by John Neal Phillips, Dallas, April 20, 1980.

Hays, Mrs. J. W. Teenaged acquaintance of Clyde Barrow. Interview by John Neal Phillips, Dallas, April 20, 1980.

Hinton, L. J. "Boots." Son of Dallas County deputy sheriff Ted Hinton. Interviews by John Neal Phillips, Dallas, May 5, 1980, August 15, 2001.

Hinton, Mrs. Ted. Ted Hinton's second wife. Interview by John Neal Phillips, Dallas, April 15, 1980.

Holmes, Ken M., Jr. Historian. Interviews by John Neal Phillips, Dallas, September 9, 1993; January 18, 1994.

Jack. Member of the Lake Dallas Gang. Interview by John Neal Phillips, Denton, Texas, February 20, 1982.

Jones, William Daniel. Barrow gang member. Interview by Kent Biffle, Houston, June 1969.

Joyner, Lorraine. Daughter of John Joyner, negotiator in the ambush of Bonnie Parker and Clyde Barrow. Interview by Dr. Robert Pierce, May 13, 1992.

Karlen, Elsie Wullschleger. Barrow robbery victim. Interview by John Neal Phillips, Dallas, January 10, 1983.

Legg, Walter, Jr. Kaufman County resident. Interviews by John Neal Phillips, Kemp, March 13, 1981; September 15, 1993.

Linder, Rhea Leen. Niece to Bonnie and Billie Jean Parker. Interview by John Neal Phillips, October 5, 2002.

Milner, Dr. E. R. Historian. Interview by John Neal Phillips, Denton, August 4, 1984.

Myers, Rose. Cafe customer of Bonnie Parker. Interview by John Neal Phillips, Dallas, January 19, 1983.

Neuhoff, Henry, Jr. Barrow robbery victim. Interview by John Neal Phillips, Dallas, February 20, 1982.

Pierce, Dr. Robert. Former director of the Texas prison archives and the Texas Prison Museum at Huntsville. Interviews by John Neal Phillips, Huntsville, November 5 and 6, 1993.

Roseborough, Robert F. Barrow auto theft victim. Interview by John Neal Phillips, Marshall, Texas, July 11, 1984.

Russell, Robert H. Biographer of Texas prison system employee Bud Russell. Interview by John Neal Phillips, Tyler, Texas, July 11, 1984.

Scoma, Luke. Former inmate at Eastham prison farm. Interview by John Neal Phillips, Dallas, August 24, 1984.

Scarles, William R. Eyewitness to Platte City gunfight. Interview by John Neal Phillips, Cassville, Mo., April 20, 1983.

Weiser, Esther. Longtime friend of Blanche Caldwell Barrow. Interviews by John Neal Phillips, September 8, 2001; October 5 and 31, 2002, April 18 and May 13, 2003.

Internet Sources

Norwich. "Unguentine," *chenangocounty.org/norwichpharmacalmuseum/*

Procter, Ben H. "Great Depression." *Handbook of Texas Online. http://www. tsha.utexas.edu/handbook/online/articles/view/GG/npg1.html.*

Roosevelt, Franklin Delano. "First Inaugural Address, March 4, 1933." *nationalcenter.org/FRooseveltFirstInaugural.html*

Schultz, Stanley K. "American History: 1865 to the Present, Lecture 19, The Great Depression and the New Deal." University of Wisconsin, 2002. *http://us.history.wisc.edu/hist102/lectures/textonly/lecture19.html*

Audio/Visual Media

Parker, Billie Jean. Interview by Jud Collins. RCA Victor sound recording, #LSP 3967, 1968.

Piper, Kurt. Video interview. *Remembering Bonnie and Clyde.* Video documentary. Tim Leone, writer and director. St. Louis: Turquoise Film/Video Productions, 1994.

Index

Barrow, Artie (Blanche's sister-in-law). *See* Winkler, Artie Barrow

Barrow, Audrey Faye (Blanche's sister-in-law), 161; Barrow-Parker harboring trial, defendant in, 291n.8

Barrow, Blanche Caldwell, 3, *4*, 7, 8, 18, *35*, *45*, *84*, *85*, *86*, 89, 94, *108*, *134*, *138*, *140*, *141*, *153*, *155*, *158*, *160*, 163, *168*, *172*, *174*, 178, *184*, *192*, *196*, *197*, *198*; animals and dolls as surrogate children, 194, 226n.3; Barrow family, conflicts with, 23, 143, 147, 161–62, 235n.23; Barrow family, living with, 234n.22; Barrow-Parker harboring trial, defendant in, 146, 164, 291n.8; and Billie Parker, 101, 183–95; and Bonnie, 25–26; Bonnie and Clyde, reaction to deaths of, 146; *Bonnie and Clyde*, 1967 motion picture, 179–83; Buck, fighting with, 83–86; Buck, first meeting with, 5, 226n.6; Buck, marriage to, 6, 8; Buck, reunion with, 17; Buck, robbery accomplice of, 227n.8, 232n.19, 235n.28; Buck and Clyde in prison, visiting, 11, 227n.9, 236n.29; Buck's crimes, prior knowledge of, 228–30n.10, 240n.10; childless, 226n.3; Clyde, fighting with, 255n.26; Clyde leaving Blanche and Buck, 286n.24; Clyde's statement to Cumie, 238n.37; cooking and food, 40, 50, 73, 81, 82, 101, 111, 112, 128, 185–86; in custody, 134–43, 149; Dallas, bus trip to, 72–74; death of, 194; and Denison police, 21–22; Dexfield Park, camped in, 124–29, 282–83nn.8–16; Dexfield Park, captured in, 132–136, 286nn.26,28, 287n.29; Dexfield Park, flight in, 285nn.21,22; Dexfield Park, separated from Bonnie, Clyde, and W. D. in, 129–32, 285n.21; Dexfield Park and Schwartz photographs, 287n.29; Dexfield Park shootout 129, 283–85nn.17–20; Dexter, escape attempt in, 287–88n.1; drinking, 44–45, 82, 111, 112, 242n.20; driving, 67, 192, 251n.10, 252n.14, 254n.21; Eastham, mistaken about Clyde's plan to raid, 236n.29, 237n.33; Eastham, plan to raid, 27–28; Eddie Frasure, marriage to, 169–83; and Esther Weiser, 175–78, 191–97; ex-convict, problems of, 170; eye, treatment of, 138, 143, 145, 151, 154, 165, 289–90n.4; father, living with, 172; father, visits to, 89–91; fishing, 185; Florida, trips to, 81–87, 259n.2; Fort

Smith, flight from, 270n.12; Fort Smith, hiding in, 98–104, 268n.16; friends, compartmentalization of, 191–92, 235n.23; hospitalization, 194; hysterical, 245–46 n.40, 277n.40, 287n.32; interrogated, 139–41, 149–50, 288–89nn.4,6; jigsaw puzzles, 44, 241n.14; John Callaway, first husband, 8, 149, 226n.3, 228n.8, 292n.2, 293n.24; Joplin, plan to visit, 29–35; Joplin, trip to, 37–40; Joplin apartment, 42–56, *43*; Joplin shootout, 36, 245nn.38,39; Kaufman County jail, visiting Bonnie and Fults in, 193, 239n.39; as Lua Talb, 161; Mary O'Dare, confused with, 181–82; and memoir manuscript, 194, 296n.40; men, protective tendencies from, 73–74, 256n.2; Missouri, extradition to, 141; Missouri court, tried in, 144–45, 150, 289nn.1–3; mother, conflicts with, 3, 161–62, 171–72, 194, 225n.1; mother, visits to, 24–35; movies and music, 44, 156–57, 293n.15; murders, reaction to, 52–54, 56, 58, 103, 108–109, 268n.14; parents, desired reunification of, 225n.2; parole denied, 292n.2; pet name "Baby," 9, 103, 109, 113, 115, 128, 129, 130, 133, 135; philosophical outlook on life, 196; photography, 153–54, 227n.10; as poet, 198; prison boyfriends, 157–60, 293nn.18,22; prison release, 166–67, 295n.38; prison years, 145–47, 150–68, 291–92nn.1,2; Ralph Fults, reunion with and memories of, 193; Raymond Hamilton, memories of, 232n.19, 235–36n.29; Red Crown, flight from, 122–24, 278–82nn.1–7; Red Crown cabins, 110–17, 272–75nn.18–28, 273n.19; Red Crown shootout, 117–21, 276–78nn. 34–50; Ruston abduction, 60–63, 247n.7; scrapbooks, 260n.6, 294n.25; Snow Ball the dog, 24, 35, *35*, 52, 55, 244n.34; and suicide, 112–13, 143; surveillance of, 175, 191; weapons, handling of, 243–44n.32, 251n.9; weight loss as fugitive, 256n.3, 288n.3; Wellington, flight from, 95–97, 263–64nn.3–9; working, 11, 14, 173, 234n.22; wounded, 105, 119–21, 278n.49

Barrow, Clyde Chestnut (Blanche's brother-in-law), 5, 13, 16, 17, 20, 21, 24, 26, 37, *41*, *51*, 76, 77, *79*, 88, 89, 93, 94, 106, 108, *118*, *127*, 137, 149, 150, 151, 154, 161, 162, 167, 177, 242n.18, 246n.43, 248–49n.15, 253nn.17,19, 255n.23; in